# PLATO AND HESIOD

# Plato and Hesiod

Edited by
G. R. BOYS-STONES AND J. H. HAUBOLD

OXFORD
UNIVERSITY PRESS

# OXFORD
UNIVERSITY PRESS

Great Clarendon Street, Oxford OX2 6DP

Oxford University Press is a department of the University of Oxford.
It furthers the University's objective of excellence in research, scholarship,
and education by publishing worldwide in

Oxford New York

Auckland Cape Town Dar es Salaam Hong Kong Karachi
Kuala Lumpur Madrid Melbourne Mexico City Nairobi
New Delhi Shanghai Taipei Toronto

With offices in

Argentina Austria Brazil Chile Czech Republic France Greece
Guatemala Hungary Italy Japan Poland Portugal Singapore
South Korea Switzerland Thailand Turkey Ukraine Vietnam

Oxford is a registered trade mark of Oxford University Press
in the UK and in certain other countries

Published in the United States
by Oxford University Press Inc., New York

© Oxford University Press 2010

British Library Cataloguing in Publication Data

Data available

Library of Congress Cataloging in Publication Data

Data available

Typeset by SPI Publisher Services, Pondicherry, India
Printed in Great Britain
on acid-free paper by the
MPG Books Group, Bodmin and King's Lynn

ISBN 978-0-19-923634-3

# Contents

# List of contributors

**G. R. Boys-Stones** is Professor of Ancient Philosophy at Durham University.

**Andrea Capra** is Research Fellow in Greek Philology at the Università degli Studi di Milano.

**Dimitri El Murr** is Lecturer in Ancient Philosophy at the Université de Paris I, Panthéon-Sorbonne.

**Andrew L. Ford** is Professor of Classics at Princeton University.

**Barbara Graziosi** is Senior Lecturer in Classics at Durham University.

**J. H. Haubold** is Leverhulme Senior Lecturer in Greek Literature at Durham University.

**Hugo Koning** is a PhD student at the Universiteit Leiden.

**Vered Lev Kenaan** is Senior Lecturer in Comparative Literature at the University of Haifa.

**Glenn W. Most** is Professor of Greek Philology at the Scuola Normale Superiore di Pisa and Professor on the Committee on Social Thought at the University of Chicago.

**E. E. Pender** is Senior Lecturer in Classics at the University of Leeds.

**Mario Regali** is a Research Fellow at the Università di Pisa.

**Christopher Rowe** is Emeritus and Honorary Professor of Greek at Durham University.

**David Sedley** is Laurence Professor of Ancient Philosophy at the University of Cambridge and a Fellow of Christ's College.

**Helen Van Noorden** is Wrigley Fellow in Classics at Girton College, Cambridge.

**Naoko Yamagata** is Senior Lecturer in Classical Studies at the Open University.

# Abbreviations

ARV$^2$ = J. D. Beazley, *Attic Red-Figure Vase-Painters*. 2nd edn, Oxford, 1963.

DK = H. Diels and W. Kranz, *Die Fragmente der Vorsokratiker*, 3 vols., 6th edn. Berlin, 1951–2.

*FGrHist* = F. Jacoby, *Die Fragmente der griechischen Historiker*, Berlin, 1923–.

KA = R. Kassel and C. Austin (eds.), *Poetae Comici Graeci*, Berlin, 1983– .

*LfgrE* = B. Snell *et al.*, *Lexikon des frühgriechischen Epos*, Göttingen, 1955–.

LSJ = H. G. Liddell and R. Scott (eds.), *Greek–English Lexicon*, revised by H. S. Jones. 9th edn, Oxford, 1940.

MW = Merkelbach and West (1967).

OCT = Oxford Classical Texts.

*PMG* = D. L. Page (ed.), *Poetae Melici Graeci*, Oxford, 1962.

*PMGF* = M. Davies (ed.), *Poetarum Melicorum Graecorum Fragmenta*, Oxford, 1991–.

*SVF* = J. von Arnim (ed.), *Stoicorum Veterum Fragmenta*. Indexes by M. Adler, 4 vols., Stuttgart, 1903–24.

# Introduction

## WHY PLATO AND *HESIOD*?

As many existing studies recognize (see for example Nightingale 1995, Levin 2001, Ledbetter 2003, Giuliano 2005), Plato has a close and complicated relationship with the Greek poetic tradition. On the one hand, he is keen to distance philosophy from the pedagogy of the sophists, largely based as it was on the study of poetry to which they showed at least notional deference; but, on the other, he needed to acknowledge and work with those same poets insofar as they represented the accumulated learning of Greece and the reference-point for the reception of his own literary output. So while Plato notoriously expelled Homer from his ideal state in the *Republic* on the ground that the epics undermined his own philosophical teaching, he also relied heavily on his readers' knowledge of the *Iliad* and *Odyssey*—as many studies of Plato attest.

But Homer was not the only poet with whom Plato engaged, and this volume aims to help widen the perspective on the issue by looking at Hesiod's presence in Plato's works. The reason for looking at Hesiod in particular is not just that, as the 'second poet' of Greece, he is the natural place to start thinking more broadly about Plato's interaction with poets and poetry. It is also because, while Homer dominated the curriculum, Hesiod was more obviously part of the didactic tradition against which Plato's works would inevitably be read. So it is, for example, that Hesiod (himself criticized along with Homer in the *Republic* for his depiction of the gods) provides important background to the cosmogony of the *Timaeus* through his *Theogony*; or, again, for Plato's account of justice and polity in the *Republic* through his *Works and Days*—which even furnishes the basis for the 'noble fiction' at the root of its new mythology

(414b7–415a2). By focusing on Plato's engagement with Hesiod in these and other dialogues, the aim of the present collection is not only to investigate some central aspects of Platonic philosophy, but also to further our understanding of the reception of Hesiod in the period between the consolidation of the archaic canon and the advent of Hellenistic poetry.

The last attempt at investigating the relationship between Plato and Hesiod in anything like a systematic manner, and an important reference-point for many of the studies in this volume, is an article by Friedrich Solmsen published in 1962. If we ask what Solmsen did not do that we might wish to do today, and what we might think of doing differently, some points immediately suggest themselves. To begin with, Solmsen was writing a survey article, which means that his analysis is of necessity selective and sometimes hurried. The present volume has the luxury of reading at a more leisurely pace (something which, in a field that has been largely neglected by classical scholars, is itself an important step forward). Another thing that Solmsen did not do, partly because he lacked the necessary space, was to consider larger contexts. He has little to say about other people's views of Hesiod, and even less about the reception of Hesiod in classical Athens more generally. Plato himself does of course remark on current perceptions of Hesiod: most famously, perhaps, he quotes Protagoras' view of him as a proto-sophist (*Protagoras* 316d3–9: the point is picked up by a number of contributors to this volume). He even (in ways discussed here by Graziosi) alludes to debates about the 'correct' use of Hesiod, for example when he introduces the problematic and highly topical notion that 'no work is blameworthy' (*Charmides* 163b4–5). So Plato clearly expects us to place his view of Hesiod within a broader intellectual context, and one aim of the present volume is to do precisely that.

But this book also has a more general, and we believe more important, objective. When Solmsen was writing in the early 1960s, reception studies as a sub-discipline of classics did not yet exist. Indeed, the groundbreaking work of Hans Robert Jauss and the Constance School (e.g. Jauss 1982, Iser 1978) was yet to be published. How much has changed since Solmsen wrote his survey becomes apparent when we look at his overall methodological framework. Solmsen sets out his stall thus towards the beginning of his essay (Solmsen 1962, 174):

By Plato's time the Greeks had long found out that the realities of life were far more complex than Hesiod had imagined them to be and they had become sufficiently realistic to accept the facts.

Solmsen suggests that things improved from Hesiod to Plato: the Greeks eventually learned to understand reality better than they had done before, and they came to express that understanding through an endorsement of Platonic philosophy. Forty-five years on, these claims are no longer tenable. For a start, there have been important changes in our perception of Hesiod (e.g. Pucci 1977, Martin 1992, J. S. Clay 2003, Stoddard 2004), as a result of which we are no longer convinced that Hesiod really was less subtle than his successors. But far more important are the changes in how we read texts and construe intertextual relationships that have taken place since the early 1960s: not only Jauss and Iser, but also Foucault, Derrida, and many others have taught us that human thought does not simply improve with time, and that the nature of a text, its meaning and value at any given moment, depends in large measure upon the meaning and value that its readers attach to it. Recent work on classical reception reflects those insights (e.g. Martindale 1993, Hardwick 2003, Martindale and Thomas 2006, Hardwick and Stray 2008). Solmsen's essay, which is still informed by the idea of a 'discovery of the mind' (cf. Snell 1953), ranks Hesiod below Plato because he precedes him in time; and on that basis fails to detect much in Hesiod that might have been of real interest to Plato. This view is in urgent need of revision.

More recent work on the reception of epic (e.g. Nagy 1990, Graziosi 2002, Ford 2002) warns us against assuming that Plato encountered his Hesiod in the form of a tidy manuscript shelved in the 'archaic literature' section (which is where Snell and Solmsen found him). Rather, Hesiodic epic came wrapped up in a complex web of glosses, audience expectations, and reading practices. The very extent of Hesiod's *oeuvre* was contested in classical Athens. Moreover, many passages from the Hesiodic corpus had already been given influential reworkings by the time Plato was active. So, for example, Plato's account of justice in the *Republic* can hardly be divorced from those of Solon and Aeschylus, even where Hesiod is ostensibly the main reference point. Sophistic readings of Hesiod provide another important filter. By the 4th century, we must also reckon with a well-developed tradition of reading by commonplace. Something of this is visible in the Attic orators who occasionally combine passages from Hesiod and other poets to illustrate a point, thereby suggesting a certain range of meanings that can be attributed to a given text or passage, and a range of contexts in which those meanings may be invoked.

This is a rich field for further investigation, and much relevant material is still waiting to be unearthed, especially in the scholia to the canonical poets. But what matters here is the more general point that reading Hesiod in the 4th century BC was a complicated, and often fraught, business. Within this context, it seems appropriate— urgent, even—to ask some fundamental questions about Plato's relationship with Hesiod: who, in Plato's view, was Hesiod and how does he place him in his own history of thought? Where and to what effect does Plato find it expedient to invoke Hesiod? Does he treat different Hesiodic texts differently? And does his attitude change from one dialogue to the next? These questions form the backbone of the present collection. They are addressed in a fairly direct manner in Part I, which includes chapters devoted to Plato's relationship with Hesiod *in general*; but they also inform the studies focused on individual Platonic dialogues to be found in Part II.

## OVERVIEW OF THE VOLUME

Reception history is never simply a given, but is itself imagined and actively shaped by those who participate in it. Part I of our volume therefore opens with two chapters on the reception of Hesiod as Plato and Hesiod themselves imagined it: Johannes Haubold argues that Hesiod shapes the history of his reception by way of an elaborate biographical narrative, leading his readers from a conception of knowledge as Muse-inspired poetry in the *Theogony* to one that centres on the human world and must be acquired through reflection and personal experience in the *Works and Days*. Haubold suggests that this vision of intellectual progress informed the reception of Hesiod in classical Athens; and that it may also have had a role to play in the wider intellectual developments of the 5th and 4th centuries BC.

George Boys-Stones approaches the same problem from a different angle, asking how Hesiod fits into *Plato's* view of intellectual history. The answer lies in Hesiod's praise of *eris*: this makes him a symbol and reference-point for the unproductive squabbling that Plato sees in much previous philosophical debate (and especially the work of the sophists); but it also provides Plato with the language to show how his own philosophical methodology differs. Boys-Stones argues that the language of *eros* which underpins the theory of Platonic 'dialectic' represents a transformation of Hesiodic *eris*, one which draws out its positive potential while freeing itself of its tendency to polemic for polemic's sake.

Chapters 3 and 4 look in more detail at the ways in which Plato engages with Hesiod. Glenn Most asks whether Hesiod for Plato was an acquired taste, and concludes with a cautious 'yes'. He looks at the pattern of Hesiodic quotations across Plato's works and suggests that Plato came to endorse especially the *Works and Days* more freely in the course of his life. Most also notes that the Hesiodic corpus, for Plato, included the *Theogony* and *Works and Days*, but not the *Catalogue of Women* and the minor works; just as the only genuine Homeric texts, for Plato, appear to be the *Iliad* and *Odyssey*. Chapter 4, by Naoko Yamagata, surveys the relationship between Homer and Hesiod in Plato's work. More specifically, Yamagata focuses on the way in which individual characters portray and invoke the two poets. She concludes that Plato depicts Socrates as a lover of Homer, whereas his interlocutors draw more freely on Hesiod. Moreover, there appears to be a tendency among Platonic speakers to be more optimistic about the truth of Homeric myths than that of Hesiodic ones.

Chapters 5–7 investigate the wider cultural and intellectual context of Hesiodic reception in classical Athens. As Hugo Koning shows, Plato's view of Hesiod is shaped not only by a critical tradition that pairs him up with Homer but also by sophistic appropriations of a more specific kind. Koning suggests that Prodicus in particular, with his concern for the 'correctness of names', recognized Hesiod as an intellectual ancestor. More generally, Hesiod could be appropriated to represent particular philosophical interests, from etymology to atomism, and so became a convenient target for Plato's attacks on precisely those approaches. Barbara Graziosi turns to more public uses of Hesiod in classical Athens, from rhapsodic performances to public speeches. She argues that Hesiodic poetry formed a battle-ground for sexual politics in the 4th century BC, and that Plato's reception of Hesiod is fundamentally bound up with ongoing de-bates about education. In this context, quotable lines from Hesiod could take on a life entirely of their own. Chapter 7, by Andrew Ford, examines the extent to which Hesiodic poetry became associated with specific contexts of reading, from the courts to school-room teaching and philosophical debate. As Ford points out, the *Theogony* and *Works and Days* acquired a very different *Sitz im Leben* by the time in which Plato encountered them. Indeed, their very status as texts 'in their own right' (i.e. outside specific contexts of consumption), and the idea of an overarching Hesiodic *oeuvre*, appear to have become rather less important to many readers than the traditions and institutions of reading that had accrued around specific passages.

Part II of the volume, looking in more detail at Hesiod's reception within individual Platonic dialogues, begins with a study by Vered Lev Kenaan of the *Symposium*. In this work, she argues, Plato not only recalls Hesiodic passages and motifs at important moments in the dialogue, but founds his portrayal of Socrates on Hesiod's Pandora. The claim is striking, paradoxical even, if one thinks of Pandora as the bringer of evils par excellence. But defined, like Socrates, by the rift between interior and exterior, essence and ap-pearance, Pandora is, like Socrates, a *marvel to behold*—and (also like him) a challenge to the intellect, the obvious prompt to philosophical enquiry.

Like other contributors to the collection, Lev Kenaan explores Plato's own understanding of how texts relate to other texts. The *Symposium*, she argues, casts the very process of reception in the form of an erotic genealogy very much in the vein of Hesiod. Helen Van Noorden takes up the idea of a deeper affinity between Plato and Hesiod in a chapter on the myth of the races of man in the *Republic*. Van Noorden's central idea is that Plato does not just 'rework' the Hesiodic narrative of the five races, but reads its contribution to the *Works and Days* as an antecedent to, and a model for, his own, self-critical practice of philosophy. In this sense, he can ask us to think of Hesiod's races as 'our own' too (546e1): it sets the pattern for continued philosophical reflection.

From the *Republic* we move to the *Timaeus–Critias*. Andrea Capra points out that the diptych of *Timaeus* and *Critias* is modelled on the rhapsodic structure of Greek epic, and especially the Hesiodic catalogues (*Theogony–Catalogue of Women*). By imitating Hesiodic rhapsody, Plato signals his ambition to create a new and philosophically better kind of 'song'. What this might mean in practice is the focus of Liz Pender's chapter on the *Timaeus*, which shows the extent to which Plato takes up and transforms central categories of the *Theogony* such as one *vs* many, male *vs* female, creation *vs* birth.

Two more chapters then investigate specific aspects of the *Timaeus* and its relationship with Hesiod. David Sedley asks what the *Theogony* can teach us about the advent of evil in the *Timaeus*, and in so doing uncovers what he calls 'a remarkably deep isomorphism' between the two texts: both, for example, introduce first the potential for evil (Hesiodic Chaos and its descendants, Platonic matter) and then its realization (Hesiodic and Platonic woman). Moving from evil to good, Mario Regali concludes the section by looking at the crucial passage in the *Timaeus* where the Demiurge addresses the gods (41a6–8). Regali shows how Hesiodic reminiscences enable Plato to combine the need for a memorable account with a claim to superior sophistication: Hesiod's well-known etymology *dia* ('through') = *Dia* (Zeus) triggers an intellectual journey from the popular surface of Hesiodic poetry to a more profound (i.e. Platonic) understanding of the world.

The final two chapters of the collection consider one of the most challenging of all Platonic myths: that of the Age of Kronos as told in the *Politicus* (268e4–274e4). Dimitri El Murr places the passage in the wider context of Golden Age imagery from Hesiod to Attic Comedy and defends the majority view of the myth as describing two distinct stages of development, neither of them unproblematically positive. Against this view, Christopher Rowe restates his reading of the myth as describing a three-stage development, from the world under Kronos, via a transitional second phase, to the present regime of Zeus. In contrast with El Murr's more wide-ranging analysis, Rowe rests his case on a close reading of the myth itself. He also suggests a reason for why Plato might have chosen not to remove any remaining ambiguities: the myth springs a trap for Athenian readers eager to fall back on their own misguided sense of superiority.

*

This volume has its roots in a conference held at Collingwood College, Durham in July 2006, where, it is fair to say, the contributors surprised even themselves at quite how much there is to say about Hesiod's importance for Plato: more, of course, than this volume can encompass in the end. But we offer it in the spirit of Plato's Hesiod (*Cratylus* 428a, citing *Works and Days* 361), and with the hope that it will not be another 45 years before the next substantial contribution to the question: *It is helpful to add even a little to a little.*

GB-S, JHH
January 2009

# Part I

# Plato and Hesiod

# 1

# Shepherd, farmer, poet, sophist: Hesiod on his own reception

*J. H. Haubold*

## INTRODUCTION

According to Plato, the sophist Protagoras regarded Hesiod as a predecessor.[1] By contrast, modern scholarship has often depicted Hesiod as an archaic peasant who formulated his 'convictions' in a chaotic and rather simplistic manner.[2] More recently, the pendulum of critical opinion has swung back in Protagoras' (and Hesiod's) favour, suggesting that Hesiod's persona is carefully tailored to his poetry,[3] and that the Hesiodic corpus represents a sophisticated attempt to understand the world and to communicate that understanding.[4] Building on these recent insights, this chapter aims to investigate a specific question: how did Hesiod envisage and shape his own reception? In the first part of the chapter, I argue that the Hesiodic corpus as a whole implies—by way of an elaborate biography of its author—a narrative of cultural and intellectual progress: Hesiod's ideal audience stands at the summit of that development. In

---

[1] Plato, *Protagoras* 316d3–9. Protagoras also mentions Homer, Simonides, Orpheus, and Musaeus in this context. The idea of Hesiod as a (proto-sophistic) teacher of virtue resurfaces in Plato's *Republic* at 600d5–e2. For Hesiod as a σοφός, see *Republic* 466b4–c3, *Laws* 718d7–719a2.

[2] E.g. West (1978), 41–59.

[3] Griffith (1983), R. Rosen (1990), Martin (1992), Most (1993), Graziosi (2002).

[4] Marsilio (2000), J. S. Clay (2003), Stoddard (2004).

the second part, I look in more detail at the Myth of Ages as an
example of the level of sophistication which the mature Hesiod of the
*Works and Days* expects of his audience. Finally, and more specula-
tively, I reflect on some possible connections between Hesiod's views
on intellectual development and those of his self-declared successors
in the 5th and 4th centuries BC. I take it as my premise that texts do,
in some measure, shape future intellectual developments and their
own reception.[5]

## BIOGRAPHY AND HERMENEUTICS

The major Hesiodic poems form a history of the world in three
stages, starting with the era of the gods (*Theogony*) and demigods
(*Catalogue*), before moving on to the world of men as they are 'now',
i.e. at the time of the audience (*Works and Days*).[6] Each text shows an
awareness of this chronology. Thus, the *Theogony* starts at the very
beginning of history (ἐξ ἀρχῆς: 115; πρώτιστα: 116), while the
*Catalogue* picks up where the *Theogony* leaves off (fr. 1 MW). The
*Works and Days*, finally, looks back to the world of the heroes as
immediately preceding its own (*Works and Days* 156–73). Although
there are inconsistencies in detail, the corpus as a whole is informed
by a fairly coherent chronological framework. This chronology is in
turn overlaid with a biographical narrative: the *Theogony* looks back
to the moment when Hesiod first acquired the gift of song (30–32).
At that time, he was still herding sheep on the slopes of Mount
Helicon (*Theogony* 22–35).[7] The narrator of the *Works and Days*,
by contrast, has not only become an expert farmer and head of his
own household (both decidedly adult roles) but looks back to the
greatest triumph of his career, when he won a singing contest at

---

[5] Feeney (forthcoming) investigates this proposition by looking at the poetry of
Horace.

[6] Graziosi and Haubold (2005), ch. 2. We need not here worry about whether the
*Catalogue of Women* was 'genuine' Hesiod. For the purposes of the present argument
it suffices that ancient readers generally regarded it as such: see the testimonia
collected in Merkelbach and West (1967).

[7] In epic, this kind of work is typically done by young men: Haubold (2000), 18.

Chalcis.[8] In this context, he also reminisces about his encounter with the Muses on Mount Helicon (*Works and Days* 659), confirming our impression of a mature man who looks back over a significant stretch of his life.

An author's biography in ancient Greece was never simply a collection of biographical facts. More often than not, its main function was rather to say something about the texts of the author in question.[9] Biography, in other words, amounted to a form of literary criticism. Archilochus' poetry, for example, was witty and aggressive, so the biographers gave him the appropriate character as an expression of what they perceived to be a crucial aspect of his poetic output. Euripides took an interest in lowly characters and was therefore mocked for his low birth. The life of the author and the meaning of his work were closely intertwined. In the specific case of epic poetry, there was even a temptation to match the time of composition with that of the poem's setting. Thus, Homer was sometimes said to have composed the *Odyssey* after the *Iliad*. As [Longinus] suggests (*On the Sublime* 9.12, trans. W. Rhys Roberts):

δῆλος γὰρ ἐκ πολλῶν τε ἄλλων συντεθεικὼς ταύτην δευτέραν τὴν ὑπόθεσιν, ἀτὰρ δὴ κἀκ τοῦ λείψαντα τῶν Ἰλιακῶν παθημάτων διὰ τῆς Ὀδυσσείας ὡς ἐπεισόδιά τινα τοῦ Τρωικοῦ πολέμου προσεπεισφέρειν καὶ νὴ Δί' ἐκ τοῦ τὰς ὀλοφύρσεις καὶ τοὺς οἴκτους ὡς πάλαι που προεγνωσμένους τοῖς ἥρωσιν ἐνταῦθα προσαποδιδόναι. οὐ γὰρ ἀλλ' ἢ τῆς Ἰλιάδος ἐπίλογός ἐστιν ἡ Ὀδύσσεια.

It is clear from many indications that the *Odyssey* was his [i.e. Homer's] second subject. A special proof is the fact that he introduces in that poem remnants of the adventures before Ilium as episodes, so to say, of the Trojan War. And indeed, he there renders a tribute of mourning and lamentation to his heroes as though he were carrying out a long-cherished purpose. In fact, the *Odyssey* is simply an epilogue to the *Iliad*.

For [Longinus], the idea of the *Odyssey* as an 'epilogue to the *Iliad*' works at several levels: the events it describes happened later; it fills

---

[8] For Hesiod's expertise in farming see *Works and Days* 383–617; for his household see *Works and Days* 37, 394–7; his victory in the song contest is described at *Works and Days* 654–62.

[9] Graziosi (2006).

gaps in the Iliadic account; and its narrator is older. This latter point
serves as a springboard into a discussion of the character of each text
(9.13, trans. W. Rhys Roberts):

Ἀπὸ δὲ τῆς αὐτῆς αἰτίας, οἶμαι, τῆς μὲν Ἰλιάδος γραφομένης ἐν ἀκμῇ
πνεύματος ὅλον τὸ σωμάτιον δραματικὸν ὑπεστήσατο καὶ ἐναγώνιον, τῆς δὲ
Ὀδυσσείας τὸ πλέον διηγηματικόν, ὅπερ ἴδιον γήρως. ὅθεν ἐν τῇ Ὀδυσσείᾳ
παρεικάσαι τις ἂν καταδυομένῳ τὸν Ὅμηρον ἡλίῳ, οὗ δίχα τῆς σφοδρότητος
παραμένει τὸ μέγεθος.

It is for the same reason, I suppose, that he has made the whole
structure of the *Iliad*, which was written at the height of his inspiration,
full of action and conflict, while the *Odyssey* for the most part consists
of narrative, as is characteristic of old age. Accordingly, in the *Odyssey*
Homer may be likened to a sinking sun, whose grandeur remains without
its intensity.

[Longinus] did not of course have any hard evidence on which
to base his claim that Homer composed the *Odyssey* after the
*Iliad*. What mattered to him was the ethos of each poem which
suggested an image of its narrator: young, strong, and passionate
in the *Iliad*, old and mellow in the *Odyssey*. Something similar
happens in the Hesiodic corpus, except that here an elaborate biography is inscribed into the text itself. Richard Martin has shown
that the story of Hesiod's father—allegedly an economic refugee
from Cyme—reflects the voice and thematic concerns of the
*Works and Days*.[10] More recently, Grace Ledbetter has studied the
biographical section of the *Theogony* as a hermeneutic framework
for that poem.[11] I would now like to ask what bearing Hesiod's
biography has on our reading of the Hesiodic corpus as a whole.
More specifically, I ask what we should make of the transition
from the poet as shepherd in the *Theogony* to the expert farmer of
the *Works and Days*.

---

[10] Martin (1992), who goes so far as to speak of a 'metanastic poetics': the fact that
Hesiod is from a family of exiles explains the openness and aggressive nature of his
advice.

[11] Ledbetter (2003), Ch. 2.

## THE SHEPHERD AND THE FARMER

At a very basic level, Hesiod's biography confirms the order of reading already implied by the setting of each text, which suggests that we
should start with the *Theogony* before moving on to the *Works and
Days*.[12] To this the biographical narrative adds a further dimension,
suggesting a different kind of narrator for each poem, a different kind
of poetry, and even a different kind of reading. Indeed, what is at
stake here is nothing short of a fully-fledged 'biographical hermeneutics', an overall framework for how to read the Hesiodic poems
and what to make of them. As Glenn Most has put it (1993, 77):

[T]he reader . . . is invited to replicate Hesiod's own trajectory by reading the
two poems in the same order as that in which they are claimed to have been
composed. Autobiography becomes protreptic: the reader is allowed to
make the same errors as the younger Hesiod did—so that, like the older
Hesiod, he may redeem them by maturer insights into a less one-sided
world.

As Most points out, the biographical narrative which Hesiod super-
imposes on the *Theogony* and *Works and Days* establishes far more
than merely a recommended order of reading.[13] Indeed, the Hesiodic
narrator quite clearly changes approach from one poem to the next.
Jenny Strauss Clay has shown that the narrator of the *Theogony* relies
on the help of the Muses to a far greater extent than that of the *Works
and Days*, who proposes from the outset to speak in his own voice
(cf. line 10: ἐγὼ δέ . . . μυθησαίμην).[14] As she also points out, each
narrator's approach, as articulated primarily in the proems to the two
texts, is appropriate to his chosen topic: whereas the narrator of
the *Theogony* must rely on divine help to recount divine matters

---

[12] Hesiodic poetry reminds us of this overall sequence by providing frequent
cross-references and other temporal markers. These are particularly common in the
*Works and Days*: see e.g. 11–12 (Eris), 42–105 (Pandora), 111 (Kronos), 156–73 (the
race of heroes).

[13] Most goes on to explain Hesiod's use of autobiography by emphasizing the
spread of writing. He may well be right, but the issue is never raised by ancient
readers and it is their views that interest me here.

[14] J. S. Clay (2003), Ch. 3.

truthfully (*Theogony* 28: ἀληθέα), that of the *Works and Days* speaks
the kind of truth (*Works and Days* 10: ἐτήτυμα) that is relevant to
human life in the Iron Age.[15] The distant past is properly the domain
of Memory and her daughters, the Muses;[16] whereas the present
circumstances of the Iron Age require not divine memory but
human knowledge and understanding. Biographical information
further enhances these differences. In the *Theogony*, the narrator is
introduced as a shepherd who as yet lacks any relevant knowledge of
his own. Shepherds in early Greek epic not only tend to be young but
also fallible.[17] No epic character ever boasts of being a shepherd.
Farmers, we have already seen, are usually older than shepherds and
hence more authoritative.[18] Their métier is also superior: thus,
Odysseus can proudly announce that he knows how to plough a
straight furrow.[19] Conversely, the proverbial fool Margites knows
nothing about farming (*Margites* fr. 2 West, with West's translation):

> τὸν δ᾽ οὔτ᾽ ἄρ᾽ σκαπτῆρα θεοὶ θέσαν οὐδ᾽ ἀροτῆρα
> οὔτ᾽ ἄλλως τι σοφόι. πάσης δ᾽ ἡμάρτανε τέχνης.

> The gods had made him neither a digger nor a ploughman,
> nor skilled (*sophos*) in any other way: he fell short at every craft.

Note that farming is here associated with the quality of being σοφός
('knowledgeable, expert'),[20] and that Margites' lack of knowledge in

---

[15] For a suggestion that ἀληθής refers to a different *kind* of truth from ἔτυμος /
ἐτήτυμος see Nagy (1990), 45; J. S. Clay (2003), 58–63; Stoddard (2004), Ch. 3.

[16] *Theogony* 53–79; cf. 915–17.

[17] Haubold (2000), 19, with ref. to *Iliad* 16.352–6. One of the most positive
depictions of a shepherd in early Greek epic can be found at *Odyssey* 13.221–7.
(Note, however, that this shepherd too is young; and that he is found at the margins
of civilized society.) Elsewhere, shepherds tend to be seen in a less favourable light:
*Odyssey* 17.246 has a proverbial ring to it. Contrast the very different standing of
shepherds in non-Greek literatures of the time.

[18] For the link between age and understanding in Greek epic cf. formulaic
πρότερος γενόμην καὶ πλείονα οἶδα (*vel sim.*) at *Iliad* 13.355, 19.219, 21.440 ('I was
born first and know more').

[19] *Odyssey* 18.375. Note that the ploughing contest (ἔρις ἔργοιο) at 18.366–75 has
its counterpart in a challenge to match Odysseus' military prowess (18.376–80). The
good farmer is also a good soldier.

[20] The adjective σοφός is rare in early Greek epic, but the noun σοφίη is reasonably
common: see *LfgrE* s.vv. σοφός, σοφίη B. For the significance of σοφός and related
terms see n. 46. For Hesiod as a σοφός in Plato see above n. 1.

matters of farming becomes symptomatic of his failure in all other fields of human endeavour (πάσῃ τέχνῃ).[21] We may therefore conclude that the Muses' insulting address to Hesiod and his fellow shepherds in the *Theogony* (26) not only contrasts divine insight with human folly but also sets up an implied contrast with the farmer of the *Works and Days* who speaks from a position of superior knowledge.[22] As we have seen, this contrast works at an intellectual level, but it also has some broader social and cultural ramifications. As Odysseus points out, a good farmer is someone who can and must control his appetite (*Odyssey* 18.366–70, trans. Lattimore):

Εὐρύμαχ᾽, εἰ γὰρ νῶϊν ἔρις ἔργοιο γένοιτο
ὥρῃ ἐν εἰαρινῇ, ὅτε τ᾽ ἤματα μακρὰ πέλονται,
ἐν ποίῃ, δρέπανον μὲν ἐγὼν εὐκαμπὲς ἔχοιμι,
καὶ δὲ σὺ τοῖον ἔχοις, ἵνα πειρησαίμεθα ἔργου
νήστιες ἄχρι μάλα κνέφαος, ποίη δὲ παρείη.

Eurymachos, I wish there could be a working contest
between us, in the spring season when the days are lengthening,
out in the meadow, with myself holding a well-curved sickle,
and you one like it, so to test our endurance for labour,
without food, from dawn till dark, with plenty of grass for mowing.

Because Odysseus is able to resist his belly and work the land, he can claim to be more than merely a social drop-out.[23] The *Works and Days* too emphasizes that, by working the land and eating in a controlled manner, one avoids having to join beggars and other

---

[21] In other ways too, Margites represents the exact counterpart to the Hesiod of the *Works and Days*: like Hesiod, he knows many 'works' (ἔργα), but unlike Hesiod he knows them all badly (fr. 3 West). His parents are exceedingly rich (fr. 4 West), whereas Hesiod's father is desperately poor (*Works and Days* 637–8). Hesiod defines the human condition through men's desire for women (*Works and Days* 57–8). Margites does not even know how to have sex (fr. 4 West) and apparently gets stuck with his penis in a chamber pot (fr. 7 West). Some ancient readers commended Margites for combining stupidity with leisure, the exact opposite of Hesiod's teachings (fr. 6 West).

[22] For Hesiod's claims to knowledge in the *Works and Days* see *Works and Days* 10, 40–41, 106–7, 293–9; compare also the references to 'foolish' Perses: *Works and Days* 286, 397.

[23] *Odyssey* 18.362–4. According to Eurymachus, Odysseus prefers to live as a beggar rather than work the land (ἔργον ἐποίχεσθαι) precisely so as to feed his insatiable belly (ὄφρ᾽ ἂν ἔχῃς βόσκειν σὴν γαστέρ᾽ ἄναλτον).

good-for-nothings who cannot so control themselves.[24] In the *Theogony*, shepherds are pointedly included in this latter group when they are insulted as 'mere bellies'.[25] By describing himself in this way, the young Hesiod of the *Theogony* renounces any claims to cultural and intellectual competence.

According to early Greek epic, human society acquires the art of farming at a relatively late stage. Indeed, it is only with the advent of farming that we become properly human: the race of gold, which is not yet fully human, does not yet work the land (*Works and Days* 109–19). Likewise, the violent men of bronze do not eat grain (*Works and Days* 146–7). As may be seen from these examples, life without farming can have positive as well as negative aspects, yet it is never unproblematically human. The nexus between human knowledge and farming in the *Works and Days* is thus fully transparent: man in early Greek epic is essentially defined as a grain-eater,[26] and expertise in farming is therefore expertise in the human condition par excellence. Shepherding, by contrast, is associated with pre- or sub-human forms of existence, as exemplified by the Odyssean Cyclops, in many ways the ultimate exponent of pre-agricultural savagery.[27]

Hesiod's biography not only helps to explain the different *types* of knowledge imparted by the *Theogony* and *Works and Days* but also encourages us to arrange them into an overarching narrative of social, cultural, and intellectual development. The *Theogony* cannot and need not yet be accounted for in human terms: what matters here is the truth imparted by the Muses, a problematic kind of truth to be sure, but one which we are in no position to challenge.[28] The knowledge of the farmer, by contrast, is civilized and fully human. It

---

[24] E.g. *Works and Days* 299–309, 314–16, 368–9, 392–5.

[25] *Theogony* 26.

[26] Cf. the formulaic descriptions of 'grain-eating men': ἐπὶ χθονὶ σῖτον ἔδοντες etc. (*Odyssey* 8.222, 9.89 = 10.101); οἳ ἀρούρης καρπὸν ἔδουσιν etc. (*Iliad* 6.142, 21.465, *Homeric Hymn to Apollo* 364–6); for discussion see Hartog (2001), 22–4.

[27] *Odyssey* 9.105–542. For discussion of the Odyssean Cyclops see Kirk (1970), 162–71; Vidal-Naquet (1986), 21–2; Segal (1994), 203; Graziosi and Haubold (2005), 77–9.

[28] Ledbetter (2003), 40–41, 44–7. She is right in saying that Hesiod's account of the Muses does not amount to a theory of fictionality (46); but her attempt to divorce Hesiod as narrator of the *Theogony* from the Muses seems to me to go too far: Ledbetter (2003), 52–3.

is a form of knowledge which can and must account for itself largely from within the life experiences of the narrator and his audience. Since the activities of Hesiod as shepherd predate those of Hesiod as farmer in terms of cultural history and the author's own life, poetry in the narrow sense of divinely inspired song about the past becomes propaedeutic to the engagement with properly human truths. Not only do we read the *Works and Days* after the *Theogony*; in reading it (or listening to it) we know that we have made progress.[29]

## THE FARMER AS TEACHER

We have seen that the persona of the author as farmer in the *Works and Days* is not that of a boorish peasant, as modern readers have sometimes assumed. On the contrary, the farmer as the 'grain-eater' par excellence appears as a fully civilized and mature man who puts humanity at the centre of his concerns. Maria Marsilio has emphasized the extent to which farming and poetry are aligned with one another in the *Works and Days*.[30] However, as Stephanie Nelson points out, ancient authors more commonly associate poetry with shepherding, while divorcing the 'dung and drudgery' of farming from the lofty realm of poetic inspiration.[31] Nelson sees this distinction primarily as a later development, but her point applies to Hesiod too: the properly poetic, Muse-inspired voice of Hesiod belongs to the shepherd who performs the *Theogony*, while the *Works and Days* is framed in terms of the farmer's essentially human wisdom. The shepherd sings what no man can know; whereas the farmer challenges us to understand our place in the world we see around us. And while the *Theogony* emphasizes the pleasurable nature of the Muses' song and praises its therapeutic powers,[32] the *Works and Days* cures its reader in a more human, and distinctly less enchanting, manner.

---

[29] One set of Hesiodic scholia suggests the opposite order of reading, starting with the *Works and Days* before graduating to the *Theogony*: cf. *Scholia Vetera in Hesiodi Opera et Dies* 1, 4 Pertusi.

[30] Marsilio (2000).

[31] Nelson (2003).

[32] *Theogony* 98–103; cf. Ledbetter (2003), 48–50.

If what has been argued so far is correct, we may ask in what ways the actual texts of the *Theogony* and *Works and Days* reflect the narrator's changing outlook and approach.[33] Starting again with the *Theogony*, the poem bears many of the hallmarks of Muse narrative.[34] In keeping with the persona established in the proem, the narrator rarely intrudes upon his story. Where he does so most conspicuously (at 369–70) it is to profess a gap in his knowledge. Much of the poem is framed as an impersonal and linear account of events set in the distant past.[35] There is only very limited room for explicit reflection on the nature and truth value of the narrative, and none at all for self-aggrandizing audience addresses. What we get instead are repeated invocations to the Muses (114–15, 965–8, 1021–2). As I have pointed out already, the narrator's reliance on the Muses is appropriate not only to his persona but also to the contents of his song. The *Theogony* is essentially about the gods, and the *pièce de résistance* of Muse narrative in early Greek epic was precisely the world of the gods.[36] The gods could only be fully known to other gods, and to the bard as the servant of the Muses. This type of knowledge defies human understanding, and as Hesiod himself emphasizes there is no real check on it. All we can do is worship the Muses and suspend our disbelief,[37] as duly happens in the *Theogony*: after the initial declaration of the Muses that they alone command truth and falsehood, the narrator never expresses any doubts about the events he recounts.

---

[33] At this point, the investigation could be broadened out to include the *Catalogue of Women*, which shows an interesting shift in tone and texture from the *Theogony*; cf. R. L. Hunter (2005). In time, the *Catalogue* too was given a biographical interpretation: Hermesianax tells us that Hesiod came to Ascra for the sake of a lover called Ehoie. The story arises from a transparent personification of the formula ἠ οἵη; and the alternative title of the *Catalogue* which derives from it. Cf. Hermesianax fr. 7.21–6 Powell.

[34] The narrative strategies of the *Theogony* are discussed in detail by Stoddard (2004). Stoddard emphasizes the autonomy and subtlety of the narrator in the *Theogony*. Here, I emphasize his relative lack of autonomy when compared to the *Works and Days*.

[35] For flashbacks, flash-forwards and other cases of narratorial intervention see Stoddard (2004), esp. Ch. 5.

[36] Graziosi and Haubold (2005), 80–4.

[37] Ledbetter (2003), 53.

The *Works and Days*, by contrast, starts precisely with Hesiod correcting the Muses' 'earlier' account in the *Theogony*.[38] This opening gambit is highly pointed: the mature Hesiod will be a very different narrator (if we can call him that) from the Muse-inspired shepherd of the *Theogony*. Hesiod in the *Works and Days* constantly and noisily intrudes upon his text, reflecting at length on the basis and nature of his knowledge (e.g. 646–62), his chosen rhetorical strategy (e.g. 106–7, 202), and even his own person (e.g. 174–5, 633–62) and that of his addressee (34–9, 396). The tone is expressly and passionately didactic. Much is at stake both for the author and the reader/addressee who is repeatedly warned that flawed thinking will lead to ruin. None of this is ἀοιδή, epic 'song', in any straightforward sense; the Muses have to do with it only very indirectly.[39] Accordingly, the *Works and Days* lacks many of the more important formal characteristics of Muse narrative: instead of a linear, 'objective' account of events, we find a barrage of injunctions, riddles, and parables which force us to delve deep in pursuit of the underlying meaning of the text: what classical Greeks might have called its ὑπόνοια.[40] The *Works and Days* is hard work for its reader, and there is no short cut. The realm of mortals that it describes is not easily grasped. Even the gods become more obscure as the poem wears on.[41]

The 'biographical hermeneutics' of the Hesiodic corpus, then, is reflected in the tone and shape of the poems themselves. The reader who follows the thread of history and biography from the *Theogony* to the *Works and Days* is expected to mature together with the narrator. The *Theogony* promises to make us forget what is difficult

---

[38] *Works and Days* 11–26; cf. *Theogony* 225–6. For discussion see Most (1993), 76–80.

[39] Although they are mentioned twice (*Works and Days* 1–2, 661–2), they are only said to sing about Zeus. Insofar as Zeus is the basis for everything else, the *Works and Days* too is a product of the Muses, albeit in a very indirect way.

[40] E.g. Xenophon, *Symposium* 3.6; Plato, *Republic* 378d.

[41] J. S. Clay (2003), 146–9. Protagoras on one occasion dismisses the gods as being beyond human comprehension: 80 B4 DK. This radical gesture, in many ways emblematic of intellectual life in 5th-century Athens, goes far beyond what we find in Hesiod. Yet, the basic idea of bringing knowledge 'down from the sky' and into the sphere of men may already be prefigured in the shape and overall educational trajectory of the Hesiodic corpus: see below pp. 29–30.

about our lives.[42] In the *Works and Days*, by contrast, forgetting our difficulties is no longer an option,[43] nor is the essentially passive approach to reading that comes with it. Whereas the shepherd-narrator of the *Theogony* expects relatively little of his audience beyond a joyful acknowledgement of the cosmogonic facts, the narrator of the *Works and Days* expects a great deal more. From the start, he asks us to reconsider, quite literally, what we thought we had already learned. That is no easy feat, and in fact the text constantly challenges its addressees (Perses, the kings, the reader) to think harder than feels comfortable: what precisely is the point of the αἶνος to the kings? What does it mean to discover the value of mallow and asphodel (41)? Why take the hard road when the easy one looks so much more inviting (286–92)? These are eminently human, non-poetic, one might even say philosophical concerns to get one's teeth into; though not before the basics are in place: as we have seen, the *Works and Days* opens with a blunt reminder of just how much knowledge of a more poetic kind it is going to assume: οὐκ ἄρα μοῦνον ἔην ἐρίδων γένος . . . [44]

If the *Theogony* marks the divinely inspired beginnings of an intellectual career, Hesiod unleashes his own, very human and self-consciously mature knowledge in the *Works and Days*.[45] It is here too that he presents himself as an expert teacher in a way that rings suggestively across the ages. At 649, Hesiod acknowledges that he is οὐδὲν σεσοφισμένος, 'not knowledgeable', in seafaring, which might imply that he is indeed σεσοφισμένος ('knowledgeable') in the other areas of life on which he pronounces. The participle σεσοφισμένος did not of course have the same implications as the noun σοφιστής in

---

[42]  *Theogony* 94–103.

[43]  Μεμνημένος εἶναι and similar injunctions to 'remember' (i.e. the difficult bits) form a constant refrain in the *Works and Days*: e.g. *Works and Days* 298, 422, 616, 623, 641, 711, 728.

[44]  More such reminders follow: the story of Pandora recalls *Theogony* 535–616. Mention of Kronos at 111 recalls the succession myth; that of the heroes (156–73) the end of the *Catalogue of Women*. All this material is pointedly *revisited*, with a view to reaching a deeper understanding of our present world.

[45]  As will have become clear, by 'Hesiod' I mean the biographical persona portrayed in the poems: I do not wish to make any claims for the historically 'real' Hesiod, however one is to imagine him.

later Greek literature.[46] Nor should we overlook the fact that Hesiod never explicitly advertises his own σοφίη ('expertise').[47] Still, we have seen that he does take on the role of teacher and educator in the *Works and Days*. Most strikingly sophistic in this connection is perhaps his attitude to what later Greeks were to call 'myths', i.e. narratives about the distant past. We recall that in the *Theogony* (and the *Catalogue of Women*) these were still the preserve of the Muses. In the *Works and Days* they have truly become a means to a pedagogical end. In the next section of this chapter, I wish to have a quick look at an example which was to become particularly influential: the so-called Myth of Ages.

## THE TEACHER AT WORK

The Myth of Ages was Plato's favourite Hesiodic passage. He rewrote it—or significant parts of it—on a number of occasions, most extensively in Book 3 of the *Republic* (414b7–415a2, trans. F. M. Cornford):[48]

Τίς ἂν οὖν ἡμῖν, ἦν δ᾽ ἐγώ, μηχανὴ γένοιτο τῶν ψευδῶν τῶν ἐν δέοντι γιγνομένων, ὧν δὴ νῦν ἐλέγομεν, γενναῖόν τι ἓν ψευδομένους πεῖσαι μάλιστα μὲν καὶ αὐτοὺς τοὺς ἄρχοντας· εἰ δὲ μή, τὴν ἄλλην πόλιν;

Ποῖόν τι; ἔφη.

Μηδὲν καινόν, ἦν δ᾽ ἐγώ, ἀλλὰ Φοινικικόν τι, πρότερον μὲν ἤδη πολλαχοῦ γεγονός, ὥς φασιν οἱ ποιηταὶ καὶ πεπείκασιν, ἐφ᾽ ἡμῶν δὲ οὐ γεγονὸς οὐδ᾽ οἶδα εἰ γενόμενον ἄν, πεῖσαι δὲ συχνῆς πειθοῦς.

---

[46] For the verb σοφίζομαι cf. Theognis 19. σοφίη in early Greek poetry can refer to the knowledge and/or skill of the craftsman (*Iliad* 15.412), horse-rider (Alcman fr. 2.6 *PMGF*), assayer (Theognis 120), poet and/or musician (Hesiod fr. 306 MW). For further passages see West (1978) *ad Works and Days* 649; and for discussion Griffith (1990), 189, and R. Rosen (1990), 102, n. 13 with further literature. Among the earliest uses of the noun σοφιστής are Pindar, *Isthmian* 5(4).28 (of the poet); Herodotus 1.29 (of the seven sages), 2.49 (of diviners); *Prometheus Bound* 62 (of Prometheus).

[47] He does appear to have praised that of his fellow poet Linus: cf. fr. 306 MW.

[48] Other relevant passages include *Cratylus* 397e5–398a2, *Laws* 713e–714a, *Politicus* 268e4–274e4, *Republic* 468e8–469a2, 546d8–e1; see also the discussions in Van Noorden, this volume, Ch. 9, El Murr, Ch. 14, Rowe, Ch. 15.

Ὡς ἔοικας, ἔφη, ὀκνοῦντι λέγειν.

Δόξω δέ σοι, ἦν δ᾽ ἐγώ, καὶ μάλ᾽ εἰκότως ὀκνεῖν, ἐπειδὰν εἴπω.

Λέγ᾽, ἔφη, καὶ μὴ φοβοῦ.

Λέγω δή - καίτοι οὐκ οἶδα ὁποίᾳ τόλμῃ ἢ ποίοις λόγοις χρώμενος ἐρῶ.

...

Οὐκ ἐτός, ἔφη, πάλαι ᾐσχύνου τὸ ψεῦδος λέγειν.

Πάνυ, ἦν δ᾽ ἐγώ, εἰκότως· ἀλλ᾽ ὅμως ἄκουε καὶ τὸ λοιπὸν τοῦ μύθου.

Now, said I, can we devise something in the way of those convenient fictions we spoke of earlier, a single bold flight of invention, which we may induce the community in general, and if possible the rulers themselves, to accept?

What kind of fiction?

Nothing new; something like an Eastern tale of what, according to the poets, has happened before now in more than one part of the world. The poets have been believed; but the thing has not happened in our day, and it would be hard to persuade anyone that it could ever happen again.

You seem rather shy of telling this story of yours.

With good reason, as you will see when I have told it.

Out with it; don't be afraid.

Well, here it is; though I hardly find the courage or the words to express it.

...

You might well be bashful about coming out with your fiction.

No doubt; but still you must hear the rest of the story.

Socrates' 'noble fiction' is one of the most blatant examples in Plato of myth employed for educational purposes. It does not matter whether or not the story is true—indeed, Socrates insists from the outset that it is false. What matters is its didactic value for the just city. At first glance, Plato's rewriting of Hesiod highlights the differences between their outlook and interests. Hesiod does not call his story a μῦθος but a λόγος.[49] And he believes in it—or so it would seem, given that he never comments on its truth value. We are apparently left with two very different scenarios: on the one hand the archaic peasant-poet who remains in the thrall of his own tall tales; and on the other the philosopher who

---

[49] In early Greek epic, the word λόγος is not normally used in the singular to mean 'story' or 'account'; cf. *LfgrE s.v. λόγος*, Verdenius (1985), 76 with n. 328; Wakker (1990), 87–8.

playfully presents his version of the ancient *logos* as a useful lie, no more.

There is, however, more to be said. Let us start by noting that Hesiod's Myth of Ages too has a transparent educational aim: it is meant to explain the wretchedness of our present situation and help us lay the intellectual foundations for the more specific advice that follows. Note too that Hesiod introduces his tale as 'another account' (ἕτερος λόγος). Within the larger context of the *Works and Days* we have just heard of Pandora and how she brought misery to mankind (42–105). Now we get a second explanation of how and why it is that we are miserable, one which focuses on the need for justice.[50] The Pandora narrative anchors the *Works and Days* in the wider Hesiodic tradition: Pandora was already important in the *Theogony* (570–616), and in the *Catalogue of Women* she stars as the first mortal partner of the immortal gods (frr. 2, 5 MW).[51] The Myth of Ages looks prima facie less Hesiodic, though the narrator is careful to coordinate the golden race with the reign of Kronos (111); and he later includes the race of the heroes, against the logic of his own narrative as many have pointed out.[52] So there are some connections here with the main body of Hesiod's work. Still, the phrase ἕτερος λόγος suggests that something unusual is afoot.

How unusual becomes clearer when we compare the Myth of Ages with the Pandora narrative. The Pandora story as told in the *Works and Days* differs from that of the *Theogony* in that it is framed as an illustration of a timeless truth (*Works and Days* 42–7, 105).[53] However, it is not radically different in essence: what we call 'myth' is still introduced as cosmogonic fact.[54] At the beginning of the Myth of Ages, by contrast, we are promised no transparent facts. Instead we

[50] Boys-Stones (this volume, p. 41 with n. 19) points out that Protagoras in the Platonic dialogue first tells a 'myth' (μῦθος) based on the Hesiodic Prometheus narrative and then goes on to give an alternative 'account' (λόγος) of his position: he may well be echoing Hesiod.

[51] Most (1993), 89, without considering the *Catalogue of Women*.

[52] West (1978), 173–4.

[53] For other differences in emphasis see J. S. Clay (2003), Ch. 5; Kenaan, this volume, Ch. 8.

[54] Note the factual statements that open the account at *Works and Days* 42 ('For the gods hid their livelihood from human kind') and 47 ('But Zeus hid man's livelihood in anger').

are told to expect 'another' *logos*; and Perses gets to hear it only if he shows commitment. The phrase εἰ ἐθέλεις—in itself common enough—introduces a telling element of choice on the part of the listener. One *could*, at least theoretically, say 'no'; which is to say that the story that is about to follow is worth listening to not so much because of its intrinsic value (its 'truth' in absolute terms), but because of the value the reader accords it.[55] At the very least, we can say that we are invited to reflect on what *we* want to learn and how we want to go about it. This sort of concern is a far cry from the Muse narrative of the *Theogony* but not so very far perhaps from Plato's noble lie in the *Republic*.

If the narrator of the Myth of Ages is unusually explicit about the commitment he demands from his audience, he is even keener to emphasize his own achievement, claiming that he will give his account 'well' (εὖ) and 'knowingly' (ἐπισταμένως). It has been suggested that the language here implies the skill and knowledge of the bard, but the more immediate association is with skilled craftsmanship.[56] As Margalit Finkelberg has shown, craftsmanship provides important models of fictionality in early Greek literature,[57] and it is probably significant that the only other passage in epic where the phrase εὖ καὶ ἐπισταμένως is used of speech refers to a carefully crafted lie.[58] Certainly, no epic bard ever says of himself that he tells (will tell or has told) his story εὖ καὶ ἐπισταμένως.[59] In fact,

[55] Compare the Homeric parallels at *Iliad* 6.150–51 and 20.213–14 (εἰ δ᾽ ἐθέλεις καὶ ταῦτα δαήμεναι ... ), both in the context of a genealogical account given for the benefit of the listener. The genealogical nature of the Myth of Ages is spelled out at *Works and Days* 108.

[56] For affinities with craftsmanship see *Iliad* 10.265 (Meriones' boar-tusk helmet), *Odyssey* 23.197 (Odysseus' marriage bed); cf. *Odyssey* 20.161 (the skilled preparation of firewood). Verdenius (1985), 77 and Wakker (1990), 90 compare *Odyssey* 11.368 and suggest that Hesiod alludes to the knowledge of the bard.

[57] M. Finkelberg (1998), esp. Ch. 4.

[58] *Homeric Hymn to Hermes* 390.

[59] The closest we come to such a claim is *Odyssey* 22.347–8; but even Phemius emphasizes that his expertise derives ultimately from the gods. At *Homeric Hymn to Apollo* 166–73 the narrator praises himself and/or Homer (Burkert 1987) not in terms of his special expertise but in terms of audience appreciation—a subtle but important difference. Contrast what he says about the Delian maidens at 163 (ἴσασιν).

bards tend to play down their expertise.[60] Our passage is quite exceptional in that respect, and the extravagant and slightly obscure verb ἐκκορυφώσω further enhances our impression that what we are about to hear is only very superficially related to the Muse-inspired account of the *Theogony*.[61]

Indeed, what follows looks like an allegorical myth *avant la parole*. Readers of Hesiod have long puzzled over the nature and significance of the metal imagery in the Myth of Ages:[62] is Hesiod perhaps hinting at the growing distance between gods and humans, from gold as the Olympian metal par excellence to iron with its associations of human toil and suffering?[63] Or should we focus on the ethical considerations that Hesiod develops in his account, given that bronze in early Greek epic is 'pitiless', and a 'heart of iron' remains unmoved in the face of even the most extreme suffering?[64] Rather than trying to answer these questions, I note that the metal imagery is clearly intended to make us think about the deeper meaning of this text. Hesiod was not alone in appreciating its symbolic potential: in the *Odyssey*, Eurylochus accuses Odysseus of

---

[60] Homer emphasizes his own lack of knowledge precisely when he is about to perform his most outrageous feat of memory; cf. *Iliad* 2.484–93 and Graziosi and Haubold (2005), 44–5. At *Odyssey* 11.368, Alcinous praises Odysseus' skills as a narrator (NB ἐπισταμένως) by comparing him to a bard; but like a true bard, Odysseus never makes any such claims for himself.

[61] I strongly suspect that ἐκκορυφόω means something like 'to perfect/bring to its peak' (thus Wilamowitz-Moellendorff 1928, 53–4; Most 1993, 91), but the meaning of the word continues to be debated. Alternative translations include 'to summarize' (West 1978, 178; Wakker 1990; *LfgrE s.v. κορυφόω*) and 'to tell from beginning to end' (Verdenius 1985, 76–7). The scholia suggest either 'to begin' or 'to finish' (48 Pertusi). The word is *hapax legomenon* in early epic; the only other passage where it occurs in Greek literature appears to be Hippocrates, *On Diseases* 4.48. The simplex κορυφόομαι (middle) means 'to rise up high' (of a wave).

[62] For recent discussion and further bibliography see Most (1997), J. S. Clay (2003), 81–95.

[63] For gold see the many divine epithets that feature this metal (e.g. χρυσάορος, χρυσείη, χρυσηλάκατος, χρυσήνιος, χρυσόπτερος, χρυσόθρονος). Gold and silver are associated with immortality at *Odyssey* 7.91–4 (the dogs of Alcinous). For bronze as the metal of heroic warfare see formulaic χαλκοκορυστής, Ἀχαιοὶ χαλκοχίτωνες, etc. For iron and the world of humans see *Works and Days* 387, 420, 743 and especially *Theogony* 764–6: Death is hateful to the gods and has a heart of iron and pitiless bronze.

[64] Most (1997), 124–5.

being 'entirely made of iron' because he never tires and even at night does not allow his companions any rest (*Odyssey* 12.279–85).[65] Odysseus is of course not literally made of iron: as a character within epic, Eurylochus is permitted a degree of rhetorical licence which the epic narrator rarely allows himself.[66] Hesiod in the Myth of Ages allows himself precisely that kind of licence, and in so doing makes an important point about the nature of his account, and our task as readers: what matters now is what we can learn about the world from other human beings; and in order to learn, we must get thinking.

All that is still part of the larger project of telling 'true things', ἐτήτυμα, to Perses (*Works and Days* 10). However, I hope to have shown that the Myth of Ages conveys truth by self-consciously alternative means. Not unlike sophistic mythmakers such as Protagoras or Prodicus—and in keeping with Socrates' noble lie in the *Republic*—Hesiod first frames and then tells his story in such a way as to alert us to the fundamentally layered nature of human speech and human knowledge. As Kathryn Morgan observes: 'philosophical myth [in Plato] achieves its intellectual power by encouraging methodological reflection and self-consciousness about the status of philosophical discourse.'[67] A similar point could be made, *mutatis mutandis*, about Hesiod's ἕτερος λόγος of the ages of man: from the perspective of the fully formed human being (the farmer, not the shepherd), the clairvoyance of the Muses has become literally a thing of the past: they taught the shepherd all he needed to know about the gods and the early stages of the universe. If we want to understand our own present lives as grain-eaters, we must learn to adopt a different approach, one that looks altogether more modern.

---

[65] Most (1997), 125. Hesiod too describes the current race of iron as one that never stops struggling, even at night (*Works and Days* 176–8).

[66] R. Scodel (2002), esp. Ch. 5, discusses the different rhetorical textures of character speech and third-person narrative specifically in Homeric epic.

[67] Morgan (2000), 164.

## CONCLUSION

I have argued that the Hesiodic corpus is structured in terms of internal chronology and in terms of its author's biography. Taken together, these suggest an order of reading and an intellectual trajectory: from divine inspiration to human knowledge, from poetry to reasoned argument. This trajectory works as a *Bildungsroman* at a personal level but, as we have seen, it also has wider implications. The shepherds of epic are not only portrayed as young but also as culturally and intellectually challenged. And farmers, as well as being more mature and socially acceptable, are also more fully human.

We have seen that some of the concerns of the mature Hesiod have striking affinities with those of later thinkers. Indeed, it would seem that in this respect, as in many others, the Hesiodic corpus sketches some of the patterns of thought that were to inform Greek intellectual life in the classical age. Recent scholarship has often emphasized the connections between archaic and classical Greek thought. Thus, Mark Griffith remarks in his discussion of 'contest and contradiction' in early Greek poetry:

Such writers as Gorgias, Protagoras, and Euripides . . . were not for the most part introducing radically new techniques or attitudes, but rather exploiting, systematizing, and exaggerating possibilities that they found already well developed by their predecessors.[68]

Griffith captures well the current distaste for grand narratives of intellectual and cultural change ('Hesiod to Plato', 'poetry to philosophy', 'myth to reason'): rather than speculating about shifts in outlook or mentality, scholars have increasingly come to concentrate on the 'exploitation' and 'exaggeration' of possibilities embedded in the work of predecessors. The present discussion firmly belongs in this context, though it also raises a question that Griffith does not consider: might it be possible that a (grand) narrative of intellectual change is itself among the possibilities that classical authors inherited from their predecessors? Antony Grafton has recently shown that the discovery of the New World was in many ways framed in terms of

---

[68] Griffith (1990), 187.

traditional canons of learning.[69] Narratives of discovery and change were already part of those canons, and the very developments that would eventually supersede canonical knowledge were in large part driven by existing intellectual templates.[70] Similarly, it might be worth considering whether the Hesiodic corpus provided a useful template for intellectual change in the 5th and 4th centuries BC. Could thinkers like Protagoras—or indeed Plato—look to Hesiod for a model of how Muse-inspired poetry gives way to more challenging, more secular, and more properly human attempts to pursue knowledge? Hesiod, and especially the teacher of the *Works and Days*, was extremely popular and highly authoritative in archaic and classical Greece. If indeed his *oeuvre* charts a recognizable development from divine to human knowledge, and from myth to reason, that must be significant: in this respect as in so many others, the intellectual revolution of the 5th and 4th centuries BC appears to be deeply rooted in archaic Greek thought.

[69] Grafton (1992); for an attempt to see Alexander's conquest of Egypt in terms of pre-existing Greek knowledge of Egypt see Vasunia (2001).

[70] E.g. Grafton (1992), 51 on Ptolemy's open-ended conception of the geographer's task.

# 2

## Hesiod and Plato's history of philosophy

### G. R. Boys-Stones

## INTRODUCTION

As other contributors to this volume note, it is part of Hesiod's interest for Plato that his work has a 'philosophical' character—that is, a character which aligns it with Plato's own construction of philosophy as an activity.[1] This is true at the level of content: the *Theogony* and *Works and Days* treat what, in retrospect, look like 'cosmological' and 'ethical' themes, respectively, for example.[2] But it is also true in terms of Hesiod's relationship with his material. Where Homer begins his epics by announcing their subject matter ('Wrath' is the first word of the *Iliad*, 'Man' of the *Odyssey*), Hesiod begins with higher-level reflection on the source of his own inspiration: the Muses and his relationship with them (see *Theogony* 1–35 and *Works and Days* 1–10: both works begin with the word 'Muses'). In the *Works and Days*, this reflection culminates in an expression of Hesiod's concern, and emphatic appropriation of responsibility, for the truth of his discourse ('I, Perses, I shall speak the truth'),[3] leading straight into what appears to be a *correction* of something he had himself said in the *Theogony* ('So there was not just *one* kind of strife,

---

[1] See variously Haubold, Ford, and Van Noorden in this volume.
[2] The *Theogony* and *Works and Days*, I mean to say, wear these themes as it were on their sleeves, though it is true that Homer's poems too could be read as exercises in ethics and physics: see Anaxagoras and Metrodorus at Diogenes Laertius 2.11 (= 59 A1.11 DK and 61 fr. 1 DK respectively).
[3] Cf. for truth and falsehood as the province of the Muses, *Theogony* 27.

but two': *Works and Days* 11–12),[4] followed shortly thereafter by a note on the motivational role played by strife in the promotion of the arts in general, and his own art, that of 'singing', in particular (*Works and Days* 24–6).

Hesiod, in short, not only has interests which Plato shares, but comes across as epistemologically self-aware in his discussion of them in a way which is characteristic of philosophy as Plato will come to understand it. So did Plato afford Hesiod a place in his history of philosophy? In what follows, I shall argue that he did—but that his view of the matter is far from straightforward. The reason for this is that Plato's view of the history of philosophy is itself far from straightforward. As I shall argue in the first part of this chapter, Plato seems to think that the conditions for the historical development of philosophy turn out—perhaps surprisingly—to be more or less detached from the conditions for the historical development of civilization in general. This means that, although one certainly can find patterns in human history, patterns in which the development of many of the technical arts will naturally find their place, they do not as a matter of fact provide a systematical template for a developmental history of philosophy. But it is in articulating just this complexity that Hesiod becomes a useful reference point for Plato. For Hesiod, as I shall go on to show, can be used both to give a voice to the cumulative tradition of inchoate and abortive attempts at philosophy which Plato sees in its past, and also to provide a foundation for the new direction in which he tries to set it for the future.

## PLATO *HISTORICUS*

That Plato has what we might call a 'historical consciousness' is evident both at a general level, in his reflections on the historical patterns governing human existence, and in the narrower sphere of his engagement with earlier thinkers as part of his own philosophical activity. The broader historical patterns I have in mind include

[4] Cf. Haubold in this volume, p. 21.

Plato's view that human civilization is something which develops in cycles, from simple, pastoral beginnings, to ever more elaborate and advanced political and technological systems—before being set back to the beginning by periodic catastrophe.[5] In its extreme form, the thesis might sound hypothetical—whimsical, even.[6] But it provides the theoretical framework for at least one concrete historical narrative, which is the account of ancient Athens offered in the *Timaeus–Critias*. Athens, we are told there, once rose to a level of technical sophistication and political eminence so great that it was able to see off the empire of Atlantis in battle—before plunging back into a dark age so total that the Athenians of the 5th century had no collective memory of their former glory at all.[7] Whether one takes this narrative at face value, or (surely better) sees it as an allegory for the more recent rise and fall of Athens, from its heyday at Marathon to its humiliation at Syracuse, the point is much the same: Plato's recognition of a cyclical dimension to human history is more than merely theoretical.[8]

As to Plato's use of his predecessors: the important thing here is not the simple fact that he refers to and engages closely with earlier thinkers, but the fact that he engages with them *as* figures in the history of his own thought.[9] Plato's dialogues, it should not be forgotten, are themselves works of historical fiction, set a generation or more before their date of composition: so long ago that Plato not only is generally absent from the conversations they record, but often enough *could not have been present*. And a sense of historical depth

---

[5] See *Timaeus* 22c–e and *Laws* Book 3 with Boys-Stones (2001), 8–14.

[6] Cf. esp. the *Politicus* myth, discussed in this volume by El Murr and Rowe.

[7] The narrative purportedly comes from the Egyptians, who are able to take the long view because Egypt is less subject to catastrophe than other areas of the world. Interestingly, Egyptians are correlatively conservative, which means that their development of the arts is not so far in advance of younger civilizations which may, in fact, outstrip them (as the author of the *Epinomis* says at 987d; cf. Plato, *Laws* 656d–657b).

[8] Note the *inevitability* of the decline to which even Callipolis is subject: γενομένῳ παντὶ φθορά ἐστιν, οὐδ' ἡ τοιαύτη σύστασις τὸν ἅπαντα μενεῖ χρόνον, ἀλλὰ λυθήσεται ... (*Republic* 546a, which goes straight on to link this inevitability precisely with *cycles* of flourishing and dying). For Atlantis as political allegory, see e.g. Vidal-Naquet (2007), Ch. 1, and Gill (1980), xiv–xxi, drawing what he takes to be the 'striking' conclusion that 'Plato is genuinely interested in history' (xx).

[9] See esp. McCabe (2000).

traced between Plato as writer and the conversations he imagines is
an important part of the dynamic of the Platonic dialogue. In the
person of Socrates, Plato seems able to collapse the decades to enter
into debate with some of the major figures of the generation before
him—Protagoras and Parmenides in the dialogues named after
them, just for example. Yet, at the same time, the very different
world in which he is actually writing makes it impossible to forget
the historical gulf between 'then' and 'now', a gulf which provides
its own, sometimes very piquant, commentary on the positions
with which Plato was engaging. Most obviously, the knowledge of
Socrates' execution constantly frames Plato's depiction of him, and
readers are invited to test Socrates' philosophical integrity against
what they know of his historical fate. But the positions of his interlocutors, particularly those associated with the political orthodoxy
of democratic Athens in its heyday, are no less framed and tested by
(for example) what Plato's readers know to have been the disastrous
conclusion of the Peloponnesian war.[10]

   In one sense, then, it is not only legitimate to ask about Plato's
history of philosophy, it is crucial for the way we approach the
dialogues. The problem comes in trying to join up Plato's history
of philosophy with his broader history of civilization. It would be
natural to assume (as Aristotle, for example, assumed) that the two
things go hand in hand: that philosophy develops and becomes more
sophisticated as civilization does.[11] After all, Platonic philosophy is,
or aspires to be, a *technē*, and the development of civilization in
Plato's view is inevitably tied closely to increasingly sophisticated
attainment in intellectual and technological fields. What is more,
Plato seems explicitly to link the development of philosophy to his
narrative of the emergence of civilization: at least, he suggests at
various times that political complexity and the development of
mathematics are prerequisites for philosophy.[12] Yet there is no clear

---

[10] An excellent case study is Gifford (2001).

[11] For Aristotle, see fr. 13 Rose.

[12] Political complexity: *Laws* 678ab (cf. Boys-Stones 2001, 13–14). Mathematics is
a grounding for philosophy in the educational curriculum of the *Republic* (and
indeed the epistemological scheme expressed by the image of the 'line' at 509d–
511e). (Elsewhere, one might note, mathematics is only an *analogue* for success in
philosophy: e.g. *Theaetetus* 148d.)

sense in Plato's dialogues that philosophy, even with these prerequisites in place, has come any measurable distance at all.

This has not stopped people looking for hints of a developmental story of philosophy in Plato, however. In particular, the real, and (as far as it goes) well-founded, sense that Plato's own philosophy treads some kind of a line between Heraclitus and Parmenides is occasionally taken as the basis for ascribing to Plato the thesis that philosophy advances—already *has* advanced—by a form of 'dialectical' progress.[13] The idea is that the kind of dialectical conversation that one might imagine conducted between two ideal Platonic philosophers—confronting and testing each other's positions in order to arrive at a synthesis which preserves the best of both—is to be found played out in historical terms between different schools of thought. The proof-text for this view comes in a lengthy stretch of the *Sophist*, which can be read as a map of the historical 'dialectic' that has led to Plato himself. The passage, which is worth quoting at length, begins with the following overview of pre-Heraclitean philosophy—described in rather Hesiodic terms, a point to which I shall be returning (*Sophist* 242cd):

It seems to me that each of them tells us a story, as if we were children. One person says that there are three things, and that some of them sometimes fight with each other, but then make it up and marry and have children and bring them up. Another person says there are two things—wet and dry, or warm and cold; and he has them live together and gets them married. Our own Eleatic people, who began with Xenophanes, or perhaps even earlier, talk in their stories as if 'everything', so-called, is really just one thing.

It is not obvious from the way Plato phrases it here, but it becomes clear in the sequel that the Eleatic Stranger, who is leading the discussion in this dialogue, thinks that, at the heart of this free-for-all over the question of how many things there are, is a fundamental encounter between the advocates of two polar extremes: those who think that there is just one thing, and those who think that there are many. The debate turns out to be, in other words, a battle between monists and pluralists. The interesting thing about this is that the polarity becomes clear just as progress appears to be made

---

[13] E.g. recently Bárány (2006); Press (2007), 168–70.

through the *synthesis* of these positions in the persons of Heraclitus (what the 'hard-line' Muses say is clearly based on Heraclitus 22 A10, B10 DK) and Empedocles (the laxer philosopher of Aphrodite and Neikos) (242d–243a):

But later, certain Ionian and Sicilian Muses realized that the safest thing was to weave both accounts together and to say that what exists is *both* many *and* one, and held together by both enmity and friendship. 'What is being drawn apart is always being brought together' say the more hard-line of the Muses—though the less strict among them relax the requirement that they are always in both states, but say that everything is, successively, now one and amicable, through Aphrodite, and now many and hostile towards itself, though some power of Neikos ['conflict'].

Having (on this view) set out one 'dialectical' advance, the Eleatic Stranger goes on at 246a–c to set up a new opposition between materialists and 'friends of forms'. This time, the battle is represented in the terms of the mythical attack launched by the race of Giants who wanted to unseat the Olympian gods (again, I shall return to the Hesiodic character of the imagery):

They are involved in a kind of Gigantomachy because of their disagreement over being . . . Some of them pull everything from heaven and the invisible realm down to earth, literally laying hold of 'stones and oak'. For clinging to things like this, they affirm that only that which offers resistance and can be touched exists. So they define being as body, and if anyone says that something else, which does not have body, exists, they absolutely despise him and refuse to hear any more . . . Those who disagree with them very cautiously defend a position somewhere up in the invisible realm, constraining true being to certain intelligible and incorporeal forms. They verbally pulverize the 'bodies' that their opponents say are true being, and refer to them as a 'process of generation', not as being. In between them there has always been an interminable battle over these questions.

The Stranger goes on to broker a deal between relatively amenable representatives of each faction, in which he demands that the claims of both are recognized (249cd). Assuming that the Eleatic Stranger speaks, more or less, for Plato (it seems reasonable enough that he does), and especially if one reads this new opposition as a clash between Heraclitean Giants and Parmenidean Olympians, we arrive at the result we wanted: Plato's own philosophy constructed as a sophisticated new synthesis of the two great movements.

The appeal of a narrative like this is very strong, not least because, as I suggested, it extrapolates its diachronic narrative from views that we know Plato holds about how advances in ordinary philosophical dialectic are achieved. Platonic dialectic precisely and explicitly deals with antithetical extremes by exploring the middle ground between them. At *Philebus* 17a, in fact, this is how 'dialectic' is distinguished from 'eristic'—eristic (about which I shall have more to say below) being, roughly, the adoption of some position for the sake of maintaining it in debate, rather than making progress in understanding.

But at the same time, the idea that the pattern set by Platonic dialectic provides the basis for Plato's history of philosophy, his view of how philosophers historically have responded to each other and collectively advanced our understanding of the world, may turn out to be an illusion. It is an old and tenacious view, to be sure: it has roots in ancient attempts to make Plato the reference point for subsequent philosophical practice by making him the summation of all that went before, in the sense of being a *synthesis* of different and at times competing strands in earlier philosophical history;[14] and its currency in the modern world is no doubt helped by its seductive assonance with the language of Hegelian 'dialectic'. But it is not at all clear that Plato himself took such a tidy view of the matter, as a closer look at the *Sophist* will show.

The 'dialectical' reading of the *Sophist* starts from the position that the engagement between monists and pluralists, who are readily identified with known historical positions, results in a synthesis of the two which represents real intellectual progress. I have already noted that their crystallization into *two* opposing camps seems not to be something in the forefront of Plato's mind when he sets up the battle: perhaps that does not matter. But the status of the resulting 'synthesis' as an intellectual *advance* is also far from clear. If the

---

[14] The late 2nd-century Platonist Atticus, for example, has him 'perfect' philosophy by uniting the various traditions of his predecessors (fr. 1 des Places); Numenius, at a similar period, talks about him 'striking a mean' between Pythagoras and Socrates (fr. 24 des Places *ad fin.*). Cf. Diogenes Laertius 3.8: 'He created a blend of Heraclitean, Pythagorean, and Socratic arguments.'

model holds, if it really were an advance (and not just another new
position to add to the pot), one should expect to see this position
further refined through further dialectical stages. Indeed, the dialectical reading of the *Sophist* is inspired in the first place by the idea
that Heraclitus, one product of the first dialectical clash, is set to
battle the Eleatic school in the Gigantomachy which follows and
which is supposed to form the immediate background to Plato's
own thought.[15] But that turns out to be a very problematic assumption indeed. It has been noted often enough that Parmenides (who is
neither named nor quoted here, as he was in the previous battle) sits
uncomfortably on the side of the Friends: Parmenides, after all,
believes that there exists just one thing, yet the Friends believe in
many things, namely the forms.[16] But, just as importantly, Heraclitus
(who is not named or quoted here either, though he too was invoked
in the previous battle) turns out to make a very awkward Giant. If we
consider what Plato says about Heraclitus in the *Theaetetus*—a work
to which the *Sophist* represents itself as a sort of sequel, and which we
are therefore expected to have in mind—he actually turns out to have
as much in common with the Friends of the Forms. He does away
with what one can grasp with one's hands (*Theaetetus* 155a), and in
doing so seems at odds with the Giants who believe that only such
things exist (*Sophist* 246a). On the other hand, he reduces bodies to
processes, so that we can refer to what is 'becoming' but not what *is*
(*Theaetetus* 156a–157b)—very much like the Friends of the Forms in
the *Sophist*, who 'pulverize' bodies and consign them to 'becoming'
rather than 'being' (246c).[17]

---

[15] Cf. L. Brown (1998), 188, assuming that Heraclitus and Empedocles are among
the Giants.

[16] As many commentators have seen, Plato may more likely have identified
members of his own school as Friends of the Forms—a view which naturally undermines from the start the idea that this passage represents a stage in the dialectical
advance towards Plato himself. See e.g. L. Brown (1998), 186. (Bárány 2006, 320
suggests that the Stranger himself makes the identification between the Friends and
Parmenides at 249cd; but this passage rather seems to distinguish between (a) those
who maintain that reality is one (sc. the Eleatics, then), and (b) those who think that
reality is constituted by the (many) forms.)

[17] Bárány (2006), 320 acknowledges, but effectively ignores, all this. It is, by the
way, no easier to find Empedocles (the other product of the first battle) among the
Giants: in according an important role to the forces of Aphrodite and Neikos, he is

The fact that the participants in the Gigantomachy are so hard to pin down, which in turn baffles any attempt to construct a clear historical relationship between the Gigantomachy and the earlier battle (beyond, that is, the historically contingent fact that one occurred before the other), points finally to the conclusion that Plato is not here trying to develop a systematical account of philosophical history after all—is not seeing patterns of development, dialectical or otherwise, which lead inexorably to the threshold of his own activity. Indeed, it seems to me that this passage points in a different direction altogether. Far from placing an emphasis on philosophical *progress*, Plato here, as again and again elsewhere, suggests that he is working against a backdrop of philosophical *stasis*. The Eleatic Stranger actually comments of the Gigantomachy, not that it is a glorious battle of the recent past, but that it is *limitless* and *perennial*: ἐν μέσῳ δὲ περὶ ταῦτα ἄπλετος ἀμφοτέρων μάχη τις, ὦ Θεαίτητε, ἀεὶ συνέστηκεν (246c). And although a narrative of development seems to be written into the previous battle (the battle between monists and pluralists from which Heraclitus and Empedocles emerged as a new stage in philosophical history), the message is undercut by the fact that Plato elsewhere goes out of his way to *deny* the historical novelty of the positions which they (specifically *they*: Heraclitus and Empedocles) espouse. In the *Theaetetus* (remembering, again, that the *Sophist* itself asks us to have this work in mind) Heraclitus and Empedocles are grouped together, by name, with Protagoras, 'all the wise men, one after another, except Parmenides', and poets including Epicharmus and Homer, as having been committed to the same position, namely that everything is in flux (152de). Much the same thesis is found in the *Cratylus* too: there, Heraclitus turns out to hold a position already maintained by Hesiod, Homer, and Orpheus (402b)—a position, we learn, which is as ancient as the Greek language itself (411b).[18] Not much, it seems, has changed after all.

---

not obviously someone who thinks that only what 'offers resistance and can be touched' is real.

[18] Cf. Sedley (2003), 28, 112, 122. Plato may be relying for the details of his Heraclitean thesis, perhaps even the idea, on the Sophist Hippias: see Balaudé (2006) (and cf. Ford in this volume, pp. 144–5).

## HESIOD *ERISTICUS*

Far from finding a narrative of progress in Plato, then, it looks more likely that he viewed earlier philosophical history in terms precisely of its *failure* to make progress, certainly its failure to keep pace with advances in other areas of civilized activity. To be sure, the perennial 'mainstream' is, appropriately enough for a broadly Heraclitean tradition, in motion while it rests: the claim can hardly be that everyone says exactly the same thing. But its contributors have failed to hit upon a modus operandi which enables their various contributions to achieve the sort of cumulative advance one sees in other arts—mathematics, for example. So they keep slipping back into the same old compromise position. From a certain perspective (that of the battle between monists and pluralists in the *Sophist* for example), Heraclitus' 'nothing-is-truer-than-anything-else' theory of flux might look like an exciting innovation. In fact it is a backward step: a relapse into something familiar and ancient.

If it is right to view matters in these terms, there are two further observations to make—observations which take me, at last, to Hesiod. The first is that Plato's construction of the 'mainstream', as I am calling it, involves the deliberate inclusion of sophists and poets alongside people whom Plato might be expected to recognize more readily as his ancestors in philosophy. These categories are not, of course, so clear-cut or well established for Plato as they are, on the whole, for us. Nevertheless, it seems right to talk of a *deliberate* conflation of different categories of thinker just because it is one for which arguments are offered—and offered by figures within as well as figures outside the tradition under construction. Protagoras, for example, makes common intellectual cause in his own voice with Homer and Hesiod (as poets), Orpheus and Musaeus (as *theologoi*), physical trainers, and musicians (*Protagoras* 316d–317a). Elsewhere it is Socrates who brings together 'philosophers' and 'poets' in a single tradition—even as he distances himself from them (*Theaetetus* 152de; *Cratylus* 402ab).

There is, then, no getting away from the fact that Hesiod is one of the people implicated in, and appropriated by, the 'mainstream'. But this leads me on to my second observation. Not only is Hesiod a member of the mainstream, it is often in his voice, quite specifically, that it expresses itself. This is true on a grand scale on at least two occasions in the material I have already been surveying—the very material, that is, in which Plato offers reflections on the stasis represented by this earlier tradition. Protagoras, for example, having established himself as the representative of a tradition of sophistry that stretches back to Homer and Hesiod, gets down to business with a distinctly 'Hesiodic' narrative offered in answer to a question about the nature of justice. His response is a tale of Prometheus, Epimetheus, and the creation of man (*Protagoras* 320c ff.)—a story which is, of course, reworked from Hesiod's own meditation on justice, the *Works and Days* (42–105). The decision to deliver himself in these terms is no accident: indeed, Plato makes some play of the fact that Protagoras might have delivered a *logos* instead of this *muthos* (320c) had his audience preferred.[19]

Hesiod is very much the reference point for the historical skirmishes of the *Sophist* as well. Indeed, both of the battles I reviewed above are set up in broadly Hesiodic terms. In the first, the battle between pluralists and monists, the antagonists 'each tell us a story, as if we were children' (μῦθόν τινα ἕκαστος φαίνεταί μοι διηγεῖσθαι παισὶν ὡς οὖσιν ἡμῖν: 242c), and their stories, we learn, encompass themes of warfare, marriage, children, the raising of offspring, and the cohabitation of opposites (242cd). These are familiar enough themes in themselves, but there is no precedent for a work containing *all* of them nearly so obvious as Hesiod—whether the *Theogony* on its own, or the *Theogony* taken together with *Works and Days*.[20] So when the clash between the 'materialists' and form-lovers later on is described as a 'Gigantomachy', Hesiod naturally comes to

---

[19] That he goes on afterwards to give a '*logos*' as well (324d: οὐκέτι μῦθόν σοι ἐρῶ ἀλλὰ λόγον) hardly undermines the point: indeed, it establishes a further parallel with Hesiod. Hesiod's narrative of Prometheus is a *muthos* (μυθησαίην at *Works and Days* 10: cf. J. S. Clay 2003: 32); but on its conclusion he continues—deferring to the possibility of audience preference, just as Protagoras does—with a *logos* on the same theme: εἰ δ'ἐθέλεις, ἕτερόν τοι ἐγὼ λόγον ἐκκορυφώσω (106).

[20] Contrast Socrates' characterization of what Hesiod (and other poets) share in common with Homer (*Ion* 531c): warfare, relationships between men, between gods, and between gods and men; celestial and infernal phenomena; the births of gods and heroes.

mind again. He is, to be sure, not the *only* obvious reference point in this case: we must certainly be put in mind of the representation of the Gigantomachy which formed a central part of the Great Panathenaea (cf. *Euthyphro* 6bc): part of the moral, no doubt, is the decisive role Athena (that is, wisdom) needs to take in the present battle too. But with the *Theogony* in mind already, it would be difficult not to be reminded of Hesiod's Titanomachy, that other assault on the heavens by creatures of earth.[21] The similarity between these battles was recognized in antiquity, to the point where the two could be easily conflated;[22] Plato's Giants and Hesiod's Titans grasp rocks as weapons with suspiciously similar language;[23] and although the Giants differ in using oak trees too, the difference is explained by an apparently traditional phrase—'oak and rocks'—which may itself have suggested Hesiod to Plato's readers.[24]

But why should Plato think of Hesiod as the natural voice of this tradition? One reason might be to do with the central place taken within this tradition by the sophists. I do not mean by this that Plato thinks that all members of it *are sophists*—as we have seen, he is careful to distinguish the different interest-groups that go to make it up. (Even Protagoras, who has a point of his own to make, acknowledges that others in the tradition *seem* not to be sophists.) But Plato

[21] It is interesting that the *Theogony* should thus be a powerful thematic presence in the *Sophist*, when the *Works and Days* plays such a central role in its sequel, the *Politicus* (see in this volume esp. Rowe; El Murr). It is unlikely to be coincidence, especially since another important pairing of Platonic dialogues replicates the pattern, namely the *Republic* (*Works and Days*) and the *Timaeus* (*Theogony*). The possibility of coincidence is further reduced if Ford is right to argue (as he does in this volume) that Plato knows Hesiod only as the author of the *Works and Days* and *Theogony*.

[22] Cf. Sanford (1941).

[23] *Sophist* 246a ($\tau\alpha\hat{\iota}\varsigma$ $\chi\epsilon\rho\sigma\grave{\iota}\nu$ $\mathring{\alpha}\tau\epsilon\chi\nu\hat{\omega}\varsigma$ $\pi\acute{\epsilon}\tau\rho\alpha\varsigma$ $\kappa\alpha\grave{\iota}$ $\delta\rho\hat{\upsilon}\varsigma$ $\pi\epsilon\rho\iota\lambda\alpha\mu\beta\acute{\alpha}\nu\upsilon\nu\tau\epsilon\varsigma$); cf. Hesiod, *Theogony* 675 ($\pi\acute{\epsilon}\tau\rho\alpha\varsigma$ $\mathring{\eta}\lambda\iota\beta\acute{\alpha}\tau\upsilon\varsigma$ $\sigma\tau\iota\beta\alpha\rho\hat{\eta}\varsigma$ $\mathring{\epsilon}\nu$ $\chi\epsilon\rho\sigma\grave{\iota}\nu$ $\mathring{\epsilon}\chi\upsilon\nu\tau\epsilon\varsigma$).

[24] Plato's Giants grasp rocks and oak ($\pi\acute{\epsilon}\tau\rho\alpha\varsigma$ $\kappa\alpha\grave{\iota}$ $\delta\rho\hat{\upsilon}\varsigma$); cf. *Theogony* 35: $\mathring{\alpha}\lambda\lambda\grave{\alpha}$ $\tau\acute{\iota}$ $\mathring{\eta}$ $\mu\upsilon\iota$ $\tau\alpha\hat{\upsilon}\tau\alpha$ $\pi\epsilon\rho\grave{\iota}$ $\delta\rho\hat{\upsilon}\nu$ $\mathring{\eta}$ $\pi\epsilon\rho\grave{\iota}$ $\pi\acute{\epsilon}\tau\rho\eta\nu$; It is true that Plato knows the phrase 'being born from oak or rock' from Homer (see *Apology* 34d with *Odyssey* 19.162–3); but it is hard to see how its occurrence in the *Sophist* could have resonance with this Homeric precedent. Hesiod's use of it is thoroughly obscure (for possible meanings, see West 1966, 167–9); but since it cuts off his report of the Muses' charge to him as a singer, there is scope to think that Plato could take the idiom to be concerned with something like, for example, foundations or basic principles (even building-blocks), which the Giants might reasonably cling to.

does seem to think that the Heraclitean 'mainstream' which constitutes the broad trend of earlier 'philosophy' is strongly contami-
nated—in fact is essentially vitiated—by the sort of futile, eristic
battles that he associates above all with sophistry. And Hesiod turns
out to be, for Plato, an ideal spokesman for this corrupting, sophistic
core. Not only could he rely on an association between Hesiod and
the sophistic movement made more widely in classical culture (we
have seen, for example, that Protagoras claimed him for a sophist,[25]
and Protagoras' claims are paralleled by the representation of Hesiod
in the *Contest*, where he is depicted in debate over topics characteristic of 5th-century sophistic debate);[26] it is also relevant that Hesiod
is one of the more ancient poets. One of the points Plato wishes
to make is precisely the way in which the mainstream never really
advances, but always relapses to its ancient roots.

So much might be said for Homer as well. But there is one more
thing that makes Hesiod an appropriate spokesman for a tradition
riddled with the vices of the sophistic (that is, the *eristic*) tradition:
his own positive comments about strife (*eris*). 'Strife' had itself been a
contentious issue before Plato: Homer wished it away from the lives
of men (*Iliad* 18.107), and Heraclitus famously attacked him for it
(22 A20 DK). Hesiod not only thought that it could be a good thing,
the spur to greater achievement, but explicitly includes his own art
(the 'singing' that was to become 'sophistry') under its patronage
(*Works and Days* 11–26):

There is not just one kind of strife, but two on earth: one you would praise if
you recognized it, but the other is reprehensible: they are quite different in
spirit. For one is cruel, and fosters the evils of war and battle: no mortal loves
her, though under the necessity of divine will they pay honour to this
troublesome Strife. The other is the first daughter born to dark Night, set
down in the roots of the earth by the son of Cronus, who sits on high and

---

[25] Strictly speaking, of course, the claim is put by Plato in Protagoras' mouth; but
there is no reason to suppose that it is done to misrepresent him. And see Koning in
this volume, pp. 100–1.

[26] Cf. Graziosi (2001). That Hesiod wins the contest on the ground that he is the
poet of peace (*Contest* §13, 207–14 West) is surely ironic: his engagement in the
*Contest* itself shows his love of a fight; he shows *phthonos* towards Homer in the
course of it (11, 148–50 West; cf. 94 ἀχθεσθείς); and on winning, he sets up a
triumphalist dedication.

dwells in the heaven, and is better by far to men. Even the good-for-nothing she rouses to work: for one feels the need to work when one sees another man rich because he is quick to plough and plant and set his house in order. A neighbour competes with a neighbour who is in pursuit of riches, and this Strife is good for mortals. Potter too hates potter and builder builder, and beggar is envious of beggar, and singer of singer.

On the basis of this passage alone, one sees how Hesiod could become for Plato the rallying voice of a tradition convergent with sophistry. Plato himself, of course, allows no such distinction between good and bad *eris*.[27] Hesiod's singers might be spurred to achievement by competition, but it is a mark of Platonic experts that they never compete to outdo each other (*Republic* 349b–350b);[28] it is sophists, not philosophers, who engage in eristic (*Sophist* 225c–226a, 231e; cf. again *Philebus* 17a), people who want to pick a fight (*Republic* 454ab; 499a). At *Critias* 109b, we are told that Eris is absent from the gods—a remark surely intended to take in Hesiod's accommodation of Eris within the divine genealogies.[29] It is particularly interesting that 'Meno's Paradox'—a man can make enquiry neither into what he knows, for he knows it already; nor into what he does not know, for he would not know when he found it—is characterized as an *eristikos logos* (*Meno* 80e, 81d). In a way it is the *eristikos logos* par excellence, for it threatens to make intellectual progress impossible: if the paradox holds, *all* enquiry is futile posturing.[30]

---

[27] If one supposes that Plato sees common cause with Solon in his thought about *eris*, particularly *eris* as a political evil, it becomes the more likely that he has Hesiod quite specifically in mind in the citations that follow. For Solon must have been thinking about Hesiod when he imagined the rule of law (*eunomiē*) bringing an end to *eris* (fr. 4. 32–9 West: note the reversion in 38 to Homer's association of *eris* and *cholos* at *Iliad* 18.107–8). Compare also fr. 13. 43 ff. West (σπεύδει δ' ἄλλοθεν ἄλλος ...) with *Works and Days* 23–4 (ζηλοῖ δέ τε γείτονα γείτων | εἰς ἄφενος σπεύδοντ'· ἀγαθὴ δ' Ἔρις ἥδε βροτοῖσιν). My thanks to Johannes Haubold for drawing this to my attention.

[28] Cf. Isocrates, *Letter* 5 (*To Alexander*) 3.1–3 for the explicit association of *eris* and *pleonexia*, which is what Plato has in his targets here.

[29] See *Theogony* 225, where Eris is a daughter of Night. Homer is culpable too, though: Eris is one of the gods at *Iliad* 11.73–7.

[30] Cf. also *Euthydemus* 275d–276b. Plato constantly returns to the attempt to vindicate enquiry and the possibility of teaching, especially when it concerns virtue. One thing that makes the sophists dangerous is that, despite offering to teach, their positions often seem to entail that teaching is impossible, e.g. because it is impossible

In general, then, Plato links Eris/eristic, and with it what I am calling the mainstream, with the impossibility of substantive teaching or learning, and so of philosophical advance. Hesiod was wrong to distinguish a futile and a productive form of *eris*: contention in the law-courts, which Hesiod and Plato alike abhor (*Republic* 499a; *Works and Days* 27–41) is of a piece with the striving of 'singer against singer'. The result in each case is the same: a waste of energy and a permanent standoff—a perpetual Gigantomachy.

## PLATO *DIALECTICUS*

From what I have said so far, it might seem that I am heading towards the conclusion that Hesiod is the villain of Plato's history of philosophy. But this cannot be quite right. As other chapters of this volume (indeed, the very existence of this volume) make clear, Plato *himself* talks in the language of Hesiod, and frequently takes Hesiod as the reference point for his own positions—or, at least, for positions which frame a critical stance towards the sophists. Indeed, if I am right to suggest that a crucial point of difference, in Plato's account, between Plato and his predecessors is the futility of *their* eristic and so, by implication, the fertility of *his* dialectic, then it is relevant that Plato at least once associates Hesiod with the possibility of intellectual progress (*Cratylus* 428a, quoting *Works and Days* 361):

Hesiod's remark seems right to me: progress can be made 'by adding little to little'.

True, Hesiod was actually talking about the acquisition of money, not wisdom; but virtue is true wealth after all (cf. *Republic* 416e), and the methodological point, in any case, is well taken: one makes progress in whatever sphere by *adding* to what went before, not by flying into contention with it. Perhaps, then, for all the faults which lead to his association with the 'mainstream', Hesiod also provides the 'little'

to contradict someone or to assert a falsehood (*Euthydemus* 285e ff.), or because the truth is relative to individuals (*Theaetetus* 152a). Note that the Heracliteans of the 'mainstream' constructed in the *Theaetetus* have no pupils and no teachers (180c).

which might have been, and in Plato might yet be, the foundation for
real intellectual progress. The question is whether we can identify
something in Hesiod that Plato will think he got *right*, such that it
will act as the basis for a more constructive tradition than that of the
eristical mainstream.

Oddly enough, it looks as if the answer might come in the very
passage that proclaims Hesiod's adherence to Eris. For on the one
occasion when Plato actually quotes this passage, he does so not to
make a point about *eris* at all but—surprisingly—about the nature
of love. Hesiod, he suggests, provides evidence that love subsists
between entities which are unlike one another (*Lysis* 215cd, Socrates
speaking):[31]

> I've just remembered: I once heard someone say that like is most hostile to
> like, and the good to the good. In fact he adduced Hesiod as evidence, saying
> that, *as potter too hates potter and singer singer and beggar beggar*, so
> necessarily with everything else: things that are like one another, especially
> when they are very alike, are full of envy, competitiveness, and enmity; but
> things very unlike each other are full of love.

There is not room here to do justice to Plato's theory of love and its
role in intellectual striving.[32] But it is enough for present purposes to
remember that a crucial aspect of it is that it involves the erotic bond
between things that are not the same but between which some
relationship of need subsists. The idea, roughly speaking, is that the
philosopher conceives a radical desire for the wisdom he does not yet
possess (the form of the 'Beautiful' in the *Phaedrus* and the *Symposium*, the 'first friend' of the *Lysis*), and in virtue of this desire
conceives a further desire for individuals who complement his own
intellectual state and are thus able to help him achieve his end

---

[31] It might be relevant to Plato's re-reading of this passage as a reflection on love
rather than *eris* (especially since he does not quote the context in which *eris* is
mentioned) that the interlocutor who immediately approves of the reading, Menexenus, has himself earlier been characterized as an *eristikos* (211b).

[32] One complication is that the present passage of the *Lysis* is concerned with
*philia* (traditionally translated 'friendship') not *erōs* ('erotic love'). For the sake of
clarity and brevity, I allow myself the liberty of glossing over the distinction in what
follows, since my point in any case is that the passage *is not* but *gestures towards* the
final theory, which (following Penner and Rowe 2005) I take to be a general theory
about our desire for the good, which in turn coincides precisely with the theory of
'eros' we get in both the *Symposium* and *Phaedrus*.

through dialectic. Erotic attraction between different individuals, and between an individual and the wisdom they are pursuing, is, then, the basis of constructive dialectic for Plato—which is precisely what Plato offers instead of eristic.

It would, of course, be going far too far to suggest that all of this is what Plato is here ascribing to Hesiod. Indeed, Socrates goes straight on to offer a disproof of the strong thesis that love subsists between unlike and unlike, for which Hesiod is invoked as a witness. But Plato clearly is ascribing to Hesiod a helpful contribution to this full theory. For Plato has, with what we might regard as some perversity, turned a passage of Hesiod famous for championing *eris* into a theory of love which functions as a useful corrective to the position (considered and rejected just before) that love is between like and like.[33] What is more, it is part of the point that, in finding something to approve in Hesiod, Plato also wants to build on it—to move on from it. Indeed, the very way in which Plato cites Hesiod draws attention to the dual dynamic of his movement *away* from Hesiod with his starting point *in* him. For he offers a quotation, but rewrites it as he does so. Hesiod considered potters, builders, beggars, and singers in that order (*Works and Days* 25–6):

> καὶ κεραμεὺς κεραμεῖ κοτέει καὶ τέκτονι τέκτων
> καὶ πτωχὸς πτωχῷ φθονέει καὶ ἀοιδὸς ἀοιδῷ.

> And potter vies with potter, and builder with builder
> And beggar envies beggar and singer singer.

Plato (though preserving the metre, and so the pretence of authenticity) drops the builders and promotes the singers:[34]

---

[33] It should be noted that what I call the 'perversity' of this reading is mitigated to some extent by the fact that, in Hesiod, love (*Philotēs*, remembering that *philia* is the word under immediate discussion: n. 32) is a sister to Eris: see *Theogony* 224–5. In any case, the reading is not *so* perverse that Aristotle was embarrassed to adopt it: *Eudemian Ethics* 1235a13–18; *Nicomachean Ethics* 1155a32–b1.

[34] The potters remain in pole position, as the anchor for the quotation. Every indication is that the misquotation is deliberate and not, for example, a variant in Plato's text of Hesiod. For one thing, no one else in antiquity who quotes this line quotes it in any form other than that in our MSS (and this includes Aristotle who seems to quote it with this passage of the *Lysis* in mind: see again n. 33). For another, Plato's version, while it scans, nevertheless leaves half a line empty. Cf. further El Murr in this volume, Ch. 14, for Plato's deliberate reformulation of Hesiod.

καὶ κεραμεὺς κεραμεῖ κοτέει καὶ ἀοιδὸς ἀοιδῷ
καὶ πτωχὸς πτωχῷ . . .

And potter vies with potter and singer with singer
And beggar with beggar . . .

It is not absurd to think that this is itself carefully manipulated to fit his conceit that Hesiod can be made to point the way to his own thesis about love and dialectic. The 'singer' would stand as usual for the (would-be) wise man, the 'beggar', not implausibly, for the person in love.[35] The message, then, starts to emerge: there is no progress in the debates of men who think they are wise already: the truly wise are in search of (in love with) what they do not have. To put this a little more in the language of the *Symposium* (but in terms absolutely consistent with the *Lysis* too): philosophy is what happens when a man who would be wise teams up with Eros.


## PLATO *EROTICUS*

The *Lysis*, I am suggesting, turns the very passage which identifies Hesiod most closely with the 'eristic' tradition into a reference point for Plato's own 'erotic' science of dialectic. The suggestion gets some support from the fact that it is possible to see Plato at work making similar corrections to Hesiod in his other erotic dialogues, the *Symposium* and the *Phaedrus*. For the *Symposium*, I rely on an observation made by David Sedley, who has argued (2006, 67–9) that Agathon's speech, in making Eros the youngest of the gods, is meant as a correction of Hesiod's genealogy, since Hesiod made Eros the first of the gods (after Chaos, that is: see *Theogony* 116–22). Sedley's suggestion is that the correction is intended to dissociate Eros from the violence inflicted by the first generations of gods on each other. If this is right, Hesiod would here too be shown to be wrong about the positive connotations of *eris* (its association with

---

[35] For lover as beggar, cf. Xenophon, *Memorabilia* 1.2.29 (= Critias 88 A17 DK); and in general for deficiency as a precondition of love, *Lysis* 215ab, 221de. In the *Symposium*, Eros is famously represented as the vagrant child of penury, always striving for what he does not have: 203cd.

the major constructive force in the cosmos), but right about the importance of *eros*.

If I am right, we should hope to find Hesiod's presence in the *Phaedrus* as well, since that dialogue is concerned precisely with distinguishing living Platonic dialectic from the moribund, unresponsive posturing of sophistic speeches and texts—replacing eristics with erotics, so to speak.[36] And the hope is justified—albeit Hesiod's presence in the *Phaedrus* is more oblique than in either the *Symposium* or the *Lysis*. It comes in the account, and then the correction of the account, of Eros with which the dialogue begins. For just as Hesiod had, in the *Theogony* (at 226) discussed Eris as a baneful divinity, but then, in the passage of the *Works and Days* before us (at 11–12), *corrected* himself with a double account including a constructive Eris ('better by far to men') alongside the negative type, so the *Phaedrus* begins with a wholly negative account of Eros in the speech of Lysias (230e–234c), but then *corrects* it in Socrates' double account of Eros, first as a negative force (237b–241d), and then as something positive (at 244a–257b). To be sure, the dynamic is not quite the same: Socrates moves *through* his negative account (the initial correction of Lysias) to the official, positive account of Eros which replaces it in turn. (Socrates, after all, is committed to the position that the gods are not responsible for anything harmful to man.)[37] But the pattern is striking enough, not least because it is hardly essential to the internal dynamic of the dialogue that Socrates should have given *two* accounts at all—there is no reason why he could not have attacked both the rhetorical form and the negative representation of Eros in Lysias' speech at a single blow. The possibility that we are encouraged to see, in Socrates' *two* corrective speeches on Eros (Ἔρως), a punning reference to Hesiod's *two* forms of Eris (Ἔρις), effecting a revision similar to the one we have seen in the *Lysis*, and for a purpose which matches the thrust of the *Symposium* perfectly, is too tempting to dismiss out of hand. Eros

---

[36] Note that the champion of eristic in this case is Lysias who—like the Perses of *Works and Days*, then?—is known for his law-court speeches. (Lysias is a *logographos*: *Phaedrus* 257c.)

[37] Cf. again *Critias* 109b on the banishment of Eris from the gods.

promises real intellectual progress, where the 'mainstream' stalled long ago in its naive fascination with Eris.


## CONCLUSION

Whatever the plausibility of the details of this (allusion is rarely amenable to proof), the basic conclusion is clear. Plato's history of philosophy is not a story of linear development to match his history of civilization and the arts more directly connected with it. Indeed, again and again it is the apparent *failure* of philosophy to develop, despite its affinity with the technical arts, that baffles and frustrates Plato. Instead of locating his own work at the culmination of what went before, Plato sees (or represents) pretty well everyone who might have had a claim to his philosophical ancestry as part of a noisy but unproductive tradition characterized by eristic. Hesiod is a convenient poster-boy for this tradition partly because he can himself be represented as an advocate of eris(tic), partly because he is recognized by the Sophists (the *eristikoi* par excellence) as one of their own, and partly because, as one of the earliest surviving representatives of the tradition, its use of his voice is a token of its failure to make any progress.

But it is not all bad news. For one thing, the fact that philosophy, for whatever reason, does *not* track 'civilization' may suggest that the philosopher has a certain freedom and autonomy which can give him hope in the most adverse political circumstances. One should remember again that Plato was writing his dialogues during a downturn in the Athenians' historical trajectory, with the disastrous outcome of the Peloponnesian war in the background. If he despaired of a civilization which had overreached itself in this way, he still saw it as a time when philosophy could begin. I mentioned at the beginning that Plato on some occasions talks as if a degree of political complexity and a certain level of attainment in the mathematical sciences might be preconditions for philosophy. But on other occasions, he is very ready to subvert the idea that philosophy requires any elaborate technical expertise at all. According to *Timaeus* 47ab, for example, a pair of eyes and a view of the stars is all that it needs to get going: after that, the theory of recollection (*anamnēsis*) reassures us that we carry the answers within us already, and dialogue (of which thinking is a species: *Theaetetus* 189e) is the only thing needed to bring them out. In the *Phaedrus*, even an art so basic to the development of civilization as writing turns out to be more of a hindrance than a help (275a–e).

Another reason not to despair is that, although most people in the past have as a matter of fact been side-tracked into eristic, it does not mean that there is nothing in the past on which we can build, nothing of value to be sifted from the mainstream.[38] A token of this is the fact that Hesiod, though a natural spokesman for the eristical mainstream, can be constructively appropriated for philosophy too. And just as the eristical tradition advertises its lack of progress by using his voice, so Plato, insofar as he *re*-reads and builds on Hesiod, can use him to measure the distance his own method has enabled him to come.

---

[38] Note that Parmenides may be exempted from it altogether: he is at *Theaetetus* 152de, anyway; and he turns up as a teacher for Socrates in the *Parmenides*, and a 'father'-figure to the Eleatic Stranger in the *Sophist* (242c). (Parmenides is also, for his monism, one of the 'story-tellers' of the *Sophist*; and in fact the rejection of his monism makes the Eleatic Stranger—for Plato?—fear 'parricide': see *Sophist* 241d with McCabe (2000), 63–4. But part of the point of its being *parricide* that is in question is that Parmenides has descendants—does leave something that can be built on.)

# 3

---

# Plato's Hesiod: An acquired taste?

## G. W. Most

The reception of Hesiod throughout antiquity is a vast—and vastly understudied—subject. As far as I know, there has been only one monograph on the subject as a whole, old and variously unsatisfactory;[1] particular aspects have been examined by a few more recent books, all of them rather limited in scope but some very useful indeed;[2] and two attempts have been made to provide a collection of at least the most important testimonia.[3] Much remains to be done if we are to understand better the structure and motivations of the reception of a poet who, while almost invariably running a more or less distant second to Homer, nonetheless enjoyed an astonishing degree of popularity and influence throughout antiquity and into the Middle Ages.[4]

When questions of reception are studied in the case of post-classical authors, for many of whom we possess extensive and detailed documentation of their private and public lives, it can often be asked, interestingly, to what extent the influence of an earlier author can be traced in chronological terms over the course of the later

---

[1] Buzio (1938).

[2] E.g. Kambylis (1965); Reinsch-Werner (1976); Cameron (1995); Fakas (2001); Musäus (2004).

[3] Jacoby (1930), 106–35; Most (2006), 154–281. Most (2006), lxiii–lxix also provides a very sketchy outline of the ancient reception of Hesiod.

[4] It is hoped that Koning and Most (forthcoming), a complete translation of the extant ancient and medieval scholia to the *Theogony*, will contribute towards a better understanding of the scholarly reception of Hesiod before the Renaissance.

author's career: for example, how did Shakespeare's understanding and exploitation of Ovid change over the decades of his production,[5] or Racine's of the Greek tragedians,[6] or Joyce's of Homer?[7] Suppose we try to transfer such a line of investigation to the domain of antiquity: might it not, likewise, be possible to examine the development during the course of his career in a single ancient author's attitudes towards Hesiod?

But as soon as we raise this question, it becomes obvious that the blessedly narrow limits of our knowledge of ancient literature—not only in terms of the exiguous number of works that have survived, but also, and above all, in terms of the scant documentation of the authors' personal circumstances surrounding those works—impose severe constraints upon the possibility of our answering it. With very few, if any, exceptions, it is never possible at all to trace the chronology of Hesiod's influence upon an ancient author. On the one hand, in the case of some authors we can be sure of the intensity of their reception of Hesiod, but for one reason or another we are not in a position to make any kind of argument about the chronology of their works: either because, as with Strabo,[8] Pausanias,[9] or Athenaeus,[10] only a single work of theirs has survived to modern times; or because, as with Aristotle[11] or Plutarch,[12] there are indeed many works of theirs still extant but, with few or no exceptions, it is

---

[5] See especially Bate (1993), and for recent collections that examine many of the issues involved, Martindale and Martindale (1990), and Martindale and Taylor (2004).

[6] See especially Knight (1950); also Niderst (1978).

[7] See e.g. now Kiberd (2008).

[8] Strabo is the source of at least eighteen fragments of ps.-Hesiod's works: frr. 11, 41, 76a, 78, 85, 88, 97, 98, 101, 111, 143, 164, 181, 214, 215, 270, 279, 287 Most.

[9] Pausanias is the source of at least ten Hesiodic testimonia (Testim. 4, 31, 35, 39, 40, 42, 103, 108–10 Most) and eleven fragments (frr. 20a, 43, 53b, 170, 185, 186, 189b, 190, 195, 196, 197a Most).

[10] Athenaeus is the source of at least six Hesiodic testimonia (Testim. 66, 68, 75, 79, 81, 85 Most) and twelve fragments (frr. 179, 204b, 207–9, 213, 223–5, 235b, 238, 243 Most).

[11] Aristotle is the source of at least six Hesiodic testimonia (Testim. 37, 102, 117a–c, 128 Most) and one fragment (fr. 303 Most).

[12] Plutarch is the source of at least twelve Hesiodic testimonia (Testim. 8, 32, 33 a–b, 38, 67, 76, 86, 101, 102, 112, 155 Most) and five fragments (frr. 9, 204e, 235a, 254, 293a Most). He wrote a commentary on the *Works and Days* (Testim. 147 Most).

impossible to establish with certainty their chronological sequence. On the other hand, there are other ancient authors of whom we have a more or less good idea about the chronology of their literary careers, like Pindar, the tragedians, Aristophanes, or Cicero—but in almost all these cases the author in question happens not to have undergone intense and prolonged influence by Hesiod. In both kinds of case it makes little sense to try to ask about Hesiod's influence in diachronic terms.

The one great exception among ancient authors, the one person about whom this question can indeed be productively asked, is Plato. For the evidence of his works demonstrates beyond any doubt that Plato was intensely concerned with Hesiod throughout his career;[13] and the fact that, at least to a certain extent, and very roughly, we have some idea of the chronological relationships among many of his works means that we can pose and perhaps even hope to answer the question whether his views of Hesiod changed over time from the beginning to the end of that career, and if so how.

To be sure, such an enquiry might well seem to be obstructed by at least two grave difficulties. The first is that, notoriously, there is no 'Plato' in Plato. With the doubtful exception of the Seventh Letter,[14] Plato published nothing written in his own voice: all of his works are dialogues, and all of the speakers are, at least formally, characters other than the author, ones who present their own views, which may or may not coincide with those of Plato himself. In the strictest terms, even if we could establish securely the exact chronology of Plato's dialogues, all that we would be able to determine on the basis of these characters' apparent views of Hesiod would be the diachronic distribution of such views among a set of fictional voices whose

[13] Plato is the source of at least seven Hesiodic testimonia (Testim. 36, 83, 99, 115, 116a–c Most) and one fragment (fr. 300a Most).

[14] Doubtful not only because of the uncertainty regarding its authenticity—although currently the pendulum seems to be swinging once again towards authenticity (see e.g. now Liatsi 2008, with extensive bibliography; more cautious, but in the same direction, Erler 2007, 314–15), the matter still remains *sub judice*—but also because, even if the letter could indeed be demonstrated to be a work of Plato's, it would still not have been published in the same sense in which his dialogues were, but would have been sent in the first instance as a private communication to an individual (though of course its author would have been aware that it would likely have gone on to circulate more widely beyond him).

connection with their author would not necessarily be any more knowable than those linking Shakespeare's characters with Shakespeare. But it does not seem to me that a justifiable fear of falling into some form of naive biographism need oblige us to adopt such a thoroughgoing agnosticism. Usually, at least in the case of the large majority of references to Hesiod in Plato's works, it is not so difficult after all to tell what value we are meant to assign to the poet in a particular passage. For one thing, such references often provide demonstrative material in support of a larger argumentative construction, and it would be very odd indeed if this material were to be thought fundamentally questionable, for this would endanger the overarching argument as a whole. And for another thing, the determinate moral or intellectual character of a particular speaker can cast a helpful light upon his use of Hesiod, orienting us in assessing how, beyond his own evaluation of Hesiod, we ourselves ought to evaluate his evaluation. For example, if Euthyphro in the dialogue of that name justifies his filial practice by citing Hesiod, this will make us suspicious, whereas if Socrates or the Athenian in other dialogues does so we will likely not be at all wary, or at least nowhere nearly so much so.[15]

The second apparent difficulty regards the exact chronology of the Platonic dialogues, on which a scholarly consensus has not yet been reached. Neither external information, nor apparent historical references, nor stylometric analyses (even computer-aided ones) have succeeded, individually or in concert, in permitting the identification of a precise sequence of Plato's works on which all scholars can agree; indeed, given the likelihood that some at least of Plato's dialogues (notably the *Republic*, probably also the *Cratylus*)[16] were revised, it may never be possible to attain full certainty on this score.[17] On the other hand, while such certainty would be welcome, were it possible, we can no doubt do without it if necessary, given that there are large

[15] For the use of Hesiod on the part of Platonic characters see also Yamagata's contribution to this volume, Ch. 4.

[16] On the *Cratylus* see now Sedley (2003), 6–16.

[17] The diversity of recent positions is well illustrated by e.g. Thesleff (1982), Ledger (1989), Brandwood (1990), with the reviews of Brandwood by Keyser (1992), of Thesleff and Ledger by Nails (1992), and of Ledger and Brandwood by Young (1994), and the exchange between Ledger and Keyser (Ledger and Keyser 1992).

areas of agreement, based upon both external and internal factors, among most (if not all) scholars, regarding a rough temporal distribution of most of Plato's dialogues into three broad groupings: an early set of mostly short, dramatically vivid, often finally aporetic writings, with Socrates as a dominant interlocutor usually asking what some $x$ is (to this set the *Apology* presumably also belongs); a middle group including the *Republic* and associated dialogues, in which the theory of Ideas is established and worked out; and a final group, including the *Laws* and associated dialogues, in which that theory is problematized or simply set aside.[18] While we cannot be certain that this broad classification is entirely free from circular reasoning or various fragile philosophical presuppositions, all in all it seems to make better sense of the dialogues to group them together in this way than in no way at all or in some radically different way, and hence this arrangement seems secure enough to provide a foundation upon which, cautiously, we may build further.

With suitable caution, a repertoire of all the passages in Plato's writings in which reference is made to Hesiod can be put together; these can be divided into very broad groups of early, middle, and late dialogues, and on this basis constant tendencies as well as differences over time can be identified. Table 3.1 then presents this repertoire in a schematic form. In both, the passages in question are divided into four groups: I. early dialogues, in alphabetical order because of the uncertainty of the sequence within this group;[19] II. middle dialogues, the *Republic* and the *Theaetetus*; III. late dialogues, the *Timaeus* and the *Laws*; IV. spurious works. For each passage, I have indicated (under 'work') the poem of Hesiod's to which reference is made, if this is identifiable; whether Hesiod is explicitly and directly linked with Homer; who the speaker is who makes reference to Hesiod; and whether, very roughly, the passage suggests that Hesiod is being taken

---

[18] This is the prudent conclusion of Erler (2007), 22–6, especially 25.

[19] I have placed the *Cratylus* (*pace* Sedley 2003) and the *Symposium* in this group, despite some misgivings, but respecting the dominant view among Platonists nowadays; if these two dialogues belong not in the first group but in the second one, they surely belong more to its beginning or middle than to its end, and in any case for the purposes of the argument in the present chapter it makes little difference whether we assign them to the middle or end of the first group, or to the beginning or middle of the second one.

as an authority or praised in some other regard, or whether instead he is being criticized for some reason. No doubt such a schematization poses the danger of a certain degree of artificial oversimplification; my hope is that, if it is handled delicately, it might still prove useful. It will be up to my readers to decide whether that hope is fulfilled.

These are the passages in question:

I. Early Dialogues:

I.1.  *Apology* 41a: Socrates hopes to meet Orpheus, Musaeus, Hesiod, and Homer in the Underworld.

I.2.  *Charmides* 163b: Critias has learned from Hesiod (*Works and Days* 311) that 'to do' and 'to make' and 'to work' are not synonymous.

I.3.a. *Cratylus* 396c: Socrates can remember some, but only some, of the genealogies of the gods in Hesiod (*Theogony*).

I.3.b. *Cratylus* 397e–398a: Socrates misquotes Hesiod on the golden race (*Works and Days* 121–3) to explain the word *daimon*.

I.3.c. *Cratylus* 402b: Socrates quotes Homer on Okeanos and Tethys, associating with him Hesiod, erroneously.

I.3.d. *Cratylus* 406d: Socrates ironically accepts Hesiod's etymology of Aphrodite (*Theogony* 195–8).

I.3.e. *Cratylus* 428a: Hermogenes cites the Hesiodic proverb (*Works and Days* 361–2) that it is useful even to add only a little to a little.

I.4.  *Euthyphro* 6a: Euthyphro, to justify his mistreatment of his own father, refers to Hesiod's account of Zeus' and Kronos' mistreatments of their fathers (*Theogony*), without naming Hesiod.

I.5.  *Ion* 531a ff.: Ion and Socrates refer to rhapsodic performances and interpretations of Homer, Hesiod, and other poets.

I.6.  *Lysis* 215d: Socrates quotes an anonymous informant who cites the authority of *Works and Days* 25 to demonstrate that like is opposed to like.

I.7.a. *Protagoras* 316d: Protagoras claims that Homer, Hesiod, and other poets were really sophists in disguise.

I.7.b.  *Protagoras* 340c: Socrates cites Hesiod (*Works and Days* 289–92) in support of the claim that it is difficult to become good.

I.8.a.  *Symposium* 178b: Phaedrus cites Hesiod (*Theogony* 116–17, 120) to demonstrate that Eros is a primeval divinity.

I.8.b.  *Symposium* 195c: Agathon disputes Phaedrus' claim at I.8.a.

I.8.c.  *Symposium* 209d: Diotima praises Homer, Hesiod, and other poets as the fathers of immortal children.

II. Middle Dialogues:

II.1.a. *Republic* 2, 363b: Adeimantus cites Homer and Hesiod (*Works and Days* 233–4) on the rewards for just conduct.

II.1.b. *Republic* 2, 364cd: Adeimantus cites and paraphrases Hesiod (*Works and Days* 287–91) on the ease of vice and the difficulty of virtue.

II.1.c. *Republic* 2, 377d ff.: Socrates says that Homer and Hesiod should be censored for their false tales of the gods, providing instances of divine misbehaviour from the latter (*Theogony*).

II.1.d. *Republic* 3, 390e: Socrates refuses to believe the archaic verse (which may or may not be Hesiodic: cf. fr. 300a, b Most) according to which gifts move gods and kings.

II.1.e. *Republic* 3, 414c ff.: Socrates' noble falsehood about the metal races is clearly indebted to Hesiod's account of the races of men (*Works and Days*).

II.1.f. *Republic* 5, 466bc: Socrates cites with approval Hesiod's proverb that the half is more than the whole (*Works and Days* 40).

II.1.g. *Republic* 5, 468e–469a: Socrates misquotes with approval Hesiod (*Works and Days* 122–3) on the fate of the golden race as a parallel to what awaits the metal heroes of his city.

II.1.h. *Republic* 8, 546d–547a: Socrates explicitly connects Hesiod's (*Works and Days* 109 ff.) and his own metal heroes.

II.1.i. *Republic* 10, 600d: Socrates claims that Homer and Hesiod were driven to become rhapsodes because they failed to teach virtue.

II.1.j.  *Republic* 10, 612b: Socrates disputes the rewards of justice defined by Adeimantus at *Republic* 2, 363 on the authority of Homer and Hesiod.

II.2.a.  *Theaetetus* 155d: Socrates approves the anonymous, but Hesiodic (*Theogony* 265–6, 780) genealogy whereby Thaumas (i.e. wonder) gives rise to Iris (i.e. philosophy).

II.2.b.  *Theaetetus* 207a: Socrates quotes with approval Hesiod's pithy reference to lengthy, circumstantial enumeration (*Works and Days* 455–6).

III.  Late Dialogues:

III.1.a.  *Timaeus* 21d: Critias claims that if Solon had written a poem on Atlantis he would have become as famous for his poetry as Homer and Hesiod.

III.1.b.  *Timaeus* 40d–41a: Timaeus says that we must accept the genealogies of the gods provided by anonymous ancient poets (certainly including Hesiod, *Theogony*) because they were children of the gods.[20]

III.2.a.  *Laws* 2, 658d: The Athenian says that old men like himself prefer Homer and Hesiod.

III.2.b.  *Laws* 3, 677e: The Athenian says that Hesiod (evidently *Works and Days*) had had an inkling of political science in theory.

III.2.c.  *Laws* 3, 690e: The Athenian cites with approval Hesiod's proverb that the half is more than the whole (*Works and Days* 40).

III.2.d.  *Laws* 4, 718e–719a: According to the Athenian, Hesiod is called wise by the many for having said that the path to virtue is difficult (*Works and Days* 289–92).

III.2.e.  *Laws* 10, 901a: The Athenian applies to lazy men the words of a poet (Hesiod, *Works and Days* 303–4).

III.2.f.  *Laws* 12, 943e: According to the Athenian, Justice is indeed a 'virgin, reverend daughter' (cf. Hesiod, *Works and Days* 256–7).

---

[20] Hesiod was said to be the son of Dius: Testim. 1, 2, 95.15, 105c Most.

IV. Spurious Works:

IV.1.    *Demodocus* 383b: One of the speakers quotes with approval an archaic verse (which may or may not be Hesiodic: cf. fr. 293a, b, c Most) according to which one should hear both sides before judging a case.

IV.2.    *Epinomis* 990a: The Athenian says that the true astronomer must not just observe risings and settings, as Hesiod did; he may be referring to the relevant portions of *Works and Days* or, perhaps more likely, to a poem called *Astronomy* or *Astrology* attributed to Hesiod (frr. 223–9 Most).

IV.3.a.  *Minos* 318de: Socrates says that Homer and Hesiod (presumably in the *Catalogue of Women*) praised Minos.

IV.3.b.  *Minos* 319a: Socrates says that Homer and Hesiod (presumably in the *Catalogue of Women*) praised Minos.

IV.3.c.  *Minos* 320cd: Socrates cites lines he attributes to Hesiod (*Catalogue of Women*, fr. 92 Most) on Minos.

IV.4.    *Epistle* 11, 358e–359a: Plato, the alleged author of this letter, cites with approval words he attributes to Hesiod (fr. 274 Most) according to which something he would say would seem trivial and hard to understand.

**Table 3.1** References to Hesiod in Plato

|            |           | Work           | Homer | Cited by      | Evaluation |
|------------|-----------|----------------|-------|---------------|------------|
| *Apology*    | 41a       |                | +     | Socrates      | +          |
| *Charmides*  | 163b      | *Works and Days* |       | Critias       | +          |
| *Cratylus*   | 396c      | *Theogony*       |       | Socrates      | +          |
|            | 397e–398a | *Theogony*       |       | Socrates      | +          |
|            | 402b      |                | +     | Socrates      | +          |
|            | 406d      | *Theogony*       |       | Socrates      | ±          |
|            | 428a      | *Works and Days* |       | Hermogenes    | +          |
| *Euthyphro*  | 6a        | *Theogony*       |       | Euthyphro     | ±          |
| *Ion*        | 531a ff.  |                | +     | Ion, Socrates | ±          |
| *Lysis*      | 215d      | *Works and Days* |       | Socrates      | +          |
| *Protagoras* | 316d      |                | +     | Protagoras    | ±          |
|            | 340c      | *Works and Days* |       | Socrates      | +          |
| *Symposium*  | 178b      | *Theogony*       |       | Phaedrus      | +          |
|            | 195c      | *Theogony*       |       | Agathon       | –          |
|            | 209d      |                | +     | Diotima       | +          |
| *Republic*   | 2, 363b   | *Works and Days* | +     | Adeimantus    | +          |
|            | 2, 364cd  | *Works and Days* | +     | Adeimantus    | +          |

| | | | | | |
|---|---|---|---|---|---|
| | 2, 377d ff. | *Theogony* | + | Socrates | − |
| | 3, 390e | [?] | + | Socrates | − |
| | 3, 414c ff. | *Works and Days* | | Socrates | ± |
| | 5, 466bc | *Works and Days* | | Socrates | + |
| | 5, 468e–469a | *Works and Days* | | Socrates | + |
| | 8, 546d–547a | *Works and Days* | | Socrates | ± |
| | 10, 600d | | + | Socrates | − |
| | 10, 612b | | + | Socrates | − |
| *Theaetetus* | 155d | *Theogony* | | Socrates | + |
| | 207a | *Works and Days* | | Socrates | + |
| *Timaeus* | 21d | | + | Critias | + |
| | 40d–41a | *Theogony* | | Timaeus | + |
| *Laws* | 2, 658d | | + | Athenian | + |
| | 3, 677e | *Works and Days* | | Athenian | + |
| | 3, 690e | *Works and Days* | | Athenian | + |
| | 4, 718e–719a | *Works and Days* | | Athenian | + |
| | 10, 901a | *Works and Days* | | Athenian | + |
| | 12, 943e | *Works and Days* | | Athenian | + |
| [*Demodocus*] | 383b | [?] | | Anon. | + |
| [*Epinomis*] | 990a | *Astronomy?*<br>*Works and Days?* | | Athenian | − |
| [*Minos*] | 318de | *Catalogue of*<br>*Women* | + | Socrates | + |
| | 319a | *Catalogue of*<br>*Women* | + | Socrates | + |
| | 320cd | *Catalogue of*<br>*Women* | | Socrates | + |
| [*Epistle 11*] | 358e–359a | uncertain<br>fragment | | Plato | + |

Under 'Work', '[?]' means that it is uncertain whether reference is being made to a Hesiodic or pseudo-Hesiodic poem at all.

Under 'Homer', '+' indicates an explicit and direct link with Homer.

Under 'Cited by' is given the speaker who makes reference to Hesiod.

Under 'Evaluation' is indicated, very roughly, whether the passage suggests a positive (+) or negative (−) evaluation of Hesiod. '±' suggests a more complicated, nuanced, or ironic evaluation.

On the basis of this material, it is possible to ascertain several constant tendencies in Plato's reception of Hesiod, and also a number of differences over time.

The first constant feature is that for Plato, Hesiod figures solely as the author of the *Theogony* and the *Works and Days*, not of the many other poems attributed to him in antiquity. It is only in the spurious *Minos* (IV.3.a, b, c) and *Eleventh Letter* (IV.4) that reference is certainly made to texts which are assigned by ancient sources to Hesiod but which are now thought by almost all scholars to be due

to other poets; in the spurious *Demodocus* (IV.1), an anonymous
verse is quoted that others sometimes assign to Hesiod; in the
spurious *Epinomis* (IV.2) it is unclear whether the reference is to
Hesiod's authentic *Works and Days* or to his spurious *Astronomy* or
*Astrology*. By contrast, there is not a single passage in all of Plato's
authentic writings in which a work of Hesiod's is referred to which is
not the *Theogony* or the *Works and Days*; the only possible exception
is not in fact one—*Republic* 3, 390e (II.1.d), in which an anonymous
verse is quoted which some ancient authors (but not Plato) attributed to Hesiod. This might seem to be a trivial observation, but it is
not at all so: it demonstrates that Plato had developed so fine a
sensitivity to the specific individual nature of Hesiod's poetry that
he was able either on his own, or following other contemporary or
earlier readers whose names we no longer know, to identify as
Hesiod's his own poems and to separate them out from the others
bearing Hesiod's name that circulated in his culture. Precisely the
same thing is found in Plato's references to Homer: whereas many
other, non-Homeric heroic epics had gradually accrued to the name
of Homer over the centuries, Plato cites as Homeric only the *Iliad*
and the *Odyssey*—evidently he had worked out not only what made
Hesiod Hesiodic but also what made Homer Homeric, though it was
left to his pupil Aristotle in *Poetics* 8 and 23 to enunciate and explain
explicitly the criteria differentiating the Cyclic epics from the *Iliad*
and *Odyssey*.[21]

The second constant trait revealed by this material is that Plato
tends throughout his career (a) to accept Hesiod's *Theogony* as an
authority on the names, genealogies, and etymologies of the gods,
but (b) to reject it for its stories of the gods' dealings with one
another. That is to say, Plato accepts the *Theogony* as a divine
encyclopaedia or lexicon but rejects it as a narrative of the gradual
establishment of the justice of Zeus: either he simply does not understand Hesiod's overarching plot—in which an early phase of divine
savagery reaches its culmination in the terrifying wars of heaven but
then yields to the peaceful and equitable tranquillity of Zeus' reign—
or else, more likely, he thinks that that end does not justify these

---

[21] Cf. Labarbe (1949) for the evidence on Plato and Homer, and Most (2005) for
the wider context of this development.

means. So (a): Socratic characters adopt with various degrees of approval Hesiodic divine names, genealogies, and etymologies in the (probably) early *Cratylus* (I.3.a, b, c, d), in the middle period *Theaetetus* (II.2.a), and in the late *Timaeus* (III.1.b).[22] To be sure, not all of these passages are free from irony or other distancing techniques, and it is hard to believe in general that Plato himself ever subscribed wholeheartedly to the project of the serious etymological study of the divine names, as it had been inherited from Homer and Hesiod and refined by Greek culture over the centuries;[23] nonetheless, the continuity in these passages suggests that Plato continued to regard Hesiod as a serious authority to be consulted on such questions (to what extent the questions themselves were serious is another issue). But (b): Euthyphro's self-justification with reference to Hesiodic tales of divine misdeeds (I.4) is, in the context of that dialogue, enough to condemn him, while leaving open the question of whether blame attaches more to Euthyphro himself or rather to Hesiod. When Plato returns to the question in much greater detail and within the context of a far more elaborate theological and poetological framework in the *Republic* (II.1.c), he closes down that question once and for all, and demonstrates the unsuitability of Hesiod's *Theogony* for the instruction of children (and presumably not only of them).

The *Works and Days*, by contrast, seems consistently to be considered by Plato as (a) a sustained reflection upon justice, elaborating a consequentialist theory he finds inadequate, and (b) an anthology of useful proverbs. If we only had Plato's evidence to go on, we might well never guess that Hesiod's poem was also about agriculture, sailing, and good and bad days—did Plato ever wonder why it was entitled the *Works and Days*, or did he perhaps know it by some other title? So (a): the final passage from Book 10 of the middle-period *Republic* (II.1.j) reverts to Adeimantus' ordinary piety, buttressed by philosophically inadmissible tales of Hesiod and the other poets,

---

[22] For Plato's engagement with Hesiodic etymology see also Regali's contribution to this volume.

[23] See now on the etymologies of the divine names in the *Cratylus* Anceschi (2007).

from the beginning (II.1.a), thereby closing the ring of that grand work and providing an answer, of sorts, to his perplexities; but the fact that the Athenian returns to the question of Hesiod and theories of justice in the late *Laws* (III.2.b), claiming that Hesiod had indeed had a dim inkling, but only that, of true philosophical justice, suggests that Plato continued into his old age to wonder from time to time just why it was that Hesiod had not managed to come up with a better justification of justice. By contrast, (b): Plato's characters frequently and unabashedly draw upon the reservoir of proverbs contained in the *Works and Days*, and they do so throughout his career. In the early dialogues: add a little to a little (I.3.e), potter angry with potter (I.6), sweat set by the gods on the road to excellence (I.7.b). In the middle period: the half bigger than the whole (II.1.f), and the hundred pieces of wood in a chariot (II.2.b). In the *Laws* finally: once again, the half bigger than the whole (III.2.c), once again sweat set by the gods on the road to excellence (III.2.d), lazy men like stingless drones (III.2.e). In Plato's eyes, the *Works and Days* seems to be a prime example of popular philosophy, with all the virtues and vices associated with that unprofessional form of reasoning: useful generalizations from everyday experience well and memorably formulated, but no really satisfactory sense of logical rigour or philosophical profundity.

It is against the background of these constant features that the diachronic differences in Plato's reception of Hesiod become most striking. There are at least three of these. (a) The first, and perhaps most significant, is that there is a certain tendency for Hesiod to be cited with approval in the early dialogues by characters of whom the reader is surely intended not to approve, while in the later works this happens with characters whom the reader is no doubt expected to identify as being closer to the author's own position. Euthyphro (I.4) is perhaps a limit case of a figure who, through his ignorance, self-ignorance, and misdirection comes close to being genuinely evil; but many of the other figures who cite the authority of Hesiod in the early dialogues are, if not positively malevolent, then certainly so variously and manifestly ignorant that it is hard not to see their references to Hesiod as indicative of a general privilege accorded to that poet in ordinary Athenian culture of which Plato himself strongly disapproves.[24] Vapid and self-congratulatory Ion (I.5), slick and self-assured Protagoras (I.7.a), bright and shallow Phaedrus (I.8. a), and so too in the middle-period *Republic* well-intentioned and confused Adeimantus (II.1.a, b)—the various characters in these early dialogues who are fond of Hesiod have evidently not managed to find in his works the kind of moral and philosophical orientation that could save them from smaller and larger errors. In Plato's later works, to be sure, there are no really bad characters, only, occasionally, relatively ignorant ones; so we should not expect to find any Euthyphros darkening the pages of the *Laws*. But what is striking about the references to Hesiod in the last period of Plato's writing is that they are entrusted to those characters who seem of all to be the closest to the author's own voice—Critias (III.1.a), Timaeus (III.1.b), the Athenian (III.2.a–f). It is hard not to see in this late tendency evidence that, as he aged, Plato had come to appreciate Hesiod more than he had when he had been younger: the poet whom he had once regarded as being typical of, and partly responsible for, a corrupt and perhaps unredeemable society had turned out later upon closer inspection to possess a degree of (admittedly amateurish) seriousness that allowed the older Plato to regard him with something approaching grudging sympathy.

(b) If this were so, we might well expect Plato to have shown, over the course of his career, an increasing concern with Hesiod himself in his difference from other authors; and to a certain extent this is just what the evidence seems to suggest. In the early period, Hesiod is cited without reference to Homer in ten passages and is associated with him in five others; in the middle period, there are six references without Homer and six with; in the final period, the ratio is six references without Homer to two with. If this admittedly scant evidence does indeed admit of interpretation, it may indicate that it was only in the middle period that Plato systematically considered Hesiod and Homer together—this is of course the period of the *Republic*, to which all of the passages in question belong, with its sustained examination of the role of all traditional poetry, especially Homer and Hesiod, in mis-educating Greek society. Before and after

---

[24] For characters quoting Hesiod as part of a recognizably 'sophistic' argument see Yamagata, this volume, Ch. 4.

this period, Platonic characters tend to cite Hesiod more without than with reference to Homer, so that the proportion in the latest works (3:1) is rather higher than in the earlier ones (2:1). Perhaps, then, after the interlude of his systematic consideration of archaic epic poetry in the *Republic*, Plato returned even more strongly to his earlier tendency to appreciate Hesiod separately from Homer.

(c) Against the background of Plato's general inclination in favour of the *Works and Days* over the *Theogony* (sixteen certain references versus nine), there is a striking shift in his preference over time: in the earliest dialogues, citations of the *Theogony* outnumber those of the *Works and Days* by six to four; but in the middle period the *Works and Days* is invoked seven times, the *Theogony* only twice; and in the last works references to the *Works and Days* are more numerous than those to the *Theogony* by five to one. It seems that, if the older Plato came to appreciate Hesiod more than he had as a young man, it was above all the Hesiod of the *Works and Days* who benefited from this development.

Perhaps this material can be summarized and interpreted as follows. Plato, like all well-educated Athenians, was of course familiar with Hesiod, as he was with Homer, from his schooldays, but he did not pay particular attention to Hesiod when he began to do philosophy: he took him as a typical representative of Greek religiosity but remembered him above all for isolated proverbs that had become part of Greek popular culture. It was only in the context of his investigation of names in the *Cratylus* and, even more, of justice in the *Republic* that Plato began to study Hesiod more closely; and when he did so, he found that he had to reject much of both the *Theogony* and the *Works and Days*, for different and compelling philosophical reasons.[25] Nonetheless, as the philosopher grew older, the poet—often thought of by the ancients as having composed his verses when he was an old man himself—came to exercise an increasing fascination upon him (this is after all what the aged Plato explicitly asserts: III.2.a), and especially the *Works and Days* seems to

---

[25] Perhaps, as Andrea Capra has suggested to me, there may even be some trace of a chronological development in Plato's attitude to Hesiod within the *Republic* itself, from Socrates' outright rejection of Hesiod as author of the greatest lies (II.1.c) to his use of a Hesiodic myth to create his own noble lie (II.1.e).

have acquired a certain importance for Plato in his last years. To a certain extent, we might say that the good Hesiod of the beginning of Plato's career, essentially the precepts of the *Works and Days*, remains the good Hesiod at its end, whereas the bad Hesiod of the beginning and middle, above all the myths of the *Theogony*, simply vanishes in Plato's later years. If this is so, then any notion that Plato is just an enemy of Hesiod must derive essentially from Book 2 of the *Republic* and, while it is not completely false, it is certainly very incomplete and one-sided.

Of course, caution is in order. An argument like this one must do without any explicit or direct evidence in its favour (but neither, for what little that is worth, is there any evidence against it), and must run various kinds of methodological risk; it can only claim a certain degree of textual, psychological, and intuitive plausibility, nothing more (though again, for what little that is worth, nothing less). But it does not seem unduly incautious to suggest that there might well be a general development in Plato's attitude towards Hesiod during the course of his career, in the direction of somewhat greater acceptance and perhaps even fondness. There is nothing in Plato's later works like Euthyphro's cynical exploitation of Hesiod (I.4) or Socrates' broad attack against Hesiod in the *Republic* (II.1.c); so too, there is nothing in the earlier works like Timaeus' apparent acceptance of Hesiodic theogony (III.1.b) or the aged Athenian's expressed fondness for Hesiod (III.2.a). Did old Plato come to accept and even admire old Hesiod? Did he come to recognize in Hesiod a certain affinity with himself in their concern with justice and teaching, a certain shared fondness for proverbs and precepts, perhaps even a discernible similarity in tone, serious, somewhat stiff, occasionally ironic, never frivolous? If so, then perhaps for Plato Hesiod did after all become an acquired taste.

# 4

## Hesiod in Plato: Second fiddle to Homer?[1]

### Naoko Yamagata

#### INTRODUCTION

When we examine references to Hesiod in the Platonic corpus we notice that Plato often mentions him in tandem with Homer, apparently without implying a hierarchy.[2] Yet references to Homer by far outnumber those to Hesiod,[3] and existing scholarship on the subject suggests that Homer was considerably more important to Plato than Hesiod.[4] If that is true, the question arises as to what function Hesiod fulfils in Plato's work that Homer does not. Is he simply Homer's junior colleague whose art and prestige are almost, but not quite, as highly regarded as those of Homer? Or does Plato see qualities in Hesiod that he does not see in Homer? My chapter is an attempt to answer these questions by looking at some of the ways in which Plato

[1] Special thanks are due to Johannes Haubold, George Boys-Stones, and the anonymous referees for this volume for their most helpful and detailed comments and suggestions which have greatly contributed to the revision of this chapter. I would also like to record my thanks to Chris Emlyn-Jones and Carolyn Price who have most helpfully read and commented on a draft of this chapter, and to the members of the audience who heard its original version in Durham in May 2006 and those who heard a later version in London in February 2008 for their useful comments and discussion.

[2] Cf. *Apology* 41a6–7, *Protagoras* 316d7, *Ion* 532a5, *Republic* 363a8, 377d4, 600d5–6, *Timaeus* 21d1–2, and *Laws* 658d6–8. I give references to different dialogues in the order of Burnet (1899–1907). Translations are my own.

[3] As we see in the Table 4.1 on p. 70.

[4] E.g. Labarbe (1949), Hobbs (2000). Contrast the virtual absence of literature specifically on Plato's use of Hesiod (Introduction, pp. 1–2 above).

refers to Homer and Hesiod, as well as some of the passages where he mentions, quotes from, and adapts the works of the two poets. I will argue that, although Hesiod does indeed play second fiddle to Homer, he also has the more positive function of offering an alternative to him, which Plato uses in subtle and surprising ways.

I would like to begin my examination with a bird's eye view of the Platonic corpus. Table 4.1 below shows my tentative counting of Homeric and Hesiodic references across the Platonic corpus. By Homeric and Hesiodic references I mean not only passages where Plato mentions the poets' names, but also quotations from their works and allusions to—or reworkings of—motifs, ideas, and characters from their poems. The criteria for selection are of course to some extent subjective: while it may seem relatively uncontroversial to classify Prometheus and Epimetheus as 'Hesiodic' figures, mention of Ajax and Achilles need not necessarily require us to think of the Homeric treatment. There will be cases where more than one intertext is at play, and cases that can be counted as both Homeric and Hesiodic.[5] Yet, despite the obvious methodological obstacles, a first, provisional attempt at sketching out the data does seem to me to be a worthwhile exercise, if only to serve as a basis for the more detailed work of interpretation carried out elsewhere in this volume.

I have sorted Plato's works into two columns, listing the dialogues fairly securely classified as genuine on the left and the others on the right.[6] Out of 28 on the left-hand side, 25 have Homeric references, whereas 19 have Hesiodic ones. Out of the seven doubtful dialogues

---

[5] To pick an example more or less at random, the proverbial expression at *Symposium* 222b7 (ὥσπερ νήπιον παθόντα γνῶναι: 'to learn from suffering like a fool') may evoke both Homer and Hesiod: cf. *Iliad* 17.32/20.198, *Works and Days* 218). Likewise, Briareus who is mentioned at *Euthydemus* 299c6 and *Laws* 795c6 features in both Homer (*Iliad* 1.403) and Hesiod (*Theogony* 149, 617, 714, 734, 817).

[6] These consist of seven doubtful and six spurious dialogues, 13 letters (all of which are widely regarded as spurious except the *Seventh* which some scholars regard as genuine), and *Definitiones* which is also regarded as spurious. Within each column I have followed the order in which Guthrie (1962–81), vols. 4 and 5, lists the works to indicate the 'traditional' chronology. *Pace* e.g. Most in this volume, I do not believe that it is possible to establish a relative chronology of Platonic works in detail, except that *Laws* was very likely his last work. I do, however, acknowledge differences in style and content on which the 'early', 'middle', and 'late' classifications are based and therefore see some value in assigning Plato's poetic references a place in the wider context of stylistic groupings.

**Table 4.1** Homeric and Hesiodic references in Plato

| | Genuine works | | | | Doubtful and spurious works | | |
|---|---|---|---|---|---|---|---|
| Title | Homer | Hesiod | Main Speaker | Title | Homer | Hesiod | Main Speaker |
| Apology | 8 | 1 | Socrates | Epinomis | 0 | 1 | Athenian |
| Crito | 1 | 0 | Socrates | Alcibiades II | 7 | 0 | Socrates |
| Euthyphro | 1 | 1 | Socrates | Clitopho | 0 | 0 | Clitopho |
| Laches | 3 | 0 | Socrates | Hipparchus | 1 | 0 | Socrates |
| Lysis | 1 | 1 | Socrates | Minos | 5 | 2 | Socrates |
| Alcibiades I | 6 | 0 | Socrates | Amatores | 1 | 0 | Socrates |
| Charmides | 2 | 1 | Socrates | Theages | 2 | 0 | Socrates |
| Hippias Major | 4 | 0 | Socrates | | | | |
| Hippias Minor | 7 | 0 | Socrates | Letter 2 | 4 | 1 | Plato |
| Ion | 45 | 5 | Socrates | Letter 7 | 2 | 0 | Plato |
| Protagoras | 9 | 4 | Socrates | Letter 11 | 0 | 1 | Plato |
| Meno | 1 | 0 | Socrates | Letter 12 | 1 | 0 | Plato |
| Euthydemus | 4 | 1 | Socrates | other Letters | 0 | 0 | Plato |
| Gorgias | 10 | 4 | Socrates | | | | |
| Menexenus | 0 | 0 | 'Aspasia' | Spuria | | | |
| Phaedo | 18 | 5 | Socrates | Axiochus | 11 | 3 | Socrates |
| Symposium | 22 | 6 | Socrates | Eryxias | 0 | 0 | Socrates |
| Phaedrus | 21 | 3 | Socrates | Demodocus | 0 | 1 | Socrates |
| Republic | 86 | 18 | Socrates | Sisyphus | 0 | 0 | Socrates |
| Cratylus | 16 | 7 | Socrates | De Iusto | 0 | 0 | Socrates |
| Parmenides | 0 | 0 | Parmenides | De Virtute | 1 | 0 | Socrates |
| Theaetetus | 14 | 3 | Socrates | | | | |
| Sophist | 3 | 1 | Eleatic Stranger | Definitiones | 0 | 0 | impersonal |
| Politicus | 3 | 4 | Eleatic Stranger | | | | |
| Philebus | 4 | 1 | Socrates | | | | |
| Timaeus | 2 | 11 | Timaeus | | | | |
| Critias | 0 | 0 | Critias | | | | |
| Laws | 29 | 11 | Athenian | | | | |

five contain Homeric references and two Hesiodic ones; among the seven spurious works, two have Homeric references and two refer to Hesiod. This broad-brush summary—and it hardly needs stressing that it really is very broad brush—reveals two striking tendencies in Plato's treatment of Homer and Hesiod. First of all, Plato refers to them both throughout his *oeuvre*, though Homeric passages are more widely distributed. Secondly, Socrates tends to be the main speaker of the works in which references to Homer and/or Hesiod are made.[7] The three dialogues among Plato's genuine works in which no Homeric or Hesiodic references occur do not have Socrates as their main speaker.[8] The pattern is different in doubtful or spurious works.

What we cannot see from the table is which Platonic speakers mention, or quote from, Hesiod and/or Homer, in what contexts, and to what effect. The main bulk of my chapter is devoted to answering these questions. I would like to start by looking at two passages from near the beginning and end of Plato's writing career. Hesiod and Homer appear at *Apology* 41a6–7, along with Orpheus and Musaeus. All four poets are praised: the fact that Hesiod is named before Homer merely reflects the preferred order in which Orpheus, Musaeus, Hesiod, and Homer were listed at the time. Indeed, if we look at the *Apology* as a whole, Homer features more prominently. Just after this passage, Socrates goes on to mention Homeric heroes, such as Ajax, Agamemnon, and Odysseus, among those people whom he would look forward to questioning after death (41bc).[9] Earlier, at 28b–d, Socrates famously compares his situation to that of the Homeric Achilles, when he says that he is not afraid of death, just as Achilles did not fear death (*Apology* 41a). Plato clearly casts Socrates in the image of Achilles, the quintessential Homeric hero.[10]

A much later passage in which Homer and Hesiod are both commended is found at *Laws* 658d6–8, where the Athenian says that poems by Homer and Hesiod (in this order) are the favourite

---

[7] Except for the doubtful *Epinomis* and spurious *Demodocus* and *Letter 11*, all works in which Hesiodic references occur also have Homeric references.

[8] Aspasia in the *Menexenus*, Parmenides in *Parmenides*, and Critias in *Critias*. The main speaker of *Menexenus* is nominally Socrates, but most of it is taken up by Aspasia's speech, which he quotes.

[9] Although Ajax, Agamemnon, and Odysseus are not exclusively Homeric characters, the Homeric resonances of this particular scenario are unmistakable: cf. *Odyssey* 11. Socrates, however, does not slavishly adhere to his model: Palamedes (41b2) is not mentioned in *Odyssey* 11.

[10] Socrates, however, modifies the quotations from the *Iliad* to suit his particular situation. Cf. A. Parry (1965), 262. See also Benardete (1963), 173–4; Stokes (1997), *ad Apology* 26b3–d9; and Hobbs (2000), 183–5.

literature of old men.[11] Interestingly, the Athenian mentions the
*Iliad* and *Odyssey* by name (without mentioning their author), but
refers to Hesiodic poetry simply as 'something from Hesiod' (τῶν
Ἡσιοδείων τι). This does not mean that the Athenian values him
more highly. If anything, there may be a hint of condescension in his
reference to 'something from Hesiod': after all, the Athenian is
discussing the relative merit of literary genres, not authors. As far
as epic is concerned, the *Iliad* and *Odyssey* clearly stand out. In fact
Homer's name has just been mentioned at 658b8, as representative of
those who would perform a rhapsody at the imaginary contest.

We are beginning to get a sense of some of the issues arising from
Plato's treatment of Homer and Hesiod. They are often mentioned
together, and in an apparently even-handed manner. Yet, on closer
inspection we tend to find that Homer does take the leading part.
Even the apparently innocent pairing of 'Homer and Hesiod'—
which was of course traditional—can be reworked in such a way as
to yield subtle and unexpected nuances of meaning.

## HOMER, HESIOD, AND OTHER POETS

A further layer of complexity is added when other poets enter into
the equation. At *Timaeus* 21d1–2, Hesiod and Homer (in this order)
are again mentioned as poets par excellence. Critias Senior used to
say that Solon could have surpassed them, and all other poets, had he
not been too busy to write down the Atlantis myth that he had
brought back from Egypt. The obvious implication of the passage
is that Hesiod and Homer serve as yardsticks for poetic excellence—
but perhaps we are also invited to reflect on the relationship between
them and Solon. The historical Solon works closely with both
Homer and Hesiod,[12] as does Plato in the *Timaeus* and *Critias*.[13]

---

[11] Cf. *Laws* 658a4–659a1. Johannes Haubold suggests to me that the influence of
the tradition of a rhapsodic contest *between* Homer and Hesiod can be seen here. For
the *Contest of Homer and Hesiod* see also Graziosi, this volume, pp. 126–8, with
further literature.

[12] E.g. Irwin (2005*a*).

[13] See Capra, this volume, Ch. 10.

The 4th-century reception of Solon is also closely intertwined with that of Homer and Hesiod.[14]

Another example of a poetic triangle involving Homer and Hesiod can be found at *Protagoras* 316d7. Protagoras claims that authors such as Homer, Hesiod, and Simonides (in this order) were in fact sophists, and merely used poetry as their cover. Once again, the order in which the poets are listed need not imply a hierarchy, but it does appear to reflect the structure of the dialogue. Homer in many ways sets the tone: at the very beginning of the *Symposium*, Socrates describes the group of sophists in Callias' house in the style of the Homeric *Nekyia*, using direct quotes from *Odyssey* Book 11.[15] Hesiod then provides the model for Protagoras' central myth that opens the first round of discussion.[16] A detailed exegesis of Simonides later in the text inaugurates the second.[17] Partly as a result of the dialogue's structure, individual characters become associated with specific poets. It is evident that Homer has a special place in the discourse of Socrates. At *Protagoras* 311e3, he asks Hippocrates what name he gives to Protagoras, given that he calls Homer a poet. Clearly, Socrates regards Homer as *the* poet, and he treats him accordingly by quoting him *verbatim*.[18] Protagoras, by contrast, draws on Hesiod to open the debate and then quotes Simonides unprompted. Socrates certainly rises to the challenge, proving himself a capable interpreter of Simonides.[19] But his way into the discussion is to enlist the help of Prodicus who, as a compatriot of Simonides, has a special connection with him.[20] Hesiod, too, resurfaces at this point in the dialogue:

[14] Cf. e.g. Plato, *Lysis*, discussed below at pp. 74–5; Aeschines, *Against Timarchus*.

[15] *Protagoras* 315b9–c1: τὸν δὲ μετ' εἰσενόησα, ἔφη Ὅμηρος, Ἱππίαν τὸν Ἠλεῖον ('and then I saw, says Homer, Hippas of Elis'); cf. *Odyssey* 11.601 (of Heracles, though what follows seems more closely modelled on *Odyssey* 11.568–71, on Minos). Also *Protagoras* 315c8: καὶ μὲν δὴ καὶ Τάνταλόν γε εἰσεῖδον ('then I saw Tantalus, too'—referring to Prodicus of Ceos). Cf. *Odyssey* 11.582. For the comical effect of the passage see Wayte (1854), 94, *ad* 315b, and Capra (2001), 67–8.

[16] *Protagoras* 320c8–322d5.

[17] *Protagoras* 339a6–347a5.

[18] As well as *Protagoras* 315b9–c8, we may note 340a4–5, 348d1–4.

[19] For the section as a sparring match see Demos (1999), 13–14.

[20] *Protagoras* 339e5–340a1. The move is all the more pronounced as Socrates uses a *verbatim* quote from Homer in order to justify it: *Protagoras* 340a2–5.

Socrates argues, against Protagoras, that Simonides does not in fact
contradict himself in the Scopas Ode because 'to be' (εἶναι) and 'to
become' (γενέσθαι) are different matters (*Protagoras* 340b3–c8). At
this point he paraphrases *Works and Days* 289–92, in a transparent
bid to bolster his alliance with Prodicus.[21] Given his tendency to
quote Homer *verbatim*, it is significant that Socrates merely paraphrases the lines, and that he does so expressly on Prodicus' behalf
(καὶ ἴσως ἂν φαίη Πρόδικος ὅδε): Hesiod is his turf, just as Homer
belongs to Socrates.[22] More generally, the *Protagoras* appears to
distinguish between a Socratic Homer and the more properly sophistic Hesiod and Simonides.

## SOCRATIC HOMER *VS* SOPHISTIC HESIOD? *LYSIS* AND *CHARMIDES*

If what has been argued so far is correct, we may ask whether it
matters more generally which Platonic characters mention Homer
and Hesiod and/or adapt their works.[23] The *Lysis* is a good test case,
for here Plato does not at first sight appear to associate individual
speakers with different poets. As Socrates and Lysis try to define
friendship, they consider passages from Solon (212e3–4), Homer
(214a6), and Hesiod (215c8–d1). In contrast with the *Protagoras*,
Socrates himself quotes all three passages. On closer inspection,
however, the *Lysis* confirms our initial findings. Hesiod is quoted
last, and is the only poet who is actually named. Once again this does
not mean that he is the most important or best loved of the three. On
the contrary, he is named as a 'witness' (215c7: μάρτυς) by an
anonymous speaker whom Socrates characterizes as rhetorically
adept (216a1–2) but intellectually suspect: his profile strongly

---

[21] *Protagoras* 340c8–d6.

[22] As we have just been reminded at *Protagoras* 340a2–5. For Prodicus' special
interest in, and affinity with, Hesiod see Koning, this volume, Ch. 5.

[23] Cf. Press (2000) which brings sharply into focus the issue of how to determine
which speaker, if any, speaks for Plato in his dialogues.

suggests what we might call a sophist in the mould of figures like Protagoras or Prodicus.[24]

The passage from Solon is introduced and discussed in a more sympathetic manner, but the possibility that he is lying (ἀλλὰ ψεύδετ' ὁ ποιητής;) is mooted even before it gets quoted.[25] Homer alone is treated with any real sympathy. 'The poets', Socrates has just said, speak 'not badly' (οὐ φαύλως) about friendship. In fact, they act as 'fathers and guides in wisdom' (214a1–2), and a line from the *Odyssey* (*Odyssey* 17.218 at 214a6) illustrates the point. Although Homer/'the poets' turn out to be mistaken about friendship, Socrates attributes to them a hidden meaning (214d4: αἰνίττονται) that seems at least worthy of serious consideration. Against this characteristically Socratic treatment of Homer, the 'sophistic'—or perhaps we should rather say eristic—use of Hesiod as a 'witness' to prop up an epideictic speech stands out as starkly un-Socratic. Whereas Socrates cares about Homer even when he is wrong, Hesiod's role is to act as a foil, much as he did in the *Protagoras*.[26]

Hugo Koning discusses in greater depth the relationship between Hesiod and prominent sophists such as Prodicus.[27] Here I simply note that the same association is also made in dialogues that do not directly juxtapose Hesiod with Homer. In the *Charmides*, Critias deploys a Hesiodic phrase to thwart Socrates' rather dubious attempt to treat ποιεῖν (doing/making) and πράττειν (doing) as exact synonyms. The sharp-tongued Critias fights back by declaring himself a pupil of Hesiod (163b3–5), who says that 'work is no disgrace' (*Works and Days* 311).[28] At the end of his speech (163c6–8), Critias

---

[24] Compare Menexenus' cautious comment that he 'seems to speak well when one hears him like that at any rate' (εὖ γε ... ὥς γε οὑτωσὶ ἀκοῦσαι) at 216a3–4.

[25] *Lysis* 212e1–2, perhaps alluding to the famous line from Solon according to which 'the poets often lie' (πολλὰ ψεύδονται ἀοιδοί); cf. Solon fr. 29 West.

[26] Johannes Haubold suggests to me that the passage may be inspired by the *Contest of Homer and Hesiod*, where Hesiod wins his competition with Homer because he teaches peace whereas Homer teaches war. He further observes that *Lysis* would then be replaying the central theme of the *Contest*, but with inverted roles: Hesiod becomes the poet of discord whereas Homer preaches harmony.

[27] Koning, this volume, Ch. 5.

[28] I adopt the common translation of *Works and Days* 311 here, but for the apparent contemporary controversy over the interpretation of this line, see Graziosi in this volume, Ch. 6.

mentions Hesiod again, saying that 'Hesiod and any other sensible person' will know that to mind your own business is what self-control is all about. Socrates associates the entire manoeuvre with Prodicus (163d3–4), thus confirming the link between that particular sophist and Hesiod that we already saw made in the *Protagoras*.

## HESIOD AMONG THE LOVERS OF HOMER: THE *ION*

Unlike the sophists and their pupils, Socrates appears to show a clear preference for Homer over Hesiod. So what happens when he encounters an even more extreme Homer enthusiast? In the *Ion*, Hesiod is mentioned at 531a–532a, but precisely in a context where Ion expresses his exclusive interest in Homer. The decisive passage has been discussed in some detail by Barbara Graziosi among others:[29] Socrates steers Ion towards admitting that Homer and other poets say the same things, though Ion insists that Homer does it better (532a). The discussion can then focus on Homer as the representative of all poetry.

The starting point for this argument is a set of three poets rather like the one we saw in *Protagoras*. This time Hesiod acts as a link between Homer and the very different poetry of Archilochus. Archilochus then falls by the wayside, and only Homer and Hesiod, the protagonists of the *Contest of Homer and Hesiod*, remain in view. As Graziosi points out, the conclusion of the *Contest* had been that Homer and Hesiod cover very different topics, namely war and peace respectively.[30] As she also points out, that view depended on regarding Hesiod primarily as the poet of the *Works and Days*. For the purposes of the *Ion*, Plato emphasizes the thematic overlap between Homer and Hesiod, which in practice means defining Hesiod as the poet of the *Theogony* and perhaps the *Catalogue*.[31] That manoeuvre is far from uncontroversial and only works because neither Socrates nor Ion has any interest in keeping Hesiod in the

---

[29] Graziosi (2002), 182–4.
[30] Graziosi (2002), 174–8.
[31] Graziosi (2002), 183.

picture. He is useful to establish that Homer represents all poetry. Once that point is made, Hesiod disappears from view.

## THE *SYMPOSIUM*

In stark contrast to *Ion* with its exclusive focus on Homer is the *Symposium*, a dialogue in which most speakers use both Homeric and Hesiodic references in their speeches. As in *Protagoras*, Socrates sets the tone by jokingly quoting from Homer.[32] And once again, the first non-Socratic speaker of the text (Phaedrus) switches to Hesiod, whom he invokes as evidence for the antiquity of Eros. The change of poet and register is marked by the only sustained quotation from the *Theogony* in the whole of Plato's *oeuvre* (178b5–7; cf. *Theogony* 116–17, 120). Otherwise, this use of Hesiod compares closely to that of the anonymous speaker in the *Lysis*: each invokes him as a witness in an epideictic speech (cf. 178b1: τεκμήριον; 178b8: σύμφησιν).

Phaedrus also quotes a Homeric phrase (ἔμπνευσε μένος: *Iliad* 10.482), and happily mixes Homeric and Hesiodic references when he describes Achilles as an example of those prepared to sacrifice their lives for their loved ones. Phaedrus refers to his love for Patroclus as in Homer (179e–180b; cf. *Iliad* 18.95–6), while at the same time locating his dwelling after death in the Hesiodic Isles of the Blessed (179e2; cf. *Works and Days* 171).[33]

The second speaker, Pausanias, combines Homer with Hesiod in a more strategic manner. He derives the main thesis of his speech from the discrepancy between the two poets' accounts of Aphrodite's birth (180de). According to Homer she was born of Zeus and Dione (*Iliad* 5. 370–430), whereas according to Hesiod she was born of Ouranos (cf. *Theogony* 190–206). The suggestion that there is not one but two gods of the same name is of course itself Hesiodic (*Works and Days*

---

[32] *Symposium* 174b3–d3. Cf. Rowe (1998*a*) *ad* 174b3–c5 and d3; Dover (1980) *ad* 174c1.

[33] As opposed to the Homeric Hades (*Odyssey* 11.465–540). If Phaedrus had wanted to use a Homeric equivalent he could conceivably have placed Achilles in the Elysian Field (*Odyssey* 4.563).

11–12). More importantly, perhaps, we note that Pausanias does the opposite of what Socrates and Ion do in the *Ion* when they write Hesiod out of that dialogue for saying essentially the same as Homer. Pausanias values the Hesiodic alternative and indeed places it above the Homeric account of Aphrodite.

Hesiod continues to play his part in the speeches that follow, with the exception of the scientific Eryximachus, albeit with reduced importance.[34] Aristophanes uses Homer to authenticate his myth (190b5–c1; cf. *Odyssey* 11.308 ff.) and, although he conspicuously fails to mention Hesiod, he alludes to Hesiod by saying that the god could not kill the round people with thunderbolts as they did with the giants (190c; cf. *Theogony* 183 ff.), and draws extensively on him for his description of how the round people of old were split.[35] Agathon, who speaks next (194e4–197e8), does mention Hesiod alongside many other poets, but only to criticize him for having given a mistaken account of Eros.[36] Immediately afterwards (195d1–8), Agathon suggests that Eros lacks 'a poet like Homer' to describe his tenderness (which he claims to be the god's true nature), quoting Homer's description of the tenderness of the goddess Ate (or rather her feet) at *Iliad* 19.92–3. Agathon himself goes on to play the role of the 'poet like Homer'.[37] The entire passage amounts to a damning indictment of Hesiod, with whom the speeches of the *Symposium* had started: he is among the very first and best known of the poets who did describe Eros, but only inadequately in Agathon's view. Hesiod does not now count as 'a poet like Homer'.

[34]  Cf. Edelstein (1945) for a detailed discussion of Plato's intentions for portraying Eryximachus as a physician in this way.

[35]  Cf. *Theogony* 570–84, *Works and Days* 60–82. In Plato, as in Hesiod, Zeus punishes mankind and creates sexual relations enlisting the assistance of one or more junior gods to finish off the job (Hephaestus, Athena, and Hermes in *Works and Days*; Hephaestus and Athena in *Theogony*; Apollo in *Symposium* 190c–191a).

[36]  *Symposium* 195b6–c6. The poets he mentions are Homer: 195b5 (cf. *Odyssey* 17.218), 195d1–6 (cf. *Iliad* 19.92–3); Hesiod: 195c2; Parmenides: 195c2; Alcidamus: 196c2–3 ('the laws that are kings of the city' is apparently Alcidamus' idea: cf. Dover 1980 *ad loc.*); Sophocles: 196d1 (from the lost play *Thyestes*: cf. Rowe 1998*a ad loc.*); Euripides: 196e2–3 (from the lost play *Stheneboea*; cf. Dover 1980 *ad loc.*); Agathon: 197c6–7 (though the echo of *Odyssey* 5.391–2 / 12.168–9 has been pointed out; cf. Rowe 1998*a ad loc.*).

[37]  Cf. Rowe (1998*a*) *ad* 195d1–2.

In the interlude that follows, Socrates signals his appreciation of Homer in a manner that recalls the opening of the dialogue (198c1–5).[38] Echoes from Hesiod do resurface in the speech of Diotima (e.g. 203a8–c6), who also mentions Hesiod in the now familiar formula 'Homer and Hesiod and *x*', with *x* being other good poets (209d1–2). That, however, is the last we hear of him. To be included among those 'good poets' who have left immortal children is flattering to Hesiod, but the emphasis is almost entirely on Homer, with Hesiod serving as little more than a convenient jumping-off point for generalization. Then the drunken Alcibiades bursts in, and with his arrival the focus shifts decisively and irrevocably to Homer.[39]

Alcibiades compliments Eryximachus with a Homeric phrase describing Machaon (214b7; *Iliad* 11.514), compares his own avoidance of Socrates to Odysseus' escape from the Sirens (216a6–7; cf. *Odyssey* 12.173–200), quotes Socrates quoting Homer (219a1; cf. *Iliad* 6.236), compares Socrates to Ajax for his invulnerability (219e2) and to Odysseus for his endurance (220c2; *Odyssey* 4.242), and mentions Achilles as one of the figures to whom you can find parallels in real life (221c6). True, he also quotes a saying that occurs in Hesiod (222b7; cf. *Works and Days* 218). But the same saying also occurs twice in Homer: hardly anyone will think of Hesiod at this stage.[40]

More perhaps than any other Platonic dialogue, the *Symposium* demonstrates how Plato would like us to see Athenian intellectuals and their consumption of Homer and Hesiod. When trying to construct an argument on a matter of cosmology or divine beings, or simply in order to impress others, they feel it necessary to cite Hesiod, either on his own or in conjunction with Homer. In such contexts, Hesiod can even be used to trump Homer (as in the speech by Pausanias). Socrates, by contrast, continues to prefer Homer. As the speeches of the *Symposium* worm their way around the room from Phaedrus to him, Hesiod fades out until we are left with the

[38] Cf. *Symposium* 174b3–d3. The allusion is to *Odyssey* 11.633–5; for discussion see Rowe (1998*a*) *ad* 198c4–5.

[39] Alcibiades was of course himself a character closely associated with Homer. Plutarch, *Alcibiades* 7.1–2 reports that in his youth he showed a special interest in Homer.

[40] Cf. *Iliad* 17.32 = 20.198.

Homeric–Socratic charade of Alcibiades' speech. All that remains for
Hesiod is the anodyne cliché of 'Homer, Hesiod, and the other great
poets', so familiar from elsewhere in Plato's *oeuvre*.[41]

## FROM THE *REPUBLIC* TO THE *LAWS*

The epideictic use of Hesiod, which is beginning to look distinctly
un-Socratic, is also found in the *Republic*. In Book 2, Adeimantus
plays devil's advocate, challenging Socrates to prove that justice is
worth practising for its own sake. He points out that Hesiod
and Homer (in this order) 'testify' (μάρτυρας ποιητὰς ἐπάγονται:
364c5–6; τὸν Ὅμηρον μαρτύρονται: 364d4–5) that justice is desirable
for the material benefit and good name it brings (363bc; cf. *Works
and Days* 232–4 and *Odyssey* 19.109–13); and that vice is easy and
easily cancelled by propitiating the gods with offerings (364cd; cf.
*Works and Days* 287–9 and *Iliad* 9.497–501). In this context, Homer
and Hesiod are quoted together, in preparation for the impending
attack on all poetry. Hesiod as the expert in justice is mentioned and
quoted first. It is difficult to gauge what precisely Adeimantus means
when he calls him 'noble' (γενναῖος: 363a8), but part at least of the
point seems to be to play on the idea of Hesiod as a natural and
innocuous witness on the subject of justice. That he is far from
innocuous, even on an issue where he was generally held to have
some authority, becomes apparent from the dangerous views that
Adeimantus extracts from his poetry.

After this prelude it is hardly surprising that, when Socrates comes
to criticize harmful stories that must not be used in the education of
the guardians, 'Hesiod, Homer, and the other poets' (in this order)
stand accused together at *Republic* 377d4–5. Significantly, Plato retains the order of names as established in the speech of Adeimantus
(i.e. Hesiod first). We have seen that the name of Hesiod can go first
when combined with that of Homer, but that it usually stands in the

---

[41] In passing, we may note that Diotima's idea of author's envy sounds distinctly
Hesiodic: cf. 209d1–2 and *Works and Days* 21–4. For a different, and more detailed,
interpretation of the passage see Lev Kenaan's contribution to this volume, Ch. 8.

middle when the name of another poet follows ('Homer, Hesiod, and
*x*'), acting as a bridge between Homer and the rest of poetry. The
order adopted by Socrates in *Republic* Book 2 is therefore marked. It
does of course reflect the fact that Socrates starts his discussion with
Hesiod, which is natural enough, given that the *Theogony* stands at
the very beginning of divine history. Yet Socrates also goes out of his
way to attack Hesiod's account of the succession myth as 'the greatest
lie about the greatest things' (377e6–378a1; cf. *Theogony* 154–210,
453–506). There may be a sense here that attacking Hesiod is a good
way of opening an attack on Homer—for the specific reason that the
Muses of the *Theogony* themselves concede that they often lie.[42] As in
the *Ion*, Hesiod and Homer are declared essentially similar in terms
of their portrayal of the gods and heroes, a move that casts Hesiod as
the poet of the *Theogony* and perhaps the *Catalogue* (cf. 377e1–2:
περὶ θεῶν καὶ ἡρώων οἷοί εἰσιν). The alleged similarity is then
exploited to achieve essentially the same rhetorical aim, which is to
deal with *all* poetry by considering Homer.

After declaring the contents of the *Theogony* unfit for prospective
guardians, Socrates turns his attention to other poets, particularly
Homer. He bans the stories about Hera being tied up by her son (i.e.
Hephaestus: 378d3),[43] about Hephaestus being thrown down from
heaven by his father (i.e. Zeus: 378d3–4),[44] and about the 'battle of
the gods in Homer' (378d4–5).[45] From this point onwards, Socrates'
attention is almost exclusively directed at Homer.[46] At 379de he
criticizes Homer's impiety for describing the gods as responsible
for the evils in the world, with a rapid succession of five quotations.
Numerous Homeric quotations and references follow—nearly 50 by
my count—throughout the rest of Book 2 and up to 412b in Book 3.
What is notable is not merely the frequency of Homeric references,
but also the concentration and intensity of the use of Homer. When
Socrates criticizes Hesiod at the beginning of the discussion he
vaguely refers to the text of the *Theogony* by outlining its plot and

[42] Cf. *Theogony* 27.

[43] Cf. the fragmentary *Hymn to Dionysus*, as reconstructed by West (2003), 28.
According to Clement, the story was also found in Pindar. Cf. Adam (1902), *ad loc.*

[44] Cf. *Iliad* 1.590–94.

[45] Cf. *Iliad* 20.1–74, 21.385–513.

[46] Cf. Murray (1996), 22 on Homer's dominance in this part of the dialogue.

mentioning some of its main characters. In the great majority of Homeric cases Socrates chooses to quote actual lines and phrases, often in quick succession.[47] One cannot help feeling that Socrates relishes the opportunity to engage closely with this particular poet.[48] Indeed, we never lose sight of the fact that Socrates is fond of Homer. Throughout the *Republic* he repeatedly expresses his admiration for Homer (cf. 383a, 391a), most notably at 595b9–c2, where he is reluctant to banish him from the city. But the better the poet, the worse the effect of his morally unsuitable lines (387b1–6): although Hesiod and Homer stand accused together, and although Hesiod is summarily dismissed first, when it comes to the exile of the poets, the only name that seems to matter is Homer's.

In this respect, as in many others, we notice an interesting contrast between the *Republic* and later Platonic dialogues. Book 2 of the *Laws* does repeat some of the criticism of poetry that we see in the *Republic,* but there is no sustained attack on Homer, Hesiod, or any other poet. Admittedly, as Rutherford says, 'the achievements of the poets are recognized but devalued: pleasure is not admissible as the criterion for judging literature, and the poets have little else.'[49] But the all-out onslaught on the poets that Socrates carries out in the *Republic* is no longer at issue. As we see from Table 4.1, references to Homer and Hesiod are not as frequent in the *Laws* as they were in the *Republic.* When the two poets are mentioned or quoted, this tends to happen simply for illustration, and mostly in a favourable way. For example, at *Laws* 690e, Hesiod (*Works and Days* 40–41: 'the half is more than the whole') is quoted as a model of frugality. At *Laws* 713b, the age of Kronos is held up as the model of ideal

[47] See 379d. Other prominent examples include: 386c–387b, where Socrates uses seven quotations to attack Homer's description of the underworld (*Odyssey* 11.489–91, *Iliad* 20.64–5, *Iliad* 23.103–4, *Odyssey* 10.495, *Iliad* 16.856–7, *Iliad* 23.100–01, *Odyssey* 24.6–9); and 388a–d, where he uses six quotations to attack Homer's depiction of excessive grief displayed by the gods and heroes (*Iliad* 24.10–13, 18.23–34, 22.414–15, 18.54, 22.168–9, 16.433–4).

[48] Xenophon (*Memorabilia* 1.2.58) reports that Socrates' accuser criticized him for constantly quoting a particular passage from the *Iliad* (*Iliad* 2.188–91, 198–202). Plato's portrayal of Socrates as a Homer-lover is certainly consistent with this testimony, though Plato's Socrates never quotes these particular lines anywhere in the corpus.

[49] Cf. Rutherford (1995), 308.

states.[50] Hesiod can be valuable after all, especially the *Works and Days*, precisely that poem which Plato largely ignored in *Republic* Book 2.[51]

## THE 'HESIODIC' MYTHS

I conclude by having a quick look at Plato's myths as arguably the most important context for his encounters with Homer and Hesiod. It is also among the most difficult to assess, and all I can do here is to whet the reader's appetite for the more detailed discussions found elsewhere in the volume. Both Homer and Hesiod contribute to Platonic myths more than any other poets. I have already touched on the Hesiodic influence on the myth of Aristophanes in the *Symposium*. There are at least four more major myths that take central ingredients from Hesiod:

1. Protagoras' myth in *Protagoras* 320c–323a.
2. The 'noble lie' in *Republic* 414b–415c.
3. Timaeus' creation myth in *Timaeus* 29 *ff*.
4. The Eleatic Stranger's myth of the cosmic cycle in *Politicus* 268c–274d.

All these are cosmological myths involving the creation or generation of mortal beings. Protagoras speaks of the creation of mortals by the gods, featuring Zeus and other Olympian gods as well as Prometheus and Epimetheus in a manner reminiscent of the Pandora narrative. The myth is in many ways Protagoras' signature piece, and the fact that it is both strikingly Hesiodic and—as it turns out—strikingly un-Socratic in character reinforces our general impression that

---

[50] At *Laws* 680c6–d3, Megillus even sings the praises of Homer after hearing a quotation from *Odyssey* 9 on the lifestyle of the Cyclopes.
[51] Already in the *Republic* Plato's attack is aimed primarily at the *Theogony*, whereas Socrates on one occasion quotes with approval from the *Works and Days*: cf. *Republic* 466c2. For the development of Plato's thought on Hesiod see Most, this volume, Ch. 3. For his different treatment of the *Theogony* and *Works and Days* see Ford, this volume, Ch. 7.

Hesiod in the *Protagoras* is associated with Socrates' sophistic interlocutors.

The one occasion where Socrates tells a very obviously Hesiodic
tale is the 'noble lie' in *Republic* 414b–415c, which closely echoes
*Works and Days* 109–201. Once again, Hesiod provides the model for
an account of how the human race came into being. Rather like
Protagoras, Socrates neither attributes the myth to Hesiod (he says it
is a Phoenician tale) nor does he claim any truth for it. Unlike
Protagoras, he goes so far as calling the story a lie (414b8–c2, e7)
and is most hesitant about producing it at all (414c9–d2).[52] Exactly
what we are to make of this text, how it relates to the *Works and
Days*, and how it fits into the context of the *Republic* as a whole are
difficult questions that are explored in greater detail elsewhere in this
volume.[53] For now we note that the one Hesiodic myth told by
Socrates is not actually attributed to Hesiod, and makes no claims
to being true.

The *Timaeus* myth raises even more difficult questions. It is by far
the most extensive and arguably the most important on Plato's list of
Hesiodic myths, but by the same token it is also the most enigmatic.
At a superficial level, it follows the pattern according to which
characters other than Socrates associate themselves with Hesiod as
part of their own, usually un-Socratic, agenda. However, this initial
assessment does very little to help us understand the relationship of
the *Timaeus* myth with Hesiodic epic on the one hand and the main
body of Platonic philosophy on the other. The precise nature of those
relationships is the subject of detailed investigation elsewhere in this
volume.[54] For now I simply note that the *Timaeus* at least does not
contradict the general trend according to which 'Hesiodic' myths are
told by interlocutors other than Socrates.

Equally complicated, though for different reasons, is the myth of
cosmic reversals at *Politicus* 268d–274d. Some of its constituent parts
are clearly Hesiodic, such as the reign of Kronos (269a7), grey-haired

---

[52] His only excuse for telling it is that it is beneficial to the state. Cf. Schofield
(2007), esp. 162.

[53] See Van Noorden, Ch. 9.

[54] See the contributions by Capra, Ch. 10; Pender, Ch. 11; Sedley, Ch. 12; Regali,
Ch. 13.

new-borns (270e; cf. *Works and Days* 181), and the gift of fire from Prometheus (274cd; *Theogony* 566–9, *Works and Days* 50–52).[55] The myth is told by the Eleatic Stranger, which conforms to the basic pattern that interlocutors other than Socrates tend to reach for Hesiod. What exactly that entails for the texture and truth of the story is less easy to determine. The Stranger himself describes it as 'child's play' (268d7–e6: παιδιά) and insists that it is his own invention (269b8–c1).[56] We have thus another example of a Hesiodic myth with relatively little pretence to truth placed in the mouth of a non-Socratic interlocutor; though, as with the *Timaeus*, the precise status and significance of the myth is complicated and will have to be investigated in more detail elsewhere in this volume.[57]

The treatment of myths based on Hesiod contrasts interestingly with the three major myths that use predominantly Homeric elements. They are:

1. The myth in *Gorgias* (523a–526d).
2. The myth of Er in the *Republic* (614b–621b).
3. The myth in *Phaedo* (108e–114d).

Unlike Plato's 'Hesiodic' myths, those based on Homeric models are all told by Socrates. In *Gorgias*, Socrates mentions the division of the world by the gods as related in the *Iliad* (523a3–5; *Iliad* 15.187 ff.), the eternal punishment in Tartarus given to Tantalus, Sisyphus, and Tityus (cf. *Odyssey* 11.576 ff.), while also noting the absence of Thersites (525e2–5). Moreover, the chief judge Minos is described with a Homeric line (526d2; cf. *Odyssey* 11.569). Socrates declares this tale to be true (523a2–3), saying that even if it might appear to be fiction (μῦθος) to others, to him it is an account grounded in reason (λόγος). The rhetoric of truth employed here contrasts interestingly with the much weaker truth claims made in all four major 'Hesiodic' myths. A similar point could be made about the myth of Er in the *Republic* which, despite being a μῦθος, is framed as an essentially believable eyewitness account (621bc). Plato first presents the re-

---

[55] It also includes non-Hesiodic elements such as the quarrel of Atreus and Thyestes and the myth of an autochthonous race. Cf. S. Rosen (1988), 67.

[56] Cf. S. Rosen (1988), 68.

[57] Compare the contributions of El Murr, Ch. 14 and Rowe, Ch. 15.

wards for the just and the punishment for the unjust after death, and then shows the process of the reincarnation of souls. The 'Odyssean' theme is unmistakable, despite a few hints of Hesiod.[58] Individual echoes aside, the myth culminates in a parade of the souls of Homeric and other heroic characters,[59] in obvious dialogue with Homer's *Nekyia*. It is striking to note that by recounting the tale, Er is cast in the role of Odysseus, and by reporting it, Socrates in that of Homer.

The myth of the judgement of souls in *Phaedo* is also presented as essentially true, though the details are not to be pressed ($\mathring{\eta}$ $\tau\alpha\hat{v}\tau$' $\dot{\epsilon}\sigma\tau\grave{\iota}\nu$ $\mathring{\eta}$ $\tau o\iota\alpha\hat{v}\tau$' $\check{\alpha}\tau\tau\alpha$: 114d2–3). The main ingredients are once again from Homer: Tartarus (111e6–112a5, quoting *Iliad* 8.14),[60] Okeanos, Acheron, Pyriphlegethon, Styx, and Cocytus (113 *ff*.; cf. *Odyssey* 10.508–14).

With due caution, then, we can conclude that not only does Plato tend to attribute strongly Hesiodic myths to speakers other than Socrates, but that those speakers also make weaker claims about their truth. If one were to speculate as to why Plato treats Homeric and Hesiodic myths in these different ways, one possible answer might emerge from Edelstein's work on Platonic myths.[61] Edelstein divides Plato's myths into two groups, one dealing with the creation of the world and the early history of mankind (*Timaeus, Critias, Politicus*), and the other dealing with the fate of the soul before and after this life (*Phaedo, Gorgias, Phaedrus, Republic*).[62] He then argues that the 'facts' in the myths of the first category, the ones concerning nature and history, remain guesswork and so can only be a 'pastime of the intellect',[63] while those in the latter category can provide more reliable knowledge because 'human reason is able to cope with its task'.[64] Put thus starkly, Edelstein's argument runs a serious risk of

---

[58] Mention of Tartarus in particular (616a3–7) may conjure up Hesiodic associations: cf. *Theogony* 682, 725, 736, 822, 868, etc. However, Tartarus is treated as Homeric at *Phaedo* 111e6–112a5; cf. n. 60 below.

[59] Such as Orpheus (620a3–6), Thamyris (620a6–7: cf. *Iliad* 2.594–600), Ajax (620b1–3), Agamemnon (620b3–5), Thersites (620c2–3), and Odysseus (620c3–d2).

[60] I have noted Tartarus among Homeric and Hesiodic passages in Table 4.1, despite the fact that Plato clearly marks it as Homeric here.

[61] Cf. Edelstein (1949).

[62] Cf. Edelstein (1949), 467.

[63] Cf. Edelstein (1949), 474.

[64] Edelstein (1949), 472.

oversimplification, but as a heuristic pointer it is not perhaps altogether uninteresting; for what it is worth, the contrast we find
between Plato's 'Homeric' and 'Hesiodic' myths matches Edelstein's
distinction to an astonishing degree: the 'Hesiodic' myths about the
early history of the world and human kind remain self-consciously
speculative. And since Socrates has long given up the pursuit of
knowledge about nature, they tend to be put in the mouths of
other speakers. Eschatological myths on the other hand directly
concern the Socratic tenet that just souls will receive just rewards.
Homeric poetry offered appropriate eschatological motifs, but more
importantly perhaps it was Socrates' favourite source of reference.
Thus it can be argued that Platonic myths that are strongly based on
Homer are appropriate to Socrates both in terms of content and
characterization, whereas the ones based on Hesiod generally speaking had to come from someone else's mouth.

## CONCLUSION

The aim of this chapter has been to ask how Plato's relationship with
Hesiod compares to his relationship with Homer. We have seen that
Plato refers to Homer and Hesiod throughout his *oeuvre*. He frequently mentions them in tandem, apparently without implying a
hierarchy. On closer inspection, however, we have found that Homer
is often the main focus of interest; and that the name Hesiod is
frequently added—and manipulated—in order to cast Homer in a
specific light. For example, Hesiod is mentioned alongside Homer so
as to allow Socrates to make a general argument about poetry while
retaining his focus on Homer (*Ion, Republic*). Mention of Hesiod
may also prepare for attacks on Homer (*Republic*). Passages from
Homer and Hesiod too are treated differently. For a start, they tend
to be quoted by different speakers and for different reasons: in the
*Symposium*, the *Charmides*, the *Lysis*, the *Protagoras*, and the *Republic*, Hesiod is invoked to prop up epideictic arguments of a dubious
nature. Homer, too, may be used in this way (*Republic*), but there is a
marked tendency in some dialogues to contrast the 'sophistic' use of
Hesiod with a more Socratic use of Homer (e.g. *Lysis, Protagoras*).

Socrates clearly prefers Homer to Hesiod even in dialogues where he makes him the main focus of his attack (*Ion, Republic*). Occasionally, the contrast between Socratic Homer and sophistic Hesiod helps to articulate the overall structure of a dialogue (e.g. *Symposium, Protagoras*). Finally, I have suggested that Plato's more 'Hesiodic' myths tend to be framed differently from the ones with a strongly Homeric flavour: the latter are all told by Socrates and are presented as relatively ambitious in terms of their truth claims.[65] By contrast, most of Plato's more 'Hesiodic' myths are put in the mouths of interlocutors other than Socrates and are framed as entertainment (*Protagoras*), play (*Politicus*), or merely likely (*Timaeus*). The one major Hesiodic myth told by Socrates is presented as a 'Phoenician lie'.

[65] See the observations of Edwards (1992), 90–1 on the myth of Er and the *Gorgias* myth.

# 5

## Plato's Hesiod: not Plato's alone[1]

### Hugo Koning

## INTRODUCTION

Who is Plato's Hesiod? One straightforward and obvious way of answering that question is to do as Most does in this volume: to draw up an inventory of passages where Plato refers to Hesiod (a surveyable total of 40 or so), and subject them to analysis. One would look for a common denominator, some element shared by all or most passages, or perhaps postulate a chronological development in Plato's attitude to Hesiod (as Most in fact does).

Such attempts, however, are not helped by the great diversity of approaches to Hesiod in the Platonic corpus. Naturally, sometimes references are nothing more than *Hilfszitate*, quotations that support or illustrate a speaker's opinion without being essential to it.[2] But even in passages that substantially address the Hesiodic corpus or persona, evaluations of Hesiod and his poetry are widely divergent. In *Republic* 377c–378a, for instance, Hesiod is attacked as a liar who concocted 'the greatest falsehood about the most important things' (τὸ μέγιστον καὶ περὶ τῶν μεγίστων ψεῦδος: 377e); his poetry is subsequently regarded as a threat to society. In *Cratylus* 406b–d,

---

[1] I wish to thank the participants in the Durham conference for their positive response and helpful remarks. I also owe thanks to Ineke Sluiter, Glenn Most, Marlein van Raalte, and Casper de Jonge for valuable comments on earlier drafts of this paper.

[2] Coined by Krause (1958), 54, *Hilfszitat* appears to have become a technical term: see e.g. Kindstrand (1973), 32 and Saïd (2000), 180.

Socrates ridicules Hesiod for his 'childish' ($\pi\alpha\iota\delta\iota\kappa\hat{\omega}\varsigma$) explanation of the name of Aphrodite, because he claimed it is related to her birth from 'foam' ($\dot{\alpha}\phi\rho\dot{o}\varsigma$). In the *Apology*, on the other hand, the mere possibility of meeting Hesiod in the underworld is said to be worth dying for, presumably because of his reputation for justice and knowledge.[3] Similarly, in *Charmides* 163bc, Hesiod is presented as an upright and generally sensible ($\phi\rho\dot{o}\nu\iota\mu\sigma\varsigma$) person giving the excellent (and Platonic) advice that one should mind one's own business. In these four examples, Hesiod changes from morally dangerous and intellectually challenged to famously wise and ethically sound.

These different and even contradictory evaluations of Hesiod in Plato's work are very striking. We can compare the above-mentioned transformations of Hesiod with those in the *Republic*. Here, Hesiod in one and the same dialogue goes from the blasphemous enemy of the state to the spiritual father of Plato's eugenics; he is attacked for the immoral purport of his poetry and praised for his ethical advice.[4] But how can the same poet be presented so differently in the same corpus? Who is Plato's Hesiod?

Some may object that we are asking the wrong question. It was common practice in antiquity to quote poetic predecessors (especially Homer) wherever possible. A citation or reference could enliven or spice up one's own text,[5] and finding a relevant line from an epic, lyric or tragic poet always testified to one's wittiness, urbanity, or erudition, not only when drinking at a symposium, but also when composing poetry oneself, or writing a serious philosophical treatise— in fact, when performing any activity one happened to be engaged in.[6] It is also perfectly normal to be in agreement with an author one

---

[3] *Apology* 41a. Hesiod is mentioned in a list of denizens of the underworld, in a middle position: after the righteous judges Minos and Rhadamanthys, and before heroes like Palamedes who met their death through an unfair trial. It is thus likely that Socrates is eager to meet Hesiod as an expert on justice.

[4] See e.g. *Republic* 377c–378a, 546e–547a, 364cd, and 466c, respectively.

[5] Hermogenes actually says of Plato's work that it attains the quality of sweetness ($\gamma\lambda\upsilon\kappa\acute{\upsilon}\tau\eta\varsigma$) because of his frequent quoting from Hesiod and Homer (*On Types of Style* 336–7 Rabe = ii. 362–3 Spengel).

[6] Diogenes Laertius mentions several anecdotes which deal with philosophers demonstrating their wit by quoting relevant verses of Homer on many different occasions: Plato when burning his poems (3.5), Xenocrates when trying to release Athenian prisoners of war (4.9), Crates when he was dragged by the heels (6.90),

time and at odds with him at another: Aristotle, to give just one simple example, can cite Hesiod's words on the barest elements of the household with approval, and disagree with him on the question of whether or not a hungry octopus eats his own tentacles.[7] Each new context constitutes a separate situation, and there is no reason why Hunter's description of the Homeric heroes in Plato as 'paradigms... to be exploited as varying contexts demanded' (R. L. Hunter 2004, 249) should not *mutatis mutandis* hold for Plato's use of Hesiod as well. There are different Hesiods in Plato because there are different contexts.

There is (at least) one reason, however, why searching for a consistent image of Hesiod in Plato is not a fool's game and *can* be worthwhile. So far, scholars seem to have regarded the dynamics of reception as consisting of two factors: (1) the creative genius of Plato, and (2) the interpretive possibilities of Hesiod's poetry.[8] It appears, however, that there is a third factor, which will be the main subject of this paper, and that is the tradition of Hesiod's reception. Plato is not the first and certainly not the only person to refer to Hesiod in his own discourse. In Plato's time, the cultural icon Hesiod had been heard, interpreted, explained to others, and used for their own particular purposes by many people for over a century at least. Hesiod had thus been deployed and formed in many ways. When Plato uses Hesiod in his own text, he is *ipso facto* joining a lively debate on who Hesiod is and what his poetry means. Plato therefore not only responds to Hesiod himself, but also to the Hesiods of others, predecessors and contemporaries. It is this factor of the tradition of Hesiod's reception, I submit, that can help us to understand better the many faces of Hesiod in the Platonic corpus.

In this chapter, I hope to demonstrate that Plato makes use of at least two different 'strands' of that tradition, something which helps

---

Anaxarchus when Alexander the Great was wounded (9.60). Diogenes the cynic does it all the time (6.52, 53, 57, 63, 66, 67).

[7] [Aristotle], *Oeconomicus* 1343[a]18–21 and Aristotle, *History of Animals* 591[a]4–6.

[8] It is perhaps useful to stress the sometimes unobserved fact that Hesiod's (or, in fact, any author's) text poses certain interpretive limitations to its recipients. What Olick and Robbins (1998), 128–30 said in the context of cultural memory studies about the ways a culture shapes its past holds true for Hesiod's reception as well: there is no 'infinite malleability' of the image of Hesiod.

to explain the different evaluations of Hesiod and at the same time allows for the fact that not all references to Hesiod are totally unrelated to each other. The two traditional Hesiods I shall discuss here are the 'Homeric Hesiod' and 'Hesiod the intellectual'. I should say beforehand that the discussion of these traditional elements is not meant to detract in any way from the uniqueness of Plato's reception of Hesiod; it is meant to show that Plato's Hesiod is a blend of both new and old elements—though it remains a uniquely Platonic blend.

## THE HOMERIC HESIOD

Following on from Naoko Yamagata's survey in Chapter 4, I will first revisit Hesiod's association with Homer. It is relevant to note at the outset that a simple quantification of Hesiodic references in Plato's corpus as a whole suggests that Hesiod is a very 'Homeric' figure: in about 40 percent of all instances in which Plato mentions Hesiod, Homer is presented as a comparable poet in the immediate context.[9] Conversely, in only about 15 percent of the instances where Homer is mentioned is he directly associated with Hesiod.[10] Turning from these mere statistics to the passages themselves, we can clearly see that Plato presents Hesiod and Homer as comparable in several ways. For instance, they treat of the same subjects. This is how Socrates summarizes the content of their poetry:

περὶ πολέμου τε τὰ πολλὰ ... καὶ περὶ ὁμιλιῶν πρὸς ἀλλήλους ἀνθρώπων ἀγαθῶν τε καὶ κακῶν καὶ ἰδιωτῶν καὶ δημιουργῶν, καὶ περὶ θεῶν πρὸς ἀλλήλους καὶ πρὸς ἀνθρώπους ὁμιλούντων, ὡς ὁμιλοῦσι, καὶ περὶ τῶν οὐρανίων παθημάτων καὶ περὶ τῶν ἐν Ἅιδου, καὶ γενέσεις καὶ θεῶν καὶ ἡρώων.

Mainly tales of war, and of how people deal with each other in society—good people and bad, ordinary folks and craftsmen, and tales of the gods,

---

[9] See further Yamagata, this volume, Ch. 4.

[10] The discrepancy is of course caused by the fact that Homer is mentioned much more frequently than Hesiod in the first place: I count 40 references to Hesiod against 96 to Homer (including the spurious works of Plato). This ratio seems to be more or less normal in antiquity, at least for the classical period. Cf. e.g. the ratio in Herodotus (4:8) and Aristotle (32:83).

how they deal with each other and with men, and of the phenomena in both the heavens and the underworld, and of the births of gods and heroes.[11]

Moreover, they say more or less the same things about those same subjects (as is indicated several times in the *Republic*),[12] and they also attract the same kind of audience: old men, as the Athenian claims in the *Laws* (658d).

What is of greatest interest to us, however, is that in the cases in which Hesiod is mentioned together with Homer a certain pattern can be discerned, a recurrent perspective that appears to supersede the individual context. The two poets, when mentioned together, are often referred to in discourse concerned with their all-embracing influence on Greek thought, that is, their prominent place in education and the collective mind of the Greeks. This position strongly resembles that of the *Torah*, the *Epic of Gilgamesh*, and the *Book of the Dead*, foundational texts[13] of other cultures which, after their 'enshrinement',[14] acquire a very strong normative value. In the case of Hesiod and Homer, the Greeks would say that their verses had become like laws. This sentiment is expressed in several ways throughout antiquity.[15]

---

[11] *Ion* 531c. All translations are from Cooper (1997), sometimes slightly altered (as here). I do not believe περὶ τῶν οὐρανίων παθημάτων καὶ περὶ τῶν ἐν Ἅιδου means 'what happens in heaven and hell' (see Murray 1996, 106).

[12] *Republic* 363a–c, 364c–e, 377d–378e, 390e (where a line attributed to Hesiod is inserted in a long list of despicable verses by Homer), 600c–e, 612b.

[13] See Assmann (2000), 43, who uses the term 'identitätsfundierend'.

[14] This term denotes the point at which a canonical text is considered 'sacrosanct': it acquires a sacred status and becomes unchangeable, exerting a strong normative and formative influence on its culture through the work of professional exegetes. See Assmann (2000), 56–9 and 142–7.

[15] There are at least four ways in which a law-like quality is attributed to the poetry of Hesiod and Homer: 1. Their poetry is more or less explicitly said to be understood as law (see e.g. Lucian, *On Grief* 2, Plutarch, *How to Study Poetry* 28B, Sextus Empiricus, *Against the Professors* 9.15). 2. The poets are associated with reputable lawgivers (see the *Apology* passage mentioned above and the *Symposium* passage discussed below). 3. The poets are often appealed to as witnesses: in the works of Plato, Xenophon, and Aristotle, for instance, there are only four poets called μάρτυρες or μαρτύρια: Homer (ten times), Hesiod (four times), and the gnomic poets Theognis (twice) and Solon (once). 4. Laws and legal documents are in some respects treated in the same way as poetry, especially that of Hesiod and Homer (in juridical speeches from the 4th century BC, for example, citations from poetry, esp. that of Hesiod and

There are, in Plato, some traces of a positive evaluation of this normative status, as in the passage from the *Apology* just mentioned; or in the *Symposium*, where Diotima tells Socrates that spiritual love is superior to bodily love, and supports her claim by pointing to the superiority of spiritual children (209cd):

καὶ πᾶς ἂν δέξαιτο ἑαυτῷ τοιούτους παῖδας μᾶλλον γεγονέναι ἢ τοὺς ἀνθρωπίνους, καὶ εἰς Ὅμηρον ἀποβλέψας καὶ Ἡσίοδον καὶ τοὺς ἄλλους ποιητὰς τοὺς ἀγαθοὺς ζηλῶν, οἷα ἔκγονα ἑαυτῶν καταλείπουσιν, ἃ ἐκείνοις ἀθάνατον κλέος καὶ μνήμην παρέχεται αὐτὰ τοιαῦτα ὄντα· εἰ δὲ βούλει, ἔφη, οἵους Λυκοῦργος παῖδας κατελίπετο ἐν Λακεδαίμονι σωτῆρας τῆς Λακεδαίμονος καὶ ὡς ἔπος εἰπεῖν τῆς Ἑλλάδος. τίμιος δὲ παρ' ὑμῖν καὶ Σόλων διὰ τὴν τῶν νόμων γέννησιν.

Everyone would rather have such children than human ones, and would look up to Homer, Hesiod, and the other good poets with envy and admiration for the offspring they have left behind—offspring which, because they are immortal themselves, provide their parents with immortal glory and remembrance. For example, those are the sort of children Lycurgus left behind in Sparta as the saviours of Sparta and virtually all of Greece. Among you Athenians the honour goes to Solon for his creation of your laws.

This passage is obviously concerned with the 'enshrined' and law-like status of Hesiod and Homer: their poems are said to be immortal (i.e. everlasting and unchanging), and the comparison with Lycurgus and Solon makes it clear that their poetry is like νόμοι with a universal appeal.[16] Moreover, this special position is described in laudatory terms: Hesiod and Homer belong to the ποιηταὶ ἀγαθοί ('good poets'—they are apparently the only ones worthy of being mentioned by name), and their poetry is compared to texts that are the 'saviours of all of Greece'.[17]

A far greater number of (explicit) references to the two poets together, however, are concerned with *attacks* on Hesiod and

---

Homer, alternated with citations of legal passages; see further Perlman 1965 and Ford 1999).

[16] The scope of Lycurgus' laws is expanded from Sparta to Greece as a whole. On the 'universality' of the audience of Homer see Graziosi (2002), 58–60.

[17] In *Symposium* 209e the poets and law-givers are ranked among those people who 'have brought a host of beautiful deeds into the light and begotten every kind of virtue. Already many shrines have sprung up to honour them for their immortal children' (ὧν καὶ ἱερὰ πολλὰ ἤδη γέγονε διὰ τοὺς τοιούτους παῖδας).

Homer, attacks that are to a considerable degree triggered by the normative status of the two poets. Much has been said about Plato's objections to poetry in the *Republic* and elsewhere,[18] and there is no need for an elaborate discussion here; instead, I will limit myself to two observations.

First, it should be noted that Hesiod's role in the otherwise very thoroughly researched Books 2, 3, and 10 of the *Republic* has so far been very poorly examined indeed. Although Plato aims his very first shot at Hesiod, since he is responsible for the 'greatest falsehood about the most important things' (*Republic* 377e), Murray still describes Plato as focusing on 'the epics of Homer, the tragedies of Aeschylus, Sophocles and Euripides', and Annas remarks with regard to Plato's view of literature that *Homer* is 'recognized [by Plato] as a major factor in many people's moral lives'. These are just two examples of a scholarly Homerocentrism that can sometimes lead to the complete disappearance of the figure of Hesiod.[19]

My second and more directly relevant point is this. Plato's objections to poetry (and art in general) are many. For example, he complains that art is an image of an image of reality (and thus brings us farther away from the Forms), and that it appeals to the emotions instead of reason. When Hesiod and Homer are coupled, however, he tends to stress that the poets tell morally pernicious stories and set the wrong example. This seems to be especially true when it concerns their supposed expertise on subjects that are notoriously difficult to gain sure knowledge about, i.e. the gods and the underworld. This

[18] See e.g. Murdoch (1977), and for a comprehensive overview the introduction of Murray (1996), 3–32.

[19] Murray (1996), 15; Annas (1982), 11. Homerocentrism is a defect of modern scholarship visible not only in Platonic studies; scholars interpreting texts very often focus exclusively on Homer, even when Hesiod provides an immediate context, and regard 'epic' as Homeric epic only. Some good examples of this persistent pro-Homeric bias can be found in the otherwise excellent studies of Robb (1994), 161, who discusses the attack of Xenophanes and Heraclitus on Homer (without mentioning Hesiod), and Zeitlin (2001), 204, who claims that Greek intellectuals regarded 'Homer (with Orpheus and Musaeus)' as 'founders of civilization and masters of paideia'. Homerocentrism seems to be waning somewhat thanks to a more general upsurge of interest in Hesiod and Hesiodic reception. However, there are still many recent studies which could benefit from a less exclusive view.

aspect of the poisonous influence of Hesiod and Homer is something to which I shall return shortly.

Apart from its actual content, there appears to be another dangerous quality to Hesiodic and Homeric poetry that bothers Plato: the fact that people (deliberately) misinterpret their verses in order to justify morally objectionable actions. Plato's ideal state is governed by a select group of specially bred and trained philosophers who with the aid of unequivocal guidelines steer the *polis* in one direction (or, perhaps, keep it firmly in the same place). In the thoroughly un-ideal Athens, however, citizens are free to interpret in their own way the 'laws' of Hesiod and Homer with which they are so familiar. In the chaos that ensues, untrained people can use the poets to legitimize their pernicious practices.

Plato is concerned about this. In the *Republic*, Hesiod and Homer are cited together twice, and in both instances Plato shows how their verses are abused. The best example is found in *Republic* 363e–364e (the other is 363ab). Here Adeimantus claims that there is an εἶδος λόγων περὶ δικαιοσύνης τε καὶ ἀδικίας ἰδίᾳ τε λεγόμενον καὶ ὑπὸ ποιητῶν, 'a type of discourse about justice and injustice employed both privately and by the poets'. According to this εἶδος λόγων, licentiousness and injustice are pleasant and easy to acquire; moreover, the rich can hurt the just and unjust alike, because priests and prophets will easily persuade the gods to serve them by means of spells and enchantments. I quote 364c–e:

τούτοις δὲ πᾶσιν τοῖς λόγοις μάρτυρας ποιητὰς ἐπάγονται οἱ μὲν κακίας πέρι,
εὐπετείας διδόντες, ὡς

τὴν μὲν κακότητα καὶ ἰλαδὸν ἔστιν ἑλέσθαι
ῥηϊδίως· λείη μὲν ὁδός, μάλα δ᾿ ἐγγύθι ναίει·
τῆς δ᾿ ἀρετῆς ἱδρῶτα θεοὶ προπάροιθεν ἔθηκαν,

καί τινα ὁδὸν μακράν τε καὶ τραχεῖαν καὶ ἀνάντη. οἱ δὲ τῆς τῶν θεῶν ὑπ᾿
ἀνθρώπων παραγωγῆς τὸν Ὅμηρον μαρτύρονται, ὅτι καὶ ἐκεῖνος εἶπεν

λιστοὶ δέ τε καὶ θεοὶ αὐτοί,
καὶ τοὺς μὲν θυσίαισι καὶ εὐχωλαῖς ἀγαναῖσιν
λοιβῇ τε κνίσῃ τε παρατρωπῶσ᾿ ἄνθρωποι
λισσόμενοι, ὅτε κέν τις ὑπερβήῃ καὶ ἁμάρτῃ.

And the poets are brought forward as witnesses to all these accounts. Some
harp on the ease of vice, as follows:

> Vice in abundance is easy to get;
> the road is smooth and begins beside you,
> but the gods have put sweat between us and virtue...

...and a road that is long, rough, and steep. Others quote Homer to bear
witness that the gods can be influenced by humans, since he said:

> The gods themselves can be swayed by prayer,
> and with sacrifices and soothing promises,
> incense and libations, human beings turn them from their purpose
> when someone has transgressed and sinned.

Modern readers notice immediately that the citations (*Works and
Days* 287–9 and *Iliad* 9.497–501) are wrenched from their original
context and imbued with a new and subversive meaning—and the
ancient reader, I submit, is meant to notice too. Even though it is far
from clear what would in the eyes of Plato amount to the correct
interpretation of a poem,[20] I think it is highly unlikely that his
audience would agree that the Hesiodic passage on the tough road
to virtue, the best-known Hesiodic passage in antiquity, quoted over
and over again to promote dedication to goodness, is in fact meant to
encourage people to embrace vice because it is so easy to do so. It is
Plato's point that ordinary citizens—who are unfit to rule or make
laws—can make the poets' sayings mean anything they want.[21] That
is why Plato says that 'what is said both privately and by the poets' is
one and the same εἶδος λόγων: the ἴδιος, the exact opposite of a
magistrate or lawgiver,[22] interprets passages from the poets (his
'witnesses', the term is mentioned twice) to support his amoral

---

[20] See, for instance, the modern debate on Socrates' exegesis of Simonides' ode to
Scopas (*Protagoras* 339a–347b); Most (1994) presents an overview and a useful
bibliography.

[21] Plato himself in fact refers to the Hesiodic passage in three other passages
(*Phaedrus* 272b, *Protagoras* 340b, and *Laws* 718a), and each time the lines on virtue
are interpreted differently. See also n. 39.

[22] See LSJ s.v. I.1; Aristotle, *Nicomachean Ethics* 1113^b21–3 contrasts individuals
'in their private capacity' (ἰδίᾳ) and 'the legislators themselves' (αὐτῶν τῶν
νομοθετῶν). Perhaps the term ἴδιος is doubly apt as it can also denote someone
without τέχνη ('knowledge', see Rubinstein 1998, 140), so that the poets (in keeping
with statements made by Socrates in *Ion* and elsewhere) are here implicitly said to
have no τέχνη either.

behaviour. By equating the λεγόμενον of poets and those not in office, Plato implicitly disqualifies the poets from being involved in the business of governing and lawmaking,[23] which in Plato's view is the exclusive domain of the philosophers.

It appears, then, that there are basically three qualities that Plato attributes to Hesiod when he is coupled with Homer. First, he is an authority with far-reaching, law-like influence, especially where matters of religion are concerned; secondly, he sets a wrong example by portraying gods engaged in activities that are particularly damaging to the *polis*; and thirdly, he is potentially dangerous as people can interpret his words wrongly and misuse his authority.

This particular Hesiod, the 'Homeric' Hesiod, is not just Plato's alone. Hesiod's normative influence, for instance, is mentioned in Herodotus, and the conduct of his gods is denounced by Xenophanes—both writers active long before the *Republic* was composed.[24] Mention of the 'abuse' of Hesiodic poetry can also be found in sources other than Plato; in fact, a most interesting example comes from his contemporary Xenophon, who reports that Socrates *himself* was accused of 'selecting from the most famous poets the most immoral passages, and using them as witnesses to teach his companions to be criminals and tyrants'.[25] These 'most famous poets' turn out to be Hesiod and Homer, who are here too described as 'witnesses'.[26]

The Homeric Hesiod, approached in either a positive or a negative way, is thus not Plato's invention—it is a traditional Hesiod that can

---

[23] Cf. *Republic* 366e, where ἴδιοι λόγοι ('private conversations') and ποίησις ('poetry') are again equated with regard to the concept of justice.

[24] Herodotus 2.53; Xenophanes 21 B11 DK (unfortunately, a more elaborate discussion of these passages is beyond the scope of the present chapter). There are some indications (such as the rise of allegoresis) that their view of Hesiod was fairly widespread at the beginning of the 5th century as well.

[25] *Memorabilia* 1.2.56: ἔφη δ᾽ αὐτὸν ὁ κατήγορος καὶ τῶν ἐνδοξοτάτων ποιητῶν ἐκλεγόμενον τὰ πονηρότατα καὶ τούτοις μαρτυρίοις χρώμενον διδάσκειν τοὺς συνόντας κακούργους τε εἶναι καὶ τυραννικούς. For further discussion of this passage and the debate about Socrates' interpretation of Hesiod see Graziosi, this volume, Ch. 6.

[26] The Homeric Hesiod is very often seen in Greek literature after Plato, a topic which goes beyond the scope of the present chapter. The Homeric Hesiod is usually under attack, mostly for the ungodly behaviour of his divinities. See e.g. Philo, *On Providence* 2.34–7; Lucian, *Menippus* 3; Dio, *Oration* 14.21; Sextus Empiricus, *Outlines of Pyrrhonism* 3.210–11; Julian, *Epistles* 423b.

be put to use in passages where Plato wants to appeal to well-known qualities of the poet; for instance, to give voice to familiar reproaches and thus contribute to a cumulative condemnation of Hesiod. In this sense, then, Plato follows tradition and so continues it. But this is not to say that Plato is merely a follower: as he is aware of the traditional association of Hesiod and Homer, he can creatively manipulate it and bend it to his will. In this sense, Plato renews and reshapes the tradition. A brief discussion of the *Ion* passage already mentioned above will illustrate this innovative aspect and end the first section of my chapter.

In *Ion*, Socrates tries to show that the τέχνη ('skill') of the rhapsode is in truth not a τέχνη at all but a divinely inspired frenzy or μανία. Since being a rhapsode is not a τέχνη, he can therefore lay no claim to knowledge either.[27] The main argument for thus disqualifying the rhapsode's art is that the 'fundamental principle applicable to any τέχνη, that he who has knowledge in a given field will know it as a whole' (Murray 1996, 107), does not apply to rhapsodizing. It is precisely the familiar association of Hesiod with Homer that Plato puts to use here: even though Hesiod and Homer write about exactly the same subjects, Ion still maintains that he knows about Homer only—therefore, rhapsodizing is not a skill.

This strategy is obvious as we re-read Socrates' summary of the content of the poetry of Homer and Hesiod: 'mainly tales of war, and of how people deal with each other in society—good people and bad, ordinary folks and craftsmen, and tales of the gods, how they deal with each other and with men, and of the phenomena in both the heavens and the underworld, and of the births of gods and heroes.' Hesiod, of course, is generally not conceived as a poet of war, nor was Homer famous for telling how the gods were born—quite the reverse: Plato is deliberately creating a blend of epic poetry in a rhetorical effort to make Hesiod and Homer as similar as possible, careful not to list their most characteristic traits next to each other (the 'tales of war' and the 'birth of gods and heroes' are at the

---

[27] Obviously, the stakes are high here as, in the words of Cooper (introducing Woodruff's translation at Cooper 1997, 937): 'the minor characters, the rhapsodes, provide Socrates entrée to a much bigger game, the poet Homer himself.'

beginning and end of the list).[28] The trap is set and poor Ion takes the bait: he agrees with Socrates' summary, but still claims to be an expert on Homer alone—and thus rhapsodizing is disqualified as a τέχνη. The traditional association of Hesiod and Homer, boosted to near-identity by Plato, causes the rhapsode's downfall.

## HESIOD THE INTELLECTUAL

I would like to proceed now to discuss another Hesiod in Plato, a Hesiod I will call 'the intellectual'. It is well-known that the sophists of the 5th and 4th centuries BC occupied themselves intensely with both Hesiod and Homer. Their extensive study, use, and re-use of poetry, especially epic poetry, was of great value to them in many ways.[29]

The clearest example of the sophists' appropriation of the poets in Plato is found at the beginning of the Great Speech of Protagoras, in the dialogue named after him. Protagoras introduces himself as a sophist and then claims a whole list of well-known educators as fellow-sophists, albeit they operated as such under cover (316de):

I maintain that the sophist's art is an ancient one, but that the men who practiced it in ancient times, fearing the odium attached to it, disguised it, masking it sometimes as poetry, as Homer and Hesiod and Simonides did, or as mystery religions and prophecy, witness Orpheus and Musaeus, and occasionally, I've noticed, even as athletics, as with Iccus of Tarentum and, in our own time, Herodicus of Selymbria . . . , as great a sophist as any.[30]

These are, strictly speaking, not Protagoras' but Plato's words, but there are several reasons for assuming that Plato's presentation of the

---

[28] This is another reason to prefer this translation to Woodruff's translation in Cooper (1997) (see n. 11): the παθήματα ('phenomena') in heaven and underworld are vague enough to include Homer *and* Hesiod.

[29] See Morgan (2000), Ch. 4, 'The Sophists and Their Contemporaries'. There is a useful summary of the sophists' work on Homer and Hesiod there at 96–7.

[30] *Protagoras* 316de. Simonides is added to the duo only because it is his poem on virtue that will be discussed later in the dialogue (see further below).

sophist comes close to the real thing. One of them is the way Protagoras claims the authority of others, which is typically sophistic,[31] and also strikingly similar to Hippias' introduction to his encyclopaedia-like *Collection*:

Some of these things are perhaps said by Orpheus, others by Musaeus, in a shorter form, this here and that there, some by Hesiod, and some by Homer, and something else again by the other poets, some in the prose-writers, be they Greeks or non-Greeks; but on the basis of the most important and interrelated passages from all these sources, I will make this new and diverse treatise.[32]

In both cases, the sophist marshals different types of knowledge, to all of which he claims to have access. It is interesting that both sophists use their list of authors as an opening gambit to a longer text, but it is more relevant to us that Homer and Hesiod in each case together represent a single category.[33] Again we witness the tradition of associating the two.[34]

What I would like to focus on now, however, is the fact that some of the sophists *do* separate Hesiod and Homer, and attribute a different kind of knowledge and expertise to each of them. I will

[31] See Morgan (2000), 89–105.

[32] Hippias 86 B6 DK: τούτων ἴσως εἴρηται τὰ μὲν Ὀρφεῖ, τὰ δὲ Μουσαίῳ κατὰ βραχὺ ἄλλῳ ἀλλαχοῦ, τὰ δὲ Ἡσιόδῳ τὰ δὲ Ὁμήρῳ, τὰ δὲ τοῖς ἄλλοις τῶν ποιητῶν, τὰ δὲ ἐν συγγραφαῖς τὰ μὲν Ἕλλησι τὰ δὲ βαρβάροις· ἐγὼ δὲ ἐκ πάντων τούτων τὰ μέγιστα καὶ ὁμόφυλα συνθεὶς τοῦτον καινὸν καὶ πολυειδῆ τὸν λόγον ποιήσομαι.

[33] In the *Protagoras* passage, the different categories are explicitly labelled (poetry, prophecy, athletics, etc.); Hippias adduces some formal criteria (such as the distinction between poetry and prose, perhaps an innovation of Hippias', and that between Greek and non-Greek), whereas Hesiod and Homer are also closely linked through word-order. Patzer (1986), 20 contrasts Hesiod and Homer with the others (poets and prose-writers), but ranks them with Orpheus and Musaeus.

[34] Hesiod and Homer are throughout antiquity coupled as a pair and opposed to other groups or genres, esp. the tragedians (see e.g. [Plato], *Minos* 318e, Plutarch, *Theseus* 16.2–3, Lucian *On Dancing* 61.2; also the scholia on *Iliad* 16.336a (A), 21.430b (A), *Theogony* 691, and *Works and Days* 3). For the common expression 'Hesiod and Homer and the other poets' see e.g. Isocrates, *Panathenaicus* 18 and 33, Philodemus, *On Music* col. IV. 83 Neubecker, Lucian, *On Grief* 2.2, Galen, *On the Doctrines of Hippocrates and Plato* 3.3.28 (v. 310.1–2 Kühn), Hermogenes, *On Types of Style* ii. 362 Spengel, Libanius, *Epistles* 181.4, and of course Plato *Timaeus* 21d, *Symposium* 209d, *Republic* 377d, and *Ion* 531c1, with Yamagata, this volume, Ch. 4.

not discuss their use of Homer here, but turn my attention to their use of Hesiod.

O'Sullivan seems to have been the first to notice that the sophist Prodicus may have had a particular interest in Hesiod. For instance, his own cosmogony resembles that of Hesiod, and his moralistic treatise on Heracles at the crossroads was clearly indebted to Hesiod's image of the roads leading to virtue and vice.[35] Furthermore, and this is especially relevant, Prodicus may have presented Hesiod as a thinker who foreshadowed his own theory concerning synonyms and the ὀρθότης ὀνομάτων ('correctness of names').[36] Prodicus' theory holds, in brief, that there is a one-to-one relationship between words and their referents, and that the phenomenon of synonymy is only apparent: people mistakenly assume that different words can have the same meaning.[37] Prodicus seems to have adopted a unique position, as most of his fellow-sophists denied the existence of such a one-to-one relationship and in fact made use of semantic 'overlap' for rhetorical purposes. Their wizardry with words often led to a 'practical relativism' (Momigliano 1929–30, 102) because they focused on terms with distinctly ethical overtones. Prodicus, however, reacted to their scepticism by looking for the single exact meaning of a word, convinced that truthful communication of knowledge through language was possible—in contrast to the views held, for instance, by Gorgias.

Plato refers to Prodicus' reconstruction and use of the 'linguistic purist' Hesiod. In the *Charmides*, for instance, it is clearly stated that Hesiod was concerned with the correctness of names as he distinguished between 'making' (ἐργάζεσθαι) and 'doing' (ποιεῖν), a procedure associated with Prodicus and taught by Hesiod.[38] In the

[35] O'Sullivan (1992), 75–9.

[36] Even though there is independent proof of Prodicus trying to distinguish alleged synonyms, the sources linking Prodicus to ὀρθότης ὀνομάτων all come from the Platonic corpus itself; we should therefore be careful not to attribute to the historical Prodicus things that are part of the theory of ὀρθότης as presented by Plato; see Fehling (1965), 216–17. It is enough for my argument, however, to deal with Plato's Prodicus, i.e. the Prodicus as he is (rather consistently) depicted by Plato.

[37] See for a more elaborate treatment of Prodicus' theory of synonyms e.g. Untersteiner (1954), 212–16 and Kerferd (1981), 69–74.

[38] *Charmides* 163bc. Charmides claims that he learnt to distinguish between such apparent synonyms from Hesiod: ἔμαθον γὰρ παρ' Ἡσιόδου (163b).

*Protagoras,* Hesiod's interest in the ὀρθότης ὀνομάτων and its link to Prodicus are again made explicit: when the men are discussing a poem by Simonides, Protagoras argues that Simonides is inconsistent as the poet in one and the same ode appears to claim that it is hard to become good and easy to be good. Socrates in turn calls in the aid of Prodicus (also present) and defends Simonides by pointing out the difference between becoming and being. What happens then is most relevant: Socrates suddenly quotes Hesiod's very well known verses on the attainability of virtue:

> The gods put Goodness where we have to sweat
> to get at her. But once you reach the top
> she's easy to have as she was hard at first.[39]

It is again Hesiod, we are supposed to infer, who has taught us to differentiate between *becoming* virtuous and *being* virtuous. When Socrates immediately afterwards remarks that the 'divine wisdom' of Prodicus is as old as Simonides, or 'even older', it is clear to whom that ἔτι παλαιοτῴρα [σοφία] (cf. *Protagoras* 341a) supposedly belongs: the archaic poet Hesiod.

The 'intellectual' Hesiod, however, is not only an expert in the correctness of names—he appears elsewhere in the Platonic corpus as well, and each time he is associated with some philosophical method that tries to make sense of the world by separating and categorizing its constituent parts. This is an admittedly vague and general observation,[40] but can be further clarified and rendered more concrete

---

[39] *Protagoras* 340d. We should note in passing that the same passage from the *Works and Days*, quoted in *Republic* 364cd to demonstrate the danger of poets, is put to use in such a different way here. Plato can easily do so because in each case he quotes only the lines he needs: *Works and Days* 287–90a in the *Republic,* and 289–92 in the *Protagoras.*

[40] The description is deliberately vague as I wish to avoid connecting Hesiod to Plato's method of *diairesis.* There are some superficial similarities that could lead to sweeping claims such as that of Solmsen (1962), 179: 'to put it simply, Hesiod's *Theogony* organizes the world of divine realities . . . whereas Plato and the Academy through their method of *diairesis* try to organize many, if not necessarily all, human and other realities.' But Platonic *diairesis* is—in contrast to Hesiod's genealogies— ultimately not about (systematical) categorization, but about (ad hoc) definition. This can be clearly seen from the fact that the method of *diairesis* creates a 'tree' in which only one branch is followed to its end (the definition), whereas Hesiod's genealogical tree tries to follow all its branches.

if we take a closer look at the passages in question. Of these philosophical approaches involving separation and categorization, I will briefly discuss two.

The first of the approaches in question is etymology.[41] In the *Cratylus*, the dialogue exploring the correctness of names and the reasons for why names are what they are, Hesiod is frequently mentioned. First of all, he features as a proto-etymologist: as I noted above, for instance, Socrates ridicules Hesiod's own explanation of the name 'Aphrodite' as 'childish'.[42] Secondly, Hesiod also supplies names on which the method of etymology can be practised.[43]

We can see such practice in action when Socrates analyses the names of Zeus, Kronos, and Ouranos in *Cratylus* 396bc.[44] He then continues (396c):

εἰ δ' ἐμεμνήμην τὴν Ἡσιόδου γενεαλογίαν, τίνας ἔτι τοὺς ἀνωτέρω προγόνους λέγει τούτων, οὐκ ἂν ἐπαυόμην διεξιὼν ὡς ὀρθῶς αὐτοῖς τὰ ὀνόματα κεῖται...

If I could remember Hesiod's genealogy, which ancestors of the gods he mentions that are even older, I would not stop investigating how correct their names are...

---

[41] A method used by Prodicus too, though how exactly is uncertain (see Untersteiner 1954, 213).

[42] See again *Cratylus* 406b–d. Presumably it is 'childish' because it is a sign of inexperience to hold on to superficial similarities when searching for an etymological explanation; older and wiser etymologists look beyond the superficial to a word's true root. Incidentally, modern scholars too see Hesiod as a 'keen etymologist and cultivator of word-play' (Miller 2001, 261; see also Leclerc 1993, 272–8).

[43] Even though this last point applies to Homer as well as Hesiod, there are some arguments for maintaining that etymology is particularly Hesiodic. For instance, Homer is mentioned seven times in the *Cratylus*, Hesiod five times (a very un-Platonic ratio), and Homer is nowhere in the *Cratylus* said to have explained names himself; moreover, Homer is generally regarded in antiquity as a founding father of practically *all* genres, sciences, and philosophies, so it would be strange if the science of etymology was not among them. But I do not wish to press this point, as it is the more specific combination of etymology and genealogy (on which see below) that I wish to connect to Hesiod in particular.

[44] Zeus, it is claimed, means 'he through whom there is life' (δι' ὃν ζῆν ἀεὶ πᾶσι τοῖς ζῶσιν ὑπάρχει). The supreme god is born from a mighty intellect, for contrary to what most people believe, the name Kronos (derived from κόρος, 'pure') signifies 'the pure and clear mind', and he is himself a son of Ouranos, 'he who looks at the things above' (from τὸ ὁρᾶν τὰ ἄνω) like a philosopher.

Hesiod's genealogy is referred to because Socrates, in etymologizing the names of Zeus, Kronos, and Ouranos, has followed the backbone of the succession myth in the *Theogony* (Ouranos—Kronos—Zeus), but in reverse order: he is retracing the origin and cause of all living creatures to an intellectual principle ('the pure and clear mind') which in turn derived from the study of astronomy ('looking at the things above').[45] The etymology linking the three gods reaffirms their genealogical connection. We should compare this practice to a passage from the *Theaetetus* (155d) where Socrates says this:

μάλα γὰρ φιλοσόφου τοῦτο τὸ πάθος, τὸ θαυμάζειν· οὐ γὰρ ἄλλη ἀρχὴ φιλοσοφίας ἢ αὕτη, καὶ ἔοικεν ὁ τὴν Ἶριν Θαύμαντος ἔκγονον φήσας οὐ κακῶς γενεαλογεῖν.

For this is an experience which is characteristic of a philosopher, this wondering: this is where philosophy begins and nowhere else. And the man who made Iris the child of Thaumas was perhaps no bad genealogist.[46]

What is of particular interest to me is that both passages suggest that the practices of genealogy and etymology are comparable and, moreover, connected to Hesiod. (The genealogist referred to is, of course, Hesiod, who calls Iris the daughter of Thaumas twice in the *Theogony*, at lines 266 and 780.)

The similarity between genealogy and etymology has been noted by modern scholars such as Sluiter, who points out that they are both 'strategies to gain control over the present' (Sluiter 1997: 156), or at least to gain knowledge of the present. Apart from their comparable goal, the two practices can be compared in at least three other respects as well. First, both attempt to organize and clarify the past. This is obvious in the case of genealogy, but etymology too, though basically synchronic and without historical interest, often searches for an original name-giver and works on the assumption that names have become less perspicuous through time; and that it is the etymologist's job to rectify distortions and restore the original structures.[47] Secondly, both practices are rather unsystematic and often

---

[45] See Sedley (2003), 91 for the wider resonance of this idea in the Platonic corpus.

[46] Socrates means that 'speaking' (εἴρω) is begotten by or comes after 'wondering' (θαυμάζω)—an etymology that is, incidentally, also present in the *Cratylus* (408a).

[47] See e.g. *Cratylus* 414cd, where Socrates says that people kept embellishing the 'first names' (πρῶτα ὀνόματα) until finally 'a name is reached that no human being

serve an ad hoc purpose. The tree-like structure of genealogy (especially when executed as systematically as in the *Theogony*) may seem incompatible with the 'anything goes' strategy of etymology, but this is only apparently so: in genealogy, derivation is similarly endless, as children can be born from one or two parents, or none at all; moreover, different pedigrees can exist side by side, grounding the present.[48] And thirdly, and perhaps rather obviously, both genealogy and etymology are usually based on a preconceived notion of what the result will be: the outcome is usually known before the investigation.

The similarity between etymology and genealogy may have been even more visible in antiquity because the mythical data used for etymology are often genealogically structured; hence the implication in the passages from *Cratylus* and *Theaetetus* just mentioned that Hesiod had knowledge of both. The *Benennungsgrund*[49] (rationale) for the names of the gods featuring in the *Theogony* is given through their ancestry. It is etymology through genealogy, or the other way round. No matter what Socrates or Plato may have thought about it, the practice referred to was very real—and Hesiod is definitely connected to it.

The second of the approaches concerned with separation and categorization that I wish to look at here is one I will call 'atomistic'. It operates on the basic assumption that the sum total of reality can be divided into, and understood from, its smallest constituent parts. This too is a view associated with Hesiod. There are some traces of this association in Plato.

One of these can be found in the *Theaetetus*. Near the end of this dialogue, which is concerned with the nature of ἐπιστήμη, knowledge

---

can understand'. The example he chooses is the word *Sphinx*, the original form of which is still visible in Hesiod's *Phix* (*Theogony* 326).

[48] One can think, for instance, of the theogonies of Hesiod, Orpheus, Musaeus, and Pherecydes, or of ad hoc theogonies like the birth of Eros from Poros and Penia in *Symposium* 203b–d. Here the link with etymology is especially apparent; see e.g. *Cratylus* 404e–406a, where no less than four equally valid etymological explanations of the name 'Apollo' are given (corresponding to the four powers of the god). The scholia abound with such multiple, mutually non-exclusive etymologies.

[49] The term is that of Herbermann (1996).

is defined as μετὰ λόγου ἀληθὴς δόξα: a 'true opinion with an account' (201d–202c). One of the three proposed ways of understanding this *logos* is as an enumeration of all the elements of the thing known (206e–207a). In order to understand first of all what is meant by this reference to elements, young Theaetetus needs an example, and Socrates cites *Works and Days* 456: 'One hundred are the timbers of a wagon.' He then explains (207a):

Now I couldn't say what they are; and I don't suppose you could either. If you and I were asked what a wagon is, we should be satisfied if we could answer 'Wheels, axle, body, rails, yoke'.

It is implied, of course, that Hesiod *does* know all the constituent parts of a wagon, and is 'the man who can explore [the wagon's] being by going through those hundred items . . . who has passed from mere judgement to expert knowledge of the being of a wagon; and he has done so in virtue of having gone over the whole by means of the elements'.[50]

Hesiod is thus quoted not only to illustrate this 'atomistic' interpretation of the *logos*, but also figures as an 'atomistic' thinker, according to whom 'it is not possible to give a knowledgeable account of a thing until, in addition to his true judgement, he has analysed it element by element' (207b).[51] This proposed interpretation of *logos*, however, is eventually rejected by means of an investigation into the smallest elements of language, i.e. its letters: it does not follow that someone who can spell (and therefore has knowledge of the letters), also knows either the syllables or an entire word (207c–208b). Similarly, knowledge of timbers will not lead to knowing a wagon.

Another example, from the *Cratylus* this time, will show several aspects of Hesiod 'the intellectual' to be closely interconnected. At one point in the dialogue (428a), Cratylus is invited to join the discussion

---

[50] *Theaetetus* 207bc: τὸν δὲ διὰ τῶν ἑκατὸν ἐκείνων δυνάμενον διελθεῖν αὐτῆς τὴν οὐσίαν . . . ἀντὶ δοξαστικοῦ τεχνικόν τε καὶ ἐπιστήμονα περὶ ἁμάξης οὐσίας γεγονέναι, διὰ στοιχείων τὸ ὅλον περάναντα.

[51] *Theaetetus* 207b: τὸ δ᾽ οὐκ εἶναι ἐπιστημόνως οὐδὲν λέγειν, πρὶν ἂν διὰ τῶν στοιχείων μετὰ τῆς ἀληθοῦς δόξης ἕκαστον περαίνῃ τις.

so far conducted by Socrates and Hermogenes alone. Cratylus, an etymologist himself, who believes that the correctness of names is determined by nature, at first declines the invitation: surely Hermogenes and Socrates do not presume to understand everything about such a large and important subject so quickly? 'No by god, I don't,' Hermogenes replies, 'but I think that Hesiod is right in saying that "If you can add even a little to a little, it's worthwhile".' It is not a coincidence that Hesiod is mentioned here; the quotation (*Works and Days* 361) is, I submit, effective on at least three levels. First, it is there for the obvious purpose of inviting Cratylus not to be shy: even if he can add only a little, he should join the others. Secondly, it is also a comment on the conversation, as Socrates and Hermogenes were engaged in a discussion of the meaning of letters, the smallest elements of language. And thirdly, it seems plausible that Hesiod, who could be interpreted as an etymologist associated with the theory of the correctness of names, was particularly appealing to Cratylus—at any rate, he eventually agrees to participate in the conversation.

It appears, then, that there is another 'consistent' Hesiod in Plato: a Hesiod associated with the 'scientific' approaches of separation and categorization, who believes in a one-to-one relationship between words and things, practises etymology, and explains reality by enumerating its constituent elements. But this Hesiod, just like the Homeric one, is not invented by Plato either—he too is traditional. We have already seen that it was Prodicus who appropriated Hesiod as a precursor of the theory of ὀρθότης ὀνομάτων, but there are other references to Hesiod splitting words or concepts.[52] Heraclitus attacked Hesiod for merely accumulating information and mistaking

---

[52] Xenophon, *Memorabilia* 1.2.56–8 (on the same distinction between 'working' and 'doing', cf. Democritus 68 B128 DK and Dio, *Oration* 7.110–11); Theognis 1.1027–8 on the difference between being and becoming refers to *Works and Days* 287–92. Hippias 86 B16 DK, Epicharmus fr. 269 Kaibel, Democritus 68 B220 DK, and Euripides, *Hippolytus* 385–6 and 630–33 all refer to Hesiod's practice of splitting concepts (like Eris and Aidos) and thus create an image of Hesiod examining the relationship between words and their referents.

that for wisdom; Xenophanes attacked Hesiod for believing that the truth could be expressed in words.[53]

But in this case too it would be wrong to regard Plato as a slavish follower of tradition, for Plato can put this Hesiod to his own use as well. One way of doing this is fairly obvious: we have seen above that Hesiod could be appropriated to represent a particular philosophical method or approach; when Plato uses Hesiod in the same way, he can beat his opponents at their own game. This is what happens when Cratylus is encouraged to build on existing wisdom in outlining his theory and so to 'add little to a little' (*Cratylus* 428a: cf. *Works and Days* 361), and when the atomists' view on language and reality is rejected as Plato rejects Hesiod's putative *logos* of the wagon (*Theaetetus* 207a ff.; cf. *Works and Days* 456).

But there is more. The sophists' own wilful affiliation with the poets, especially Hesiod and Homer, plays into Plato's hands as he can so easily connect them to a *paideia* to which he was already seriously opposed in the first place. This is most apparent in the *Protagoras*, where tracing Prodicus' theory of ὀρθότης back to Hesiod is part of a general strategy to lump together the poets and the sophists: one might think, for instance, of Socrates comparing the sophists to denizens of the Homeric underworld, or the oblique reference to Protagoras' scholarly work on Homer during the discussion of Simonides' poem,[54] itself a sophistic practice. It is exactly Socrates' point later on that *paideia* based on the poets is misleading: 'we should put the poets aside and converse directly with each other, testing the truth and our own ideas.'[55] The sophists and their approach to education, firmly rooted in

[53] Heraclitus 22 B40 DK (and 57 and 106); Xenophanes 21 B35 DK referring to *Theogony* 27–8 (cf. Morgan 2000: 51). In the post-classical period (of course in part dependent on Plato), references to this particular Hesiod abound. The view is perhaps best summed up by a Stoic, presumably Zeno, who said that Hesiod belonged to 'the ancients who organized the entire universe' (παλαιοὶ καὶ τὰ ὅλα διακοσμήσαντες: *SVF* ii. 501).

[54] *Protagoras* 315cd and 340a (cf. Capra 2005).

[55] *Protagoras* 348a: τοὺς τοιούτους μοι δοκεῖ χρῆναι μᾶλλον μιμεῖσθαι ἐμέ τε καὶ σέ, καταθεμένους τοὺς ποιητὰς αὐτοὺς δι' ἡμῶν αὐτῶν πρὸς ἀλλήλους τοὺς λόγους ποιεῖσθαι, τῆς ἀληθείας καὶ ἡμῶν αὐτῶν πεῖραν λαμβάνοντας.

poetry, cannot meet the demands of eristic and dialectic. Plato thus uses their own appropriation of the poets to disqualify them as teachers.


## CONCLUSION

I started this chapter with four contradictory views that Plato takes of Hesiod at various points in his work: a lying author of morally pernicious tales, a cosmological thinker of no account, a man of enviable wisdom, and a decent, upright citizen. It has been my purpose to show that these qualifications are not in any literal sense 'invented' by Plato, but reflect older traditions of reading, interpreting, and understanding Hesiod. In no way, however, does this mean that Plato merely adopts this tradition: he reshapes it to suit his own needs, as we have seen in the passage from the *Ion*, or his explanation of Hesiod's line on the wagon and its timbers. In such cases Plato employs the traditional Hesiod against those promoting the importance of the poets to education and morality.

Plato's Hesiod, therefore, is always a blend of Plato's genius, the possibilities of the Hesiodic text, and a third factor: the traditional Hesiod, i.e. the Hesiod used and formed by others. The relative importance of these three ingredients varies from case to case. It is an obvious hypothesis that the share of the traditional Hesiod is minimal in those cases where we encounter the poet in connection with notions that are strictly Platonic; one can think of the significant place of Hesiodic ideas in the education of the Guardians of the Ideal State, and of course of the Noble Fiction itself, based on Hesiod's distinction between the races of gold, silver, bronze, and iron.[56] Plato thus fits Hesiod into a philosophical, political, and rhetorical agenda of his own—and so adds yet another dimension to the ever—changing Panhellenic symbol that is Hesiod.

---

[56] As explored elsewhere in this volume: see especially the contributions of Haubold, Ch. 1 and Van Noorden, Ch. 9.

# 6

## Hesiod in classical Athens: Rhapsodes, orators, and Platonic discourse

*Barbara Graziosi*

### INTRODUCTION

This chapter investigates the place of Hesiod in classical Athenian culture. It focuses, in particular, on rhapsodic performances and public speeches, because it is through listening to rhapsodes and orators that most Athenians came into contact with Hesiod's poetry. It then asks how popular perceptions of Hesiod in 4th-century Athens relate to Plato's treatment of this poet's work. For reasons of space, I focus on three Hesiodic passages that seem to have been especially popular and frequently cited: they are of limited significance when compared to the more diffuse yet palpable influence of Hesiod in Athens, but I hope they may serve as a concrete starting point for a discussion of Plato's Hesiod.

When considering the question of how the Athenians came into contact with the poetry of Hesiod, we must, in the first place, consider the impact of rhapsodic performances. We know that professional rhapsodes recited poetry for a fee, both at public festivals and in private venues. Several sources mention public performances at festivals like the Panathenaea and the Brauronia, or in the *agora*, as well as more intimate recitals in the private homes of wealthy citizens like Nicias.[1] It is difficult to determine exactly which works by which authors were performed by the rhapsodes, but Hesiod certainly featured in their repertoire. Some of the evidence for this comes from Plato himself: in the *Ion*, at 531a1–2, Socrates asks the famous rhapsode whether his repertoire includes Hesiod and Archilochus, or whether he specializes in Homer only. This question fits Socrates' own agenda: in the course of the dialogue, he narrows down the expertise of the rhapsode first to Homer, then to military tactics, and then nothing at all. But Socrates' question also fits the context of 4th-century Athenian culture. We know that, at the most important city festival, the Great Panathenaea, rhapsodes were allowed to perform 'Homer only'.[2] Ion—who, in the dialogue, has just arrived in Athens in order to perform at the Pantathenaea—turns out to be a Homeric specialist, but Socrates' question implies that some rhapsodes regularly performed Hesiod and Archilochus too. That Hesiod featured prominently in the rhapsodic repertoire emerges also from another Platonic passage: *Laws* 658d6–9. When discussing the most popular form of entertainment, the Athenian stranger points out that the answer depends on whom you ask: young children prefer the puppet show, older ones comedy, young men and educated women tragedy: 'but we old men have the greatest pleasure in hearing a rhapsode recite well the *Iliad* and the *Odyssey*, or one of the Hesiodic poems.' Hesiod, then, is closely associated with Homer (though typically treated as second best), and is backed by the sound moral judgement and the authority of 'old men'.[3]

We can safely assume, then, that many Athenians were familiar with the poetry of Hesiod through listening to the rhapsodes. Various sources inform us that rhapsodic shows were hugely popular in Athens, and Martin West has calculated that some rhapsodes commanded very handsome fees: their earnings confirm the popularity of their work.[4] This does not mean, of course, that every Athenian knew

---

[1] For public performances see Kotsidu (1991). For private recitation see, for example, Xenophon, *Symposium* 3.5.

[2] Lycurgus, *Against Leocrates* 102, discussed in Graziosi (2002), 196.

[3] On Hesiod being second to Homer, see Yagamata in this volume, Ch. 4.

[4] West (1992), 368.

Hesiod's poems by heart: Isocrates suggests that only half the people cared to stay awake during rhapsodic performances (*Panegyricus* 12.263)—for those who slept, Hesiod's poetry was just a droning background noise. Even so, rhapsodic performances ensured that Hesiod's name, authority, and reputation were widely known, and that many Athenians had the opportunity to listen to his poems, whether or not they could afford to go to school. Those who did attend school studied Hesiod's works in greater detail: Aeschines, *Against Ctesiphon* 135 confirms that Hesiod featured in the school curriculum.[5] For those who could afford a more expensive education beyond basic schooling, the sophists provided further training in the study and interpretation of poetry.[6] According to Plato, the sophist Protagoras claimed: 'The most important part of a man's education is to be an acute (δεινός) critic of that which the poets have said' (*Protagoras* 339a). Why the ability to interpret poetry was such a highly prized skill in classical Athens is an important and complex question.[7] In this chapter I want to offer one specific answer. We know that the educated elite quoted, selected, and interpreted passages of ancient poetry in their public lives: poetry was used to illustrate and support a wide variety of points made in the courts and the assembly. It seems to me that there is an obvious connection between the education of public speakers and the work of the rhapsodes. The educated elites could harness the authority and popularity of ancient poetry for their own ends: appeals to a poet like Hesiod were effective because the Athenians could be assumed to be familiar with his poetry—whether or not they had received any formal education. The orators could thus create the impression that they were building on common knowledge, and treat their public to a demonstration of how poetry was studied and discussed in schools and sophistic circles—all could follow because, notionally at least, they knew their epic poetry from listening to the rhapsodes.

---

[5] On Hesiod in Athenian school education, see further Ford, this volume, Ch. 7.

[6] For Hesiod and the sophists see also Koning, this volume, Ch. 5.

[7] For a thorough investigation of this question, see Ford (2002); cf. also the Introduction to this volume.

## WORKS AND DAYS 763–4: THE POWER OF RUMOUR

A good example of how the orators offered poetry tutorials in the course of their speeches, and thereby increased the authority and persuasiveness of the points they were making, can be found in an exchange between Aeschines and Demosthenes on the correct interpretation of Hesiod's *Works and Days* 763–4.

In his speech *Against Timarchus*, Aeschines argued that the defendant had prostituted himself and should therefore be excluded from public life on a charge of disgrace (ἀτιμία).[8] In order to mount his case, Aeschines discussed and interpreted a wide range of laws and passages of poetry.[9] The intent was evidently to emphasize the gap between Timarchus' behaviour and the wisdom and authority of Solon, Homer, Hesiod, and Aeschines himself (who was able to marshal such ancient authorities at will).[10] The speech clearly played to the jury's anxieties about the education of the young; but the problem, for Aeschines, was that there was no hard evidence for Timarchus' prostitution. Aeschines had to rely on rumour.[11] So he pointed out that Rumour—according to Hesiod—was a goddess, and thus worthy of honour (*Against Timarchus* 129–30):

ὁ δ' Ἡσίοδος καὶ διαρρήδην θεὸν αὐτὴν [sc. τὴν φήμην] ἀποδείκνυσι, πάνυ
σαφῶς φράζων τοῖς βουλομένοις συνιέναι· λέγει γάρ·
    φήμη δ' οὔτις πάμπαν ἀπόλλυται, ἥντινα λαοὶ
    πολλοὶ φημίξωσι· θεός νύ τίς ἐστι καὶ αὐτή.
καὶ τούτων τῶν ποιημάτων τοὺς μὲν εὐσχημόνως βεβιωκότας εὑρήσετε
ἐπαινετὰς ὄντας· πάντες γὰρ οἱ δημοσίᾳ φιλότιμοι παρὰ τῆς ἀγαθῆς φήμης

---

[8] For an up-to-date introduction to the speech see Fisher (2001), 1–68; for Aeschines' use of poetry in it, see the excellent study by Ford (1999).

[9] The supposed excerpts from actual laws that appear in the manuscripts of the β group are generally agreed to be spurious: Fisher (2001), 68 with further literature.

[10] Fisher (2001), 286–7, with full bibliography.

[11] Compare the remarks in Fisher (2001), 54–8 and 270, who suggests that Aeschines is alluding to Timarchus' nickname 'the whore' (*pornos*). For gossip in classical Athenian culture, see V. J. Hunter (1990) and (1994), Ch. 4, esp. 104–6 (on this speech).

ἡγοῦνται τὴν δόξαν κομιεῖσθαι· οἷς δ᾽ αἰσχρός ἐστιν ὁ βίος, οὐ τιμῶσι τὴν θεὸν
ταύτην· κατήγορον γὰρ αὐτὴν ἀθάνατον ἔχειν ἡγοῦνται.

Hesiod even explicitly represents it (rumour) as a goddess, speaking very
clearly to those willing to understand. He says: 'Rumour never dies out
completely, one which many people rumour. She too is somehow a goddess.'
You will find that men who live decorously are admirers of these poems. All
men who are ambitious for public honour believe that they will gain their
reputation from positive rumour about them; but those whose life is
shameful do not honour this goddess, because they think they have her as
their immortal accuser.

When quoting Hesiod, Aeschines flatters his audience: note his
reference to 'anybody who is willing to understand what Hesiod is
saying'. He also states that good people admire Hesiod's poetry and
pay attention to his teachings. The audience can thus choose whether
to be like the good Aeschines, or like the bad Timarchus: if they care
to understand Hesiod, they are like Aeschines, and like all upright
people. The interesting thing, here, is that Aeschines crops his Hesiodic quotation so as to make it mean something quite different from
what Hesiod implies in the *Works and Days*. These are Hesiod's lines
in their original context 753–64 (I follow West's text and translation,
with minor modifications):

> μηδὲ γυναικείῳ λουτρῷ χρόα φαιδρύνεσθαι
> ἀνέρα· λευγαλέη γὰρ ἐπὶ χρόνον ἔστ᾽ ἐπὶ καὶ τῷ
> ποινή. μηδ᾽ ἱεροῖσιν ἐπ᾽ αἰθομένοισι κυρήσας
> μωμεύειν ἀίδηλα· θεός νύ τε καὶ τὰ νεμεσσᾷ.
> ὣδ᾽ ἔρδειν· δεινὴν δὲ βροτῶν ὑπαλεύεο φήμην·
> φήμη γάρ τε κακὴ πέλεται κούφη μὲν ἀεῖραι
> ῥεῖα μάλ᾽, ἀργαλέη δὲ φέρειν, χαλεπὴ δ᾽ ἀποθέσθαι.
> φήμη δ᾽ οὔ τις πάμπαν ἀπόλλυται, ἥντινα πολλοὶ
> λαοὶ φημίξουσι· θεός νύ τίς ἐστι καὶ αὐτή.

Let not a man cleanse his skin with a woman's washing water, for that too
carries a grim penalty for a time. And do not, when you come upon a
burning sacrifice, balefully criticize it: the god resents that too. Do as I say;
and avoid being the object of men's dreadful rumour. Rumour is a dangerous thing, light and easy to pick up, but hard to support and difficult to get
rid of. Rumour never dies out completely, one which many people rumour.
She too is somehow a goddess.

For Hesiod, rumour is something to be feared and avoided; Aeschines, by contrast, suggests that it is worthy of worship.[12] In fact, he goes as far as identifying himself with the goddess Rumour: he presents her as an immortal and invincible prosecutor. It was quite common for orators and other classical authors to quote poetry out of context and wilfully distort its meaning. Clearly, Aeschines did not expect his audience to remember the context of Hesiod's lines or query his interpretation of them. In this case, however, he miscalculated: his use of Hesiod came under public scrutiny.

In his speech *On the False Embassy*, Demosthenes revisited Aeschines' interpretation of Hesiod, and attempted to use the same lines in order to condemn Aeschines' own behaviour (*On the False Embassy* 243–4):

Ἀλλὰ μὴν καὶ ἔπη τοῖς δικασταῖς ἔλεγες, οὐδένα μάρτυρα ἔχων ἐφ' οἷς ἔκρινες τὸν ἄνθρωπον παρασχέσθαι·

φήμη δ' οὔ τις πάμπαν ἀπόλλυται, ἥντινα λαοὶ
πολλοὶ φημίξωσι· θεός νύ τίς ἐστι καὶ αὐτή.

οὐκοῦν, Αἰσχίνη, καὶ σὲ πάντες οὗτοι χρήματ' ἐκ τῆς πρεσβείας φασὶν εἰληφέναι, ὥστε καὶ κατὰ σοῦ δήπουθεν "φήμη δ' οὔ τις πάμπαν ἀπόλλυται, ἥντινα λαοὶ πολλοὶ φημίξωσι".

But you even quoted poetry at the judges, because you had no witness to bring forward in support of the things for which you were prosecuting the man: 'Rumour never dies out completely, one which many people rumour. She too is somehow a goddess.' And now, Aeschines, all these men say that you made money out of your embassy; so, you see, it counts against you too that 'Rumour never dies out completely, one which many people rumour'.

Demosthenes turns Aeschines' rhetorical ploy on its head, arguing that his opponent only quoted poetry because he had no actual witnesses. Moreover, he uses the same passage from Hesiod to cast doubt on Aeschines' own reputation, thus entering into a veritable contest of Hesiodic interpretation. Demosthenes' use of the passage is much closer to the original warning issued by Hesiod in the *Works and Days*: rumour needs to be avoided, rather than worshipped.

---

[12] Fisher (2001), 269–70 notes that Aeschines misrepresents Hesiod and suggests that he may be reading him through the lens of Bacchylides: cf. Bacchylides 2.1–3, 5.191–4, 10.1–3.

Demosthenes thus implies that Aeschines misunderstood Hesiod's poetry and—more importantly—that he failed to apply its moral to his own life.

In his own defence speech, Aeschines did not let the matter go, but decided to treat his audience to a full exegesis of Hesiod's words (*On the False Embassy* 114–15):

ἐτόλμησε δ᾽ εἰπεῖν ὡς ἐγὼ τοῖς ἐμαυτοῦ λόγοις περιπίπτω. φησὶ γάρ με εἰπεῖν, ὅτ᾽ ἔκρινον Τίμαρχον, ὅτι πάντες κατ᾽ αὐτοῦ τὴν τῆς πορνείας φήμην παρειλήφασι, τὸν δ᾽ Ἡσίοδον ποιητὴν ἀγαθὸν ὄντα λέγειν,

φήμη δ᾽ οὔ τις πάμπαν ἀπόλλυται, ἥντινα λαοὶ
πολλοὶ φημίξωσι· θεός νύ τίς ἐστι καὶ αὐτή.

τὴν δ᾽ αὐτὴν ταύτην θεὸν ἥκειν νῦν κατηγοροῦσαν ἐμοῦ· πάντας γὰρ λέγειν ὡς χρήματα ἔχω παρὰ Φιλίππου. εὖ δ᾽ ἴστε, ὦ ἄνδρες Ἀθηναῖοι, ὅτι πλεῖστον διαφέρει φήμη καὶ συκοφαντία. φήμη μὲν γὰρ οὐ κοινωνεῖ διαβολῇ, διαβολὴ δ᾽ ἀδελφόν ἐστι συκοφαντία. διοριῶ δ᾽ αὐτῶν ἑκάτερον σαφῶς.

But he dared to say that I am tripped up by my own words. For he says that when I prosecuted Timarchus, I said that everybody knew he had a reputation for prostituting himself and that Hesiod, a good poet, says: 'Rumour never dies out completely, one which many people rumour. She too is somehow a goddess.' He says that this very same goddess now comes and accuses me; since everybody says—according to him—that I received money from Philip. But, Athenian citizens, you know very well that there is a great difference between rumour and sycophancy. Rumour has nothing to do with slander; whereas slander and sycophancy are brothers. I will distinguish both terms clearly.

Aeschines remains faithful to his original interpretation: Rumour is a divine prosecutor—but a divine prosecutor is no sycophant or slanderer. The distinctions he makes echo Hesiod's genealogical language: 'slander and accusation are brothers' sounds Hesiodic, but in fact is not in Hesiod at all.[13] The exact meaning and nuance of Hesiod's *Works and Days* 763–4 is thus made to fit Aeschines' argument, with the help of a saying that sounds Hesiodic.

This exchange between Aeschines and Demosthenes neatly illustrates how poetry could be used and abused in the public arena. Orators, and the sophists who trained them, could quote the same

---

[13] Genealogies are typical of the *Theogony* rather than the *Works and Days*: this is an interesting case where an appeal to the poet's *oeuvre* is implied.

lines of poetry in order to support very different positions and arguments. In the *Protagoras*, at 316d3–9, Plato has Protagoras claim Homer, Hesiod, and Simonides as predecessors, or 'sophists in disguise': according to the sophist, they too were teachers and educators, even if they avoided calling themselves 'sophists', because the term attracted criticism.[14] This close association, or even identification, between poets and sophists clearly influenced Plato's own views on poetry: his most insistent criticism of it is that its meaning cannot be determined. In the *Ion* he suggests that, even if the ancient poets themselves could be asked what they meant, they would not offer reliable answers, because poets compose under the influence of divine inspiration, and without true knowledge of what they are saying.[15] In their ignorance and persuasiveness, as well as their fickleness, poets turn out to resemble sophists and orators.

Plato radically distanced himself from dominant approaches to poetry in classical Athens. Yet, at the same time, he was intensely aware of them and often mirrored quite precisely the concerns, and quotations, of his contemporaries. Here is an example. In the *Laws*, Megillus asks the Athenian stranger how he would prevent citizens from having homosexual relationships. The Athenian stranger claims that φήμη—rumour—is the best deterrent. Fear of rumour already effectively prevents people from having sex with their own relatives and—if public opinion were unanimous in condemning homosexuality—it would be equally effective in preventing sexual relationships among men. Megillus answers (*Laws* 838c8–d2):

Ὀρθότατα λέγεις τό γε τοσοῦτον, ὅτι τὸ τῆς φήμης θαυμαστήν τινα δύναμιν εἴληχεν, ὅταν μηδεὶς μηδαμῶς ἄλλως ἀναπνεῖν ἐπιχειρήσῃ ποτὲ παρὰ τὸν νόμον.

You are right about that, at least, that rumour really has some kind of astonishing power, in cases where nobody would ever dare to breathe anything against convention.

---

[14] See further Haubold, Boys-Stones, and Koning in this volume, Ch. 1, Ch. 2, Ch. 5 respectively.
[15] See especially 533c9–535a2.

Megillus seems to be evoking our Hesiodic passage here—though his wording does not quite commit him, or Plato, to the notion that rumour is an actual goddess: she simply has 'an astonishing power' when people unanimously think that men should refrain from certain types of behaviour.[16]

Megillus, like Aeschines, remembers the Hesiodic line about rumour when discussing sexual relationships between men. This deserves some attention: Hesiod does not treat the topic at all in the *Works and Days*. In its original context, the passage about the power of rumour concludes a long section of ritual and moral prohibitions, none of which relates to male homosexuality or prostitution. It is noteworthy that, by contrast, in classical Athens, Hesiod's words on rumour repeatedly appear when male homosexuality is under debate. The orators quote Hesiod when discussing the possibility that Timarchus prostituted himself to older men; and Megillus paraphrases the lines when legislating against the corrupting influence of homosexual relationships between older and younger men. We may well ask whether these different texts are directly related. It is possible that Aeschines remembered Megillus' words and made full use of the Hesiodic reference in his case *Against Timarchus*; but it seems to me more likely that both Plato and the orators independently responded to the same cultural context: they thought of Hesiod's lines in relation to sex between men, because they lived in the same city, and responded to similar circumstances and concerns—the rumours about male homosexual flings and affairs, the education (sexual and otherwise) of boys and young men, the old values embodied in Hesiod's poetry (an educational text), and the new moral challenges faced by young men and their instructors and/or lovers. Further evidence confirms that, in classical Athens, Hesiod's name featured in debates about male prostitution: I discuss some relevant passages below. For now, however, I would like to emphasize quite how in tune Plato was with classical Athenian discourse—he invoked the same Hesiodic lines when discussing the same issues as Aeschines and Demosthenes.

[16] Detienne (2002), 76–7 implies that Plato is paraphrasing Hesiod here, though he does not discuss the matter explicitly.

## *WORKS AND DAYS* 311: DISGRACEFUL WORK

That the correct interpretation of poetry was a matter of public concern also emerges from sources directly linked to the trial of Socrates. Shortly after 394/5 BC, Polycrates wrote a literary *Accusation of Socrates* in which he claimed that Socrates had used poetry in order to promote his antidemocratic ideology. If we compare what remains of Polycrates' *Accusation* with Xenophon's attempt to defend Socrates in his *Memorabilia*, it becomes clear that one of the issues at stake was the correct interpretation of Hesiod.[17] According to his accusers, Socrates had used *Works and Days* 311 in order to justify any kind of work, however immoral:

ἔργον δ' οὐδὲν ὄνειδος, ἀεργίη δέ τ' ὄνειδος.

No work is a disgrace, idleness is.

The original context of the quotation suggests that Hesiod took οὐδέν with ὄνειδος: 'Work is no disgrace at all, idleness is.' Yet our classical Athenian sources take the line to mean: 'No work (of any kind) is a disgrace, idleness is.' This reading most likely reflects Socrates' own interpretation of the line, hence my translation.

In his *Memorabilia*, 1.2.56–7, Xenophon defended Socrates from the charge that he misused Hesiod by claiming that, in Socrates' definition, 'work' meant 'morally good work':

ἔφη δ' αὐτὸν ὁ κατήγορος καὶ τῶν ἐνδοξοτάτων ποιητῶν ἐκλεγόμενον τὰ
πονηρότατα καὶ τούτοις μαρτυρίοις χρώμενον διδάσκειν τοὺς συνόντας
κακούργους τε εἶναι καὶ τυραννικούς, Ἡσιόδου μὲν τὸ
     ἔργον δ' οὐδὲν ὄνειδος, ἀεργίη δέ τ' ὄνειδος·
τοῦτο δὴ λέγειν αὐτὸν ὡς ὁ ποιητὴς κελεύει μηδενὸς ἔργου μήτ' ἀδίκου μήτ'
αἰσχροῦ ἀπέχεσθαι, ἀλλὰ καὶ ταῦτα ποιεῖν ἐπὶ τῷ κέρδει. Σωκράτης δ' ἐπεὶ

---

[17] The relevant source for Polycrates' *Accusation of Socrates* is the scholia to Aelius Aristides, iii. 480.29–481.2 Dindorf: from it we can reconstruct the fact that Polycrates criticized Socrates' endorsement of Odysseus' behaviour in *Iliad* Book 2. Xenophon is widely taken to have replied to Polycrates' accusations point by point: at *Memorabilia* 1.2.56–8 he defends Socrates' interpretation of both *Iliad* 2 and *Works and Days* 311: in all likelihood, Polycrates had discussed Socrates' interpretation of both poems.

διομολογήσαιτο τὸ μὲν ἐργάτην εἶναι ὠφέλιμόν τε ἀνθρώπῳ καὶ ἀγαθὸν εἶναι, τὸ δὲ ἀργὸν βλαβερόν τε καὶ κακόν, καὶ τὸ μὲν ἐργάζεσθαι ἀγαθόν, τὸ δ᾽ ἀργεῖν κακόν, τοὺς μὲν ἀγαθόν τι ποιοῦντας ἐργάζεσθαί τε ἔφη καὶ ἐργάτας ἀγαθοὺς εἶναι, τοὺς δὲ κυβεύοντας ἤ τι ἄλλο πονηρὸν καὶ ἐπιζήμιον ποιοῦντας ἀργοὺς ἀπεκάλει. ἐκ δὲ τούτων ὀρθῶς ἂν ἔχοι τὸ "ἔργον δ᾽ οὐδὲν ὄνειδος, ἀεργίη δέ τ᾽ ὄνειδος".

The prosecutor also said that Socrates selected the most evil passages of the most famous poets and used their testimony to teach his followers to be workers of evil and tyrannical. He is supposed to have explained Hesiod's line 'no work is a disgrace, idleness is' as meaning that the poet tells us not to refrain from any work, however unjust or shameful, but to do those things too for our own gain. But since Socrates would concede that being a worker is useful to human beings and good, whereas being idle is damaging to them and bad, and that working itself is good and being idle bad, he defined those who do good as working and being workers, whereas he called gamblers and others who do evil and illegal things idle. From which arguments it follows that the line 'no work is a disgrace, idleness is' holds true.

By redefining the meaning of ἔργον, Xenophon not only defended Socrates, but also asserted the truth and morality of Hesiod's own words. His concluding remark makes that much very clear and suggests that those who accuse Socrates also fail to appreciate Hesiod's wisdom. His rhetorical stance is thus not so different from that of Aeschines, who likewise invited his audience to side with him and Hesiod against Timarchus.

Plato was very well aware of the controversy over *Works and Days* 311, and offered his own, oblique perspective on it in the *Charmides*. Socrates, Critias, and the young and modest Charmides debate the nature of σωφροσύνη ('right-mindedness', 'temperance', 'restraint') in this dialogue, and consider the possibility that it might amount to 'doing one's own business' (τὸ τὰ ἑαυτοῦ πράττειν: 161b6). Socrates objects that cobblers and other artisans do not just make things for themselves, but provide shoes and other goods for others as well: this does not necessarily entail that they lack σωφροσύνη. At this point in the argument, Critias draws a distinction between 'doing' and 'making', πράττειν and ποιεῖν, and then adds an apparently gratuitous digression on 'working', ἐργάζεσθαι, as well. Socrates reports his exchange with Critias on this issue at 163b1–d7:

Εἰπέ μοι, ἦν δ᾽ἐγώ, οὐ ταὐτὸν καλεῖς τὸ ποιεῖν καὶ τὸ πράττειν;

Οὐ μέντοι, ἔφη· οὐδέ γε τὸ ἐργάζεσθαι καὶ τὸ ποιεῖν. ἔμαθον γὰρ παρ᾽ Ἡσιόδου, ὃς ἔφη ἔργον [δ᾽] οὐδὲν ὄνειδος. οἴει οὖν αὐτόν, εἰ τὰ τοιαῦτα ἔργα ἐκάλει καὶ ἐργάζεσθαι καὶ πράττειν, οἷα νυνδὴ σὺ ἔλεγες, οὐδενὶ ἂν ὄνειδος φάναι εἶναι σκυτοτομοῦντι ἢ ταριχοπωλοῦντι ἢ ἐπ᾽ οἰκήματος καθημένῳ; οὐκ οἴεσθαί γε χρή, ὦ Σώκρατες, ἀλλὰ καὶ ἐκεῖνος οἶμαι ποίησιν πράξεως καὶ ἐργασίας ἄλλο ἐνόμιζεν, καὶ ποίημα μὲν γίγνεσθαι ὄνειδος ἐνίοτε, ὅταν μὴ μετὰ τοῦ καλοῦ γίγνηται, ἔργον δὲ οὐδέποτε οὐδὲν ὄνειδος· τὰ γὰρ καλῶς τε καὶ ὠφελίμως ποιούμενα ἔργα ἐκάλει, καὶ ἐργασίας τε καὶ πράξεις τὰς τοιαύτας ποιήσεις. φάναι δέ γε χρὴ καὶ οἰκεῖα μόνα τὰ τοιαῦτα ἡγεῖσθαι αὐτόν, τὰ δὲ βλαβερὰ πάντα ἀλλότρια· ὥστε καὶ Ἡσίοδον χρὴ οἴεσθαι καὶ ἄλλον ὅστις φρόνιμος τὸν τὰ αὑτοῦ πράττοντα τοῦτον σώφρονα καλεῖν.

Ὦ Κριτία, ἦν δ᾽ἐγώ, καὶ εὐθὺς ἀρχομένου σου σχεδὸν ἐμάνθανον τὸν λόγον, ὅτι τὰ οἰκεῖά τε καὶ τὰ αὑτοῦ ἀγαθὰ καλοίης, καὶ τὰς τῶν ἀγαθῶν ποιήσεις πράξεις· καὶ γὰρ Προδίκου μυρία τινὰ ἀκήκοα περὶ ὀνομάτων διαιροῦντος. ἀλλ᾽ ἐγώ σοι τίθεσθαι μὲν τῶν ὀνομάτων δίδωμι ὅπῃ ἂν βούλῃ ἕκαστον· δῆλου δὲ μόνον ἐφ᾽ ὅτι ἂν φέρῃς τοὔνομα ὅτι ἂν λέγῃς. νῦν οὖν πάλιν ἐξ ἀρχῆς σαφέστερον ὅρισαι...

So tell me, I said, you don't think 'making' and 'doing' are the same thing?

Not at all, he said, no more than working and making are the same thing. That much I learnt from Hesiod, who said that 'no work is a disgrace'. Now do you imagine that, if he had meant by working and doing such things as you just mentioned, he would have said that there was no disgrace in making shoes, selling dried fish, or sitting in a brothel? That, Socrates, cannot be supposed. Rather, Hesiod too, it seems to me, distinguished between making things and doing and work, and thought that making could sometimes become a disgrace, when it did not go together with what is noble, while no work at all was ever a disgrace. For he called works those things that are made nobly and usefully, and doing those things he called works and actions. Moreover, he must have supposed that only those things were one's own business, and that all those that were damaging were not. So we must suppose that Hesiod, and any other sensible man, would call temperate those who mind their own business.

Critias, I said, as soon as you started I recognized the speech: I knew you would call one's own business good, and the doings of good people actions; for I have heard Prodicus make a million such distinctions about words. But I'll let you define each word as you wish; just be clear about how you apply whichever word you use. Now, then, start again from the beginning and mark things out more clearly...

Like Xenophon, Critias defines 'work' as 'good work', and thus defends the Hesiodic line (and hence, implicitly, the posthumous reputation of Socrates) from Polycrates' accusation. Plato's Socrates acknowledges that this is a famous issue ('as soon as you started I recognized the speech'), but then distances himself from it: Prodicus might teach such subtle lexical distinctions; as for Socrates (Plato's Socrates), the only important thing is that Critias knows what he is saying, and engages in a serious investigation of σωφροσύνη.

This passage is a complex response to the controversy over Socrates' interpretation of Hesiod's *Works and Days* 311: in order to unpack what Plato is saying here it is important to consider the internal and external chronology of the *Charmides*. Xenophon and Polycrates were writing about *Works and Days* 311 in the years following Socrates' death—which is also when the *Charmides* was written.[18] Within the dialogue, however, Plato depicts an earlier time: the conversation between Socrates, Critias, and Charmides purportedly takes place in the early 420s. It seems that, when he presents that conversation, Plato adopts two different strategies in response to Polycrates' accusation. In the first place, he claims that Socrates learnt the different possible meanings of Hesiod's line a long time ago, from Prodicus, an older sophist famous for his lexical work.[19] Those who now claim Socrates used Hesiod in order to promote bad work are simply unaware of his sophistication: Socrates knew, of course, that 'work' was open to different definitions, and therefore could not possibly have quoted Hesiod as naively as his accusers now suggest. Plato's second strategy, in this passage, is to stress that the whole debate about the meaning of Hesiod's line is beside the point: it does not add anything useful to the discussion of σωφροσύνη and is, in fact, introduced as an idle digression. Critias should not be distracted by subtle lexical distinctions or the interpretation of poetry, but rather concentrate on his discus-

[18] Polycrates' *Accusation* was written shortly after 394/3. The *Charmides* is generally dated in the 380s: see Kahn (1981). The *Memorabilia* was probably taking shape at around that time too, though it does not seem to have been completed until 371 BC.

[19] Koning, this volume, Ch. 5, discusses Prodicus' expertise in the 'correctness of names', and his special interest in Hesiod.

sion with Socrates—Plato's Socrates—in the interests of serious philosophical advancement. The interpretation of Hesiod's *Works and Days* 311—a matter, let us not forget, explicitly linked to Socrates' indictment and execution in the texts written after his death— is thus presented by Plato's Socrates, in the *Charmides*, as an utter irrelevance.

There is one further detail in this passage that seems important when considering Plato's Hesiod, and that is the arresting reference to male prostitution (ἐπ' οἰκήματος καθημένῳ) in the middle of Critias' speech. Socrates has just argued that σωφροσύνη is compatible with making and selling shoes.[20] Critias now uses Hesiod in order to make the opposite point: according to Critias, *Works and Days* 311 cannot possibly refer to humble, paid work at all; for, he says, we cannot suppose that Hesiod saw no disgrace in making shoes, selling dried fish, or selling oneself in a brothel. Critias' interpretation of Hesiod is flamboyantly aristocratic, and rather unconvincing. Even a superficial acquaintance with the *Works and Days* suggests that Hesiod does value humble, manual work. Critias' point seems to carry weight only in relation to male prostitution: that Hesiod should condone that activity seems, indeed, unlikely. But selling shoes is not at all like selling oneself: Plato exposes Critias' interpretation as preposterous and undemocratic. According to Socrates, making shoes is compatible with σωφροσύνη; Critias, by contrast, claims that making shoes is as disgraceful as prostituting oneself. That Hesiod should be marshalled in support of that view illustrates, once again, Plato's main point: that the poets can be used to make any claim whatsoever. At the same time, it also defends Socrates from Polycrates' main accusation: in Plato's portrayal, he emerges as having good democratic values.

So much for what the passage tells us about Plato's engagement with contemporary depictions of Socrates; if we ask what it tells us about Hesiod and his reception in classical Athens, it seems to me that one point emerges clearly. Even Critias' preposterous interpretation is built on one broadly shared assumption:

---

[20] Plato, *Charmides* 161e10–162a2.

Hesiod could not possibly condone male prostitution. I have just discussed how Aeschines used Hesiod against Timarchus, a young man who was accused of prostituting himself to older men. I then explored Plato's allusion to Hesiod in the *Laws*, in the context of legislating against homosexual intercourse and the corruption of the young. Now, in the *Charmides*—a much earlier dialogue concerned with the σωφροσύνη, or sexual restraint, of a beautiful young man—we again find Hesiod condemning male prostitution. This is not something that comes from Hesiod's own work: as I have said, there is nothing there about male homosexuality, or prostitution. This is an Athenian preoccupation, and we see it shape the reception of Hesiod for almost half a century.[21] As Plato himself points out, Hesiod stood for the old-fashioned morals of worthy old men.[22] The morality of up-and-coming youths like Charmides and Timarchus had to be measured against the norms of Hesiod and, indeed, those of Solon—another figure explicitly evoked both in the *Charmides* and in *Against Timarchus*.[23] What we have here is a dynamic typical of the processes of reception: the poetry of Hesiod was contested, debated, and interpreted in many ways. Yet at the same time the plurality of Hesiodic voices reinforced the normative authority of the poet. The youths and, indeed, young ideas had to be measured against it.

## WORKS AND DAYS 383–92: PEACE IS BETTER THAN WAR

I have so far outlined two contexts in which the poetry of Hesiod was heard in classical Athens: professional rhapsodic performances, and re-performances of selected passages on the part of public speakers educated in what we might broadly term sophistic strategies of

---

[21] The *Charmides* is generally dated no later than the second half of the 380s; Aeschines' *Against Timarchus* was delivered in 346 or 345 BC; Demosthenes and Aeschines delivered their speeches *On the Embassy* in 343.

[22] Cf. *Laws* 658d6–9, discussed above p. 112.

[23] Plato, *Charmides* 155a2–3; Aeschines, *Against Timarchus* 6, 25–6.

reading. I argued that one reason why it made sense, for the elite, to learn how to select and interpret Hesiod was that ordinary Athenians were familiar with his poetry through rhapsodic performances. This suggestion, however, implies too simple a picture: the rhapsodes did not just deliver straight recitations for the benefit of the masses, they also actively engaged in the intellectual developments of their time. Plato's *Ion* may seem irredeemably stupid, but even he aims to be on a par with the most famous Homeric professors of his age: he wants to explain poetry, not just memorize and perform it (see esp. *Ion* 530c7–d3). There is one text, in particular, that invites us to consider the ways in which the rhapsodes engaged with the intellectual debates of classical Athens: the *Contest of Homer and Hesiod*. I have discussed this text in greater detail elsewhere,[24] so I can be brief here: I offer an outline of the intellectual context of the *Contest*, and then focus on the way Hesiod quotes his own work at the end of his competition with Homer.

It is very difficult to establish the exact date and circumstances of composition of the *Contest*: the text we have grew and expanded over many centuries. The opening mentions the emperor Hadrian, but the central sections seem to be closely based on Alcidamas' *Musaion*, a 4th-century BC text.[25] Alcidamas in turn collected earlier stories and anecdotes, some of which circulated already in the 6th century.[26] The text is grounded in the epic tradition and is clearly shaped by rhapsodic performers: Hesiod's challenges to Homer in the *Contest* are based on a detailed knowledge of hexameter versification, and upon the deliberate and malicious breaking of a rule on which epic composers and performers relied much of the time. In early epic, individual hexameter lines tend to contain units of thought which can stand on their own, or become the subject of further elaboration in the next line.[27] The rule is not absolute but, broadly speaking, the

---

[24] Graziosi (2001).

[25] Nietzsche (1870–73), West (1967), 444, O'Sullivan (1992), 63–6, Graziosi (2001), 59.

[26] Graziosi (2001); scholars disagree about how much of the *Contest* story can be traced back to the archaic period: see West (1967) and Richardson (1981).

[27] Graziosi (2001), 64–5; more recently Collins (2005), 185–91 emphasizes some of the continuities between the manipulation of the hexameter in the *Contest* and the Homeric poems.

epic bard can choose either to start a new sentence at the beginning of the line, or continue the previous one in what is called unperiodic, i.e. non-essential, enjambement.[28] In other words, the performer can pause at the end of each line, collect his thoughts and then continue either with an elaboration in enjambement or with a new sentence altogether. In the *Contest,* by contrast, Hesiod creates a series of lines that cannot stand on their own: they need to be 'rescued' by the immediate composition of an appropriate run-over—a feat that Homer manages to accomplish only because of his virtuoso skills. We know that epic performers recited in relay, taking over from one another.[29] We cannot reconstruct where they broke off, but there are certainly more or less comfortable places at which to hand over the recitation of hexameter epic. Lines in necessary enjambement are, of course, the most uncomfortable: bluntly put, Hesiod's challenges in the *Contest* are the rhapsode's nightmare—and the techniques Homer uses to overcome the problem demonstrate extraordinary ease with hexameter versification. But the exchange between Homer and Hesiod does not just explore rhapsodic techniques of composition and performance; it also engages with fashionable topics and debates. I have argued elsewhere that Hesiod's lines in the *Contest* explore Homeric grammar and epic diction, the morality of the epic gods, the diet of the heroes, and the size of the Trojan expedition—all of which were topics of conversation in classical Athens.[30] It seems, then, that in the *Contest* Homer and Hesiod are not only presented in the guise of rhapsodes *extraordinaires,* but are also fully conversant with classical Athenian educated discourse.

The final section of the *Contest* confirms that the two poets are consummate sophists as well as rhapsodes: they are asked to compete in selecting the best passage from their works. It is on that ability of selection, so valued by the sophists and their pupils, that their merits as poets will ultimately be judged. Hesiod chooses *Works and Days* 383–92, a famous passage which starts with

---

[28] The phenomenon was first described by Parry (1929). Since then, many further investigations have appeared: e.g. Lord (1960), Higbie (1990), Bakker (1990), Clark (1994) and (1997). The idea of 'violent enjambement', a label that suits the practice in the *Certamen,* is proposed by Kirk (1966).

[29] Collins (2001*a*), (2001*b*), (2005), 167–202.

[30] Graziosi (2001).

128                          *Barbara Graziosi*

the rising Pleiades and describes the farmer's year. Homer answers
with *Iliad* 13.126–33 and 339–44, lines which—to Athenian ears
at least—described hoplite warfare.[31] Homer's selection seems designed to appeal to classical Athenian sensibilities—and indeed his
listeners, in the *Contest*, cheer his performance and demand
his victory. The judge, however, chooses Hesiod because he recom-
mends agriculture and peace, rather than wars and slaughter (*Contest*
§13 West):

θαυμάσαντες δὲ καὶ ἐν τούτῳ τὸν Ὅμηρον οἱ Ἕλληνες ἐπῄνουν, ὡς παρὰ τὸ
προσῆκον γεγονότων τῶν ἐπῶν, καὶ ἐκέλευον διδόναι τὴν νίκην. ὁ δὲ βασιλεὺς
τὸν Ἡσίοδον ἐστεφάνωσεν εἰπὼν δίκαιον εἶναι τὸν ἐπὶ γεωργίαν καὶ εἰρήνην
προκαλούμενον νικᾶν, οὐ τὸν πολέμους καὶ σφαγὰς διεξιόντα.

Full of wonder, the Greeks praised Homer also in this case, and asked that he
be granted victory, because the verses were even better than could be
expected. But the king crowned Hesiod, saying that it was just that the
poet who recommended agriculture and peace, rather than the one who
described wars and slaughter, should win.

This verdict confirms and strengthens Hesiod's reputation as the wise
poet—he may not be as popular or exciting as Homer, but he is
morally sound.

When mounting his attack against poetry in the *Ion*, Plato avoided
any direct criticism of the wise Hesiod, poet of the *Works and Days*,
though his presence can be felt throughout the dialogue. At the
beginning of their discussion, Socrates and Ion agree to focus their
discussion on Homer, because—they concur—all poets treat roughly
the same topics, but Homer is by far the best (*Ion* 531c1–d11):

ΣΩ. Τί οὖν ποτε περὶ μὲν Ὁμήρου δεινὸς εἶ, περὶ δὲ Ἡσιόδου οὔ, οὐδὲ τῶν
ἄλλων ποιητῶν; ἢ Ὅμηρος περὶ ἄλλων τινῶν λέγει ἢ ὧνπερ σύμπαντες οἱ ἄλλοι
ποιηταί; οὐ περὶ πολέμου τε τὰ πολλὰ διελήλυθεν καὶ περὶ ὁμιλιῶν πρὸς
ἀλλήλους ἀνθρώπων ἀγαθῶν τε καὶ κακῶν καὶ ἰδιωτῶν καὶ δημιουργῶν, καὶ
περὶ θεῶν πρὸς ἀλλήλους καὶ πρὸς ἀνθρώπους ὁμιλούντων, ὡς ὁμιλοῦσι, καὶ
περὶ τῶν οὐρανίων παθημάτων καὶ περὶ τῶν ἐν Ἅιδου, καὶ γενέσεις καὶ θεῶν
καὶ ἡρώων; οὐ ταῦτά ἐστι περὶ ὧν Ὅμηρος τὴν ποίησιν πεποίηκεν;

---

[31] Graziosi (2002), 175–7.

*ΙΩΝ. Ἀληθῆ λέγεις, ὦ Σώκρατες.*

*ΣΩ. Τί δὲ οἱ ἄλλοι ποιηταί; οὐ περὶ τῶν αὐτῶν τούτων;*

*ΙΩΝ. Ναί, ἀλλ', ὦ Σώκρατες, οὐχ ὁμοίως πεποιήκασι καὶ Ὅμηρος.*

*ΣΩ. Τί μήν; κάκιον;*

*ΙΩΝ. Πολύ γε.*

*ΣΩ. Ὅμηρος δὲ ἄμεινον;*

*ΙΩΝ. Ἄμεινον μέντοι νὴ Δία.*

*Socrates*: Then how can it be that you are clever concerning Homer, but not Hesiod and the other poets? Does Homer speak of other subjects than are treated by all the other poets? Does he not, above all, go through tales of war, and of how people deal with one another in society, good people and bad, those with a skill and those without one? And of how the gods deal with one another and with human beings, and about what happens in heaven and in Hades, and the births of gods and of heroes? Are these not the subjects of Homeric poetry?

*Ion*: That is true, Socrates.

*Socrates*: And what about the other poets? Do they not treat the same topics?

*Ion*: Yes, Socrates, but not in the same way as Homer.

*Socrates*: How then? Less well?

*Ion*: Far less well.

*Socrates*: Homer does it better?

*Ion*: Far better, by Zeus.

In the course of his speech, Socrates stealthily moves from Homer's area of expertise (war) to Hesiod's poetry: 'the births of gods and heroes' is a perfect description for the *Theogony* and the *Catalogue of Women*. What he fails to mention, because it would make his argument more difficult, is the sphere that defines Hesiod as essentially different from Homer, that is to say, the works of agriculture and peace that are central to the *Works and Days*. Hesiod as the poet of peace, however, implicitly shapes the dialogue. When pressed, Ion concedes that Homer essentially teaches war (again the verdict of the *Contest*); and, after that concession, Socrates proves that Homer is actually no military expert. By the same token, we can conclude for ourselves that Hesiod would turn out not to be a real expert in peace or agriculture; but the argument against Hesiod remains implicit—and for a good reason. The *Works and Days* cannot easily be dismissed as mimetic or even Muse-inspired, and this makes it impervious to Socrates' main line of attack in the *Ion*.[32] The points he makes about divine inspiration, and about the enchantment of audiences, have little or no force when applied to the *Works and Days*. Plato's relationship to Hesiod thus remains, in this dialogue, less explicit and more complex than his full-scale attack on Homeric epic.

## CONCLUSION

I have focused on three Hesiodic passages that seem to have been particularly popular and contested in classical Athens. A full investigation of Hesiod's influence on classical Athenian discourse would need to be much broader, and lengthier; but I wish to draw some conclusions at this point, and ask whether my three examples matter at all for our understanding of Plato and, indeed, Hesiod.

As far as Hesiod is concerned, I think the material discussed may offer a useful perspective on his work. The modern reception of Hesiod is a story of extremes: on the one hand, he is often depicted as an archaic peasant incapable of expressing a coherent line of thought; on the other, he is the inspiration behind some of the most far-reaching and controversial theories of modernity—such as Bachofen's elaboration of the *Theogony* in *Das Mutterrecht*,[33] or the appeal to Hesiod's Earth Mother in Gaian theory, one of the most far-reaching and controversial scientific hypotheses in the last forty years.[34] This schizophrenic attitude towards Hesiod stems from the very different receptions of his two main poems: the *Works and Days* is primarily treated as a shambolic assemblage of evidence useful to those interested in archaic Greek society; the *Theogony*, by contrast, is central to contemporary approaches to Greek mythology, and is often assumed to contain some deep truths about humanity and

---

[32] For Hesiod's relationship with the Muses in the *Works and Days*, see J. S. Clay (2003), 72–6; and Haubold and Boys-Stones, this volume, Ch. 1 and Ch. 2 respectively.

[33] Bachofen (1861). For a recent assessment of his work see Borgeaud (1999). For Bachofen's influence on psychoanalysis see Burston (1986).

[34] On Gaian theory, see Lovelock (1979) and (1988). Midgley (2001) and (2007) and Schneider *et al.* (2004) discuss in detail Lovelock's appeal to Gaia.

the world at large. The evidence from classical Athens suggests that the *Works and Days* was more highly regarded in antiquity than it is today. I did not set out to focus on that poem, but discovered, in the course of my research for this chapter, that the *Works and Days* was quoted more explicitly and more prominently than the *Theogony* in many contexts. It seems that the traditions of wisdom embedded in the poem were of particular interest to the orators, rhapsodes, sophists, and philosophers of classical Athens. The *Theogony* could be treated together with the Homeric poems and traditional myth-making more generally, but the *Works and Days* was useful when discussing the quintessential Hesiod, the champion of human wisdom and morality.

As far as Plato is concerned, the material discussed invites us to probe further into his relationship with his contemporaries. We know that hundreds of texts featuring Socrates were written by dozens of authors in the years following his execution.[35] Except for the works of Xenophon and Plato himself, hardly any trace of them remains. One reason for their disappearance is that Plato successfully replaced all other literature on Socrates. But in classical Athens this had not yet happened: Plato engaged closely, if obliquely, with other contemporary representations of Socrates. An example of how he went about challenging and replacing other portrayals of Socrates emerges from my discussion of *Charmides* 163b1–d7, where Plato persuasively suggests that the Socrates of Xenophon and Polycrates is simply too naive, too uninterested in serious philosophical enquiry, to be credible. The same determination to engage with, but also elevate, current intellectual discourse can be seen in Plato's treatment of other topics too, such as the use and abuse of poetry in the public arena. The passages I have discussed demonstrate a precise and conscious engagement with popular perceptions of Hesiod in classical Athens. Plato quoted and discussed the same passages that interested his contemporaries, and yet at the same time fundamentally questioned their authority. It

---

[35] On our evidence for Socratic literature see Giannantoni (1990), D. Clay (1994), and Kahn (1996); as well as the excellent discussion in Vegetti (2006).

seems, then, that our understanding of both Plato and Hesiod changes when we consider them together—and that, in some ways, they start resembling one another. Hesiod becomes more authoritative as a moral guide; and Plato becomes more competitive, more obviously engaged in the debates of his time.

# 7

## Plato's two Hesiods

### Andrew L. Ford

## INTRODUCTION

Friedrich Solmsen's path-breaking study of Hesiod's influence on Plato focused on 'motifs' common to the two authors. Concerned to bring out the 'threads of continuity' in their ethical thought, Solmsen explicitly set aside the evidence of quotation, explaining that '[b]y and large, Plato is moving on a level of thought on which direct contact with the Hesiodic legacy could serve little purpose' (Solmsen 1962: 179). There is no doubt that Plato found Hesiod 'good to think with' in a general way, but the evidence of his quotations of the poet is surely worth looking at as well. The present study is one of several in this volume to take up this material, which heretofore has been studied principally for text-critical reasons (Howes 1895). My concern will be to understand a simple pattern in the evidence: of the fifteen occasions on which Plato quotes specific Hesiodic lines or phrases (as against 146 quotations from Homer), fourteen come from the *Works and Days*; the *Theogony* is quoted once, though specific genealogies are referred to on a few other occasions.[1] Whether a disproportion of this sort in such a small

---

[1] Brandwood (1976), 996–1001; Howes (1895), 161–74; cf. Most's list of passages, pp. 57–61 above. I am not counting three doubtfully Platonic texts: *Minos* 320d (*Catalogue of Women*: 144 MW), *Demodocus* 383c (338 MW; cf. 293 Most), and *Epistle* 11, 395a (324 MW; cf. 223 Rzach). All are accepted by Schwartz (1960), 580–82.

sample is significant may be doubted, but it is no idiosyncrasy of
Plato's: Aristotle takes fourteen of his seventeen Hesiodic quotations
from the *Works and Days*; in addition, his three quotations from the
*Theogony* all come from the same passage (*Theogony* 116–20), which
is the very one quoted in Plato.[2] Explanations of the phenomenon are
readily imaginable: the *Works and Days* is inherently a more 'quotable' work, replete as it is with aphorisms and precepts; Plato and
Aristotle are more likely to quote it because they write more often
about ethical and social issues than mythology or theology. But a
closer look at these passages will suggest that the disparity is not
fortuitous but reflects the fact that the two principal Hesiodic works
occupied different niches and played different roles in the cultural life
of late classical Athens. What follows is an attempt to delineate these
two Hesiods and to explain their presence in Plato.

It must be conceded at once that, in themselves, verbatim quotations can tell at best only a part of the story of *Hésiode et son influence*
(to quote the title of the volume in which Solmsen's essay appeared).
Yet quotations provide literary history with precious evidence for
how the poet's actual words were recalled and interpreted. The detail
they add will require us to nuance claims for Hesiod's authority in
the 4th century, and should make us pause before attributing to
classical Greece certain hermeneutical approaches to Hesiod we
take for granted. Modern literary and philosophical studies of Hesiod, whether they regard him as an historical person or as the name
of a tradition, usually define his *oeuvre* as consisting of the *Works and
Days* and the *Theogony* (to which some would add the *Catalogue of
Women* either as a continuation or sequel);[3] moreover, these core
works are treated as mutually explicative, as in Jenny Strauss
Clay's recent *Hesiod's Cosmos* (J. S. Clay 2003), which describes
them as 'parts of an organic whole, a diptych, as it were in which
each component illuminates the other'.[4] It might seem legitimate to

---

[2] Bonitz (1870), s.v. Ἡσίοδος; cf. Howes (1895), 168–72. Hesiodic quotations by
Xenophon, Isocrates, and the orators (see Graziosi, this volume, Ch. 6) also come
from the *Works and Days*, but are too infrequent to be statistically significant.

[3] On the relation of *Catalogue* to *Theogony* see West (1985), 124–7; Hamilton
(1989), 96–9; R. L. Hunter (2005).

[4] J. S. Clay (2003), 6. In J. S. Clay (2005) she acknowledges the *Catalogue* as a
'supplement' to the diptych.

attribute the same hermeneutic stance to Plato, since the evidence of quotation shows that he 'apparently is the earliest author who cites from Hesiod exclusively in the *Theogony* and the *Works and Days*.'[5] Yet a closer look at these passages indicates that the texts had little to do with each other in practice, and comparing the evidence of Plato's contemporaries suggests we should recognize two distinct Hesiods in the 4th century BC, each with his own place in the culture and his own kind of authority. Putting the two beside each other will give us a fuller and more realistic picture of Plato's encounter with Hesiod, not as a timeless conversation between Olympians but as part of the processes by which the meaning of an old corpus of poetry was shaped and circumscribed by the social institutions that preserved it. My study will analyse the quotations of *Theogony* 116–20 and then give an overview of uses of the *Works and Days*; but I begin by reviewing two well-known 5th-century testimonia to show that it was possible to cite Hesiod as the author of one poem without the other being in view.

## THE POET OF THE *THEOGONY* AND THE POET OF THE *WORKS AND DAYS*

Herodotus pairs Hesiod with Homer as proof that the Greeks acquired their picture of the gods relatively recently: 'Hesiod and Homer are in my estimation no more than 400 years earlier than I. And they are the ones who made a genealogy of gods for the Greeks, attributing names to the gods, distributing their honours and spheres of activity and indicating their forms. The poets alleged to be earlier than these were, in my view, born later' (2.53).

---

[5] Most (2006), 243. The hexameter quoted at *Republic* 390e, which is ascribed to Hesiod by the Suda (fr. dub. 361 MW = 272 Rzach), complicates the question, as does the reference to Hesiod as the author of astronomical poetry in *Epinomis* 990a (p. 148 MW = T 72 Most). I note that I do not include cross-references to the valuable editions of Rzach and Most except when they provide differences of emphasis or interpretation worth considering.

Two points in this famous passage are worth underscoring. First, it is as the poet of the *Theogony* that Hesiod is in view. We will see that this is usually the case when Hesiod and Homer make a pair.[6] Some would go on and infer from the fact that Herodotus names Hesiod before Homer (twice in 2.53) that he thought him chronologically earlier. The ancient debate over their relative dates had possibly already begun (cf. Xenophanes 21 B13 DK), but Herodotus' main point here is to make other religious poetry, notably that of Orpheus and Musaeus, whose earliness had been accepted by Hellanicus, postdate Homer and Hesiod.[7] A more likely reason why Herodotus puts Hesiod before Homer is that he is thinking of their works in terms of what Walter Ong called a 'topical poetic', a Greek way of organizing long hexameter poems from the archaic age according to how the stories they told lined up along a continuous 'path' (οἴμη) of narrative (Ford 1992: 40–48). In this perspective—which was wide-spread, traditional, and useful in the absence of indisputable evidence about authors and dates—Hesiod's narrative poetry tended to get detached from the gnomic *Works and Days* and to be located next to the epic cycle on the path of songs about early history. The poet of the *Theogony* naturally claimed precedence over Homer since he recounted the ultimate antecedents and (in the *Catalogue*) the ancestors of the heroes who fought at Troy. The need to bracket Hesiod's best known other work offered no difficulty to this view, since in Greek terms the non-narrative, hortatory *Works and Days* was a fundamentally different kind of song (Ford 1997: 409–11).

The second point worth underscoring in this passage is that Hesiod's authority is far from absolute. Herodotus takes the poets as early and influential sources of Greek ideas about the gods, but keeps his distance from endorsing their theogony.[8] His only other explicit reference to Hesiod is a remark in the Scythian ethnography

---

[6] So, I believe, already in Xenophanes 21 B11 DK reprehending 'Homer and Hesiod' for attributing 'thieving, adultery and deceiving each other' to the gods; cf. 21 B12.2 DK with Sextus Empiricus, *Against the Professors* 1.289.

[7] Hellanicus, *FGrHist* 4 F5a, 5b (= 5a, 5b Fowler).

[8] Burkert (1990), 26. Herodotus' attitude toward Hesiod (and Homer) is well epitomized by Veyne (1988), 33: 'as the investigator cross-checks information he imposes the need for coherence on reality. Mythical time can no longer remain secretly different from our own temporality. It is nothing more than the past.'

that 'the Hyperboreans are mentioned by Hesiod, and by Homer too in the *Epigonoi*—if Homer in fact is the author of that poem' (4.32; cf. Schwartz 1960: 575). On the common but risky assumption that Herodotus' reference is to be tied to a specific passage in the Hesiod we possess, the only candidate is a brief mention of the Hyperboreans in the *Catalogue of Women* (150.21 MW; cf. 209 Rzach); if so, the sentence implies that Herodotus regarded the *Catalogue* as Hesiodic poetry (whether he saw it as separate from the *Theogony* we cannot tell). The 'Hesiod' in which Herodotus is interested, then, is an early poet whose poems may be consulted for information about early beliefs and peoples. He gives no sign of being interested in the *Works and Days*.[9]

The poet of the *Works and Days* appears in a different kind of list from Aristophanes' *Frogs* (1030–36). 'Aeschylus' there defends the social utility of poetry by showing 'how the most excellent among poets have been of service' (1031: ὡς ὠφέλιμοι τῶν ποιητῶν οἱ γενναῖοι γεγένηνται): civilization is indebted to Orpheus for mysteries and taboos on killing; Musaeus revealed healing rites and prophetic arts; Hesiod follows as the one who taught 'working the earth and the seasons for harvesting and ploughing' (1033–4: Ἡσίοδος δὲ | γῆς ἐργασίας, καρπῶν ὥρας, ἀρότους); last comes 'godlike' Homer, whose honour and fame derive from his teaching 'marshalling troops, courageous acts, and the arming of men' (1036). Hesiod is represented by the *Works and Days* and Homer by the *Iliad* for contrast, and to mark steps in Aeschylus' evolutionary scheme. These interpretative reductions fit the logic of the speech, which is a parody of sophistic disquisitions on progress in the arts. Many in Aristophanes' audience may have thought this list reflected actual chronology—the view Herodotus argued against—but the main function of its implicit topical poetic is to organize notable early hexameter corpora into an intelligible hierarchy: the *Works and Days* is located after poetry dealing with the most basic requisites for

---

[9] The fact that the last line of the oracle quoted at 6.86γ2 ('an oath-abiding man's race is better in aftertimes') happens to be the same as *Works and Days* 285 is no proof of Herodotus' knowledge of the latter. Herodotus' quotations of non-Homeric poetry tend to lyric: Alcaeus (5.95.2), Sappho (2.135.6), Simonides (5.102.5, etc.), and a little disquisition on the wisdom of a Pindaric tag (3.38).

human society but before the *Iliad*, because war depends on the wealth and social grouping that agriculture makes possible. The same basic outlook can be seen in the sophist Hippias who wrote a discourse which collected excerpts from, as he lists them, Orpheus, Musaeus, Hesiod, and Homer, along with other poets and prose writers (86 B6 DK, see below).

## THE POET OF THE *THEOGONY*

One might have expected that Plato would be closely engaged with the poet he paired with Homer as the leading purveyors of harmful stories to the Greeks (*Republic* 377d), yet references to Hesiod in the *Republic*'s notorious censoring of poetry are brief and vague. Socrates begins with 'the greatest lie' about the greatest matters, 'what Ouranos wrought, and how Kronos punished him and the deeds and sufferings of Kronos at the hands of his son' (377e). Thereafter Hesiod drops from sight, for Plato is proceeding topically: when Socrates turns from the succession myth to stories of gods struggling against each other (378b–d), he turns to Homer and other sources for examples.[10] The vagueness with which the *Theogony* is paraphrased is probably a sign of Socrates' piety, reflecting his conviction that such stories are harmful for the young even to hear; other speakers in and out of Plato do not scruple, in referring to these tales, to use the contemporary medical language of 'castration' where Hesiod speaks metaphorically of 'reaping' (ἤμησε: *Theogony* 181) or generally of 'cutting off' (ἀποτμήξας: 188).[11]

When Socrates says that such stories are not redeemed by finding 'under-meanings' in them (ἐν ὑπονοίαις: 378d), we may infer that allegorical defences of divine violence in the *Theogony* were circulating at the time, as they were for Homer's theomachy and the Orphic cosmogony in the Derveni papyrus. Support comes from *Euthyphro*:

---

[10] Commenting on the same theme in Isocrates' *Busiris* 35–7, Livingstone (2001), 171–6 also provides valuable notes on Plato's ostensible references.

[11] Agathon at *Symposium* 195c (ἐκτομαί); Isocrates, *Busiris* 38 (πατέρων ἐκτομάς), noted by Livingstone (2001), 175. So too Euthyphro (ἐκτεμεῖν) in *Euthyphro* 6b.

its title character, an expert in matters divine, has contempt for 'people' (οἱ ἄνθρωποι) who criticize him for indicting his father and yet believe that great Zeus bound his father, who in turn 'gulped down' his children (*Euthyphro* 6b). Euthyphro objects not only to the inconsistency of people's views but to their literal understanding of the *Theogony*.[12] Often taken as a sort of Orphic, Euthyphro boasts an esoteric knowledge of 'divine matters' (3e; cf. *Cratylus* 396d) and offers to tell Socrates 'things yet more marvellous, which the many do not know' (6b: θαυμασιώτερα, ὦ Σώκρατες, ἃ οἱ πολλοὶ οὐκ ἴσασιν).

The passage from the *Theogony* that seems to have drawn the most attention in Plato's time was the beginning of its story, the account of the rise of Chaos and the primordial elements (see the *apparatus criticus* at Rzach 1902: 21–5). Hesiod's version was drawn upon, along with theogonies like the Derveni's (Betegh 2004: 153–69), to concoct the 'correct' theogony preached in the parabasis of Aristophanes' *Birds* (esp. 691–4). Hesiod's opening lines in particular were often quoted, but always selectively, so it may be helpful to set out the text:

| | |
|---|---|
| ἤτοι μὲν πρώτιστα Χάος γένετ'. αὐτὰρ ἔπειτα | 116 |
| Γαῖ' εὐρύστερνος, πάντων ἕδος ἀσφαλὲς αἰεὶ | 117 |
| ἀθανάτων οἳ ἔχουσι κάρη νιφόεντος Ὀλύμπου, | 118 |
| Τάρταρά τ' ἠερόεντα μυχῷ χθονὸς εὐρυοδείης, | 119 |
| ἠδ' Ἔρος, ὃς κάλλιστος ἐν ἀθανάτοισι θεοῖσι. | 120 |

Now it was Chaos that arose at the very first, and thereupon
broad-chested Earth, steadfast eternal seat of all
the immortals who hold the peaks of snowy Olympus,
and misty Tartarus in a recess of the wide-wayed land
and Eros, who is the fairest among the immortal gods.

Plato's Phaedrus quotes from this passage in the *Symposium* as part of his praise of Eros.[13] Editors have rearranged the text, but we have a better chance of following Phaedrus' logic by staying with the paradosis:

---

[12] Euthyphro's 'gulped down' (κατέπινεν) suggests he is thinking of Hesiod's version in particular (*Theogony* 459, 467, 473, 497).

[13] See also the discussion of Kenaan, this volume, Ch. 8.

γονῆς γὰρ Ἔρωτος οὔτ' εἰσὶν οὔτε λέγονται ὑπ' οὐδενὸς οὔτε ἰδιώτου οὔτε
ποιητοῦ, ἀλλ' Ἡσίοδος πρῶτον μὲν Χάος φησὶ γενέσθαι —

> αὐτὰρ ἔπειτα                                          [116]
> Γαῖ' εὐρύστερνος, πάντων ἕδος ἀσφαλὲς αἰεί,   [117]
> ἠδ' Ἔρος                                              [120]

φησὶ <δὴ> μετὰ τὸ Χάος δύο τούτω γενέσθαι, Γῆν τε καὶ Ἔρωτα.
Παρμενίδης δὲ τὴν γένεσιν λέγει —

> πρώτιστον μὲν Ἔρωτα θεῶν μητίσατο πάντων.

Ἡσιόδῳ δὲ καὶ Ἀκουσίλεως ὁμολογεῖ. οὕτω πολλαχόθεν ὁμολογεῖται ὁ Ἔρως
ἐν τοῖς πρεσβύτατος εἶναι.[14]

For Eros has no begetters, nor are any recorded by laymen or poets; Hesiod
rather says that Chaos was the first to arise—

> 'and straight upon
> broad-breasted Earth, seat of all, unmoving always,
> and Eros.'

And so he says that after Chaos these two arose, Earth and Eros. But
Parmenides recounts his origin:

> '[she] contrived Eros as first of all the gods.'

But Acusilaus agrees with Hesiod. And so it is agreed on all sides that Eros is
among the oldest of gods.

Phaedrus quotes selectively, but his omissions are not designed to
fudge the evidence. He perhaps leaves out verse 118 because its
proleptic description of Earth as 'the seat of the immortals' might
obscure the earliness of Eros. Similarly, Tartarus at 119 might seem to
interpose another divinity between Chaos and Eros (as the verse did
for Plutarch, *On the Fortune of Alexander* 343C and Pausanias
9.27.2); it could be fairly passed over if Tartarus were regarded
as only a part of Earth (*pace Theogony* 729–819: see West 1966:
192). Phaedrus quotes enough Hesiod to show that no parents are
mentioned when Eros 'arises' in verse 120, and that, no matter what
source you follow, Eros comes early in the cosmos.

---

[14] *Symposium* 178bc. *Pace* Wilamowitz-Moellendorff (1920), ii. 341, and Dover
(1980), 90–91, I agree with R. L. Fowler (2000), 5 that it is unnecessary to transpose
φησὶ μετὰ . . . Ἔρωτα to follow Ἡσιόδῳ . . . ὁμολογεῖ. (The change seems ruled out by
Fowler's reconstruction of Acusilaus' genesis: Chaos–Erebus–Night–Aether–Eros–
Metis.)

Phaedrus can be called an over-reader, as interested in what can be inferred from what Hesiod says as in what Hesiod says. A lack in the text, Hesiod's non-mention of anthropomorphized antecedents to Eros, counts as much for proof as his explicit testimony. Such authority as Hesiod may have is not sufficient to override Parmenides (28 B13 DK), for Phaedrus leaves open the question of whether Eros is the first or is among the first gods. He brings in Acusilaus (*FGrHist* 2 F6a = 6a Fowler), not to settle the matter but as a prose source. One may further suggest that Acusilaus is cited in part to make a trio of witnesses, a rhetorical gesture in which a number of 4th-century references to Hesiod appear. Triads are of course inherently shapely in Greek, but they also carry a certain logical force: one witness proves only that a poet held the view in question; two may be a case of common error; a debater cultivated enough to muster three witnesses—and so much the better if one can find poets in agreement with prose writers— can then conclude with Phaedrus, 'on all sides it is agreed...' Adeimantus' challenge to Socrates in the *Republic* to recommend justice for its own sake is a similar rhetorical performance, arguing that fathers teach their children the opposite view when they recommend justice by citing 'noble Hesiod and Homer' (γενναῖος Ἡσίοδός τε καὶ Ὅμηρος: *Republic* 363a) for the idea that prosperity is the gods' gift to just kings (*Works and Days* 233–4; *Odyssey* 19.109, 111–13), and capping them with Musaeus' promise that virtuous people will enjoy an everlasting symposium in the afterlife (363bc). The texts suggest both that Hesiod was still a name to conjure with in the 4th century BC, and that claims for his wisdom by Plato and his contemporaries may be rhetorical or hyperbolic.

This sole passage from the *Theogony* quoted by Plato is also found, as noted, three times in Aristotle, and in a pseudo-Aristotelian work as well. Closest to the *Symposium* is *Metaphysics* 1.4 where Aristotle is considering whether Anaxagoras was the first to look beyond material causes and seek a cause of motion and order. Among possible predecessors is Hesiod ($984^b$23–31; cf. T 117(c)ii Most):

ὑποπτεύσειε δ᾽ ἄν τις Ἡσίοδον πρῶτον ζητῆσαι τὸ τοιοῦτον, κἂν εἴ τις ἄλλος
ἔρωτα ἢ ἐπιθυμίαν ἐν τοῖς οὖσιν ἔθηκεν ὡς ἀρχήν, οἷον καὶ Παρμενίδης· καὶ
γὰρ οὗτος κατασκευάζων τὴν τοῦ παντὸς γένεσιν

        ‘πρώτιστον μέν’ φησιν ‘ἔρωτα θεῶν μητίσατο πάντων’,
Ἡσίοδος δὲ

        ‘πάντων μὲν πρώτιστα χάος γένετ’, αὐτὰρ ἔπειτα  [116]
        γαῖ’ εὐρύστερνος ...                       [117]
        ἠδ’ ἔρος, ὃς πάντεσσι μεταπρέπει ἀθανάτοισιν’,  [120]
ὡς δέον ἐν τοῖς οὖσιν ὑπάρχειν τιν’ αἰτίαν ἥτις κινήσει καὶ συνάξει τὰ
πράγματα.

One might suppose that Hesiod was the first to inquire into such a cause, along with anyone who like Parmenides made love [*eros*] or desire a first principle in things: for Parmenides too in his rendition of the origin of the universe says,

        ‘first of all the gods (s)he contrived Eros,’
and Hesiod says,

        ‘Of all things now first of all Chaos arose, and thereupon
        broad-breasted Earth, seat of all, unmoving always,
        and Eros’
as though there must be some cause in things which moves them and brings them together.

The fact that Aristotle combines the same passage from the *Theogony* with the same verse from Parmenides may suggest that he is quoting the *Symposium*. But slight differences indicate that if Aristotle was reading Plato he was also reading (or remembering) Hesiod. Whereas Phaedrus paraphrased the first two thirds of 116, Aristotle quotes the verse entire. In his version of the line (which is also quoted at *Physics* 208[b]27–32), the asseverative particle ἤτοι is omitted, converting didactic precept into self-contained proposition; replacing it with πάντων makes it clearer that Hesiod is talking about the same thing as the philosopher, the ultimate origin of cosmic motion (984[b]22: ὅθεν ἡ κίνησις ὑπάρχει τοῖς οὖσιν). (It is to show that the line from Parmenides is on the same point that Aristotle glosses it as an account of ‘the origin of the universe’.) As to verse 117, quoted in whole by Phaedrus, Aristotle stops after the name and epithet of Earth have been given: this omits any distracting mention of ‘all’ in 117b, which also would have been otiose after his ‘all’ beginning 116. Like Phaedrus, Aristotle takes no account of 118–19, jumping to 120;

but he quotes this line entire, in a variant form stressing the pre-eminence of Eros rather than his beauty (Howes 1895, 173). It may be that this boiled-down understanding of *Theogony* 116–20 was standard in the Academy and the Lyceum: a similar citation of *Theogony* 116, 117, and Aristotle's version of 120 is found in the pseudo-Aristotelian treatise *On Melissus, Xenophanes, and Gorgias* and applied to the question of whether something can come from nothing (see 975$^a$9–14; cf. Melissus 30 A5 DK); *Physics* 4.1, 208$^b$29–35, quotes 116–17a to ask if Chaos ('chasm') precedes Earth as an intimation of the doctrine that space is the precondition for 'bodies'.

Complicating the triangular relation between Aristotle, Hesiod, and Plato is the likelihood of a further source to which both philo-sophers respond. The evidence is at *Cratylus* 402b where Socrates is trying out the idea that the original maker of the gods' names held a Heraclitean view of the universe. Etymologies of Rhea as 'flow' (ῥέω) and Kronos as 'spring' (κρουνός) suggest as much, as do a trio of cosmogonic passages in old poetry:

Just as Homer speaks of
  'Okeanos, the origin of gods, and mother Tethys',
I think Hesiod does so as well (οἶμαι δὲ καὶ Ἡσίοδος); and Orpheus some-where says:
  'fair-streamed Okeanos was the first to marry
  and espoused Tethys, his sister by the same mother.'

The Homeric proof-text is from the *Iliad* (14.201 = 302: Ὠκεανόν τε θεῶν γένεσιν καὶ μητέρα Τηθύν), with Tethys etymologized to mean pure water (402cd). The curiously non-committal mention of Hes-iod makes it hard to specify the reference, but *Theogony* 337 is usually adduced: 'and Tethys bore to Okeanos the whirling rivers' (Τηθὺς δ' Ὠκεανῷ ποταμοὺς τέκε δινήεντας).[15] Though that line's fluidity is suitably Heraclitean, nothing in it suggests that the watery union is primordial (Okeanos is child of Earth and Sky). This may be why Aristotle appealed to a different Hesiodic context when he treated the same topic in a slightly earlier part of the *Metaphysics*. Considering possible antecedents to Thales' 'watery' first principle, Aristotle cites

---

[15] Cf. Orpheus 1 B2 DK with note; Howes (1895), 167–8.

'some people' who held that a similar view of nature is found among those who 'made the first accounts of the gods' (πρώτους θεολογήσαντας) in ancient times: 'they made Okeanos and Tethys the parents of creation (τῆς γενέσεως πατέρας), and they described the oath of the gods as being by water, to which they give the name of Styx' (*Metaphysics* 983ᵇ28–32 = T 117(c)i Most). Aristotle drops the evidence of Orpheus, but refers to the same passage from Homer;[16] the passage from Hesiod to which Socrates evasively referred is identified as the gods' swearing by Styx (*Theogony* 775–806), a text Aristotle makes cosmically significant by the specious argument that 'what is oldest is most venerable, and what is most venerable is oath' (τιμιώτατον μὲν γὰρ τὸ πρεσβύτατον, ὅρκος δὲ τὸ τιμιώτατόν ἐστιν). Whether this citation is due to 'some people' or is Aristotle's improvement on a reference to Okeanos and Tethys at *Theogony* 337 we cannot tell, for he closes the question as admitting no answer.

In an important analysis of the doxography on Thales, Bruno Snell (1944, 178–80) argued that both the Platonic and Aristotelian passages made use of Hippias' anthology, which had connected tags from Homer, Hesiod, and Orpheus with Thales' naming of water as the primordial element. Snell's powerful argument certainly chimes well with Hippias' description of that work (86 B6 DK):

Of these things, some perhaps have been said by Orpheus and others by Musaeus, briefly, by this poet here and that poet there, some by Hesiod and some by Homer and by many other poets, and by prose writers, Greek as well as foreign. From all these, my novel and genre-crossing discourse will put together the parts that are most important and suited to each other.[17]

Aristotle would thus have taken the Homer–Thales connection from Hippias, along with his reference to Hesiod (or perhaps substituted his own as better); Plato in *Cratylus* downplayed Hesiod (perhaps

---

[16] *Pace* Most (2006), 247, who suggests that Aristotle is thinking less about the *Iliad* than about the offspring of Okeanos and Tethys catalogued at *Theogony* 337–70; but the progeny of Hesiod's Okeanos and Tethys are confined to rivers and springs, whereas θεῶν γένεσιν at *Iliad* 14. 401 is closer to Aristotle's gloss, 'parents of generation' (τῆς γενέσεως πατέρας).

[17] I take as genuine the final sentence of 86 B6 DK: ἐγὼ δὲ ἐκ πάντων τούτων τὰ μέγιστα καὶ ὁμόφυλα συνθεὶς τοῦτον καινὸν καὶ πολυειδῆ τὸν λόγον ποιήσομαι. For the significance of Hippias for Plato's relationship with Hesiod see also Koning, in this volume, Ch. 5.

euphemistically avoiding mention of Styx), but preserved Orpheus (15 Kern = 1 B2 DK = 22 Bernabé), all the while transferring the context from Thaletan hydrogony to the flux of Plato's *bête noire* Heraclitus.

Few though they are, these quotations suggest two preliminary observations about the use of the *Theogony* in the 4th century BC. In considering Hesiod's influence on Plato we should not imagine them as two talking heads raising their voices above history and addressing each other directly. Readers like Plato doubtless read and re-read all of Hesiod (possibly more than all), but Hippias' was one of many works—others lie behind the parodic theogony in *Birds*—that mediated the *Theogony* for contemporaries, focusing on particular passages and suggesting contexts within which to interpret them. Aristotle's engagement with the poet was shaped by these and by Plato as well.

A second point to note is that, for all their nods to poets as wise men, thinkers of the Academy seem to have been interested in Hesiod's antiquity as much as his authority. Phaedrus, of course, is less a philosopher than an after-dinner speaker manipulating putative authorities to exalt his object of praise. His use of Hesiod is confuted later in the *Symposium* by Agathon, on the not altogether serious grounds that if Eros arose before the other gods, 'there would have been no castrations and bindings and other such violence among them' (195c). Aristotle shows the poem being used in a lecture hall: he is willing to consider possible philosophical implications of its cosmogony, but always in the optative mood: one 'might suppose' Hesiod discovered motive causes (*Metaphysics* 1.4, $984^b23$–4); he 'might seem to have spoken correctly' in putting Chaos (i.e. space) first (*Physics* $208^b27$–8); the idea that ancient poets preserve ancient truth is attributed to 'some people' (*Metaphysics* 1.3, $983^b27$–30).[18]

To be sure, the idea that the ancients were wise—even uncannily so—was widely proclaimed in the culture, and Plato elsewhere shows Socrates extracting from the *Theogony* theses he thinks worth defend-

---

[18] [Aristotle] in *On Melissus, Xenophanes and Gorgias* is less reserved, citing Hesiod as 'not just anyone but one of those esteemed for wisdom' ($975^a6$–7: οὐχ ὅτι οἱ τυγχάνοντες, ἀλλὰ καὶ τῶν δοξάντων εἶναι σοφῶν).

ing in philosophical discussion. But Plato never presents Hesiod's word as adequate warrant for adopting a belief. So Socrates praises the unnamed genealogist—i.e. Hesiod in *Theogony* 266, 780—who made Iris the daughter of Thaumas, but this wisdom stems less from the poet's insight than from Plato's own ingenuity in discovering 'speech' (ἐρῶ) in Iris and 'wonder' (θαυμάζω: *Theaetetus* 155d) in Thaumas. When in *Cratylus* 406c Socrates agrees to accept Hesiod's derivation of Aphrodite's name from her being born from foam (*Theogony* 197–8) this is a 'playful' (παιδικῶς) etymology (and one for which Aristotle preferred a naturalistic explanation, based on the fact that semen is foamy: *On the Generation of Animals* 736ᵃ18–21). Though the etymologies of *Cratylus* have in recent years been acknowledged as philosophically suggestive, Plato insists and never retreats from the position that we know nothing about divine names and can at best play with the names men have given (*Cratylus* 400d–401a). David Sedley observes that in the end etymology for Plato was 'not a dependable route to the truth',[19] and the same can be said for reading the *Theogony*. Plato's playfulness toward that text is established early in the discussion when Socrates etymologizes Zeus, Kronos, and Ouranos but declines to go further back into 'Hesiod's genealogy', claiming he cannot remember the earlier part (ἐμεμνήμην: 396c). The suggestion is that we have to rely on our own memory and powers, not Μνημοσύνη's daughters the Muses, however well hymned they are in *Theogony* 1–116.

## THE POET OF THE *WORKS AND DAYS*

The poet of the *Works and Days* is not only quoted far more frequently in 4th-century prose, he is also, unlike the poet of the *Theogony*, attested as taught in schools. In a rare description of the classical elementary curriculum, Plato's Protagoras observes that letter-teachers 'set before their students on their benches works of good poets and compel them to learn them by heart, in which

[19] Sedley (2003), 34; cf. 30–34 on the 'anthropological basis' in Plato's day for taking poetic testimony seriously.

there are many admonitions and detailed narratives, panegyrics and eulogies of the good men of the past' (*Protagoras* 325e– 326a: παρατιθέασιν αὐτοῖς ἐπὶ τῶν βάθρων ἀναγιγνώσκειν ποιητῶν ἀγαθῶν ποιήματα καὶ ἐκμανθάνειν ἀναγκάζουσιν, ἐν οἷς πολλαὶ μὲν νουθετήσεις ἔνεισιν πολλαὶ δὲ διέξοδοι καὶ ἔπαινοι καὶ ἐγκώμια παλαιῶν ἀνδρῶν ἀγαθῶν). Assuming that Hesiod was already stan- dard school reading (as he was later: Cribiore 2001: 197–8), the only term here that can apply to Hesiodic rather than epic poetry is 'admonitions', suggesting that it was his gnomic verse that featured in school texts. Support can be found on a *kyathos* from the begin- ning of the 5th century, one of our earliest representations of Greek book rolls: there a youth sits holding an open papyrus roll while two youths with walking sticks stand on either side of him listening; on top of a box in front of the reading youth is another volume inscribed 'Chironeia'.[20] The boy is clearly equipped to read didactic poetry like the Hesiodic *Precepts of Chiron* (frr. 283–5 MW), very possibly that work itself: the pedagogic suitability of Hesiod's *Precepts* was rein- forced by its 'plot', which consisted of a series of precepts from the noble centaur to young Achilles.

Further support comes from a protreptic passage in Isocrates' *To Nicocles* (42–4) which additionally gives an insight into popular attitudes toward Hesiod's gnomic poetry:

Everyone believes that texts that offer advice, whether in poetry or prose, are very useful, but by no means do people listen to them with pleasure; their attitude toward them is rather the one they take toward people who rebuke them. For they also praise these people, but prefer to associate with fellow sinners and not those who would correct them. An example would be the poetry of Hesiod, Theognis, and Phocylides. For people say that they are excellent advisors about human life, but while they say these things they prefer to pass their time with the inanities of others and not their precepts. Moreover, if one should pick out from the top-ranked poets the so-called maxims, on which they have lavished such effort, people would be similarly disposed toward these—for they would listen with more pleasure to the cheapest comedy than to things so artistically composed.

---

[20] ARV² 329.134, on which see Beazley (1948), 337; on Chiron-literature, Kurke (1990), 192.

Hesiod is here ranked with other authors of maxims and 'advice about life'. People apparently are willing to pay lip-service to the worthiness of such texts, but few care to spend more time with them than they are obliged to. Homer's narratives do not fall into this class, even if, as Isocrates suggests, Homer was among the 'top-ranked poets' from which 'so-called maxims' could also be culled (εἴ τις ἐκλέξειε τῶν προεχόντων ποιητῶν τὰς καλουμένας γνώμας).[21] But the occasional nugget of anthologizable wisdom was hardly typical of epic, and Isocrates goes on to group Homer with the tragedians as a dramatic poet who pleases audiences by the vivid presentation of myth, undiluted by admonition and advice (*To Nicocles* 48–9).

The typical schoolbook, then, was more likely to contain extracts from Hesiod's gnomic poetry than his *Theogony*. Such 'treasuries that wise men of old wrote and left behind in books' were likely to be what Xenophon's Socrates used to 'unroll with friends and go through, picking out whatever strikes us as good' (ἀνελίττων κοινῇ σὺν τοῖς φίλοις διέρχομαι, καὶ ἄν τι ὁρῶμεν ἀγαθὸν ἐκλεγόμεθα: *Memorabilia* 1.6.14). We find Socrates interpreting an extract from the *Works and Days* for his students in Polycrates' *Accusation of Socrates*, which charged that he corrupted them by 'extracting from the most esteemed poets their most corrupt passages' (τῶν ἐνδοξοτάτων ποιητῶν ἐκλεγόμενον τὰ πονηρότατα) and using them to teach his associates to be tyrannical (*Memorabilia* 1.2.56–7). The example is *Works and Days* 311, 'work is no disgrace but not working is a disgrace', which Socrates was held to interpret as 'no deed is disgraceful', a deliberately perverse construal of ἔργον δ᾽ οὐδὲν ὄνειδος. This same Hesiodic half verse is also subjected to hair-splitting analysis in Plato's *Charmides* to distinguish banausic from liberal activity (*Charmides* 163b).[22] The fact that the interpreter is none other than Critias, Socrates' tyrannical associate, suggests that Plato and Xenophon are not in direct dialogue with Hesiod but are triangulating his name with a 4th-century rhetorical text and other sources—very possibly including Prodicus (*Charmides* 163d; cf. *Birds* 692). Like the *Theogony*, the *Works and Days* depended for its

---

[21] Cf. Aristotle's discussion of maxims in *Rhetoric* 2.21 where examples are taken from Homer (but not Hesiod).

[22] Cf. Koning and Graziosi, this volume, Ch. 5 and 6 respectively.

continuing relevance on a para-literature that excerpted it and gave it point.

The practice of extracting tags from the *Works and Days* and adapting their meanings can be seen already in Pindar, who quotes the first half of *Works and Days* 412 ('devotion, you know, furthers the work', μελέτη δέ τοι ἔργον ὀφέλλει) in an epinician honouring a son of Lampon of Aegina: 'In his "devotion to work" Lampon truly honours that saying of Hesiod, which he quotes when exhorting his sons' (*Isthmian* 6.66–7: Λάμπων δὲ <u>μελέταν</u> | <u>ἔργοις</u> ὀπάζων Ἡσιόδου μάλα τιμᾷ τοῦτ᾽ ἔπος). Nothing could seem more respectable than a prominent aristocrat quoting Hesiod to his sons, but Pindar's Hesiod is subtly updated: in the language of the *Works and Days*, μελέτη means the sort of assiduous care required in agricultural labour (ἔργον); Pindar's Lampon uses it, however, in the sense of 'practice', a meaning the word acquired when it was adopted by the highly esteemed professional trainers to refer to their athletic exercises. The word appears in the name of the famous Athenian trainer Melesias, and Bacchylides describes the trainer of Lampon's sons as 'Menander, whose exercises bring benefit to mortals' (μελέτα[ν τε] βροτωφ[ε]λέα Μενάνδρου 13.154–5). Indeed the compound epithet βροτωφελέα, unique to Bacchylides, suggests that his own phrase is also an adaptation of the Hesiodic motto: its second element brings Hesiod's verb ὀφέλλω—'to increase' or 'enlarge' in a sense appropriate to agricultural prospering—into the orbit of ὠφελέω—'to be of use to', a word for a person providing a service for another (cf. ὠφέλιμοι in *Frogs* 1031 quoted above). Even in traditionalist circles, Hesiodic vocabulary needed constant adaptation.

Xenophon's Socrates stands in this tradition when he explicates another half line from the *Works and Days*. Defending Socrates from charges of nonconformity with civic religion, Xenophon explains that he held small sacrifices to be in no way inferior to exorbitant ones (*Memorabilia* 1.3.3–4):

He was an admirer of this verse, 'in accordance with your power make sacrifices to the immortal gods' [*Works and Days* 336: κὰδ δύναμιν δ᾽ ἔρδειν ἱέρ᾽ ἀθανάτοισι θεοῖσι], maintaining that 'acting according to one's powers' was also good advice for dealing with friends, guest-friends, and the rest of life.

The story shows that Socrates was pious and also that he was willing to reinterpret Hesiod's memorable old phrase by extending the meaning of ἔρδειν from 'sacrifice' to 'acting' in general. A sophistic discourse summarized in Plato's *Lysis* uses the poet similarly: defending the thesis that the like is the greatest enemy of the like, the 'eloquent' speaker first called on Hesiod as a witness—'potter strives against potter, singer against singer I beggar against beggar' (215c, compressing *Works and Days* 25–6)—and then went on to extend this widely quoted maxim (four times by Aristotle alone: Howes 1895, 162) and to apply it to everything, not excluding the physical elements (215e). As Aristotle would say, Socrates differs from Polycrates or from the unnamed sophist as a reader of the *Works and Days* only in moral intent, not in method.

Plato's *Protagoras* suggests how a sophist like Prodicus handled one of the most popular passages from the *Works and Days*, Hesiod's allegory of *aretē*. In much-quoted verses (already paraphrased by Simonides: 579 *PMG*), Hesiod explained that Baseness or Misery (κακότητα) is always nearby and easy to be found, whereas Excellence or Prosperity (ἀρετῆς) dwells at the end of a long, steep road and is not reached without sweat (287–92). According to Socrates, 'Prodicus and many other people agree with Hesiod that *becoming* good is hard, for "in front of excellence" the gods have put "sweat", but when one "reaches the top, then it is easy, difficult though it is" to acquire' (340d: 'εἰς ἄκρον ἵκηται, ῥηϊδίην δήπειτα πέλειν, χαλεπήν περ ἐοῦσαν', ἐκτῆσθαι). We may infer that Prodicus used this text to display the value of his skill in distinguishing the meanings of words; the reading attributed to him also resolves the meaning of Hesiod's final line, which is ambiguous enough to be rendered quite differently by Most: when one 'reaches the top, then it is easy, difficult though it still is'.[23]

If a sophist read this familiar text as proving that attaining *aretē* requires expenditure, Plato's 'beggar-priests' seem to have used it differently. Adeimantus says these priests explained that even the virtuous (and rich) may require expiatory rituals because, as Hesiod shows, the gods send misfortunes to good people (*Republic* 364b–d). Not wanting to alienate potential clients, they quoted only Hesiod's

---

[23] For further discussion of the passage see Yamagata, this volume, Ch. 4.

lines about the prevalence of Misery (*Works and Days* 287–9), leaving out the bit about achieving excellence by sweat (290–92). Able speakers, the priests also had Homer to cite for the idea that gods are swayed by gifts (quoting *Iliad* 9.497–500), and they made a trio of witnesses by adding a 'bushel of books' from Orpheus and Musaeus on expiatory rites (cf. Koning, this volume, pp. 100–1). Contrary to what a philologist might suppose, the currency of the passage made its meaning less determinate: Hesiod's allegory appears in humbler company making a simpler claim when Xenophon's Socrates combines the lines with the consensus of athletic trainers and the verse of Epicharmus to argue that it takes steadfast commitment to achieve fine works (*Memorabilia* 2.1.20). I suspect we come close to Plato's own reading when *Works and Days* 289–92 are given a mischievous twist by the Athenian stranger: 'the many prove that Hesiod was wise' when he said that there is no great abundance of people who are zealous for virtue, the proof consisting in the scarcity of excellence among them (*Laws* 718e).

The authority of a poet treated in this way can only be notional or negotiable. Socrates adduces the poets to help define friendship because 'they are to us like fathers and guides to wisdom' (*Lysis* 214a), but in the event they offer no clear guidance: they first suggest the thesis that friendship is an affinity bestowed by the gods, 'which they express, as I think, thus: "god always draws like to like" and makes them familiars' (214a, citing a hexameter found at *Odyssey* 17.218 and treated by Aristotle as a proverb: *Rhetoric* 1371b). But the opposite case can also be supported from the poets, as Socrates notes in recalling that Hesiod's lines on strife were used to argue that the like is the enemy of the like (215c). Accordingly, Plato's Socrates, like Xenophon's, usually approaches the *Works and Days* by extracting a phrase or verse and examining it in isolation to see if the poet's reputation for wisdom is deserved. Experience will show 'if Hesiod was in fact wise' (*Republic* 466c) or 'was correct after all' (*Laws* 690e) when he said 'half is more than a whole' (*Works and Days* 40). On matters of which we lack certain knowledge, we may rely on the poets. So, for example, Socrates will adopt the Homeric custom of feasting heroic men with choice cuts of meat and wine (*Republic* 468d–e, quoting *Iliad* 7. 321 and 8.162, and adding that warriors need good nutrition); when such men die on campaign, he will 'believe Hesiod' and quote *Works and Days* 109 in affirming that they belong to the 'golden race' (468e; note 'gold' is interpreted in *Cratylus* 398a as 'noble'); he will add *Works and Days* 121–2 to show they have become protective spirits (469a).[24] Sometimes, of course, we don't believe him (cf. *Republic* 468e quoting and rejecting *Works and Days* 122–3).

Quotations suggest that for readers of Plato's time Hesiod's *Works and Days* was usually encountered in pre-selected, often pre-interpreted excerpts. To be sure, rhapsodes could perform 'something from Hesiodic poetry' (*Laws* 658d: τι τῶν Ἡσιοδείων), though we do not know which of his works were included (along with Homer and Archilochus) in their repertoire.[25] Isocrates speaks of 'sophists' haunting the Lyceum during the Great Panathenaia and 'discussing the poets, especially the poetry of Hesiod and Homer, saying nothing original about them, but merely chanting their verses and repeating from memory the cleverest things which certain others had said about them in the past' (*Panathenaicus* 18).[26] There is no evidence in Plato and Xenophon to support the assumption that they presented Hesiod's poems in full or read the one against the other; their methods are far more likely to have been those that Isocrates complains they applied to his own works: 'misreading them in the worst possible way, dividing them incorrectly and ruining them by picking them to pieces' (ibid. 17).

## CONCLUSIONS

Hesiod's two most popular works were in two different genres, and in the classical age genre continued to be tied to occasion of performance. Extracts from his wisdom poetry were commonly taught at

[24] Noting how often Hesiod's verses on the races and the *daimones* were rewritten, Solmsen (1962), 184–5, 195 claimed only 'a certain authority' for them.

[25] Cf. *Ion* 531a. Hesiod himself was thought of as a rhapsode: *Republic* 600d. See also Graziosi in this volume, Ch. 6.

[26] Although the Aristotelian school produced a book of 'Hesiodic questions' (ἀπορήματα, in the Hesychian *Vita*, no. 143 Rose), I do not think Isocrates' 'Lyceum' points to Peripatetics particularly: it is festival time and many intellectuals–teachers–writers are working the crowd.

school, where many learned to repeat the claims of pedagogues that Hesiod was a valuable adviser even as they found the poetry tedious. Sayings from the *Works and Days* could be presented as venerable wisdom, though in practice the old maxims usually needed a bit of interpretative legerdemain to be made relevant to contemporary situations. Works like the *Accusation of Socrates* or the sophistic piece of natural philosophy described in *Lysis* highlighted certain passages of the poem as especially interesting or problematic. As a result, the *Works and Days* was encountered most often in the form of isolated titbits that were quoted, by sophist and layperson alike, to see if Hesiod's reputation as a wise counsellor was deserved.

The *Theogony* was probably more often encountered through presentations by rhapsodes than at school. The poem was acknowledged as one very early and influential account of the gods (for some, influential merely because early), and like most poetry treating such matters, was allegorized, etymologized, and 'philosophized' in certain circles. The *Theogony* was seen as a complement to Homeric epic in providing an account of the gods that was coherent and recognizable throughout Greece. In this perspective, the poetic pair could be set against Orpheus and his like, whose mystical theogonies were less Panhellenic in aspiration and less amenable to exploitation by civic religion. Nevertheless, Orphic poetry, like its eschatology and soteriology, claimed enough popular adherents that the *Theogony* did not attain the dominant position in *theologia* that Homeric epic did in heroic song (or that the *Works and Days* did in gnomic verse). Hence it was also possible to combine Hesiod and Homer with Orpheus and Musaeus as forming a sort of summa of ancient wisdom.

As for Plato, he must be allowed to have been one of the subtlest readers of his time, but his encounter with Hesiod was shaped by the ways in which Athenian culture preserved and institutionalized this old poetry. Although the question of which of the many works ascribed to Hesiod were really by him was never unanimously answered in antiquity (cf. Most 2006: 188–215), Plato seems to have focused, as we do, principally on the *Theogony* and *Works and Days*. Yet our documented 4th-century readings do not treat Hesiod as the author of a coherent and self-explanatory *oeuvre*, and never appeal from one work to another to explicate Hesiod's ideas. We can only guess, of course, at what went on in esoteric interpretative communities, but it is notable that the two Hesiods do not meet even in the well-read Plato. I submit that this is because he wrote not only as a creative thinker engaged with the poetry of the past, but also as a social critic, observing and critiquing the musical culture of the society for which he wrote. Plato thus provides an important challenge to those assertions of Hesiod's timeless value he quotes. His texts are precious because they frequently adopt, sometimes parody, and always represent the many curious ways in which the poet's actual words were put to work.

# Part II

# Individual dialogues

# 8

## The seductions of Hesiod: Pandora's presence in Plato's *Symposium*

*Vered Lev Kenaan*

### INTRODUCTION

The *Symposium* is among those Platonic dialogues that are very obviously interested in Hesiod: Plato quotes directly from him and borrows Hesiodic motifs and ideas at crucial points in the text. Moreover, as Naoko Yamagata shows elsewhere in this volume, Plato in the *Symposium* uses references to Hesiod in order to articulate a broader intellectual shift from epideictic speech-making to Socratic enquiry.[1] In this chapter I would like to revisit the dialogue by a slightly different route. Rather than discussing individual cases of borrowing, my aim is to understand better some of the underlying affinities between the *Symposium* and Hesiodic epic. My argument is in two parts. I start by asking how Plato construes the relationship between authors and texts in the *Symposium*, and what that might mean specifically for his relationship with Hesiod. Taking the speech of Diotima as my point of departure, I argue that literary reception in the *Symposium* appears primarily as a genealogy of erotic inspiration; and that the *Symposium* exemplifies Diotima's theory by virtue of its Hesiodic theme and structure. I then turn to the figure of Socrates in the *Symposium* as the erotic character par excellence. I argue that Socrates is conceived as a Pandora figure, somebody who instils

---

[1] Yamagata, this volume, Ch. 4.

wonder and thereby sets us on a path towards philosophical reflection. Like Pandora, the 'beautiful evil' (καλὸν κακόν) of Hesiodic epic, Socrates is characterized by a striking contrast between appearance and being. In Hesiod, that contrast exemplifies the dire necessities of human life: Pandora teaches us to mistrust the world of phenomena. Socrates too inspires reflection but, in contrast with Pandora, he holds out the prospect of hidden truth. Like Pandora, he sets us on a path towards deeper understanding by virtue of his appearance and speech; but unlike her, he puts us back in touch with the divine truths that we thought we had long lost.

## EROTIC INTERTEXTUALITY

A text is not a text unless it hides from the first comer, from the first glance, the law of its composition, and the rules of its game. A text remains, moreover, forever imperceptible. Its law and its rules are not, however, harboured in the inaccessibility of a secret; it is simply that they can never be booked, in the *present*, into anything that could rigorously be called a perception. (Derrida 1981, 63)

Hesiod's influence on Plato is especially apparent in the *Symposium*. Plato not only cites from the *Theogony* and refers to Hesiod in cosmological and divine matters, but also praises him through the words of Diotima (209cd):[2]

Everyone would rather have such children than human ones, and would look up to Homer, Hesiod, and the other good poets with envy and admiration for the offspring they have left behind—offspring, which, because they are immortal themselves, provide their parents with immortal glory and remembrance.

Diotima commemorates Hesiod as a literary father, an admired creator of immortal poetry. She singles out Hesiod (and Homer) among the good poets (ποιητὰς τοὺς ἀγαθούς) who are worshipped like heroes. Like Hesiod's demigods (ἡμίθεοι at *Works and Days* 160) who escape a nameless death in Hades (νώνυμνος at *Works and Days*

---

[2] All translations from the *Symposium* are from Nehamas and Woodruff (1989).

154), Homer and Hesiod gain immortal glory (ἀθάνατον κλέος) and remembrance (μνήμην).

It is in the context of Diotima's discussion of *eros* and immortality that she refers to the figure of the literary father as a model for imitation. Homer and Hesiod were motivated by an erotic drive in creating beautiful works of art but, as we shall see, their effect on the reader (or listener) is also primarily erotic. Indeed, according to Diotima, any process of giving birth, whether physical or mental, depends on a bond between two parental figures. The lover of wisdom, beauty, and goodness, she says, becomes productive through contact with a man whose soul incites and reflects the lover's desires. In being close to his source of inspiration the lover 'remembers that beauty, and in common with him he nurtures the newborn' (209c).

That process is also apparent in the interaction between authors and their readers; and in so far as authors are themselves readers of other texts, it affects how we view the relationship between authors and their literary sources. As a result of a prolonged familiarity with other texts, the reader 'conceives and gives birth to what he has been carrying inside him for ages' (209c). A text is therefore always a product of more than one author. Diotima's erotic approach to intertextuality thus provides a lens through which we can investigate the *Symposium*'s own literary ancestors. In this chapter, I would like to take my cue from her and ask whether Socratic philosophical discourse too has more than one parent. What kind of textual bonds beget the Platonic dialogue? And how does Platonic philosophy respond to the possibility of nurturing its ideas in common with poetry?

Diotima uses the language of love as she describes the effect of the author on the reader: 'Everyone would rather have such children than human ones, and would look up to Homer, Hesiod, and the other good poets *with envy and admiration* for the offspring they have left behind' (209d). In turning the reader into a viewer who gazes (ἀποβλέψας) with envy and admiration at the poet, Diotima effectively characterizes him as a lover (ἐραστής). As the lover conceives and becomes an author in his own right, his infatuation with the model might create its own problems. In the *Phaedrus*, for example, Socrates alerts us to the manipulation of the passionate lover who turns a beloved into a complete dependent (πάντα ἀποβλέπων εἰς τὸν ἐραστήν: 239b). Alternatively, the lover himself might be paralyzed by the object of his desire, as happens to the admirers of Charmides (*Charmides* 154c). Yet the reader of the *Symposium* is not an all-powerful manipulator, nor is he simply paralyzed by the great poets' achievement, for he is also motivated by a desire to emulate (ζηλοῦν) them. Recalling Hesiod's analysis of the good Eris in *Works and Days* (esp. 23–4), Plato suggests that we see the reader's rivalry as an ambition to conceive better children.

Plato's competitive relationship with *Homer* as a charismatic father figure is obvious throughout his work. It is particularly pronounced in the *Republic*, which culminates in the myth of Er as Plato's attempt to replace the famous Homeric description of the underworld (*Odyssey* Book 11). By contrast, Plato does not appear to explore his relationship with Hesiod in that dialogue with a high degree of intensity.[3] The *Symposium*, however, does seem to me to do precisely that. I am not primarily thinking here of passages, themes, or ideas that Plato borrows from Hesiod, though these are obvious enough and are discussed elsewhere in this volume.[4] Rather, I argue that Hesiod's poetry is embroidered into the *Symposium* in a more subtle way. In reading Plato's *Symposium* with Hesiod we may hope to see what, in the words of Derrida, 'hides from the first glance'; and perhaps discover some hidden threads that are important to the *Symposium*'s unique textual fabric.

The way I propose to approach Plato's reception of Hesiod, then, is through the metaphor of giving birth in beauty. However, that metaphor is unstable, for the bond of friendship (φιλία) between Plato and Hesiod cannot be entirely equal. In fact, Plato's reception of Hesiod betrays signs of tension between old and new ideas, external and internal sources that participate in the shaping of the *Symposium*. The question of what the *Symposium* can tell us about its literary parents is certainly not answered merely by looking at how Plato 'uses' Hesiod at the level of quotation and appropriation. But it is not only a matter of harmonious symbiosis either. Rather, I suggest that the *Symposium* allows us to see the mirror-play between the two fathers, Plato and Hesiod, within the very fabric of the text. Herein, it seems to me, lies the crux of their intertextual bond.

---

[3] See, however, the contributions to this volume of Yamagata and Van Noorden, Ch. 4 and 9 respectively.

[4] Compare the discussion by Yamagata, this volume, Ch. 4.

Birth and the origin of things are central issues in the *Symposium*. From the very beginning, the dialogue presents the question of a primary source as inherent not just to its 'contents', but to its very form of writing. Who among the different narrators of the *Symposium* can be considered a reliable source? And what is the relation between a historical event and accounts of that particular event? These are questions that we are challenged to consider from the outset. The problem of origins arises with particular clarity from Socrates' enigmatic relationship with his admirers, Aristodemus and Apollodorus. It surfaces again in the attempt to identify who initiated the discussion, and becomes relevant whenever individual speakers discuss their respective sources. Thus, for example, Eryximachus calls Phaedrus 'the father of the *logos*' (177d); and Socrates recalls Diotima's teaching in order to establish her as the mother of his own erotic knowledge (201d, 212b). In displaying a plurality of originators, however, the *Symposium* does not seem particularly interested in the rivalry between them over who owns what ideas. The dialogue rather emphasizes the discursive contact that shapes its own textual process. Thus, Socrates remarks ironically at the beginning of the dialogue that it would be wonderful 'if the foolish were filled with wisdom simply by touching the wise' (175d), thereby pre-empting Diotima's notion of erotic contact. Both Socrates at the beginning of the dialogue and Diotima at its end capture the *Symposium*'s inner structure of a community of authors whose creativity lies in the very fact that they do *not* operate in isolation.

By showing us various ways in which different sources intersect with their copies (e.g. Socrates and his followers, literary sources and their epigones) Plato in the *Symposium* creates a textual fabric that very largely depends on the transformation and absorption of multiple texts. Readers of *Republic* Book 10 may well ask whether mimetic art does not obstruct our access to true sources. Ought we not to safeguard the distinction between an origin and a work of imitation?[5] Yet in the *Symposium*, a work that displays its similarity to an admired origin is not considered a mere copy of its appearance. On the contrary, such a work, Diotima tells us, reflects a desire for a

---

[5] See *Republic* 601c, where the imitator is said to know only the appearance of things.

source that is invaluable in the search for wisdom. Similarities between authors and their predecessors are therefore welcome: they
help us search for an essence that is born afresh each time a new
procreator joins the genealogy of texts. There is nothing whimsical or
superfluous about this process: the erotic force of human genealogy,
Diotima suggests, lies precisely in its capacity to preserve mortal
things beyond death (208ab):

And in that way everything mortal is preserved, not, like the divine, by
always being the same in every way, but because what is departing and aging
leaves behind something new, something such as it had been.

According to Diotima, even a radically new text is bound to its place
in the evolutionary chain of human creation, and in that sense
appears as a transformation of earlier texts, despite its originality.


## THE EROTIC SUBJECT

The genealogical framework of Diotima's theory reflects the overall
structure of the *Symposium*, as different speakers explore the genealogy of Eros. And it is specifically through an elaboration of this
theme that Plato resembles Hesiod most. At the most general level,
he inherits from Hesiod an interest in genealogy and the meaning it
engenders. In the *Theogony*, which is both a genealogy of the Greek
gods and a cosmological epic, Hesiod makes this request to the
Muses (*Theogony* 108–15):

Tell how in the first place gods and earth were born, and rivers and bound-
less sea seething with its swell, and the shining stars and the broad sky above,
and those who were born from them, the gods givers of good things; and
how they divided their wealth and distributed their honors, and also how
they first took possession of many-folded Olympus. These things tell me
*from the beginning* (ἐξ ἀρχῆς), Muses who have your mansions on Olympus,
and which one of them was born first (πρῶτον).[6]

------

[6] All translations of Hesiod are taken from Most (2006).

At the beginning of his genealogical account, Hesiod does not so much aim to see beyond all things, but rather to recover a picture of the world as yet empty of things. And since he cannot avoid seeing rivers, sea, stars, and sky, he turns to the Muses for help. Aided by their divine knowledge, Hesiod attempts to reconstruct a lost picture of absolute beginning (ἀρχή) that is otherwise beyond our grasp. And so we begin with four primordial beings: Chaos, Gaia, Tartarus, and Eros. Other entities soon join them, but the four cosmic principles do not disappear, nor do they lose their constitutive qualities. Thus, although the world at large, the Olympian gods, and human beings are not identical with the original four beings, they descend from them, and inherit from them important qualities. In so far as they never entirely shed that legacy, the four primordial beings come to be our main source for inquiring into the meaning of the world.

For the purposes of the present chapter, the most significant of Hesiod's primordial forces is Eros. He is introduced last of the four, and alone among them receives three full hexameter lines (*Theogony* 120–22):

And Eros, who is the most beautiful among the immortal gods, the limb-melter—he overpowers the mind and the thoughtful counsel of all the gods and of all human beings in their breasts.

Eros in many ways differs from the other primordial forces.[7] Whereas Chaos, Gaia, and Tartarus constitute space and matter, Eros is devoid of their material and spatial dimensions. Moreover, his contribution to the world is yet to come. To some extent that is also true of Gaia, who is introduced as the 'secure seat forever of all the immortals who occupy the peak of snowy Olympus' (*Theogony* 117–18). Yet only Eros looks ahead to both gods *and* humans, and hence to the fully formed world as it presents itself to Hesiod's readers. That point, I would argue, is in fact fundamental: Hesiod makes it quite clear that if we wish to understand the nature of Eros we cannot stop at lines 120–23 of the *Theogony*, but need to familiarize ourselves with *all* the cosmic processes through which he works his transformative power.

---

[7] In what follows I develop a few of the themes that are central to my discussion of Hesiod and Plato in Lev Kenaan (2008), Chs. 1 and 3.

Among those processes two stand out for their significance in defining the nature of Eros: the birth of Aphrodite and that of the first woman, Pandora.[8] It is these two figures above all others who embody the power of Eros to 'subdue' the minds of gods (Aphrodite) and humans (Pandora); and it is also Aphrodite and Pandora who help to define the power of Eros in visual terms—and hence introduce a theme that will be of crucial importance for Plato's engagement with Hesiod.

Hesiod first makes a connection between erotic attraction and visual impact in his reference to the beauty of Eros. That beauty, however, remains largely abstract, for Hesiod never gives a description of the god's appearance: all he says about him is that he is 'most beautiful of the gods' (*Theogony* 120). With the birth of Aphrodite, visual impact becomes more obviously an aspect of the erotic, though as yet Hesiod remains relatively restrained. He does call Aphrodite a 'beautiful goddess' (*Theogony* 194) and her feet 'slender' (*Theogony* 195). Moreover, he describes her as 'well-wreathed', if we allow line 196 to stand. However, it is with the advent of Pandora as the first woman that visual impact truly comes to the fore.

Since the feminine, being under the divine influence of its beautiful patron goddess Aphrodite, represents the visible world more than the male does, femininity is, in fact, the prime representative of the erotic phenomenon in the human world. And so the ultimate stage of the process that began with the abstract force of Eros and led to the emergence of the world of phenomena is marked in the *Theogony* by the creation of the ultimate phenomenon, the first woman.

Aphrodite is not directly responsible for Pandora's creation in the *Theogony*, though she does play a significant role in shaping her beauty in the *Works and Days*.[9] However, shared features suggest that, on a semantic level at least, Pandora is a direct descendant of Aphrodite.[10] Indeed, she appears as the final link in the erotic development of the cosmos, which started with the primordial erotic

[8]  See Vernant (1990).

[9]  Yet even in that version Pandora is, first and foremost, the result of a male conceptualization.

[10]  This female line of descent is suggested by Bergren (1989).

principle and continued with the divine Aphrodite.[11] Pandora brings the erotic genealogy to its culmination, not only in the sense that she asserts the power of Eros in the human realm, but also in the sense that with her the erotic is most fully associated with visual impact, thus marking a crucial stage in the development of the phenomena.

Hesiod's unique construct of an erotic genealogy deeply informs the ways in which Eros is discussed in the course of the *Symposium*. Plato too takes us from the divine principle of Eros in Phaedrus' opening speech (178b) to its main human conduit and representative in the closing speech by Alcibiades (namely Socrates). Along the way, Diotima recapitulates the general movement of the dialogue from primordial Eros to its human embodiment, charting a path from the mythical son of Poros and Penia to the figure of the lover. Diotima clearly points ahead to the human lover of wisdom when she describes Eros as someone 'between wisdom and ignorance' (204a). More specifically, we recognize in her portrayal of Eros some of Socrates' typical features, such as his awareness that he lacks knowledge, his love of wisdom, and his constant wavering between ignorance and knowledge.

Indeed, it is widely recognized that the figures of Socrates and Eros are symbolically tied together in the *Symposium*. Socrates is very obviously behind Diotima's mythic portrayal of Eros as a δαίμων (202d–203d),[12] and the connection is further strengthened by Alcibiades, who not only adopts the term δαιμόνιον in addressing Socrates, but depicts his physiognomy, personality, and philosophical disposition in a manner that recalls crucial aspects of the figure of Diotima's Eros. Like Eros, Socrates is barefoot and loves wisdom and beauty.[13] Moreover, his vocation as a teacher of love is realized in his (erotic) role as mediator between the human and the divine, the ephemeral and the eternal. The resemblance between Socrates and Eros is crucial for understanding the nature of the *Symposium* as a

[11] On the relationship between Aphrodite and Pandora as disrupting the primal harmony that reigns among men in Hesiod's *Theogony*, see duBois (1992), esp. 102. A. S. Brown (1977) shows how Pandora's visual impact in Hesiod's works manifests an intentional resemblance to the figure of golden Aphrodite, as principally displayed in Pandora's golden diadem.

[12] See Nehamas and Woodruff (1989), xxiii.

[13] *Symposium* 203d.

seductive text. More specifically, it goes to the heart of the relationship between Plato's *Symposium* and Hesiodic epic.

We have seen that Eros is key for understanding the emergence of
the world of phenomena in the *Theogony*. He initially appears as an
abstract primordial force, but with the maturation of the perceptible
world, erotic attraction comes to be increasingly realized through
beauty and visual impact (Aphrodite). This tendency culminates in
the appearance of Pandora as the ultimate erotic phenomenon. Now,
Plato never mentions Pandora in his dialogues, though he does
allude to her on several occasions.[14] However, there is an intrinsic
connection between his writing and the Hesiodic myth of the first
woman; and much of the force of that connection depends on Plato's
main literary persona, Socrates.

On the face of it, Socrates and Pandora may seem very different
figures indeed. How can the pursuer of truth and wisdom be related
to the archetypal figure of the *femme fatale*, the beautiful symptom of
a misogynist culture? Yet, we have already seen that both the *Theogony* and the *Symposium* conceive of their protagonists as descendants
of Eros. In fact, the relationship between the first woman and the
Platonic ideal philosopher arguably goes beyond the *Symposium*. In
the *Apology*, for example, Plato presents Socrates as a divine gift. As
Socrates asks his judges and audience to recall what his presence
means for their city, he challenges them to consider whether he is
'really the sort of person who would have been sent to this city as a
gift from God ($\delta\epsilon\delta\acute{o}\sigma\theta\alpha\iota$)'.[15] Socrates suggests that he should be
viewed as a divine gift to a city that has forgotten its noble origins.
But what an odd gift he is, this annoying gadfly that harasses a large
and noble horse (*Apology* 30e).

The image of Socrates as a gadfly makes him into a nuisance who
harangues ($\pi\rho\sigma\sigma\kappa\epsilon\acute{\iota}\mu\epsilon\nu\sigma\nu$: 30e) a self-indulgent Athens. Although
Plato does not employ the Hesiodic term $\delta\hat{\omega}\rho\sigma\nu$ in this context, his
formulation at 30d7, $\tau\grave{\eta}\nu$ $\tau\sigma\hat{\upsilon}$ $\theta\epsilon\sigma\hat{\upsilon}$ $\delta\acute{o}\sigma\iota\nu$, 'god's gift', nevertheless

---

[14] The Hesiodic myth is present in several Platonic dialogues. For example, I take
*Philebus* 59e and 61c to be direct allusions to Hesiod's creation of Pandora in *Works
and Days*. Within the *Symposium*, the myth of Aristophanes takes up crucial elements
of the story. See Yamagata in this volume, Ch. 4.

[15] Plato, *Apology* 31b, as translated by Tredennick in Hamilton and Cairns (1961).

recalls the epithet of Pandora in *Works and Days*, δῶρον θεῶν, 'gift of the gods' (85). Both Hesiod's *Works and Days* and Plato's *Apology* describe a divine gift that society would rather do without. For Plato, condemnation of Socrates is indicative of society's shortcomings. In other words, Socrates as a gift is misunderstood and misused. His hostile reception on the part of the Athenians is not unconnected to an important ambiguity in Socrates' character and behaviour: his alleged care for the soul of his interlocutors often embarrasses them. His goodness, that is, assumes the form of an annoyance. Socrates, therefore, becomes a gift whose usefulness remains concealed from the majority of Athenians. The city cannot understand that his annoying behaviour is in fact the essence of his usefulness.

Returning to Hesiod, we see a number of connections with the divine gift of Socrates in the *Apology*. Pandora too is an ambiguous gift. In the *Theogony*, but especially in the *Works and Days* with its more immediate interest in human affairs, she signifies a break from a golden past, an ideal state in which men lived like gods. Pandora's gift inaugurates the present human condition, which is characterized by scarcity of resources, disease, labour, and careful advance planning. This last point is important, for men's new relationship with the gods and their new position in the world also creates the need for self-reflection. Like her Socratic successor, Pandora stimulates humankind to perceive its own being as distinct from the world and the gods who embody it. Pandora's enlightening force is to lead her beholders to revise their past vision of the world and their place in it.

As I have already pointed out, the challenge that Pandora poses has predominantly ethical implications in the *Works and Days*, with its more immediate interest in the question of how we should lead our lives. In the *Theogony*, it is more properly of an epistemological nature. Her different roles within each text become clearer once we consider at what point she appears in them. Pandora in the *Works and Days* acts as a preamble to Hesiod's ethical teachings. In the *Theogony*, by contrast, she marks almost exactly the midway point of the cosmological narrative.[16] This is an interesting narrative choice, and will turn out to be significant, though in order to appreciate its

---

[16] See Zeitlin (1996), 73 and n. 35.

significance we need to return to the opening section of the *Theogony*'s cosmological narrative one more time.

We have seen that the initial state of Hesiod's world is much reduced: four primordial entities constitute a universe that is dark and largely undifferentiated. As the cosmological narrative unfolds, the world begins to look increasingly like the place we know, dotted with rivers and mountains, the sea, a sky overhead, a sun and moon. What Hesiod does not give us until very late is any clear outline of the world as a whole;[17] and even when he does attempt a more synthetic description, he emphasizes the terrible and gloomy aspects of the cosmos.[18] Towards the end of the poem, and in anticipation of the last stage of evolution, the basic building-blocks once again come to the fore, this time in order to articulate an overall picture of the world for which, as West remarks (1966, 363), 'no single expression yet existed' (*Theogony* 736–9; cf. 807–10):

That is where the sources and limits of the dark earth are, and of murky Tartarus, of the barren sea, and of the starry sky, of everything, one after another, distressful, dank, things which even the gods hate.

While this picture arises from a description of the despicable underworld, it is distinctive in the way it develops, seemingly for the first time in the *Theogony*, a sense of cosmic unity. Yet a similar attempt to grasp the world as a whole is already found earlier in the text, and here I refer precisely to that moment when the first woman is presented to the assembled gods and men.

In contrast to the physical world of the *Theogony*, Pandora has a creator, and her creation has a purpose. She is, above all, the product of Zeus's thoughts, who is otherwise not directly responsible for forming the universe. But being thus differentiated from the world, Pandora is also related to it. In fact, she in many ways represents a miniature version of the world: the creatures pictured on her diadem populate earth and sea, and are themselves metonymic of these cosmic realms (*Theogony* 581–4). Moreover, Pandora is physically

---

[17] In contrast, for example, with Plato's *Timaeus*, which derives the world's overall goodness from its pleasant appearance.

[18] Cf. Plato, *Timaeus* 29a–c and 92c, where the emphasis is on the visual impact of the world, which satisfies its beholder and maker.

made of earth, and her head is appropriately wreathed in grass and flowers (*Theogony* 571, 576). As well as being an offspring of Gaia, the second primordial deity, we have already seen that Pandora has strong connections with Eros, the fourth. Long before Hesiod builds up the invisible structures of the world from its gloomy third element, Tartarus (*Theogony* 713–819), he shows us a mirror image of the visible world of appearances in a nutshell, an image that combines the second element (Gaia) with the fourth (Eros). A creature of both Earth and Eros, Pandora mediates between men and the world in a uniquely challenging and seductive manner.

Seen as a miniature of the world, the philosophical core of Pandora in the *Theogony* becomes readily apparent. Nowhere else does the *Theogony* present the visible world to the reader in quite the same way as an object of meditation and admiration. Only with the appearance of the first woman is it possible for us to contemplate—and thereby see beyond—the phenomena. The episode therefore marks a crucial turning point in Hesiod's cosmology. Although the poem never outlines or even names the cosmos as a whole, the lack of any unifying conception is, to some extent, compensated for by the experience of gazing at Pandora whose depiction holds out the possibility of grasping the world of appearances.

Pandora, then, is the first object to impress upon the human mind the understanding that what it perceives is the world of phenomena. We may recall in this context that she is introduced as a substitute for fire (*Theogony* 570). Interpreters who are guided by notions of feminine passion conceive of Pandora as a symbol of women's unquenchable passion.[19] Yet while fire does signify heat, its main association in the context of early Greek epic is with light.[20] The connection is particularly clear in the Pandora narrative of the *Theogony*, where fire is introduced very much in visual terms.[21] Moreover, the connection between fire and visual impact is entirely

---

[19] Cf. Vernant (1980), 180. Vernant refers to Palladas of Alexandria, who, while commenting on Pandora as a substitute for fire, suggests that, unlike fire which can be quenched, the fire of women is inextinguishable.

[20] In Homeric poetry, as Prier has shown (1989, 46–50), fire is associated with the appearance of powerful objects or heroes.

[21] Cf. *Theogony* 566, 569: πυρὸς τηλεσκόπος αὐγή, 'the far-shining gleam of fire'. Note also that Zeus 'sees' the fire at *Theogony* 569. The emphasis is slightly different in

appropriate in this context, for one of the distinctive features of the feminine image in early Greek culture is its radiance. Given that the overall appearance of Hesiod's universe as outlined at *Theogony* 713–819 is murky and dark, the female form provides a moment of illumination, a source of enlightenment. Pandora quite literally pours forth streams of light that are derived from her finery and divinely bestowed charm.[22] And since her figure gives off light, the gods and men nearby not only behold her, but also see the world by her. Gazing at Pandora is erotic not just in the trivial sense that she is sexually seductive, but also in the more profound, Platonic, sense that she challenges us to enquire into the enigmatic nature of things.

The starting point for any such enquiry is the response that Pandora elicits: her radiant appearance is, as the *Theogony* tells us more than once, 'a wonder to behold' ($\theta\alpha\hat{v}\mu\alpha$ $i\delta\acute{\epsilon}\sigma\theta\alpha\iota$).[23] Pandora as a source of wonder recalls the place assigned to wonder in Platonic philosophy. 'This sense of wonder is the mark of the philosopher,' Socrates explains to the young Theaetetus: 'philosophy indeed has no other origin.'[24] In making the point, Socrates invokes the authority of Hesiod: 'and he was a good genealogist who made Iris the daughter of Thaumas.'[25] At one level, the reference to Hesiod merely reflects Plato's appreciation of Hesiodic cosmology, which reveals hidden meanings through its family ties. Yet it also places the starting point of philosophy squarely in the realm of visible phenomena. The rainbow not only strikes the eye with its beauty, but calls for an explanation as well. And even when an explanation is at hand, and we understand how the rainbow is created, there remains a sense of

---

*Works and Days*, but Hesiod's insistence on 'hiding' once again suggests that fire is primarily thought of in visual terms.

[22] See Prier (1989), 83, stating this in reference to the visible force of *charis* that is recurrent in Homeric poetry: 'The gods, in fact, are expert at surrounding the human being with the necessary "grace" to induce sight-wonder.' For examples in Homer see Prier (1989), 83–4.

[23] *Theogony* 575, 581; cf. 584, 598.

[24] Plato, *Theaetetus* 155d, as translated by Cornford in Hamilton and Cairns (1961). Aristotle famously took up the idea: Aristotle, *Metaphysics* 982$^b$11–12.

[25] Plato, *Theaetetus* 155d, referring most probably to Hesiod, *Theogony* 265–6. Homer never mentions Iris' parentage, although at *Iliad* 11.201 she refers to Zeus as 'our father'.

wonder at the appearance of a world whose mystery cannot ulti-mately be reduced to our (human) understanding.[26]

The fact that Pandora shocks and dazzles is not, therefore, in itself an indication of her destructiveness. Rather, her appearance also sharpens our minds. That aspect of her existence is particularly prominent in the *Works and Days*, where Pandora becomes an object-lesson in Iron-Age thinking: we *must* develop insight into the hidden nature of things or else suffer dire consequences. But even in the *Works and Days*, with its fairly transparent moral mes-sage, there is no sense that we could ever hope to solve the riddle that Pandora represents. In that respect, Pandora and Socrates affect their viewers in a fundamentally similar way: both the beautiful woman and the ugly philosopher strike others with a sense of wonder that they cannot fully overcome, because it is based on an unresolved tension between exteriority and interiority, what is traditionally called appearance and essence.

This brings me finally back to the *Symposium*. In the *Symposium*, the connections between eros, wonder, and philosophical enquiry become most fully apparent when Alcibiades contemplates his tea-cher Socrates. As Alcibiades enters Agathon's house he is at first unaware of Socrates' presence. He is drunk and wears a beautiful wreath made of fresh flowers and ribbons with which, he announces, he will crown the head of the most intelligent and best-looking man (212e). He naturally turns to the handsome Agathon, the acclaimed winner of the festival. But then he suddenly notices Socrates and cries out (213bc):

Good lord, what's going on here? It's Socrates! You've trapped me again (ἐλλοχῶν αὖ με ἐνταῦθα κατέκεισο)! You always do this to me—all of a sudden you'll turn up out of nowhere where I least expect you!

Caught by surprise, Alcibiades once again experiences the erotic effect of Socrates and accuses him of playing the old game of hunting

---

[26] Pandora's splendour refers the spectator to another *sēma*, the stone established by Zeus as a memorial in Delphi. This stone originally served as a substitute for baby Zeus, when Kronos wanted to swallow him. Once vomited up from Kronos' intes-tines, it was granted the glorious appearance of a *thauma* by Zeus (*Theogony* 500). In a similar way, Pandora's illuminating power resides in her capacity to elucidate meanings buried deep within cosmic beginnings.

him.[27] It is an old game, and Socrates is an old acquaintance. Yet Alcibiades is still shocked when he sees him, so much so that he strips Agathon's head of the ribbons he has bestowed on him and places them instead on Socrates, proclaiming his to be the most wonderful of heads, θαυμαστὴ κεφαλή (213e).[28] In so doing, he not only pronounces Socrates to be the cleverest man on earth, but unexpectedly declares him the most beautiful of men too, κάλλιστος (212e).

Alcibiades' response to the sight of Socrates is surprising. Far from ignoring his ugly appearance, Alcibiades cheerfully declares Socrates beautiful and assigns to him a strong erotic appeal. It is of course not easy to take this judgement at face value, especially when we recall that Alcibiades himself also describes this 'most beautiful' man as an ugly and grotesque Silenus or Satyr (215b, 221d). How, we may ask, is it possible that Socrates' appearance stupefies his beholders in a manner so similar to the effect of Pandora? For ugliness in itself has no appeal, even if it belongs to a brilliant mind.[29] Plato says as much when he introduces the figure of Theaetetus, the bright and young, but ugly, thinker. Theaetetus is described to Socrates by his teacher, Theodorus, in the following manner (*Theaetetus* 143e–144a):[30]

Yes, Socrates, I have met with a youth of this city who certainly deserves mention, and you will find it worthwhile to hear me describe him. If he were handsome, I should be afraid to use strong terms, lest I should be suspected of being in love with him. However, he is not handsome, but—forgive my saying so—he resembles you in being snub-nosed and having prominent eyes, though these features are less marked in him. So I can speak without fear. I assure you that, among all the young men I have met with—and I have had to do with a good many—I have never found such admirable gifts. The combination of a rare quickness of intelligence with exceptional gentleness, and of an incomparably virile spirit with both, is a thing that I should hardly have believed could exist.

---

[27] See the opening of the *Protagoras* (309a), where Socrates is described as hunting after the beauty of Alcibiades. On the hunting metaphor in Plato, see Nussbaum (1986), 92.

[28] Alcibiades addresses Socrates as a wonderful man in 219c and refers to his wonderful interiority in 217a.

[29] On the history of Socrates' portrait see Zanker (1995), 32–9.

[30] The translation is by Macdonald in Hamilton and Cairns (1961).

Theaetetus is physically unattractive, though thanks to his intelligence he does make a positive impression. His patron Theodorus commends him to Socrates with great enthusiasm. He is aware that his passionate description of the young man may suggest a merely sexual interest, but he also knows that there is no real scope for misunderstanding: nobody will suspect Theodorus of being physically attracted to the boy because he is so ugly. Now Theodorus goes out of his way to point out how similar Theaetetus is to Socrates. Yet the physical idiosyncrasies that they share do not make Theaetetus another Socrates.[31] So the question remains how Socrates' ugliness can be considered beautiful. What is the secret of his erotic charm in the *Symposium*?

In order to understand better Socrates' allure let us consider briefly the manner in which he beholds others. In the *Charmides*, Socrates expresses his interest in those young men distinguished for their wisdom ($\sigma o\phi i\alpha$) or beauty ($\kappa\acute{\alpha}\lambda\lambda o\varsigma$) or both (*Charmides* 153d). When Socrates catches a glimpse of Charmides he captures his beauty by calling it 'wonderful' ($\theta\alpha\upsilon\mu\alpha\sigma\tau\acute{o}\varsigma$). The tantalizing effect of his appearance turns Charmides' beholders into lovers. Their desire, Socrates explains, does not only mean that they see Charmides as a beautiful sculpture ($\acute{\alpha}\gamma\alpha\lambda\mu\alpha$):[32] it also stupefies their mind as they become smitten and confused by his appearance (154cd). Socrates' response is no less erotic but differs from that of other spectators in that he searches for the invisible essence of Charmides' beauty. Looking at Charmides involves for Socrates an urge to discover what his beautiful body hides, his soul ($\psi\upsilon\chi\acute{\eta}$: 154e).

With that in mind, let us look again at Socrates through the eyes of Alcibiades. Alcibides' gaze in the *Symposium* turns Socrates into a Pandora figure, that is to say, somebody whose exterior challenges us to search for a hidden interior. As he beholds Socrates, he undergoes a visual experience similar to that of the men in Hesiod as they gaze at Pandora (215b):

---

[31] Ruby Blondell discusses the likeness between Socrates and Theaetetus in Blondell (2002), 260–313.

[32] For the objectification of Charmides as the beloved, see Steiner (1996), 91.

Look at him! Isn't he just like a statue of Silenus? You know the kind of statue I mean; you'll find them in any shop in town. It's a Silenus sitting, his flute or his pipes in his hands, and it's hollow. It's split down the middle, and inside it's full of tiny statues of the gods.

As human embodiments of Eros, Pandora and Socrates share a similar structure: their form of selfhood rests on a thoroughgoing tension between appearance and being. Both Pandora and Socrates challenge their beholders to grapple with their enigmatic being and to look for 'truth' behind their appearances. If beauty is the touch of transcendence in the phenomenal, if it is a form of visibility that carries within itself a promise of the invisible, then we might say that Pandora and Socrates are each, in their own way, beautiful.

Of course there are also differences. Granted, the hidden interiors of Pandora in Hesiod and of Socrates in Plato's *Symposium* both direct the beholder to go in search of an inner truth. However, in Hesiod, both the circumstances and the outcome of that search are unhappy: god-given beauty leads us towards the discovery of deception, human misery, and ugliness. In this respect, Plato liberates the Hesiodic image of Pandora from its stigma, sublimating the anxiety associated with her as an image of hiddenness and turning the ultimate symbol of disillusionment and suspicion into an invitation to engage in a passionate search for truth and beauty. To say that Plato 'reworks' the Hesiodic image hardly does justice to what is at issue here: rather, if what I have argued is right then Alcibiades' portrayal of Socrates in the *Symposium*—and Socrates' own oblique relationship with Pandora in the *Theogony* and *Works and Days*—should be seen as a prime example of erotic intertextuality of the kind that Socrates himself develops only moments before, when reporting the speech of Diotima.

## CONCLUSION

I have argued that Plato in the *Symposium*, as well as quoting and reworking Hesiodic passages and themes, develops a much more ambitious model of intertextuality as erotic genealogy. Within this model of how authors and texts relate to one another, Hesiod plays a crucial role, not least, as I hope to have shown, as a source of inspiration for Plato's portrayal of Socrates. Like so many others before him, Plato must have marvelled at the Hesiodic Pandora; but unlike most others, who could see in her little more than the source and symbol of human disillusionment, Plato was able to turn the marvel into a truly erotic event of philosophical inspiration, resulting in the character of Socrates as portrayed in the *Symposium*.

The legacy of Pandora, however, extends beyond the creation of the Socratic persona. Indeed, it becomes symptomatic of the *Symposium*'s very character as a text, for it is not only Socrates' physical appearance that points beyond itself. His utterances too are based on a tension between concealment and disclosure (222a). As Alcibiades tells us, one needs 'to go beyond the surface' in order to understand Socrates' words. Once more, we see Plato comment obliquely on the character of his own writing: the *Symposium*, like Pandora and like Socrates, is a phenomenon whose visible surfaces reflect a residue of what remains hidden, calling upon the reader to engage in the endless pursuit of meaning.

# 9

## 'Hesiod's races and your own': Socrates' 'Hesiodic' project[1]

*Helen Van Noorden*

### 9.1. INTRODUCTION

This chapter approaches the question of Hesiod's importance for Plato by reassessing the use of 'Hesiod's races' in the *Republic*. Critical evaluations of the ways in which Platonic *philosophia* itself 'invokes, confronts and absorbs poetic texts' (Halliwell 2000, 95) have often begun from the discussion of *mimēsis* in *Republic* Book 10, in which Socrates[2] seems to have nothing to say about Hesiod that distinguishes him from Homer, 'leader and teacher of the tragedians' (e.g. 595c1–3).[3] By focusing on a different section of Socrates' dialogue with Glaucon and Adeimantus, however, this chapter aims to show why it is insufficient merely to bracket Hesiod with Homer in his importance for Plato's construction of 'philosophical' discourse.[4]

[1] I would like to record my thanks to Clare College, to the editors and to those who responded to my thoughts on Plato and Hesiod before, during, or after the Durham conference; in particular George Boys-Stones, Robert Fowler, Richard Hunter, Hugo Koning, Alex Long, Malcolm Schofield, and David Sedley, for their illuminating comments.
[2] All references to 'Socrates' are to Plato's 'Socrates'.
[3] Cf. e.g. Murray (1996), Burnyeat (1999).
[4] For further discussion of this issue see Yamagata and Koning, this volume, Ch. 4 and 5 respectively.

Socrates in the *Republic* is set the challenge of proving the value of justice, but without mentioning its material rewards, *unlike* Hesiod, Homer, and other poets (363b ff.). Yet, as I shall argue in section 9.2, Hesiod's poetry in particular is recalled when his narrative of successive metallic 'races/eras' (γένη: *Works and Days* 106–201) is appropriated for Socrates' 'noble lie'. The connection is acknowledged in *Republic* Book 8, in the Muses' enigmatic discourse on the inevitable decline of Callipolis. Continuing their narrative in political terms, Socrates' analysis of the 'faulty' constitutions, maligned by readers since Aristotle,[5] has rarely been considered in relation to *Republic* Book 3.[6]

Renewed attention to the framing and emphases of the two passages (section 9.3 below) reveals how echoes of 'Hesiod's races', particularly of the heroic and 'iron' *genē*, appropriate for the *Republic* the urgency of the wider ethical exhortation in the *Works and Days*. I go on to argue (section 9.4) that Socrates redirects towards Glaucon and Adeimantus the combination of explanation and warning, in Hesiod's silver race, by which personal choice is linked to just or unjust societies. Further (section 9.5), such 'readings' of the Hesiodic context in *Republic* Books 8–10 arguably appropriate Hesiod as a forerunner to Socrates' own multifaceted argument for justice.

In this, Socrates' 'Hesiodic' pretensions may appear to resemble those of the sophists, but, as section 9.6 emphasizes, the framing use of inscrutable Muses to explain the initial decline from Callipolis connects the *Works and Days* with the poetic voice in the *Theogony*, interpreted as knowingly fallible. In conclusion, I suggest that Plato's use of the races in the *Republic* exploits Hesiod's *conscious* re-articulation of the way things are as a starting point for the repetition and variation characterizing Socrates' 'philosophical' redefinition of the route to virtue.

---

[5] Cf. *Politics* 1316$^a$1–$^b$2; Annas (1981), 294 ff. judges *Republic* Books 8–9 'both confusing and confused'.

[6] One exception is Schofield (2009), 108–9. Solmsen (1962), 182 claims that *Republic* Book 8 adds no new elements of meaning, and that the temporal presentation of Hesiod's metallic myth 'could not serve Plato's purpose'.

## 9.2. SOCRATES' CASE FOR JUSTICE: A 'HESIODIC' PROJECT?

The basic task that aligns Socrates in the *Republic* with the speaker of Hesiod's *Works and Days* is that of persuading certain individuals, who are inclining towards injustice, to choose to be just. However one reconstructs the situation behind the *Works and Days* (Most 2006, xliv–xlv), it is clear that the speaker ('Hesiod') is concerned to warn his brother Perses away from 'gift-eating' kings who, if they are not actively abusing their status, at least 'do not know how much more the half is than the whole' (*Works and Days* 40). The discourse on justice is applied also to the kings. Compare the danger that motivates Socrates in the *Republic*: Glaucon and Adeimantus in *Republic* Book 2 demand to know why they should not aim merely for the appearance of justice, and practise injustice in secret (367c2).

In response to this challenge, Socrates proposes to work from the larger image to the smaller, and embarks on the theoretical foundation of a city (369a1) in order to see where justice and injustice come to be in it. Having outlined the just city and its counterpart, the man in whose soul every part does its own work (443b), he then has to pause to defend controversial aspects of his vision (the common possession of wives and children). Not until *Republic* Book 8 does the framing project come back into view; Socrates explicitly aims to identify and contrast the most just and the most unjust constitutions to determine which corresponding individual would be happier (544a6–7), in order to know whether to practice injustice or justice (545b1–2).

As an argumentative strategy with which to urge a moral choice for individuals, images of utopian and dystopian cities appear first in the *Works and Days* (225–37 and 238–47) pointedly juxtaposed (*Works and Days* 225–7, 232–4, and 238–42):[7]

> Those who give straight judgments to foreigners
> and fellow-citizens and do not turn aside from justice at all,
> their city (πόλις) blooms and the people in it flower...

[7] All translations of Hesiod are from Most (2006).

For these the earth bears the means of life in abundance, and on the
mountains the oak tree bears acorns on its surface, and bees
   in its center;
their woolly sheep are weighed down by their fleeces...
But to those who care only for evil outrageousness ($ὕβρις$)
   and cruel deeds,
far-seeing Zeus, Cronus' son, marks out justice [i.e. penalty].
Often even a whole city ($πόλις$) suffers because of an evil man
who sins and devises wicked deeds. Upon them,
Cronus' son brings forth woe from the sky...

Within Hesiod's poem, these images function as part of a cumulative
case for the good life (A. S. Brown 1998, 389–90). It is in the 'myth of
the races' that the contrast between justice and *hybris* begins, thereafter developed through allegory, personification, images of cities,
and then warnings addressed to kings. If Plato's text can be shown to
prompt comparisons between Socrates' project and this didactic
context in Hesiod, Socrates' city–soul analogy emerges as, in part, a
radical transformation of Hesiod's application of such a mixture of
images to his audiences. To establish the legitimacy of this view is the
final goal of the present chapter: in this section, it is argued that
within the *Republic*, the prompt to keep in mind the argumentative
course of Hesiod's text is found in appropriations of 'Hesiod's races'.

It is of course important that it is precisely for the presentation of
justice in the *Works and Days* that Hesiod is initially mentioned in the
*Republic*. Adeimantus adduces part of Hesiod's presentation of the
just city (233–4) to show that it connects justice with material
prosperity (363a8 ff.). What is now required from Socrates is an
entirely different basis for advocating justice. The *Works and Days*
is first in focus, then, as an argument with which Socrates' own
procedure is to be compared.

The context of this reference, however, means that in itself it will
not guide Plato's readers back to Hesiod in particular. Adeimantus
cites his argument for justice only alongside something 'similar'
($παραπλήσια$) in Homer (*Odyssey* 19.109 ff. on the good king, cited
at 363b5 ff.).[8] If Homer's poetry too can thus be classified as an
'argument for justice', the mere citation of Hesiod by Adeimantus

---

[8] Cf. Erler (1987) on ancient responses to the 'good king' motif.

does not in itself indicate that Plato, through Socrates, is about to engage seriously with an argumentative method recognized as specifically 'Hesiodic'.[9]

True, Socrates himself cites from the *Works and Days* with approval (466b); he asserts, against Adeimantus, that a good guardian will understand 'that Hesiod was really wise in saying that the half is worth more than the whole' (*Works and Days* 40). Plato may well expect his readers to recall that in the *Works and Days*, this advice was addressed to rulers who were disregarding justice (Halliwell 1993 *ad loc.*). Given broader Greek traditions of gnomic wisdom, however, claims for significant connections between the *Republic* and the *Works and Days* must be based on echoes of Hesiod that distinguish him from the 'noisy throng of books by Musaeus and Orpheus' (364e3 ff.) and from more recent predecessors for Plato's thoughts about civic justice, such as Solon[10] or Aeschylus, or (to an extent) *any* discussion of monarchy and justice after the *Works and Days* and *Theogony*.[11]

One series of allusions to Hesiod *does* achieve this distinction— Socrates' references to Hesiod's narrative of races (*Works and Days* 106–201). This particular representation of human history is not in Homer, nor in what is extant of Solon, Aesop, or Aeschylus. In the *Works and Days*, as an 'alternative' (ἕτερον λόγον: *Works and Days* 106) to the narrative of Prometheus and Pandora, the speaker presents gold, silver, bronze, heroic, and iron *genē* as a chronological but discontinuous sequence. In the *Republic*, the metallic *genē* reappear as contemporaneous human races in Socrates' notorious 'noble lie' for Callipolis (414b–415c), which states that the citizens were born from the earth with gold, silver, and bronze or iron in their souls, and should accordingly be kept in three distinct classes; the rulers of each generation must guard the composition of each class, since an oracle has stated that the city will be ruined if it has an iron or bronze guardian. The relevance of this 'noble lie' of natural hierarchy to the

---

[9] But cf. O'Connor (2007) on how the *Republic* fuses references to the *Odyssey* with Hesiodic themes.

[10] Cf. Irwin (2005a), 163: Solon's focus on *Works and Days* 213–326 fashions 'a certain image of Hesiod'.

[11] Cf. *Theogony* 89 ff.

project of portraying Callipolis is forcefully signalled by the fact that
the metallic men of the myth are transferred directly *into* the potentially ideally just community: 'Let's arm these earthborn men and
bring them forth, led by their rulers' (415d5–6).[12]

In itself, however, Socrates' initial combination of myths, billed
as 'something Phoenician' (414c4),[13] does not yet proclaim his use
of *Hesiod's* narrative (rather than oriental metallic sequences or
other archaic tri-functional schemes)[14] as the basis for the sketch of
Callipolis. Its Hesiodic inspiration is indirectly acknowledged by
*Republic* 468e5–469a3, where Socrates derives a post-mortem title
for *all* outstanding 'guardians' in Callipolis from Hesiod's statement
that the golden race after death became *daimones*, 'guardians'
(φύλακες) of current mortals (*Works and Days* 122–3; cf. 252–3).[15]
At the time, however, this is perhaps more readily seen within traditions of debate about Hesiod's *daimones*;[16] its full significance for
the *Republic* (especially given the similarly synchronic reinterpretation of these lines at *Cratylus* 397e5–398b7) does not emerge until
Hesiod is still more explicitly credited with the metallic myth, as the
framing project recommences in Book 8.

Here, Socrates presents a warning from 'the Muses' that Callipolis will decline through civil strife when the metallic classes mix.
According to the Muses, this will happen after the rulers, through
ignorance of the 'geometric number' which identifies the cycle of
human fertility, will engineer marriages in the citizen population at
the wrong time. Their descendants, born at unpropitious times,
will begin to neglect the Muses, and, as rulers, will fail to test τὰ
Ἡσιόδου τε καὶ τὰ παρ' ὑμῖν γένη (547a1: literally, 'the races of
Hesiod, which are also those among you [citizens]'). The consequent

---

[12] Ophir (1991), 75 notes the 'impossible infusion of a myth told *in* the city with a myth told *about* it'.

[13] On this label, cf. Schofield (2006), 284.

[14] Hence Hartman (1988), demonstrating the 'Hesiodic roots' of the classes in Callipolis without reference beyond *Republic* Book 4, recalls the races myth only through Vernant (1960) and Nagy (1979).

[15] West (1978), 181–2 offers reasons why Plato's memory of the text differs from our MSS. On Hesiod and Plato's 'guardians', cf. e.g. Solmsen (1962); Fago (1991), 230.

[16] Cf. Heraclitus 22 B63 and 119 DK with Guthrie (1962–81), i. 483. On the *Dämonisierungstopos*, present also in *Laws* Book 4, cf. Gatz (1967), 56–7.

*stasis* (547a1–6) will result in a compromise between the money-making, property-owning impulses of the iron / bronze types, and the impulses of those 'rich in their souls' towards virtue (547b2 ff.). Socrates takes over the account with his question at 547c6–7, rephrasing the Muses' description in political terms: 'Then, isn't this constitution a sort of midpoint between aristocracy and oligarchy?' Applying the city–soul analogy, he sketches out four 'diseased' constitutions—timocracy, oligarchy, democracy, and tyranny—as hypothetical stages in a continuous decline.

By emphasizing that the preservation of Callipolis depends on 'testing' the metallic races, the Muses reaffirm the centrality of the 'noble lie' in Socrates' project to sketch the extremes of justice and injustice. Plato's reason for connecting the races back to Hesiod at this juncture, however, is not immediately obvious. The next section begins to address the question of what is gained by raising Hesiod's profile in *Republic* Book 8.

## 9.3. AN URGENT CHOICE

I shall first argue that Socrates' account of constitutional decline appropriates for the *Republic* the urgency of choosing justice that underlies Hesiod's address to Perses and the Kings. In view of Socrates' stated goal of identifying and comparing the *extremes* of justice and injustice in cities and men, his detailed analysis of the intermediate constitutions has been termed 'needless complexity' (Pappas 1995, 165). Leo Strauss, however, observed and briefly puzzled over the fact that when Socrates rephrases the Muses' account of decline in political terms, his sketch of constitutional decline recalls Hesiod's temporal sequence of gold, silver, bronze, heroic, and iron races (Strauss 1964, 130–32).[17] In retrospect, the

---

[17] Compare too Socrates' retrospective view of this sequence ('excessive action in one direction usually sets up a reaction in the opposite direction', *Republic* 563e9–10) with J. S. Clay (2003), Ch. 4 on Hesiod's *genē* as consequences of divine trial and error in creating the ideal human race.

re-introduction of Hesiod's name just beforehand does seem to invite comparison (Callataÿ 2005, 186 n. 28).[18]

For Strauss, the main point of interest in such a parallel is that the 'odd one out' in each five-part series is the fourth stage, the heroes and the democracy respectively, each of which apparently interrupts a sequence of increasing degeneration. After the 'sick body' of oligarchy (556e4), Socrates introduces democracy as 'perhaps the most beautiful of the constitutions' (557c4) with its emphasis on freedom and pleasure. So in Hesiod, the generation of heroes is 'more just and better' (*Works and Days* 158: δικαιότερον καὶ ἄρειον) than their predecessors, the hyper-aggressive men of bronze, and while the bronze race descend to Hades and become 'nameless', some heroes, at least, obtain a care-free afterlife on the Blessed Isles. The variety within this, the only non-metallic race in Hesiod's sequence (cf. Most 1997, 117–18 on their different fates), also seems significant for Socrates' vision of democracy not as a coherent constitution but rather as a 'supermarket of constitutions' (557d6: παντοπώλιον ... πολιτειῶν). Strauss concluded from this that democracy is the only constitution other than Callipolis in which philosophers could survive undisturbed. Bringing in circumstantial evidence from other dialogues, he and his followers suggest that the main point to draw from a parallel with Hesiod's races narrative is that Plato was not as anti-democratic as has been thought (Strauss 1964, 131; Hanasz 1997–8).

As an analysis of Hesiod's role in *Republic* Book 8, this purely political conclusion is unsatisfactory for two reasons. First, apart from the fact that we cannot detect anything reliable about Plato's own political views from the poetic allusions in his dialogues, such an assessment of what Plato took from Hesiod does not illuminate the particular pattern of references to Hesiod's races in this dialogue. The foregoing reference to 'Hesiod's races *and those among you*' recalls the present context, Socrates' argument for Glaucon and Adeimantus, which should guide interpretations of Socrates' vignettes. Given Socrates' selective applications of 'Hesiod's races' in his 'noble lie',

---

[18] E.g. Hanasz (1997–8), 40 notes that in Socrates' vision, oligarchy, in which rich and poor communities coexist, collapses in mutual destruction, like Hesiod's bronze race.

there is no reason to assume that the Muses' expression sets up nothing more and nothing less than one-to-one correspondences between the sequences. Indeed, such an assumption obscures aspects of Socrates' presentation and their potential as clues to the *use* of Hesiod's narrative in the service of Socrates' argument.

This can be seen from a second objection to Strauss, namely that his emphasis is misleading. For a parallel with the heroic afterlife as depicted by Hesiod can indeed be identified in Plato's text, but it is one that *depends* for the most part on a rather sinister irony,[19] comparable to that with which Socrates will speak about the 'happy and blessed' tyrant. In democracy, a criminal condemned to death or exile walks around the city 'like a hero' (558a8: ὥσπερ ἥρως) although meant to be, like Hesiod's heroes, dead or removed from men (cf. *Works and Days* 167). Only 'women and children' judge democracy the 'finest and most beautiful' of the constitutions, as they would a multicoloured cloak (*Republic* 557c5–9). Its pleasure is 'divine' but temporary (558a1–2: θεσπεσία καὶ ἡδεῖα . . . διαγωγὴ ἐν τῷ παραυτίκα). In Socrates' description, far from conveying approval of democracy, evocations of the heroic afterlife according to Hesiod work to heighten the discomfort.

On closer examination, the discomfort is reinforced by other details that recall, not the heroes, but Hesiod's vision of the 'iron' future. According to Hesiod, the arrival of humanity's final stage will be marked by the birth of grey-haired babies; family harmony will be lost and its traditional hierarchy disregarded (*Works and Days* 180–82, 185):

> Ζεὺς δ' ὀλέσει καὶ τοῦτο γένος μερόπων ἀνθρώπων,
> εὖτ' ἂν γεινόμενοι πολιοκρόταφοι τελέθωσιν.
> οὐδὲ πατὴρ παίδεσσιν ὁμοίιος οὐδέ τι παῖδες . . .
> αἶψα δὲ γηράσκοντας ἀτιμήσουσι τοκῆας . . .

> But Zeus will destroy this race of speech-endowed human beings too,
> when at their birth the hair on their temples will be quite gray.
> *Father* will not be *like-minded* with sons, nor sons at all . . .
> They will *dishonour their aging parents* at once . . .

---

[19] *Pace* Hanasz (1997–8), 41: 'His presentation is full of irony, sarcasm, and grotesquerie but does not seem to be very hostile.'

This finds an echo in Socrates' image of the tyrant as parricide, and 'harsh nurse to old age' (569b7–8: χαλεπὸν γηροτρόφον). Compare too, however, the description of how, as democracy increases to extremes of freedom, artificial attempts at 'likeness' indicate that the hierarchy of old and young is suspended or reversed (*Republic* 8, 562e6–563a1 and 563a7–b3, trans. Grube and Reeve):

A father accustoms himself to behave like (ὅμοιον) a child and fear his sons, while the son behaves like a father, feeling neither shame nor fear in front of his parents (μήτε αἰσχύνεσθαι μήτε δεδιέναι τοὺς γονέας), in order to be free... And, in general, the young imitate their elders and compete with them in word and deed, while the old stoop to the level of the young (οἱ δὲ γέροντες συγκαθιέντες τοῖς νέοις) and are full of play and pleasantry, imitating the young for fear of appearing disagreeable and authoritarian.

In so far as this description recalls or even rationalizes the 'grey-haired babies' who announce the nadir in Hesiod's vision, the proportions of Socrates' sequence call attention to the fact that in Hesiod's account, the vision of the 'iron' future receives almost twice as much space as any of the past races. In the *Works and Days*, this ratio functions as a rhetorical strategy, marking the speaker's response to the immediate threat of unjust behaviour from Perses and the Kings.[20] With this in mind, the shape and content of Socrates' sketch of decline makes sense as a response to the analogous pressure from Glaucon and Adeimantus in *Republic* Book 2. His extended descriptions of both tyranny and democracy,[21] partially intertwined,[22] accelerate the sense of decline by implying that democracy is to be viewed as part of the long final deterioration.

The precise aim of such 'colouring' may be inferred from closer analysis of Socrates' account. Without claiming that 'Hesiodic'

---

[20] Indeed, Querbach (1985) argues that *Hesiod* added the iron race to a pre-existing narrative of four races in order to emphasize the devastating effects of *hybris*.

[21] Tyranny extends over fifteen Stephanus pages (565c–576b), and democracy over thirteen (557a–565c); the preceding stages of decline from Callipolis number ca. fifteen pages in total.

[22] Having announced the topic of tyranny, Socrates elaborates on democracy (562a10–11, 564a10–b1).

overtones prevail over more recent associations,[23] it seems that recollection of a context in Hesiod illuminates the function of at least one detail in the current rhetorical project: the sudden appearance of the term *hybris* in the democratic constitution functions as a 'Hesiodic' reminder of the urgency of making an ethical choice. In Socrates' vision of the democratic soul, positive and negative qualities are starkly re-valued and re-named (from *Republic* 8, 560d–561a, trans. Grube and Reeve):

Won't they call reverence foolishness and moderation cowardice, abusing them and casting them out beyond the frontiers . . . ? Having thus emptied and purged these from the soul of the one they've possessed . . . they proceed to return insolence (ὕβριν), anarchy, extravagance, and shamelessness from exile . . . They praise the returning exiles and give them fine names, calling *insolence* good breeding, anarchy freedom, extravagance magnificence, and shamelessness courage.

*Hybris* stands out here, since the noun occurs in the *Republic* only at 400b2, 403a2, and in the description of the democratic constitution (again at 572c7). Its repeated presence is all the more striking given the context of inverted values, which recalls the redirection of praise and blame in the era that Hesiod presents as the final stage of humankind (*Works and Days* 190–92):

οὐδέ τις εὐόρκου χάρις ἔσσεται οὐδὲ <u>δικαίου</u>
οὐδ᾽ ἀγαθοῦ, μᾶλλον δὲ κακῶν ῥεκτῆρα καὶ <u>ὕβριν</u>
ἀνέρα τιμήσουσι . . .

Nor will there be any grace for the man who keeps his oath,
  nor for the *just* man
or the good one, but they will give more honor to the doer of evil
and the *outrage* man.

In the *Works and Days*, this is a key stage in Hesiod's argument, for the exhortation to justice is developed in parallel with an injunction to avoid *hybris*. The word appeared first in Hesiod's account of the silver race (*Works and Days* 134: as adults, they could not keep themselves from mutual *hybris*) and was a defining feature of the bronze race (146: they cared only for acts of war and *hybris*).

---

[23] Cf. e.g. Roscalla (2005), 398–413 on the 'drone' featuring in the worst three constitutions.

Following the account of how *hybris* supplants *dikē* in the worst era of iron, these terms become the two poles of the present choice laid before Perses and the Kings.[24] Personifications of *Hybris* and *Dikē* are envisaged as running a race (213 ff.), before details from the golden and heroic races are resituated in the images of the just (δικαίου) city, and aspects of the silver, bronze, and iron races are recalled by the fortunes of 'those who care only for evil outrageousness (ὕβρις τε μέμηλε κακή) and cruel deeds' (238). In the context of the city–soul analogy, therefore, *hybris* is arguably recalled as a 'Hesiodic' term (Hanasz 1997–8, 44), whose effect is to draw attention to Socrates' sketch of decline as, like the 'myth of the races' in the *Works and Days*, a story that sets up a stark ethical choice for its audiences.

It is important to emphasize that Socrates' use of the term *hybris* works to stress the urgency of making the right choice, not merely a sense of impending doom. In Hesiod, *hybris* is a feature of every post-golden *genos except* the fourth, 'more just and better' race. It seems no accident that immediately after re-introducing the term *hybris*, Socrates repeats the possibility of halting one's personal decline (561a), raised first at 560a. These 'notes' of despair and hope reinforce in Socrates' portrait of democracy the provocative mixture of motifs from Hesiod's generations of heroes and iron, described above. Socrates thereby harnesses for his address to Glaucon and Adeimantus one implication of the sharp contrast between the heroes and the iron generations in Hesiod's five-stage narrative: his listeners *today* have a choice to go down either path.

Moreover, Hesiod's races are picked up arguably with an eye to the social status of Socrates' current audience. The opposition of *hybris* to 'good breeding' (εὐπαιδευσίαν: 560e5) not only supports arguments that *hybris* was in classical Athens typically an activity of the *top* classes and also a vice of the young,[25] but in this context brings the whole account closer to Glaucon and Adeimantus as youthful elites in a 'democratic' reality. In the following section, I argue that prompts in the *Republic* to recall Hesiod's silver race are constructed so as to suggest that Plato has 'read' the metallic narrative in Hesiod with Socrates' internal audience in view.

---

[24] Cf. the structuralist analysis of Vernant (1960).
[25] Fisher (1992), 1, 195. He finds its appearance here in the *Republic* reminiscent of Alcibiades: see 457–8.

## 9.4. TARGETING THE SECOND-BEST TYPES

The start of the sequence draws attention to Socrates' interlocutors. Adeimantus, before he has heard details of the timocratic character, volunteers Glaucon as an example of it, citing his 'love of victory' (φιλονικία: *Republic* 548d8–9). Socrates only half agrees to this idea, judging Glaucon more cultured than the timocrat (548e ff.)—a correction which serves to clarify the limitations of the city–soul analogy and to re-emphasize its status as a didactic model more than a story about real constitutions.[26] Yet Socrates' subsequent presentation implies that Adeimantus was rightly ready to see his brother in the descending sequence of individuals in Book 8, in so far as it is the tarnishing of souls such as their own that Socrates aims to prevent.[27] A closer look at the pattern of references to Hesiod's races in the *Republic* reveals Socrates' particular anxiety about keeping in check those powerful citizens who are not (yet) philosopher rulers. It is then argued that verbal echoes tie this focus to the context of Hesiod's races as a complex exhortation to Perses *and* 'crooked-judging' kings.

If the Muses' reference to the metals at 547a is what first marks Socrates' sketch of decline from timocracy to tyranny as a sequel to his earlier appropriations of Hesiod's races, one image at the nadir of Socrates' sequence recalls his striking characterization of the silver race in particular. The evolution of democracy's popular champion into a paranoid tyrant, figured also as a transformation into a wolf (565e1, 566a4), picks up and expands Socrates' greatest fear, confided to Glaucon and Adeimantus at the end of Book 3, that the (silver) auxiliaries, these 'pedigree dogs' (cf. 375d11 ff.), will become 'like wolves to their own flock' (416a5–6). A ban on contact with mortal 'gold or silver' is needed (416d4–417a5), for if corrupted by mortal possessions, the guardians would destroy the city from within: 'fear-

---

[26] Despite timocracy's label as the 'Cretan' constitution, on which cf. Calabi (2005); on the Laconizing thread in Plato, cf. Schofield (2006), 35 ff.

[27] Cf. e.g. G. R. F. Ferrari (2003), 21. As he notes (35), it is within the Straussian tradition of reading the *Republic* that one finds the fullest treatment of these interlocutors as characters. Cf. Craig (1994), *passim*.

ing internal enemies more than external ones' (417b2–4). Only the capacity for corruption in silver characters explains the urgency of the 'noble lie' that balances fraternity and hierarchy:[28] the welfare of the community is under threat unless Socrates reconciles spirited 'guardians' to their newly-defined status as 'auxiliaries' to golden 'rulers'.[29]

The need to control the soldiers (Coby 2001) becomes more explicit and is connected with Hesiod's narrative in *Republic* Book 5, where post-mortem promotion to the golden race is suggested among other incentives for auxiliaries to serve the city (Halliwell 1993, 188 *ad loc.*). Socrates shrewdly applies to the silver citizens who die with distinction Hesiod's last words on the *golden* race, that upon their death 'some become *daimones* . . . , guardians (φύλακες 469a2) of mortal men'. Plato's readers may well recall the contrasting fate of Hesiod's silver men ( *Works and Days* 127–42):[30]

> Afterwards those who have their mansions on
> Olympus made a second race, much worse, of silver,
> like the golden one neither in body nor in mind.
> A boy would be nurtured for a hundred years at the side of his
>     cherished mother (παρὰ μητέρι κεδνῇ) playing in his own house,
> a great fool (μέγα νήπιος).
> But when they reached adolescence and arrived at the full
>     measure of puberty,
> they would live for a short time only, suffering pains
> because of their acts of folly. For they could not restrain
>     themselves from wicked outrage against each other, nor were they
>     willing to honor
> the immortals or to sacrifice upon the holy altars of the blessed ones,
> as is established right for human beings in each community. Then
> Zeus, Cronus' son, concealed these [men] in anger, because they did
> not give honors to the blessed gods who dwell on Olympus.

---

[28] Schofield (2006), 286 emphasizes that love for the city (unlike the belief that its interest coincides with one's own) is not in the *Republic* presented as achievable by rational argument.

[29] Throughout the 'noble lie', a division between rulers and auxiliaries occurs, if at all, only within larger syntactical and rhetorical suggestions of unity.

[30] For the assumption that entire passages can be recalled through quotation, cf. Halliwell (2000), 96 ff.

> But since the earth covered up this race too,
> they are called blessed mortals under the earth—
> in second place (δεύτεροι),[31] but all the same honor attends
>     upon these as well.

Since the importance of this narrative as a stage within Hesiod's argument has gone un-remarked, it is worth highlighting the fact that this story combines two aspects often noted in discussions of Socrates' account of constitutional decline. The first is the sense of targeted explanation. In Hesiod's narrative, the silver race is the only one before our own to decline and to suffer the wrath of Zeus (Nelson 1998, 69). Arresting syntax—sentences linked by ἀλλά (130, 132, 142), αὖτε (127) or αὐτάρ (140)—supports other indications that this narrative, unlike that of the eternally prosperous and youthful golden men,[32] should catch the attention of Hesiod's lazy brother. As scholars note, μέγα νήπιος (*Works and Days* 131) is later twice applied to Perses (286, 633; and cf. 397),[33] who needs to hear how a foolish and weak individual becomes part of a lawless society.[34]

At the same time, the fact that the silver people are created *already* 'like the golden [race] neither in body nor in mind' signals that, despite the story's framing as human history,[35] its point in the argumentative context of the *Works and Days* is ultimately not explanation of decline but a cautionary tale. It is fitting to find a grotesque echo of those long-lived silver children in the grey-haired babies who will be a sign of doom for the speaker's contemporaries (*Works and Days* 180–81), since the fall of the silver men into *hybris*

---

[31] Its unparalleled repetition (from the *chronological* sense at 127) may have inspired Socrates' hierarchical conception of the silver race.

[32] If not already traditional (cf. Baldry 1952), the golden lives will sound familiar (hence the smoother δέ 116, 117, 118) because *Works and Days* 90–2 has already prepared the ground for the idea of a lost paradise.

[33] On the 'education of Perses', cf. Schmidt (1986), 31–40; J. S. Clay (1993); and Calame (2004), 77.

[34] The scholia to *Works and Days* 130–1 (citing Laws 3, 694c ff.) infer that the *hybris* of the silver adults results from maternal solicitude in their upbringing.

[35] It professes to show that/how [something] has come about (ὡς . . . γεγάασι at *Works and Days* 108).

operates as dramatic warning for Hesiod's audiences, in so far as they are in between, or with the potential for, both *hybris* and *dikē*.

Although never yet considered in relation to Hesiod's silver race, the generation gap in Socrates' portrait of timocracy in *Republic* Book 8 similarly both suggests and withholds explanation for decline. Critics have been troubled by Socrates' description of the *starting point* of degeneration in terms that recall 'the world as it is' (Annas 1981, 298), because this appears to weaken both his claim to explain the genesis of constitutions[36] and the validity of the city–soul analogy.[37] Socrates charts the demise, not of the individual corresponding to Callipolis, but of the timocrat envisaged as the *son* of a good father (πατρὸς ἀγαθοῦ: 549c1–2) living in a badly-governed city (οὐκ εὖ πολιτευομένῃ: 549c2) in which men who live quietly are considered of little account and their opposites are praised. The father shuns positions of office and lawsuits (δίκας), and minds his own business even when this will put him at a disadvantage (549c3–5). For this, he is chastised by his wife, who feels 'disadvantaged...among other women' (549c8–d1); she and the servants exhort the son to be more of a man than his father.

On one level, the son's corruption by those around him is perfectly in accord with Socrates' observation, back in Book 6, that philosophers cannot flourish *as things are now*, since sophists and others tend to corrupt 'the philosophical nature' in promising young people (491e–492a). Given the earlier reference to 'Hesiod's races' in *Republic* Book 8, however, the intriguing prominence of the mother[38] in developing the timocrat's appetitive and spirited parts (θυμοειδές: 550b3) arguably triggers comparisons also between Socrates' account of timocratic downfall and the most idiosyncratic part of Hesiod's races narrative: the silver children each παρὰ μητέρι κεδνῇ ('at the side of his cherished mother'), and their subsequent fall into *hybris*.[39]

---

[36] Cf. 544e1 with Vegetti (2005b), 147–51 and Coby (1993), 22–7. By contrast, the 'noble lie' of metallic races and divine creation removes the *need* for explanation or argument for different human capacities.

[37] However, Lear (1992), 207 notes that generational decline in the story supports Plato's philosophical point: only the just constitution is entirely stable, and hence analogous between city and man.

[38] On the syntax of 549d1–6, cf. Adam (1902), *ad loc*.

[39] West (1978), 174 notes that (only) the silver race has no counterpart in legend.

It may be that recalling 'Hesiod's races' to begin a narrative of decline into tyranny is itself sufficient to recall that in the *Works and Days* the five-stage account, although addressed initially to Perses, underlies a complex argument aimed also at those whose actions have an impact on the community.[40] Hesiod's remarks for 'gift-eating' kings (*Works and Days* 39, 264), 'who think baneful thoughts and bend judgements to one side by pronouncing them crookedly' (261–2), converge with the exhortations to 'foolish' Perses first in the images of just and unjust cities (to which the kings are summoned to listen at *Works and Days* 248). As was noted above (p. 187), details from all the metallic races resurface in these passages for which Hesiod was first cited in the *Republic* (363b ff.). Their explanatory/warning force in Hesiod's argument, however, rests on the link between individual and society, first apparent in the tragedy of the silver race. It is ultimately due to this race that Hesiod can emphasize personal choice as a decision of real consequence for the communities of which his audiences form a part (*Works and Days* 240: 'Often even a whole city suffers for an evil man . . .').

If Socrates' appropriations of the races in the construction of *his* ethical argument recall the corresponding part of Hesiod's exhortation, they may also draw inspiration from its double target. The timocrat-to-be, as the son of an aristocrat immune to society's perversion of values, recalls not just 'the world as it is' but, more pointedly, the danger embodied by Socrates' interlocutors Glaucon and Adeimantus, whose cynical scenario of a supremely just man in an unjust world prompted Socrates ironically to adapt contemporary praise of *them* as 'sons of Ariston' (367e5–368a5). These brothers, unlike Thrasymachus, are on Socrates' side, yet, elite and talented as they are, they present a threat to the community[41] until convinced that justice is worth practising for its own sake. In this respect, they resemble those guardians at 'one remove from the best' who are critical to the success of Callipolis. The use of these powerful individuals as

---

[40] J. S. Clay (2003), 38–42 notes that the complex progress of Hesiod's argument is due to the need to persuade each audience that its self-interest lies in the joint practice of justice.

[41] According to Coby (1993), 35, Glaucon and Adeimantus are wondering 'whether they should choose a life of tyrannic lawlessness'.

an audience, then, perhaps reflects back on the role of Hesiod's silver race in highlighting for Perses and the Kings the communal significance of a personal ethical choice.

## 9.5. 'READING' AND APPROPRIATION

By 'reading' connections between different parts of Hesiod's multi-faceted argument for justice, including the sections addressed to the Kings, Socrates' use of the races alerts us to his appropriations of other ideas both small and large in the *Works and Days*. For example, the city–soul analogy suggests, against Adeimantus, that Hesiod too is concerned not just to offer 'instruction on how to live in society' (G. R. F. Ferrari 2003, 79), but to some degree addresses the individual *qua* individual. Having warned the kings that Zeus 'is well aware just what kind of justice this is which the city has within it' (268–9), Hesiod adds (*Works and Days* 265–6):

> οἵ τ' αὐτῷ κακὰ τεύχει ἀνὴρ ἄλλῳ κακὰ τεύχων,
> ἡ δὲ κακὴ βουλὴ τῷ βουλεύσαντι κακίστη.

> A man contrives evil for himself when he contrives evil for
>     someone else,
> and an evil plan is most evil for the planner.

That self-harm results from injustice to others is the central idea with which Socrates answers the brothers' challenge of proving the intrinsic value of justice.[42]

A second 'Hesiodic' moral picked out by Socrates' city–soul analogy is a reminder of the relationship between justice and humanity. After addressing to an unnamed individual the story of Prometheus and Pandora (42–105) and the 'myth of the races', Hesiod directs towards 'mindful' kings an *ainos* ('moral story'?) of a hawk exacting

---

[42] It is tempting to suppose that the *Republic* provides early evidence for, or even helps to create, the idea of the *Works and Days* as a poem about morality. Cf. R. L. Hunter (2008) on Callimachus' choice of *Works and Days* 265–6 apparently to evoke the *whole* of the *Works and Days*, in the *Aetia* (fr. 2.5 Pfeiffer).

physical 'justice' on a nightingale (202–12). Later, however, Hesiod addresses to Perses what is apparently a belated 'correction' of the *ainos*—humans are not truly human unless they behave with justice; without Zeus' law of justice, they would be 'fish and wild beasts and birds' (276–80).[43] In Plato, Socrates' sequence of constitutions discredits Thrasymachus' 'hawkish' argument (*Republic* 338c3: justice is 'the advantage of the stronger'),[44] by presenting it as the logic of the tyrant-wolf (569b1–2), the culmination of a slide into constitutions that are not distinctively human (beginning with the 'drones' in oligarchy). This perspective, expanded in the presentation of the tripartite soul and reworked again in the myth of Er, creatively fuses the presentations of humanity in Hesiod's races both with the *ainos* and with the wider argument in Hesiod.[45]

It turns out, then, that, although forbidden to argue like Hesiod and Homer, Socrates does use the races as a prompt to draw various points out of Hesiod's wider argument for Perses and the Kings. In so far as 'testing' the metallic races is identical with preserving Callipolis (as the Muses' reference to τὰ Ἡσιόδου τε καὶ τὰ παρ' ὑμῖν γένη implies), 'testing' the potential applications of the races in their Hesiodic contexts is an expression of Socrates' parallel aim of preserving the potential for just rule in Glaucon and Adeimantus. *Republic* Books 8–9, incorporating the languages of metals, social functions, constitutions, and psychological characters, picks up several possible connections between the images with which Socrates, like Hesiod, argues for justice.

It may be objected, however, that such a view of Socrates' 'Hesiodic' pretensions attributes to him precisely the kind of reconstruction and appropriation of Hesiod's didactic authority displayed by Protagoras and other sophists.[46] In the *Protagoras*, the eponymous sophist's fusion of Hesiodic myths for didactic purposes (320d ff.)

---

[43] For ways in which this 'moral' recontextualizes the *ainos*, cf. Mordine (2006), with bibliography.

[44] Cf. R. L. Hunter (2008), 158–9 on post-Platonic interpretations of the *ainos* and *Works and Days* 274 ff.

[45] For allusions to Hesiod's argument about virtue in the myth of Er, cf. O'Connor (2007), 76–7.

[46] Cf. Koning and Graziosi, this volume, Ch. 5 and 6. The discussion of Simonides in *Republic* Book 1 encourages comparison and contrast with the *Protagoras*.

was countered by Socrates' own appropriation of Hesiod's Prometheus for 'forethought' about his *own* life (361cd).[47] In the *Republic*, the framing of Socrates' account in Book 8 more explicitly calls attention to the epistemological self-consciousness that makes Hesiod in particular a poet worth appropriating as well as correcting.[48] The key lies in Socrates' use of Muses to begin the project of explaining Callipolis' decline.

## 9.6. THE MUSES OF HESIOD AND SOCRATES

I shall now argue that the Muses, by recalling the openings of the *Theogony* and the *Works and Days*,[49] connect Socrates' discourse with a voice identified as 'Hesiodic'. Socrates appeals to the Muses 'like Homer' to declare 'how civil war first broke out' (*Republic* 545d8–e1); his recourse to divine authority promises to lend his account an explanatory power usually beyond human reach (McCabe 2000, 9). That promise is withdrawn, however, by his emphasis on the overwhelmingly poetic, teasing manner of the Muses' reply (545e1–3, trans. Grube and Reeve):

φῶμεν αὐτὰς τραγικῶς ὡς πρὸς παῖδας ἡμᾶς παιζούσας καὶ ἐρεσχηλούσας, ὡς δὴ σπουδῇ λεγούσας, ὑψηλολογουμένας λέγειν;

Shall we say that they speak to us in tragic tones, as if they were in earnest, playing and jesting with us as if we were children?

Further, the Muses' answer to the riddle of Callipolis' downfall is that humans *cannot* explain and so hold on to perfection, expressed in mathematical terms whose notorious obscurity (Adam 1902, *ad loc.*) reinforces the message. It is at this point that they recall 'Hesiod's races' and describe the initial decline (from 547a2–6, trans. Grube and Reeve):

---

[47] On this contest, see further Morgan (2000), 147–53 with bibliography.

[48] On the 'correction' of Hesiod, see Fago (1991), 224.

[49] 'Muses' begin each poem, as Boys-Stones notes at p. 31 of this volume.

The intermixing of iron with silver and bronze with gold ... will engender
lack of likeness and unharmonious inequality, and these always breed war
and hostility wherever they arise. Civil war ... is always and everywhere 'of
this lineage'.

By citing from Glaucus' declaration of ancestry in *Iliad* 6, Socrates'
Muses appropriate for Callipolis' tragedy his famous exchange of
gold armour for bronze.[50] In addition, however, their perspective
combines the metals with the language of intercourse and generation
familiar from the beginning of the *Theogony*,[51] a context evoked also
by the reaction to, and characterizations of, the Muses' speech.
Glaucon remarks: 'We'll declare that the Muses reply [to your prayer]
accurately.' Socrates replies: 'Necessarily, since they are Muses'
(547a7–8). Given their initial depiction, this is certainly a 'wry comment' (Allen 2006, 266 *ad loc.*); these Muses are not Homer's guar-
antors of truth. Rather, their pseudo-earnest voices, emphasizing
human fallibility, recall the words of Hesiod's Muses in the *Theogony*
(26–8):

> 'Field-dwelling shepherds, ignoble disgraces, mere bellies:
> we know how to speak many false things similar to genuine ones,
> but we know, when we wish, how to proclaim true things.'

The fact that an idea of useful 'falsehoods like the truth' (*Republic*
382d3–4), within a critique of Hesiod,[52] earlier formed the seeds of
Socrates' own 'noble lie' of metallic races strengthens the case for a
second allusion to *Theogony* 27 before the Muses' reference to 'Hesiod's races and your own'.[53]

If Socrates' Muses are here recalling and fusing Homeric and
Hesiodic poems, one effect is arguably to deflate Hesiod's claims to
distinction. In the *Works and Days*, Hesiod confidently instructs
Perses about sailing, recalling the limits of his own sailing experience

---

[50] O'Connor (2007), 79 notes that Socrates elsewhere refers to this, now proverbial as a poor bargain.

[51] ὁμοῦ ... μιγέντος σιδηροῦ ἀργυρῷ ... ἀνομοιότης ἐγγενήσεται: 547a2–3 (*Theogony* 56, 46); ἐγγάηται: 547a4; τίκτει πόλεμον: 547a5 (*Theogony* 45, 60); 'ταύτης τοι
γενεᾶς ... εἶναι στάσιν': 547a5–6. Compare the 'Hesiodic' Muses at *Sophist* 242c ff.

[52] Belfiore (1985) argues that Plato interprets these lines so as to attack Hesiod's
own poetic ability.

[53] For this translation, cf. e.g. Grube and Reeve (1992) with LSJ *s.v.* παρά.

just to recall that he beat other poets at a competition in Aulis because the Muses on Helicon granted him privileged knowledge (*Works and Days* 646–62). By contrast, Socrates' detailed depiction of the Muses' speech points out that the Muses of the *Theogony* were in fact capriciously declaring their epistemological superiority to Hesiod even as they inspired him.[54] Plato has Socrates ironically refigure himself as 'Hesiod' through a consciousness of the *limitations* of human understanding.[55]

At the same time, however, the combination of material from the *Works and Days* with the language of the *Theogony*, in the Muses' speech, in so far as it recalls the relation between the two, indicates that for Socrates, 'Hesiod' is precisely not a figure who claims a once-and-for-all understanding of the world. Indeed, as a 'lineage' of *stasis* fusing the language of two Hesiodic poems, *Republic* 547a2–6 on the decline of Callipolis recalls (and perhaps rivals) the *Works and Days'* opening revision of the *Theogony's* genealogy of Strife (*Eris*) (*Works and Days* 11–12: 'after all [ἄρα], there was not just one *genos* of Strifes, but on the earth there are two').[56] From Socrates' perspective in *Republic* Book 8, this line would be worth picking up for its implication that Hesiod too is concerned to differentiate forms of disunity. Its position directly after the proem, moreover, in which Hesiod firmly demarcates his task from that of Zeus, suggests that 'conscious revision' will play an important role in the *Works and Days*. Recalled in the Muses' speech, 'Hesiod's races' may be seen to provide just such an emphasis, on several levels; the discontinuous *genē* reflect not only the status of the story as a whole, as 'alternative' (ἕτερον at *Works and Days* 106)[57] to the tale of Prometheus and Pandora, but the fact that this account in turn is a variation of that in the *Theogony*.[58] Perhaps, then, in the Muses' speech, Plato has Socrates connect his reprise of the 'myth of the races' to the openings

---

[54] Stoddard (2004), Ch. 3 surveys many interpretations of *Theogony* 26–8, and argues that it is such a taunt.

[55] Not for the first time in the *Republic*: cf. Van Noorden (forthcoming) on 450b as a 'Hesiodic' (de)construction of Socrates' authority.

[56] J. S. Clay (2003), 33.

[57] On the status of these presentations as self-consciously alternative see also Haubold, this volume, Ch. 1.

[58] On Hesiod's multiple approaches to Pandora, see first Rowe (1983).

of *each* Hesiodic poem in order to signal his use of this story in its context as an emblem of Hesiod's consciously plural, ever-revised view of the cosmos.[59]

A final argument for drawing a positive significance from the 'Hesiodic' aspects of Socrates' Muses is that the health of the soul's constitution depends on cultivating these Muses; they ascribe political decay to the guardians' becoming *amousoteroi* (546d5–7). A description of fully-grown timocrats as those who have neglected 'the true Muse—that of discussion and philosophy' (548b8–c1) makes clear in retrospect that the Muses of 546–7 are those of philosophy, whose command of the ideal city has been sketched out in *Republic* Books 5–7.[60] This chapter has argued that their evocation of Hesiod's races suggests not so much a rejection of his poetry as a new appropriation of it. Just as the 'noble lie' builds on a recategorization of the top classes in Callipolis (p. 189 above), so now in Book 8 Hesiod's metallic races again appear as focal points for a recategorization, this time of discourses (no longer purely 'poetic' and 'political') in Socrates' definition of the route to *aretē*.

## 9.7. CONCLUSION

In the *Republic*, at least, the 'myth of the races' is not a free-floating piece of poetic lore that just happens to come from Hesiod rather than Homer,[61] and Socrates' repeated use of 'Hesiod's races' does not simply correct, or express sympathy with, Hesiod on particular points. On one level, it picks up the races reinvented *within* the *Works and Days* as a dichotomy between two communities. Socrates exploits the iron and silver races in particular in reapplying the lesson to Glaucon and Adeimantus. Beyond this, however, the multiple appropriations of Hesiod's sequence of decline point to Hesiod as a

---

[59] For this view of Hesiod's corpus, cf. J. S. Clay (2003).

[60] See *Republic* 499d3–4, with Murray (2004), 374 ff. on Plato's appropriation of Muses for philosophy.

[61] The final reference to Hesiod in the *Republic* (612b) does not distinguish him from Homer, but Socrates is here recalling his *interlocutors'* objection to Hesiod's argument.

model for the repeated reconfiguration of ideas within an urgent ethical argument.[62] Through Socrates' use of 'Hesiodic' Muses, revealed to be those of philosophy, Plato signals his interest in rewriting Hesiod's *multiple* articulations of the 'world as it is', as epistemological self-consciousness in the service of progress towards ethical truth.[63]

Those who translate τὰ Ἡσιόδου τε καὶ τὰ παρ' ὑμῖν γένη (*Republic* 547a1) as 'Hesiod's races and your own', referring to Socrates-as-poet and his *knowing* construction of the 'noble lie', are assuming that Plato appropriates Hesiod on some level.[64] In fact, in connecting Hesiod's metals with the self-conscious use of 'myths' and with explorations of the boundary between divine, human, and animal *genē*, the *Republic* paves the way for the *Statesman*'s more radical experimentation with the 'philosophical' possibilities of Hesiod's narrative of the races.[65] Perhaps, then, it is ultimately in highlighting the 'philosophical' repetition and revision of material characterizing the Platonic corpus as a whole[66] that the *genē* may truly be recalled in Plato as 'Hesiod's races and your own'.

---

[62] This view of the *Works and Days* perhaps resolves in some measure the debate concerning the extent to which the *Republic* is genuinely 'dialectical' in its exhortation towards justice. Against Roochnik (2003), Rowe (2006), 9 emphasizes in the *Republic* the serious claim that 'justice pays'.

[63] For Hesiod's invitation to progress towards the truth see Haubold, this volume, Ch. 1.

[64] By contrast, Solmsen, who argues Plato's *limited* use of Hesiod's myth (cf. n. 6 above), translates 'the races which you have distinguished in conformity with Hesiod' (1962, 183).

[65] Cf. El Murr and Rowe, this volume, Ch. 14 and 15 respectively; and Van Noorden (forthcoming).

[66] Cf. Morgan (2004), 369 f.: its repetition helps to 'refocus attention on important points'.

# 10

## Plato's Hesiod and the will of Zeus: Philosophical rhapsody in the *Timaeus* and the *Critias*[1]

*Andrea Capra*

### INTRODUCTION

The horrifying stories of divine struggles and killings, which feature so prominently in Hesiod's *Theogony*, are the very first target of Plato's notorious attack on poetry in the *Republic*.[2] According to Plato, such stories simply reflect Hesiod's no less horrifying ignorance about the nature of the gods. Later in the *Republic*, Plato's focus shifts to Homer's gods and especially to his heroes, whose behaviour

---

[1] I started thinking about the subject of this chapter after reading Cerri's masterly analysis of *Republic* 10 (Cerri 2000). However, Cerri's essay devotes to the *Timaeus–Critias* no more than three lines: Plato's *Republic* 10 and *Timaeus–Critias*, he says, aim 'alla esemplificazione di poemi *politically correct*, esemplificazione contenuta nello stesso libro X (poema escatologico), nel *Timeo* (poema cosmogonico-cosmologico) e nel *Crizia* (poema eroico)' (34). I would like to thank Graziano Arrighetti, Rudolf Carpanini, Pierluigi Donini, Johannes Haubold, Stefano Martinelli Tempesta, Aglae Pizzone, and Maria Michela Sassi for their help and advice in preparing this chapter. Thanks are due also to the participants in the Durham conference, and to all those who took my course SILSIS at the University of Milan in 2006/7: it was helpful, and a pleasure, to discuss the topic with them. Translations of the *Timaeus* and *Critias* in this chapter are taken from Bury (1929), and translations of the *Theaetetus* from H. N. Fowler (1921). For the *Iliad* I have used Butler (1898). All other translations are my own.
[2] *Republic* 377e ff. Cf. *Laws* 886b; *Euthyphro* 5e.

is bitterly censured—and indeed censored too.[3] The poets' representation of men, as opposed to gods and heroes, is on the agenda too, but the subject is dropped for want of a satisfying definition of justice (392a ff.), and is never resumed afterwards. Yet Plato's dissatisfaction with the treatment of post-heroic men in epic poetry, that is with Hesiod's *Works and Days*, is no less explicit.[4] Thus, the very fathers of Greek mythology, to quote Herodotus (*Histories* 2.52), are censured by Plato because of their misconception of the three main categories relevant to epic poetry, namely gods, heroes, and men.

So far, so good, but how does Plato's ban on mythology square with his own myths? Ever since antiquity, readers of Plato have been ready either to emphasize or play down this apparent contradiction. Traditionally, scholars tend to explain away Plato's contradictions by resorting to the notion of an 'evolution' in Plato's thought; and by pointing out that he often changed his mind in the course of his writing career. Yet such a reading can hardly apply in the case of the *Republic*, since that dialogue itself famously ends with an eschatological myth.[5] As has been suggested, however,[6] a possible solution lies in the introductory words of the myth (614a):

I won't tell you one of Alcinous' (Ἀλκίνου) tales, but one of a strong man (ἀλκίμου).

'Alcinous' tale(s)' was of course the traditional title of Books 9–12 of the *Odyssey*, and the pun Ἀλκίνου/ἀλκίμου marks a self-conscious opposition between Homer's myth and Plato's own. Earlier in the *Republic*, Socrates had sharply criticized Homer's frightening portrayal of the underworld because it inevitably instils fear of the afterlife and, ultimately, cowardice (386a ff.). Thus Plato's myth has been plausibly interpreted as a revised version of Homer's underworld scenes, specifically designed to inspire courage in death, provided one has led a pious and just life. Rather than a fully-fledged

---

[3] Gods: 378d ff.; 379d ff.; 386a ff. Heroes: 386a–392a.

[4] Hesiod is not able to praise justice for its intrinsic value (*Republic* 612a ff.). See Solmsen (1962), 174 ff.

[5] This contradiction was criticized already in the 3rd century BC by Epicurus' pupil Colotes. See Cerri (2000), 25.

[6] See Segal (1978); Cerri (2000). Cf. Halliwell (1984) and Dalfen (2002).

new 'poem', the new myth of the *Republic* can thus be construed as a paradigm, a sample of a new kind of poetry (379a and *passim*).

It is in fact telling that Plato chooses to rework Homer's portrayal of the underworld, given its pivotal role in the *Odyssey*. It has been argued convincingly that Odysseus' *katabasis* forms the very centre of his adventures, quite possibly staging Homer's own implicit reflections on other poetic traditions.[7] From a structural and metapoetic point of view, then, the very core of Homer's *Odyssey* provides Plato with a starting point for a new form of poetry. Moreover, the notion of *katabasis* seems to shape the whole of the *Republic*. Its very first word is κατέβην ('I descended'), and the katabatic motif, by way of textual echoes, is later resumed in the Odyssean myth of the cave and finally capped at the very end of the dialogue, where reference is made to the philosopher's ascending road.[8] From the heart of the *Odyssey*, then, to the heart of the *Republic*.

The reshaping of poetic tradition is a fairly common phenomenon in Plato's dialogues.[9] What is peculiar to the *Republic*, however, is its unmistakably Odyssean flavour, all the more notable in a dialogue so openly critical of both Homer and Hesiod. So what about Hesiod? Socrates himself reveals that he has modelled the 'noble lie' of the three political classes on the Hesiodic myth of the five races of man (546e), and occasional echoes from Hesiod's poems can be found elsewhere too,[10] though they do not have the same structural impact on the dialogue as the *Odyssey*.[11] Yet my focus in this chapter is not the *Republic* but the *Timaeus* and the *Critias*, two dialogues which are openly, if ambiguously, introduced as a kind of sequel to the *Republic*. I shall start by arguing that they too can be seen to rewrite epic on an ambitious scale. Secondly, I shall try to show why Plato's 'reformed' versions of epic song are superior to traditional epic by Plato's own standards. Finally, I will of course discuss the major role that Hesiod plays in this context.

---

[7] See Most (1989) and (1992) with bibliography.

[8] See Vegetti (1998*b*), with bibliography. The idea that Plato's *Republic* is a kind of philosophic *Odyssey* is popular in Straussian circles. See e.g. Howland (1993).

[9] For a useful discussion, see Giuliano (2004), 240 ff., with extensive bibliography.

[10] See e.g. Solmsen (1962).

[11] But see Van Noorden, this volume.

## THE EPIC FRAME OF THE *TIMAEUS*
## AND THE *CRITIAS*

'One, two, three': so runs the famous beginning of the *Timaeus*. Three are the hosts of Socrates, namely Timaeus, Critias, and Hermocrates, who invite him to a banquet of speeches.[12] Accordingly, three should be the number of speeches delivered in honour of the guest, to pay him back for his own previous speech, which—as summarized by Socrates himself—closely recalls the more political books of the *Republic*.[13] Timaeus delivers the first one, which may be described as a cosmo-theogony recounting the birth and nature of the world, the gods, and mankind. A direct sequel to the *Timaeus*, the *Critias* contains the beginning of Critias' speech. Its ostensible subject is the mythical war between Atlantis and ancient Athens, which Critias readily identifies with Socrates' ideal city (esp. 26cd). It is important to note that according to Critias both cities were then inhabited by children of the gods.[14]

The *Critias* appears to be unfinished and breaks off just as Zeus is about to trigger the war, so we do not have a single word of the speech originally assigned to Hermocrates. This is very strange, and leaves room for much speculation as to why Plato did not bring the Atlantis story to an end.[15] Yet one can make a reasonable guess at least as to the contents of the missing speech. In Thucydides, the Syracusan general Hermocrates features as an implacable critic of Athenian imperialism (4.58). Accordingly, his role in Plato's unfinished trilogy might have been to make an unfavourable comparison between contemporary Athens and the virtuous city described in Critias' myth.[16]

It seems that Plato's unfinished trilogy was conceived as a triptych depicting three distinct eras, namely the creation of the gods and

---

[12] See *Timaeus* 17a with Slaveva-Griffin (2005).

[13] *Timaeus* 17c ff. For the ambiguous link between the *Timaeus* and the *Republic*, see Vegetti (2000).

[14] *Timaeus* 24d (παιδεύματα θεῶν); *Critias* 113c ff.; cf. 120e.

[15] See Nesselrath (2006), 34 ff., with bibliography.

[16] See Brisson (1970), 404; D. Clay (1997); Naddaf (1994); Pradeau (2001); Iannucci (2002), 8 ff.

nature, the wars and death of the demigods or heroes, and the dismal era of contemporary men. Such an arrangement is immediately reminiscent of epic poetry, because Greek epic poems and entire cycles are set in one of these three eras, according to a tripartite structure that seems to have been a common feature of Greek thought.[17] As we have seen, even Plato chooses to arrange his attack on poetry into three categories, namely gods, heroes, and men.

So much for epic content; but there is surely more to the 'poetry' of the *Timaeus–Critias*. For a long time the *Timaeus* was the only Platonic work known in the West, a circumstance that still affects its exceptionally rich reception. The *Timaeus* inspired such artists as Lorenzo de' Medici and Raphael, whose *School of Athens* depicts the opening of the dialogue, with Socrates facing one-two-three characters.[18] Paul Shorey has even called the *Timaeus* a 'hymn of the universe', while reminding us that in early 19th-century France Plato was often imagined reciting the work at Cape Sounion (Shorey 1938, 104, 166). To be sure, such remarks are as impressionistic as they are fascinating, and are usually made in passing.[19] Contrast the tradition of philosophical commentary whereby the *Timaeus* is regarded (*inter alia*) as Plato's 'physics', or Plato's 'ethics' in physical disguise, or even as Plato's philosophy *tout court*. (Cf. Sedley, p. 246 below.) More recently, however, Gregory Nagy has aptly remarked that the *Timaeus–Critias* often reflects the vocabulary of rhapsodic performance, and he collects a number of relevant passages (2002, Ch. 2). In this chapter, I would like to add some further details to Nagy's very useful discussion.

According to Critias, the Atlantis story was recorded by the Egyptian priests in their archives, then recounted to Solon, then to Critias Senior, then to Critias Junior, and finally to Socrates (21a ff.). All in all, we have four accounts of the same story in different settings. Let us now take a closer look at this curious chain of stories.

---

[17] See Haubold, Ch. 1 in this volume.

[18] Lorenzo wrote a poem modelled on the *Timaeus* (Shorey 1938, 110 ff.). For Raphael's Plato, see Most (2001).

[19] Hadot (1983), Laplace (1984), and D. Clay (2000) have some good remarks on the poetic quality of the *Timaeus–Critias*.

The first account, set in Egypt, is delivered in honour of Athena and is arranged as a continuous exposition (πάντα... ἐξῆς διελθεῖν: 23d; ἐφεξῆς... διέξιμεν: 24a). The language here corresponds neatly to that of epic performance as described in the *Hipparchus*, where on the occasion of the Panathenaea the rhapsodes perform Homer's poems by way of a continuous exposition (ἐφεξῆς αὐτὰ διιέναι: 228b).[20] Moreover, the rhapsodes obviously perform Homer in honour of Athena, and I should add that in both the *Timaeus* and *Hipparchus* such a performance is described as a liberal display of wisdom (φθόνος οὐδείς: *Timaeus* 23d; cf. οὐδενὶ... φθονεῖν: *Hipparchus* 228c).

The second account is set in Athens, and is preceded by Solon's attempt to turn the story of Atlantis into poetry. Unfortunately, his political activity prevented him from fulfilling his ambition. Had he not left his poem unfinished, however, Solon 'would have surpassed in fame Hesiod, Homer and any other poet' (21de).[21] Such at least is the claim of Critias Senior.

The third account is again set in Athens, during the festival called the 'Apaturia', at a time when Critias Senior was an old man and Critias Junior still a young boy. As was customary on this occasion, Athenian boys competed with one another in a rhapsodic contest, and many of them would sing Solon's poems, which were new and fashionable at the time.[22]

The fourth account is set on the day of the Panathenaea—that is, on the very same occasion when Homer's poems were performed. Far from being coincidental, this circumstance is clearly alluded to by Critias, when he presents Timaeus' and his own speech as a sort of hymnodic praise to be performed in honour of Athena on the day of her festival (21a).[23] Moreover, both Timaeus and Critias, and, by implication, Hermocrates too, begin their speeches with a traditional invocation to the gods and the Muses (*Timaeus* 27cd; *Critias* 108cd). Last but not least, I should add that Timaeus' speech is intriguingly equipped with a proem preceding the speech itself. Note that the

[20] Cf. Nagy (2002), 66.
[21] Cf. Nagy (2002), 55–6.
[22] *Timaeus* 21a, 26e. Cf. Nagy (2002), 54.
[23] Cf. Nagy (2002), 53 ff.

words προοίμιον, νόμος, and ἐφεξῆς are used,[24] once again echoing the vocabulary of rhapsody and more generally of literary beginnings.[25]

All of this allows us to reach a twofold conclusion. First, *all* Platonic accounts or 'performances' of the Atlantis story revolve around rhapsody and epic poetry. Secondly, Timaeus' speech is given the very same epic features as the story of Atlantis. This last point is important, but it is hardly surprising. The *Timaeus* and the *Critias* share the same prologue and are clearly conceived as a whole, 'the city of Athens standing as microcosm over against the universe as macrocosm'.[26]

So far, I have tried to cast light on the way in which the *Timaeus–Critias* is entangled with epic poetry. To some extent at least, the speeches of Timaeus, Critias, and Hermocrates must be conceived as epic performances, or as models for epic performances, not unlike the final myth of the *Republic*. This conclusion can—and partly will—be further developed in the course of my argument through a closer examination of the *Timaeus–Critias*. Yet my main focus will now shift to a different question: why should Solon's poem—that is, the *Critias*, and by implication the *Timaeus* as well—be superior to the poems of Hesiod and Homer?


## PLATO'S CLAIM TO POETIC EXCELLENCE

We are prepared for Solon's alleged superiority to Hesiod and Homer by a crucial remark made by an acquaintance of Critias Senior (*Timaeus* 21c):

Solon was not only the wisest of men in all else, but in poetry also he was of all poets the most liberal (ἐλευθερώτατον—or 'free': ἐλευθεριώτατον).

---

[24] See *Timaeus* 29d (not discussed by Nagy).

[25] Cf. e.g. *Theogony* 108 ff.

[26] Hackforth (1944), 8. Cf. Welliver (1977), Naddaf (1997), Ayache (1997), Johansen (2004), 7 ff.

This remark is puzzling. Solon's wisdom is not in question, but what does it mean to say that he was of all poets the most 'liberal' (according to the manuscripts) or 'free' (according to the indirect tradition)?[27] I believe that an appropriate answer to this question can be found in the famous digression at the centre of the *Theaetetus*, where Socrates compares his ideal of the philosopher to its antitype, the orator (172c ff.). The latter is short-sighted, pressed for time, and always absorbed in trivial minutiae. By contrast, the wise philosopher is always at his leisure, hovers in the sky, broadens his perspective to include the universal, and from that somewhat metaphysical vantage point can fully appreciate the pettiness of human affairs.[28] Consider the concluding remarks of one important section (175d–176a):

Such is the character of each of the two classes of men, Theodorus. On the one hand, the man who has truly been brought up in freedom and leisure, whom you call a philosopher. This one may without censure appear foolish and good for nothing, when he is involved in menial services. For instance, he does not know how to pack up his bedding, much less to put the proper sweetening into a sauce or a fawning speech. On the other hand, the second type of man can perform all such services smartly and quickly, but he does not know how to wear his cloak properly (or: 'strike a song to the right': ἀναβάλλεσθαι . . . ἐπιδέξια/ἐπὶ δεξιά) in a free way (or: in a liberal way: ἐλευθέρως/ἐλευθερίως), still less to acquire the true harmony of speech and hymn aright the praises of the true life of gods and blessed men.

Textual and exegetical problems make this intriguing passage a difficult one to understand.[29] The whole passage is arguably dominated by the imagery of the symposium and revolves around the opposition between footmen, that is the orators, and free symposiasts, that is the philosophers. The former prepare the table-beds, serve at table, and flatter their masters, whereas the latter—as was expected from any civilized Greek attending a symposium—know how to play and pass the song to their right, praising piously the gods and heroes.[30] But even if this reading were incorrect, it is still remarkable, and

[27] This detail is left unexplained in Welliver (1977) and David (1984).

[28] For the metaphysical (and 'metasocratic') implications of the digression, see Sedley (2004), 65 ff. ('Broadening perspectives'!) See also Sassi (1986), 115.

[29] See Campbell (1883), *ad loc.*

[30] Cf. Xenophanes, fr. 1 West.

sufficient for my present purposes, that the crowning touch of the comparison is the image of the free (or, again, 'liberal') philosopher singing the praises of gods and heroes at his leisure.[31] As we shall see, the philosopher who hymns gods and heroes corresponds neatly to Plato's Solon, who is equally wise and free (or liberal).

According to the *Theaetetus*, then, only the free/liberal philosopher is able to hymn gods and heroes or 'blessed men', provided he has the leisure to do so. With this in mind, we are now in a position to appreciate fully an important remark by Socrates in the *Timaeus*. In the prologue to that dialogue, he says that the praise of blessed citizens is the province of men like Timaeus, Critias, Hermocrates, and especially Solon.[32] Only such men are equipped with the appropriate wisdom, whereas the sophists are too busy wandering from client to client, while traditional poets *were brought up with wrong values* and could not conceive anything beyond the petty interests of their fellow citizens (19d). The sophists and the poets of the *Timaeus*, then, are very much like the orators of the *Theaetetus*, too slavish to weave an appropriate song about gods and heroes.

What I have argued last raises an obvious question: in what respect is the philosopher's song superior to that of the poets? Again, the *Theaetetus* is a very good starting point. Unlike the orators and the traditional poets, the philosopher *has been brought up with the right values* (175d: note the use of τρέφω and its cognates, as in the *Timaeus*). Consequently, as we have already noted, he has a broader perspective on the cosmos, and he is not at all impressed by the seemingly vast estates of his fellow citizens, nor by their allegedly extended genealogies (174e ff.). Thus, he addresses his song of praise only to the gods and to truly blessed men—that is, the heroes.

Such a broader perspective, then, looks like a crucial requirement for good, philosophical poetry. Now, according to the *Timaeus* Solon has his eyes opened by the Egyptian priests. Their Atlantis story, so grand and venerable, holds an explicit lesson for him: namely, that the world of antiquity *was a much vaster thing* than we might suspect (24e ff.) and, most of all, that *Greek genealogies are just childish stories*, limited in scope and time (23b ff.; cf. 22c). As a result,

---

[31] See e.g. Butti de Lima (2002), 33 ff.
[32] *Timaeus* 19c–e. Cf. David (1984).

Solon has acquired a far broader perspective on space and time, and has thus become the ideal poet-philosopher. By now, he closely resembles the pious symposiasts in the *Theaetetus* and the divine artist who, in the *Republic*, paints his masterpiece with an eye to the sublime world of the Forms (500e ff).[33] Not surprisingly, he is fully entitled to take part in the banquet of speeches of the *Timaeus*.

A second, more obvious requirement for good poetry is easily provided by many passages in the *Republic* (e.g. 379a): the gods are always good and blameless—something that is a crucial premise for Plato's attack on traditional poetry. Needless to say, the gods of Hesiod and Homer are far from blameless, whereas Plato's own eschatological myth in the *Republic*, which is designed to reshape Homer's underworld, lays a special emphasis on the blameless nature of god (esp. 617e). More generally, the *Republic* teaches that poets must represent gods, heroes, and men in a correct, that is, in a moral, way.

What Plato requires of good poetry, then, is a correct representation of gods, heroes, and men, as well as—much less obviously—a broadening of the reader's perspective. I shall be referring to these requirements as the 'moralizing rule' and the 'broadening rule' respectively. With that in mind, we can now revisit the *Timaeus–Critias* from a truly Platonic point of view. Are these works really superior to traditional poetry? To tackle that question I turn to the third section of my chapter, and, finally, to Hesiod.

## PLATO'S HESIOD AND THE WILL OF ZEUS

Let me begin with a brief comparison between Timaeus' speech and Hesiod's *Theogony*. There is little need to discuss Plato's and Hesiod's very different handling of the 'moralizing rule': according to the *Republic*, Hesiod's violent gods are 'the biggest of all lies' (377e), whereas Timaeus stresses that god is always blameless (e.g. 42d), his

---

[33] Cf. 472d and 484c; and see Giuliano (2005), 95 ff., with bibliography.

behaviour being invariably aimed at what is best (29a and *passim*). Admittedly, the Demiurge hints that he *could* destroy Ouranos, Kronos, and Zeus, if he wanted to; but of course he will not want to destroy them, precisely because his will (*boulēsis*) is perfectly good (41ab). Thus, the Demiurge distances himself from the horrifying battles of Hesiod's gods. As Mario Regali points out in this volume (p. 261), the Demiurge himself etymologizes his name so as to make him the cause (*di' emou*) of all things (*erga*). Plato here alludes to the proem of the *Works and Days*, where Hesiod etymologizes Zeus (*Dia*) as the cause (*dia*: the 'through whom') of human affairs. However, Hesiod's Zeus emphatically causes *both* good *and* bad things, whereas the Demiurge brings about only good things. By the criterion of the 'moralizing rule', Plato's entirely 'good' Demiurge clearly outperforms Hesiod's often 'bad' Zeus.

If we now turn to the 'broadening rule', it might initially seem as though the *Theogony* does rather well in this category, given the vastness of its perspective. After all, the *Theogony* is about the birth of the mighty gods and their role throughout the world, from the time of the primeval chaos up to the reign of Zeus: it would seem that Hesiod encompasses the entirety of time, space, and divine power. In fact, he himself appears to have been rather proud of the range of his narrative. According to Jenny Strauss Clay (2003, 180–81, commenting on *Theogony* 653–9), Hesiod 'invites us to compare his poetry to that of Homeric epic', in order to show that his vision is 'far more universal and complete'. Hesiod's Muses know past, present, and future, and apparently there can be nothing vaster than that. Even a cursory comparison with the *Timaeus*, however, cannot but prompt second thoughts.

To begin with, both the *Theogony* and the *Timaeus* explore the order of the cosmos as a whole, but according to the latter our world is nothing but a sensible copy of an intelligible cosmos lying far beyond (28a ff.). Secondly, in the *Timaeus*, time is just a device designed to equip this copy with a physical imitation of real eternity (37d ff.). Thirdly, even in our second-rank world the traditional gods are just second-rank entities. Far from being the supreme beings of Hesiod's *Theogony*, the gods are not even immortal in their own natures (41b), and they need directions from a superior, the

Demiurge.[34] A direct quotation, from *Timaeus* 40d–41a, may be in order here:

Concerning the other divinities, to discover and declare their origin is too great a task for us, and we must trust those who have declared it aforetime, they being, as they affirmed, descendants of gods and knowing well, no doubt, their own forefathers.[35] It is, as I say, impossible to disbelieve the children of gods, even though their statements lack either probable or necessary demonstration; and inasmuch as they profess to speak of family matters, we must follow custom and believe them. Therefore let the genera-tion of these gods be stated by us, following their account, in this wise. Of Ge and Ouranos were born the children Okeanos and Tethys; and of these, Phorkys, Kronos, Rhea, and all that go with them; and of Kronos and Rhea were born Zeus and Hera and all those who are, as we know, called their brethren; and of these again, other descendants.

These few lines hastily summarize the content of entire poems such as the *Theogony*.[36] Plato glosses over the embarrassing struggles of the traditional gods, and there is not the slightest hint that they could ever aspire to rule the world. Subsequently, the traditional gods are even lectured by a patronizing Demiurge, who turns out to be the very model they are supposed to imitate.[37] Among other things, the Demiurge states that any cosmogony is incomplete if it fails to account for the creation of mankind (41b ff.). Plato thus 'corrects' Hesiod in another important way, because anthropogony is precisely the 'strange omission' of the *Theogony*, to quote Walter Burkert (1999, 101).[38] Compared to the *Timaeus*, Hesiod's is really a small world.

Let us now turn to the Atlantis story. Plato no doubt drew inspira-tion from various sources, and in many ways the historians provided

---

[34] The precise meaning of these directions has been debated since antiquity, with readers wavering between literal and figurative interpretations. On the ancient debate, see Berti (1997). For a sensible compromise, see e.g. Donini (1988), 37 ff., Partenie (1998), and Mesch (2002). Lloyd (1966, esp. 222 ff. and 282 ff.) and Pender (2000, esp. 100 ff.) discuss the problem within a broader context.

[35] Possibly a reference to *Works and Days* 299 (Hesiod's *dion genos*).

[36] Cf. Sedley in this vol., p. 247 with n. 3. See further *Laws* 886c and *Epinomis* 988c, with Sassi (1997), 232.

[37] See *Timaeus* 41a ff., 42e; Pender (2000), 105.

[38] Cf. Classen (1962) and Haubold (2002). *Contra*, see J. S. Clay (2003), 95 ff.

an important model. To begin with, it has been argued that Atlantis
and mythic Athens in fact stand for two distinct historical stages of
Athens itself.[39] On this view, the Athens of the myth broadly stands
for old rural Athens, as it used to be until the first Persian war. This
innocent and no doubt idealized city undergoes a dramatic change
at the time of the second clash with the Persian empire, when,
according to Herodotus (7.143–4; cf. 8.41), Themistocles persuaded
his fellow citizens to abandon their homes and 'become maritime'.
Moreover, Thucydides (1.143–5) tells us that Pericles fantasized
about Athens becoming a powerful island. As the 'Old Oligarch'
remarks bitterly (2.14 ff.), Athens became in fact an aggressive and
somewhat insular empire. Plato's Atlantic island, then, is nothing but
a disguised and fantastic version of Athenian imperialism, in which
the dream of Pericles—or perhaps Plato's nightmare—comes true.[40]
Thus, the Atlantis story is actually a metaphorical civil war between
old rural Platonized Athens and its new maritime counterpart.

The Persian wars, as recounted and interpreted by the historians,
function as a model in a second, no less important way. The clash
between Athens and Atlantis, with the former playing the role of little
David defeating Goliath, clearly follows the pattern of the Persian
wars.[41] Very much in the vein of Herodotus' *Histories*, Plato's mythic
Athenians are presented as the saviours of Greece against a huge
barbarian empire (*Critias* 109a). However, the war between Athens
and Atlantis features open divine interventions (120d ff.), and was
fought 9,000 years ago (*Timaeus* 23e), by two peoples referred to as
children of the gods. In other words, the war is set in the era of the
heroes, when mortals were stronger and had frequent exchanges with
the gods. By Greek literary standards, this is just what distinguishes
epic from historical or pseudo-historical narrative,[42] and Aristotle
was apparently well aware that in this respect the Atlantis story was

---

[39] See, most recently, Vidal-Naquet (2005), with bibliography. For Plato's use of
historiographical catchwords, such as *tekmērion*, see Sassi (1986), 119.

[40] See Pradeau (1997), 106.

[41] See e.g. Dusanic (1982) and Morgan (1998).

[42] See e.g. Gill (1977), 293 and—more generally—Hornblower (2001). The emphasis on names (see *Critias* 113ab) is probably a further hint at the poetic quality of
the text (see Aristotle, *Poetics* 1451[a]36–[b]23 with Tulli 1994, 99 ff.).

very much like the *Iliad*.[43] This is, of course, in full accordance with the epic frame of the *Timaeus–Critias*.[44]

Like the cosmology of the *Timaeus*, then, the Atlantis story is in some ways a new kind of epic, to be read against the background of traditional poetry, and especially of Hesiod and Homer, who are explicitly—and unfavourably—compared to Solon. Unfortunately, we have only a rapid summary of the war in the prologue of the *Timaeus*, from which we merely learn that Athens eventually defeated the Atlantic Armada and that afterwards the sea swallowed up both the island and the Athenian troops.[45] More information is provided by the *Critias*, which features a description of both Atlantis and ancient Athens. After a long period of peace, the Atlantic people succumb to greed and vice, thus provoking this reaction from Zeus (121bc):

And Zeus, the god of gods, who reigns by law, inasmuch as he has the gift of perceiving such things, marked how this righteous race was in evil plight, and wanted (βουληθείς) to inflict punishment upon them, to the end that when chastised they might strike a truer note. Wherefore he assembled together all the gods into that abode which they honour most, standing as it does at the centre of all the Universe, and beholding all things that partake of generation, and when he had assembled them, he said . . .

The assembly of the gods is a quintessentially epic scene, but, unfortunately, it is just at this point that the *Critias* breaks off, so that we do not hear the words of Zeus. No less epic in flavour is the motif of the 'will of Zeus' (Διὸς βουλή), clearly alluded to by the verb βουληθείς, as Taylor noted.[46] It is, of course, a divine assembly summoned by Zeus that triggers the action of the *Odyssey* (see 1.19 ff.),[47] and it is again the will of Zeus that marks the beginning of the *Iliad* (1.1–5):

---

[43] See Rowe (1998*b*), 142, discussing Strabo 2.3.6; 13.1.36.

[44] For the merging of history and poetry in the *Timaeus–Critias*, see Arrighetti (1991), Brisson (1992), 319 ff., and Nagy (2002), 67 ff. (an allusion to Herodotus' and Thucydides' proems is palpable at *Critias* 107de and 121a).

[45] This implicitly raises a problem of theodicy, which is aptly discussed in Broadie (2001).

[46] Taylor (1926), in his very short discussion of the *Critias* at the end of the chapter devoted to the *Timaeus*. See also Nagy (2002), 66.

[47] As is noted by D. Clay (1997), 52.

> Sing, o goddess, the anger of Achilles son of Peleus,
> that brought countless ills upon the Achaeans.
> Many a brave soul did it send hurrying down to Hades,
> and many a hero did it yield a prey to dogs
> and vultures, for so was the will of Zeus ($\Delta\iota\grave{o}\varsigma\ldots\beta o\upsilon\lambda\acute{\eta}$) fulfilled.

Intriguingly, the *Critias* breaks off exactly where a traditional epic poem should begin. So, what exactly is the will of Zeus? Plato applies to it the by now familiar 'moralizing rule', for in the *Critias* the will of Zeus has an ethical slant, clearly echoing the good will of the Demiurge in the *Timaeus* (41b).[48] In the *Iliad*, however, the will of Zeus has decidedly nasty implications and probably even conceals a larger scope than the wrath of Achilles. Ever since antiquity, readers of Homer have detected behind *Iliad* 1.5 the hint of a divine plan to destroy the human race by means of war or natural catastrophe.[49] This theme is familiar in both Greek and Near Eastern epic poetry and has survived in a number of texts.[50] Among these, I would like to look for a moment at the concluding fragment of the Hesiodic *Catalogue of Women* (204 MW).[51] These poorly preserved lines raise thorny problems of interpretation which I cannot discuss here, so I will just explain what I take to be its general meaning.[52]

After a lengthy list of Helen's suitors and her marriage to Menelaus (41–95), the gods are ready to quarrel (*eris*), because Zeus is planning 'astonishing things' (95–8). Zeus, in fact, wants to do away with a large part of mankind, with the *prophasis*—an ambiguous word meaning either 'excuse' or 'motivation'—of destroying the demigods (98–100).[53] From here on, the papyrus is badly damaged, but it appears to mention the sons of the gods because it is they who most obviously represent a situation of close contact between

---

[48] It makes sense that Zeus should act in a similar way to the Demiurge, because Zeus and the gods have to 'imitate' him (42e).

[49] See e.g. the scholia to *Iliad* 1.5; R. Scodel (1982), 39 and 46 ff.; Mayer (1996), with bibliography. Cf. Euripides, *Orestes* 1639–42; *Electra* 1282–3; *Helen* 36–41.

[50] See e.g. Kirk (1972), 79.

[51] The *Catalogue's* authorship does not affect my argument. However, see e.g. Dräger (1997) and Arrighetti (1998).

[52] For alternative interpretations, see Cerutti (1998) and Hirschberger (2004), 407 ff.

[53] On *prophasis*, see now J. S. Clay (2005), 29 ff. Platonic scholars usually quote Thucydides 1.23.6: cf. Nesselrath (2006), 429.

mortals and gods. This situation was first established in the proem of the *Catalogue*, but must apparently come to an end in fragment 204 MW. As a consequence, the demigods must be removed, either through death or a happy exile to the Blessed Islands.[54] When the fragmentary text resumes, we hear of heroes sent to Hades, in language reminiscent of the *Iliad* (118–19). We also hear that the mind of Zeus is inscrutable (116–17). The war marks the beginning of a new era, with an arresting scene that recalls the so-called 'nuclear winter' in post-atomic scenarios. The first ever autumn and winter— or at any rate 'a major disturbance in nature' (R. Scodel 1982, 39)— descend upon the earth, bringing further misery to the surviving mortals (124 ff.). After a mysterious section devoted to the life-cycle of snakes, the text is interrupted again, though it is probably nearing its end at this point anyway. In fact, the catastrophe 'brings the curtain down on the age of the heroes' (West 1985, 43), and puts an end to the affairs between gods and mortal women, which is the very subject of the *Catalogue*.

In the *Timaeus*, the Egyptian priests make fun of Solon because he naively tells them the childish myths of Phoroneus, Niobe, Deuca- lion, and Pyrrha, the survivors of the Greek Flood (22a ff.). Now, Niobe was the first woman ever to be loved by Zeus (Acusilaus fr. 25 Fowler), and all of these stories featured prominently in the *Catalo- gue of Women*.[55] Moreover, our Hesiodic fragment is linked through Helen to the genealogy of the Atlantids, mentioned earlier in the *Catalogue* (see West 1985, 43). Thus, there is a strong likelihood that in the *Timaeus–Critias* Plato refers back to Hesiod.[56] It is all the more intriguing, therefore, that the *Critias* should likewise mention the *prophasis* of Zeus for the war (120d):

[54] See Cerutti (1998), 166 ff. The poem thus comes full circle, in a way that is echoed in Catullus 64 (see Pontani 2000). In the *Works and Days*, that is, after the catastrophe, gods and humans no longer interact closely with one another (see e.g. Arrighetti 1978).

[55] See frr. 2, 4, 5, 6, 7, 123, 234. The presence of *this* Niobe in the *Catalogue* is conjectural but very likely. See West (1985), 76 and D'Alessio (2005), 202.

[56] One cannot rule out the influence of other genealogies, but Hesiod's were among the most famous and appear to have been close to Attic traditions. For genealogical literature, see West (1985), 3 ff. For the *Catalogue*'s connections with Athens, West (1985), 168 ff. and Irwin (2005*b*). For Plato's knowledge of the *Catalogue*, cf. *Symposium* 219e, *Laws* 944d, 948b with Schwartz (1960), 580–81.

Such was the magnitude and character of the power which existed in Atlantis at that time; and this power the God set in array and brought against these regions of ours on some such *prophasis* as the following, according to the story.

A particularly brilliant instance of the 'moralizing rule' is at work here. The *prophasis* of Zeus has of course become a just one, namely the impiety of the Atlantic people, whose divine nature succumbs to the mortal part of their soul. So Zeus does not remove the demigods as in the *Catalogue*. Rather, *they* stifle their divine nature and are punished for that reason. Moreover, Zeus wants to reform rather than destroy them, as we have seen; and his thinking, far from being inscrutable and causing quarrels among the other gods, as in Hesiod, will be made clear to everyone in the divine assembly just before the *Critias* breaks off. All this is part of a larger project to improve on the old story pattern: as early as 109b, Critias states in the most emphatic way that there can be no quarrelling (*eris*) among the gods in this text.[57]

Let us now turn briefly to the 'broadening rule' in *Critias* and the *Catalogue of Women*. Once again, Plato emerges as the clear front-runner. For one thing, Deucalion's Flood probably played a major role in the *Catalogue*, which may explain Critias' apparently casual remark that it is merely the latest in a whole series of even vaster catastrophes (112a). On this count alone, the chronological scope of the *Catalogue* appears very narrow when compared to the *Critias*. Moreover, the war between Athens and Atlantis took place no less than 9,000 years ago, and the latter was an island larger than Asia and Europe put together, lying beyond the pillars of Heracles and facing a still larger landmass referred to as the 'true continent' (*Timaeus* 24e–25a; cf. *Phaedo* 109a ff.). More than a century before Plato, Aeschylus had colourfully depicted the huge size of the Persian army and the fabulous extent of the Persian empire. Even Thucydides had tried painstakingly to demonstrate that after all the Peloponnesian War was greater and more important than the Trojan War. However, given its fantastic size and remoteness in both space and time, 'the city that repulsed Atlantis is displayed as immemorially

---

[57] Cf. *Laws* 715e–716b (and Nesselrath 2006, 431).

senior to any historical version, and as unsupersedably archetypal.'[58]
The Trojan War—and for that matter the Persian wars and the
Peloponnesian conflict as well—are no match for the Atlantis story.

## CONCLUSIONS

Plato reshapes Hesiodic patterns and motifs for a number of reasons
and in a number of ways, many of which would repay closer examination.[59] By way of conclusion, I would like to emphasize just
three general points that have a bearing on the literary status of the
*Timaeus–Critias*.

First of all, the surprisingly emphatic claim to truth of Plato's
*Timaeus* may well be ascribed to the influence of the *Theogony*,
where Hesiod famously makes an equally bold claim.[60] After all,
Hesiod's truth becomes 'the biggest of lies' in the *Republic*, and
Socrates expresses his satisfaction about the 'true *logos*' of Atlantis
as opposed to some 'made up myth'. In so doing, he may be referring
to Hesiod's opposition between his own true poetry and the 'lies
resembling truth' (*Timaeus* 26e–27b; *Theogony* 27),[61] which are presumably meant as the hallmark of Homer or his like.[62] As we have
seen, Plato's claim to truth is based on his attempt to moralize and
broaden Hesiod's cosmos.

Secondly, in both Hesiod and Plato, the will of Zeus brings about
the end of the heroic world by way of a disastrous war followed
by a natural catastrophe.[63] Afterwards, the surviving mortals are
trapped in an impoverished world, as is made clear by Plato's astonishing comparison between the lush Attic countryside of yore and its

---

[58] See Broadie (2001), 27–8, quoting *Timaeus* 34b10–c6 for seniority = dignity.

[59] See e.g. Pender and Sedley in this volume.

[60] Compare *Timaeus* 21d, 26cd, and 26e with *Theogony* 28.

[61] Both passages are followed by a cosmogonic *propositio* and share manifold
analogies.

[62] Cf. Arrighetti (1998), xix ff., and Szlezák (1993), 234. For alternative views, see
Nagy (1996) and J. S. Clay (2003), 58 ff.

[63] Cf. *Timaeus* 25d, possibly a Hesiodic echo (see Sassi 1986, 112 and cf. R. Scodel
1982, with bibliography).

contemporary counterpart, arid and eroded like 'the bones of an ill body' (*Critias* 111a ff.). All that is fully consonant with the spirit of epic poetry, which constantly, if implicitly, compares the vastness of the heroic world to a diminished and disappointing present.[64]

Finally, the *Catalogue* and the *Theogony* were stitched together by way of divine marriages between gods and mortal women, so as to form one continuous rhapsody embracing the gods, the demigods, and the end of the heroic world. In the same vein, Plato stitches together the *Critias* and the *Timaeus*, as Critias 'receives' the song-speech from Timaeus, once again resorting to the vocabulary of rhapsody, which of course literally means 'stitching of songs'.[65] Moreover, it cannot be accidental that he attributes the foundation of Atlantis to the marriage between Poseidon and a heroine explicitly referred to as a 'mortal woman' (*Critias* 113c). Thus, the *Timaeus* and the *Critias* are one and two works at the same time: regardless of its manifold implications,[66] such a 'rhapsodic' arrangement is once again modelled on Hesiod.

Plato's literary agenda was no doubt an immensely complex and ambitious one. However, one thing is clear: a careful observance of the 'moralizing' and 'broadening' rules fully vindicates Plato's claim to poetic excellence and his later fame as a sublime writer—if not his alarming ambition to replace all existing literature. After all, to quote [Longinus] (*On the Sublime* 35.2–3), Plato 'transcends the boundaries of the world surrounding us' and 'inspires an inextinguishable passion for what is eternally vast and divine'.

---

[64]  See e.g. Griffith (1983) and Graziosi and Haubold (2005).

[65]  See *Critias* 106b, where the tell-tale expressions τὸν ἑξῆς λόγον and δέχομαι are used. As Nagy (2002) argues, δέχομαι is used in *Iliad* 9.191 of the song being passed from one rhapsode to the next. Cf. Aristophanes, *Wasps* 1222 ff.

[66]  At least since Wilamowitz-Moellendorff (1920) (i: 590–2; ii: 255 ff.), the relationship between the *Timaeus* and the *Critias* has been a much-debated issue. The manuscript tradition has been studied by Jonkers (1989), and Prof. G. J. Boter is going to publish the new OCT edition of the *Timaeus*, along with Slings' *Clitophon* and *Critias*. However, the study of the textual tradition does not allow any positive conclusions (see Haslam 1976).

# 11

---

# Chaos corrected: Hesiod in Plato's creation myth

*E. E. Pender*

## INTRODUCTION

Respect for Greek cultural tradition is evident in Plato's dialogues.
But countering this is the writer's keen competitive spirit, reinforced
by his confidence in the progressive achievements of philosophical
reasoning.[1] Hesiod's *Theogony* held a highly influential position in
Plato's Athens as the most venerable of ancient, surviving, Greek
myths of creation. In composing his new account of the birth of the
universe, Plato selected the best of models to emulate and, crucially,
to contest. Although Plato's *Timaeus* diverges markedly from the
*Theogony*, it reveals a deep engagement with it. Hesiod is named,
alongside Homer, in the prologue. In the cosmology Plato incorporates and adapts various narrative features of Hesiod's myth, including the use of personified primal figures, the dominant motif of
lineage, and various supporting polarities. Further, at key transitional
passages of Timaeus' exposition, direct allusions are used to accentuate Plato's response to Hesiod's account. Through these abundant
allusions and parallels, the formative influence of the *Theogony* is
acknowledged and the *Timaeus* is situated within a specific genealogy
of creation stories. Plato's myth is born from the Greek tradition. But
it must depart from it. For the radical innovations of teleology

---

[1] Though cf. Boys-Stones in this volume.

demand that *Timaeus* correct its predecessors' fundamental errors—
on the nature of the gods, the created universe, and the relationship
they share.

## MAINTAINING TRADITION

The introductory discussions of *Timaeus* evince Plato's complex
response to the Greek poetic tradition. In the opening conversation,
Socrates addresses the theme of the best city and its exploits, declares
his own inability to celebrate such a city, and hands over the task
to his friends. In these preliminary exchanges Socrates refers to the
limitations of poets (19d3–e2) and Critias asserts the potential superiority of Solon over Hesiod and Homer.[2] These brief asides signal the
Athenian cultural context, but also point obliquely to Plato's own
credentials as both story-teller and reformer. Plato challenges established Greek thought but remains mindful of ancient authority,
especially in matters relating to the gods. The tension between tradition and innovation first appears when, in support of Socrates'
revolutionary proposals for the ideal city (17c1–19a6), his friends
offer as their worthy sequel an ancient tale. Moreover, Critias trans-
poses the 'imaginary citizens' of Socrates' ideal state from 'myth' (ἐν
μύθῳ: 26c8) to historical 'truth' (ἐπὶ τἀληθές) as he claims them as
their own actual ancestors (προγόνους ἡμῶν: 26d3)—the Athenians
of long ago.

The prologue of *Timaeus* is dominated by a concern with the past,
with telling stories about the past, and with genealogies. Critias
explains how he heard the Atlantis story as a boy from his grandfather (also named Critias) who was close to 90 years old (21b1).[3]

---

[2] *Timaeus* 21d1–3 (Critias on Solon): κατά γε ἐμὴν δόξαν οὔτε Ἡσίοδος οὔτε
Ὅμηρος οὔτε ἄλλος οὐδεὶς ποιητὴς εὐδοκιμώτερος ἐγένετο ἄν ποτε αὐτοῦ. The text
of *Timaeus* used is that in Burnet (1899–1907), vol. iv; the translation is from
Cornford (1937).

[3] *Timaeus* 21a7–b1: Ἐγὼ φράσω, παλαιὸν ἀκηκοὼς λόγον οὐ νέου ἀνδρός. ἦν μὲν
γὰρ δὴ τότε Κριτίας, ὡς ἔφη, σχεδὸν ἐγγὺς ἤδη τῶν ἐνενήκοντα ἐτῶν, ἐγὼ δέ πῃ
μάλιστα δεκέτης.

The grandfather had inherited the tale from his father, Dropides, who had heard it from its original author: his 'relative and close friend' Solon (20e1–2).With the aged grandfather and great-grandfather Plato stresses that Critias is the third generation of his family to hear Solon's tale.[4] Further, the tale itself tells how even those former Athenians who told their 'most ancient' stories (τὰ ἀρχαιότατα: 22a5) were not aware of a pre-history dating back still further. Critias tells how Solon had travelled to Egypt and conversed at Sais with the priests, the guardians of ancient knowledge (21e1–22a2). Solon had recounted to the priests the ancient Greek legends of the first humans and the survivors of the flood—Deucalion and Pyrrha—and had traced the pedigree of their descendants (γενεαλογεῖν: 22b2). In response, a 'very old' Egyptian priest had reproached him (22b4–5): 'Ah, Solon, Solon . . . you Greeks are always children (ἀεὶ παῖδες); in Greece there is no such thing as an old man (γέρων).' The priest sees the Greeks as lacking a 'store of old belief based on long tradi-tion' (22b7–8) and criticizes Solon's genealogies (γενεαλογηθέντα: 23b4) as 'little better than nursery tales'. The problem, he explains, is that interruptions in their literary tradition have left the Greeks unaware of their true history. Indeed the Athenians do not realize that they are in fact descended from the bravest race in the world (23b6–c2). The priest goes on to relate the story of the first Athe-nians, born 9,000 years earlier at the point when Athena 'took over the seed of your people from Earth and Hephaestus'.[5]

This emphasis on the transmission of knowledge down the gen-erations is further reinforced by the circumstances of the retelling of the Solon narrative. For Critias remembers how he heard it from his grandfather as they were celebrating the festival of Apaturia. More-over, he names the specific occasion—'Children's Day' (21b1–5):

We were keeping the Apaturia; it was the Children's Day. For us boys there were the usual ceremonies: our fathers offered us prizes for reciting. Many poems by different authors were repeated.

---

[4] *Timaeus* 20e1–4: [Σόλων] ἦν μὲν οὖν οἰκεῖος καὶ σφόδρα φίλος ἡμῖν Δρωπίδου τοῦ προπάππου . . . πρὸς δὲ Κριτίαν τὸν ἡμέτερον πάππον εἶπεν, ὡς ἀπεμνημόνευεν αὖ πρὸς ἡμᾶς ὁ γέρων.

[5] *Timaeus* 23e1–2: ἐκ Γῆς τε καὶ Ἡφαίστου τὸ σπέρμα παραλαβοῦσα ὑμῶν.

The Apaturia celebrated the 'Brotherhoods' (*Phratriai*) of Athenian society, communities which claimed long descent from a common male ancestor. Children's Day was the time when Athenian children were inscribed on the register of their clan and so introduced to their *Phratria*. Critias remembers the 'usual ceremonies'—the competitions in reciting traditional poetry—by which the Athenians sought to preserve their literary inheritance alongside their family lines.[6] Since the Critias portrayed here is Plato's own great-grandfather, Plato is here preserving and paying respect to his own noble family line, reaching back to Solon and beyond. In these various ways the prologue of *Timaeus* brings into sharp focus the issues of family tradition, genealogies, and the transmission of cultural knowledge from the distant past to the present. The lineage motif therefore not only sets the scene for a new account of the divine birth of the universe but also indicates that Plato as author is keenly aware of his own myth's place in the Greek genealogy of creation stories.

The prologue's concern with the preservation of traditional knowledge further raises the question of authority in recounting matters ancient and divine. When the Egyptian priest delivers the tale of Atlantis, he refers to the founding of Athens as a divine creation, born of Hephaestus through Athena. Despite this evidently mythological reference, Socrates responds to Critias' retelling of the story by approving it as 'no fiction, but genuine history' (26e4–5): μὴ πλασθέντα μῦθον ἀλλ' ἀληθινὸν λόγον. The ultimate authority for Critias' story is the Egyptian priest. But when Timaeus in turn delivers his account of events still older than these, who will be his authority? Will Timaeus' account of divine creation also be genuine history? The challenge of revealing the divine beginnings of the whole universe is implicit in Timaeus' invocation of the gods at the opening of his speech. Socrates bids him call on the gods 'as custom requires' (κατὰ νόμον), and Timaeus replies (27c1–d1):

That, Socrates, is what all do, who have the least portion of wisdom: always, at the outset of every undertaking, small or great, they call upon a god. We who are now to discourse about the universe—how it came into being (ᾗ γέγονεν), or perhaps had no beginning of existence (ἀγενές)—must,

---

[6] Plato's use of the Apaturia as situational allusion is discussed in Pender (2007).

if our senses be not altogether gone astray, invoke gods and goddesses with a prayer (ἐπικαλουμένους εὔχεσθαι) that our discourse throughout may be above all pleasing to them and in consequence satisfactory to us. Let this suffice, then, for our invocation of the gods.

In this traditional gesture, Timaeus calls on the gods to support his discourse and re-enacts the familiar invocations of epic, including Hesiod's invocation to the Muses at *Theogony* 104–15. When addressing the matter of authority regarding the birth of immortals, Hesiod's stance is to claim that he received his account directly from the Muses on Mount Helikon. But even with this very bold move, the poet still feels it necessary to draw attention to the truth-status of the account they deliver. Therefore in the prologue to *Theogony* he has the Muses say to the poet as representative of human beings (26–8):[7]

> ποιμένες ἄγραυλοι, κάκ' ἐλέγχεα, γαστέρες οἶον,
> ἴδμεν ψεύδεα πολλὰ λέγειν ἐτύμοισιν ὁμοῖα,
> ἴδμεν δ', εὖτ' ἐθέλωμεν, ἀληθέα γηρύσασθαι.

> Shepherds that camp in the wild, disgraces, merest bellies:
> we know to tell many lies that sound like truth,
> but we know to sing reality, when we will.

The Muses make clear their contempt for mankind and stress the gulf between their own knowledge and power and that of the poor shepherds, subject to all the usual human limitations. As a result of the Muses' caprice (28) a question mark remains: will they wish to tell the truth *this time*? Before his theogony proper begins, then, Hesiod raises the vexed question of authority when recounting divine origins.

Similarly, Plato flags early in his text the same question of authority and truth in telling a creation story. For the issue of historical truth is raised both in the prologue itself and in the very opening of Timaeus' cosmology. But Plato's approach to the truth-status of his discourse takes a different turn as he famously establishes that it is merely a 'likely story'.[8] Two reasons are given. First, since the cosmos

---

[7] The text of *Theogony* used is Solmsen (1970), with translation by West (1988).

[8] Timaeus' cosmology as 'likely' story: 29d2; 44d1; 48d2; 53d5; 55d5; 56a1; 56b4; 56d1; 68b7; 72d7; 90e8.

itself is merely a likeness, the account of it cannot be as secure as an account of the actual model and must therefore itself be merely likely (29c2). But as the explanation continues, a more familiar reason also emerges (29c4–d3):

If then, Socrates, in many respects concerning the many things—the gods and the generation of the universe (θεῶν καὶ τῆς τοῦ παντὸς γενέσεως)—we prove unable to render an account at all points entirely consistent with itself and exact, you must not be surprised. If we can furnish accounts no less likely than any other, we must be content, remembering that I who speak and you my judges are only human (φύσιν ἀνθρωπίνην ἔχομεν), and consequently it is fitting that we should in these matters, accept the likely story (τὸν εἰκότα μῦθον), and look for nothing further.

Here the limitations of human knowledge and the gap between human and divine become a further reason why the tale is merely likely. This gap recalls the Muses' taunts to the human shepherds, and the same theme of human limitations sounds later at *Timaeus* 40d6–e4.[9] As he concludes his exposition on the creation of the planets, Timaeus raises again the question of the truth-status of such accounts of divine beings (40d6–7):

Περὶ δὲ τῶν ἄλλων δαιμόνων εἰπεῖν καὶ γνῶναι τὴν γένεσιν μεῖζον ἢ καθ' ἡμᾶς.

As concerning the other divinities, to know and to declare their generation is too high a task for us.

Whereas at 27c1–d1 Timaeus had recourse to an invocation of the gods, here he adopts a different strategy for managing the subject of divine generation (40d7–e4):

We must trust those who have declared it in former times: being, as they said, descendants (ἐκγόνοις) of gods, they must, no doubt, have had certain knowledge of their own ancestors (προγόνους). We cannot, then, mistrust the children of gods (θεῶν παισίν), though they speak without probable or necessary proofs; when they profess to report their family history (οἰκεῖα), we must follow established usage and accept what they say (ἑπομένους

---

[9] This gap between divine and human knowledge is also stressed at 53d6–7, where knowledge of the remote beginnings of matter is said to be only open to the gods themselves or to those especially favoured by the gods.

τῷ νόμῳ πιστευτέον). Let us, then, take on their word this account of the generation (γένεσις) of these gods.

At this point Plato introduces a direct allusion to the *Theogony*. The myth-makers of former times who claimed divine descent are such figures as Orpheus and Musaeus, but the particular theogony recalls that of Hesiod's poem. At *Theogony* 132–8, Earth and Heaven produce their first generation of divine children:

But then, bedded with Heaven, she [Earth] bore deep-swirling Oceanus... and Rhea... and lovely Tethys. After them the youngest was born, crooked-schemer Kronos most fearsome of children, who loathed his lusty father.

The second generation, born from Rhea and Kronos, is detailed later at 453–8:

Rhea, surrendering to Kronos, bore resplendent children: Hestia, Demeter, and gold-sandalled Hera, mighty Hades...and the booming Shaker of Earth, and Zeus the resourceful, father of gods and men, under whose thunder the broad earth is shaken.

The allusion to Hesiod is evident as Timaeus sets out the traditional divine family (40e5–41a3):

As children of Earth and Heaven were born Okeanos and Tethys; and of these Phorkys[10] and Kronos and Rhea and all their company; and of Kronos and Rhea, Zeus and Hera, and all their brothers and sisters whose names we know; and of these yet other offspring.

The positioning of this Hesiodic allusion at 40e5–41a3 marks one of the various transitions between Plato's two modes of speaking about the cosmos—the scientific and the mythological. From 38c3 to 40d5, Timaeus has narrated the creation of the divine planets, culminating with the earth at 40b8. He honours planet earth by personifying it as 'our nurse' (τροφόν) and as 'the first and eldest/most venerable (πρεσβυτάτην) of the gods in heaven', a personification consistent with Hesiod's theogony. The creation of earth completes Timaeus' account of the generation of the planets (40d4–5): 'here let our account of the nature of the visible and generated gods come to an end (τέλος).' In the next lines (40d6–e4), Timaeus recognizes that

[10] At *Theogony* 237 Phorkys is the son of Pontos and Gaia.

speaking about the generation of other gods is beyond him, which necessitates his recourse to the Hesiodic theogony of Earth and Heaven as parents of the traditional gods (40e5–41a3). From there the narrative moves immediately into a new sequence as the Demiurge instructs the lesser gods, his children,[11] to arrange the birth of humankind (41a5–d3). Thus Timaeus resumes the story of the personified creator who was last notably evident at 37c6–d2, rejoicing as a father at the birth of his offspring. The presentation of the Demiurge as father recedes to make way for the scientific account of the creation of the planets, but then is resumed at 41a5 once that section is complete. Therefore Timaeus' Hesiodic theogony at 40e5–41a3 defers to poetic tradition in the matter of the birth of the Titans and Olympians. But this is carefully placed after the creation of the divine planets and so secondary to it, thus enabling Plato to accentuate his own rival account of the nature and status of earth. Further, Timaeus' use of the traditional mythology of Earth and Heaven as parents of the gods also works to smoothe the internal transition between the scientific account and the new mythological sequence of the Demiurge as father of gods and men. Finally, the reference to following established custom ($\tau\hat{\omega}$ $\nu\acute{o}\mu\omega$: 40e3) provides a structural parallel with the invocation to the gods at 27b9 ($\kappa\alpha\tau\grave{\alpha}$ $\nu\acute{o}\mu\omega\nu$), underlining that in both cases Timaeus looks back to Greek tradition to help overcome the difficulties of revealing divine origins. Thus Plato shapes the Hesiodic allusion to fit his own exposition and indicates that he is content to maintain and respect his predecessors' accounts, so long as they can be blended with his own.

## A NEW STORY TO TELL

Despite the affinity between the *Timaeus* and traditional stories, Plato's account is new and aims to replace the moral chaos of established creation myths. Plato must correct Hesiod's *Theogony*

---

[11] *Timaeus* 41a7: Θεοὶ θεῶν, ὧν ἐγὼ δημιουργὸς πατήρ τε ἔργων. For the lesser gods as children of the Demiurge, see also 42e6 and 69c4. For discussion of this passage, see Regali's contribution to this volume, Ch. 13.

since it gives a distorted picture of the gods as engaged in wrong-doing. He simply cannot accept stories of divine plotting, deception, and acts of violence. Plato's criticism of ancient myths at *Laws* 886c applies directly to the *Theogony*, and Hesiod is named explicitly at *Republic* 377d4 as Plato explains why such tales of wrongdoing are unacceptable. Indeed, Hesiod is singled out for specific criticism with his story of Kronos' castration of his father (377e) and battles of Giants (378c). The actual distortion is then spelled out at 379a7–b2: since god is definitively *good* (ἀγαθός), stories of wrong-doing do not offer a truthful account of the divine nature. As the *Republic* passage continues (379bc) god is identified as the cause (αἴτιον) not of all things but only of good, since his nature will not allow him to cause evil or harm. The identification of the Demiurge as the cause (αἴτιον) of the universe at *Timaeus* 28c2–30c1[12] recalls and builds on the *Republic* passage. Here the cause of the universe is explicitly identified as good and working with entirely virtuous motive (29d7–e2):

Λέγωμεν δὴ δι᾿ ἥντινα αἰτίαν γένεσιν καὶ τὸ πᾶν τόδε ὁ συνιστὰς συνέστησεν. ἀγαθὸς ἦν, ἀγαθῷ δὲ οὐδεὶς περὶ οὐδενὸς οὐδέποτε ἐγγίγνεται φθόνος.

Let us, then, state for what reason becoming and this universe were framed by him who framed them. He was good; and in the good no jealousy in any matter can ever arise.

The emphatic negatives and repetition of ἀγαθός stress the god's wholly virtuous nature, and at 29e4 this drive towards goodness is identified as the ἀρχὴ κυριωτάτη, 'the supremely valid principle', of becoming and the whole cosmos. Unlike Hesiod's Ouranos, Kronos, and Zeus, Plato's supreme god is not seeking to create a world order that will allow him simply to gain and then hold on to power. This god and those he creates are themselves good and their aim is to create further goodness. Thus the dynastic strife and political power-play of Hesiod's myth must be firmly set aside.

---

[12] *Timaeus* 28c2–5: 'But again, that which becomes, we say, must necessarily become by the agency of some cause (ὑπ᾿ αἰτίου). The maker and father (ποιητὴν καὶ πατέρα) of this universe it is a hard task to find, and having found him it would be impossible to declare him to all mankind.'

In revealing a universe built on principles of goodness, Plato has a
new story to tell. But while this cosmology will be rational and
scientific, there is no sense that it is expected to be anything less
than entertaining. Indeed, the prologue is insistent on this point,
with repeated use of the metaphor of the proposed speeches as
friendly entertainment and feasting.[13] Plato's own myth must not
only correct the faults of the poets but also rival their impact. He
must remove the villains, the trickery, and the violence but retain the
interest of his audience. A major part of his approach is to incorpo-
rate from Hesiod's *Theogony* a storyline based upon procreation and
lineage, and supported by narrative motifs of polarities and their
resolution. Thus, under Hesiodic influence, Plato presents the generation of the cosmos within the context and dynamics of a divine
family.

## FATHERING AND MOTHERING THE UNIVERSE

Plato's account challenges Hesiod's creation myth by revealing radically different starting points at the birth of the cosmos, leading to
contrasting modes of development. But despite their differences,
Plato follows Hesiod in using primal figures to personify the creative
forces and events, and polarities to structure the tale. Let us begin
with Hesiod.

### Primal figures in *Theogony*

After the invocation to the Muses at the close of proem (104–15),
Hesiod's theogony proper begins at 116–22:

> Ἤτοι μὲν πρώτιστα Χάος γένετ᾽· αὐτὰρ ἔπειτα
> Γαῖ᾽ εὐρύστερνος, πάντων ἕδος ἀσφαλὲς αἰεὶ

---

[13] *Timaeus* 17a2–3: δαιτυμόνων, ἑστιατόρων 17b2–4: ξενισθέντας, ξενίοις,
ἀνταφεστιᾶν; 20c1: ξένια; 27a2: ξενίων; 27b8: ἑστίασιν.

ἀθανάτων οἳ ἔχουσι κάρη νιφόεντος Ὀλύμπου,
[Τάρταρά τ' ἠερόεντα μυχῷ χθονὸς εὐρυοδείης]
ἠδ' Ἔρος, ὃς κάλλιστος ἐν ἀθανάτοισι θεοῖσι,
λυσιμελής, πάντων τε θεῶν πάντων τ' ἀνθρώπων
δάμναται ἐν στήθεσσι νόον καὶ ἐπίφρονα βουλήν.

First came the Chasm [Chaos]; and then broad-breasted Earth, secure seat
for ever of all the immortals who occupy the peak of snowy Olympus; [and
misty Tartara in a remote recess of the broad-pathed earth]; and Eros, the
most handsome among the immortal gods, dissolver of flesh, who over-
comes the reason and purpose in the breasts of all gods and all men.

I follow the view that Tartara is here the interior of Earth,[14] and that
there are therefore three primal figures: Chaos, Gaia (Earth), and
Eros.[15] While Hesiod's account of the actual beginnings does not give
much detail, there is nevertheless no indication that Gaia and Eros
are generated out of Chaos. Rather the three seem to have been
generated independently but with Chaos as the first to come into
existence. The Greek word 'Chaos' means 'chasm', its grammatical
gender is neuter, and different interpretations have been offered as to
its nature. The most secure point is that Chaos is a gap or 'yawning
space'.[16] At the very first moment of the universe, then, there is for
Hesiod one entity in existence—a gap—but this one does not on its
own generate the many beings that will follow. So there is no one/
many relationship here of the sort that is found in the various Milesian philosophers, where the whole universe arises out of a single
entity as 'starting point' (ἀρχή).[17] Chaos does, however, initiate its
own family-line by producing from itself two offspring: Erebos and
Night. Erebos (darkness) is grammatically neuter but notionally
male. Night is female, and the two children join in the first sexual

[14] Whether 'misty Tartara' is one of the primal entities has been debated since
antiquity. See J. S. Clay (2003), 15–16.
[15] The summary of Hesiod's lines at *Symposium* 178b3–9 supports this view. But
see also Kenaan, this volume, Ch. 8.
[16] Looking forward to lines 736–45 and 807–14, West (1966) and others interpret
it as dark and gloomy. Stokes, following the implication of line 742–3, posits that 'a
further attribute that may with probability be applied . . . is internal motion' (1963,
21). But aside from the buffeting storm winds in line 742 there is no other suggestion
that *Chaos* denotes disorder.
[17] See Stokes (1962) and (1963).

union of many in the story and produce their opposites Aither and Day (*Theogony* 123–5). The sexual union and reproduction of Chaos' children is made possible by the prior existence of Eros who, notably, gives birth to no line of his own. Vernant considers the place of Eros in Hesiod's trio of primary entities and observes (1990, 466):

Eros makes explicit . . . that which is implicitly contained in the confused unity of the ancestor . . . he makes manifest the duality, the multiplicity, included in the unity.

On this reading, the force of Eros is active at the first stage of existence, exerting his influence over others and making reproduction possible.[18] Both Chaos and Gaia reproduce from within themselves, and thus in each case a multiplicity comes forth from an original unity. Looked at from the point of view of the later universe, there are two primal parents who each produce independently from within themselves. The polarities of one/many and male/female are at work in the first stages of the gods' birth, but that of male/female will become more dominant in the story of Gaia and Ouranos.

Of Hesiod's primal beings, it is Gaia who is by far the most prolific and the chief generator of the many beings to come. Under the force of Eros, Gaia reproduces her male partner (126–8, with West's translation, adapted):

> Γαῖα δέ τοι πρῶτον μὲν ἐγείνατο ἶσον ἑωυτῇ
> Οὐρανὸν ἀστερόενθ᾽, ἵνα μιν περὶ πᾶσαν ἐέργοι,
> ὄφρ᾽ εἴη μακάρεσσι θεοῖς ἕδος ἀσφαλὲς αἰεί

Gaia bore first of all one equal to herself, starry Ouranos, so that he should cover her all about to be a secure seat for ever for the blessed gods.

Although Gaia will continue to reproduce by parthenogenesis and with other partners, Ouranos is Gaia's most important partner, and this marriage of 'Earth' and 'Heaven' stands at the head of the dominant genealogy that will lead to the birth of Olympian Zeus. The marriage of Gaia and Ouranos is one of 'incessant copulation' driven by 'a sort of raw desire, a blind and ongoing cosmic compulsion' (Vernant 1990, 466), which in time produces the 'holy family' (ἱερὸν μένος: 21 and 105;

---

[18] For Hesiodic Eros see also Kenaan's contribution to this volume, Ch. 8.

see also 43–6). The respective roles of male and female are in some sense balanced in this procreation but, as J. S. Clay has shown, there is a pattern in the story whereby it is the female principle that constantly promotes change. In the context of the succession myth of the *Theogony*, Gaia and Ouranos are set in conflict with each other due to Ouranos' desire to block the birth of their children. The male prefers continued sexual access and no generational change, while the female wishes to secure birth and consequent future generations. Commenting on the castration story, Kronos' later swallowing of his children, and Zeus' swallowing of his wife, Metis, J. S. Clay notes the repeated power struggle between male and female (2003, 17–18):

Gaia will always be on the side of birth and of the younger against the older generation . . . Left to itself, procreation would continue, infinitely multiplying and proliferating without brakes. Countering this force for constant change, however, is the male principle, first embodied in Uranus . . . In fact, the history of the gods as a whole can be viewed as an account of the various attempts on the part of the supreme male god to control and block the female procreative drive in order to bring about a stable cosmic regime.

This male/female conflict in the succession story is resolved by the victory of Zeus, and the continued regulation of the female principle through various marital arrangements. Zeus' dynastic marriages help to strengthen his powerbase and earn him the honorific title of 'father of gods and men' (e.g. *Theogony* 47 and 457).[19] As father of all, the single patriarch therefore provides stability and order. Bearing in mind these male efforts at containment and regulation of the prolific female, let us return to the creation myth of *Timaeus* to compare the primal figures presented there.

## Primal figures in *Timaeus*

Plato's cosmology starts with the eternal beings already present. While for Hesiod the cosmos begins with the coming into existence of the three primal figures, for Plato the cosmos is created by specific interactions between pre-existing, ungenerated beings.

[19] See also *Theogony* 468, 542.

Plato's narrative presents a complicated array of eternal entities. Following the order of the narrative and including the grammatical gender (m/f/n) of their names, the full cast-list of Plato's primal figures is:

1. the eternal model for the universe, also identified as the 'Form of Living Creature' (n);
2. the Demiurge, the male creator who works as a craftsman (m);
3. Reason (m);
4. Necessity (f);
5. the Wandering Cause (f);
6. the Receptacle of Becoming (f);
7. disorderly Proto-Matter variously described, e.g. plural 'powers' (f); and
8. Space (f).

Much critical effort has gone into trying to interpret the precise nature of each of these entities. My reading focuses on 'who does what' in Plato's creation story. To understand the functions and roles of the primal figures, it helps to consider both their place within the order of the cosmology story and their inter-relationships.

The narrative structure of *Timaeus* is complex. Plato takes different approaches to explaining the cosmos and beginning with a Prelude at 27c1–29d6 accordingly divides his main exposition into three distinct parts: Part I (29d7–47e2) sets out the work of the Demiurge in creating the components of the universe that are to be everlasting; Part II (47e3–69a5) presents the irrational factors that Demiurge/Reason has to contend with—factors subsumed under the title of 'Necessity'; and Part III (69a6–92c3) tells how Reason and Necessity co-operate to create the human body in all its detail.[20] The most difficult transition in the account is that between Part I and Part II, as Timaeus switches from narrating the work of the rational Demiurge to explaining the effects of irrational Necessity. This transition occurs at 47e3 where Timaeus is explicit about his new theme (47e3–48a2):

---

[20] Cornford's commentary follows the internal structure of Plato's account (1937, xv–xviii).

Now our foregoing discourse, save for a few matters, has set forth the works wrought by the craftsmanship of Reason (τὰ διὰ νοῦ δεδημιουργημένα); but we must now set beside them the things that come about of Necessity (τὰ δι' ἀνάγκης γιγνόμενα). For the generation of this universe was a mixed result of the combination of Necessity and Reason (ἐξ ἀνάγκης τε καὶ νοῦ συστάσεως).

Moreover, he explains that the switch from Reason to Necessity is so marked that it will require a whole new beginning (48a7–b3):

So we must return upon our steps thus, and, taking, in its turn, a second principle (ἑτέραν ἀρχήν) concerned in the origin of these same things, start once more upon our present theme from the beginning (ἀπ' ἀρχῆς), as we did upon the theme of our earlier discourse.

The significance of this new start is further underlined by a second divine invocation,[21] to match that of the Prelude (27c1–d1). Thus parallel invocations launch the accounts of Parts I and II. The Form as eternal model is introduced at the start of Part I (28a7, 30c5–8 and 37c8), followed closely by the Demiurge (28c3, 29a3). In the transition to Part II, the content of Part I is summarized as 'the craftsmanship of Reason' (47e4). Therefore before Part II gets underway, Plato has identified three eternal entities: the Form, the Demiurge, and Reason. The other five primal figures are then introduced in Part II. Indeed, they arrive in quick succession at its opening. Necessity is mentioned first at 47e5, and the Wandering Cause a mere seven lines later, at 48a7. The Receptacle makes its first appearance at 49a6, soon followed by Space at 52a8 and by the disorderly Proto-Matter at 52e2, which is anticipated at 49e.

The careful placing of the primal figures reinforces their distinct roles and relationships in the creation narrative. The perfect Form of Living Creature is the unchanging model for the universe. As the original prototype, the Form plays the first fundamental role. Through the striking phrase 'the craftsmanship of Reason' (47e4), the Demiurge and Reason are given the same function of creating

---

[21] *Timaeus* 48d4–e1: 'So now once again at the outset of our discourse let us call upon a protecting deity to grant us safe passage through a strange and unfamiliar exposition to the conclusion that probability dictates; and so let us begin once more.'

*E. E. Pender*

and organizing the universe. As the leading actor in creation, then, the Demiurge as craftsman-father is the second fundamental entity. Plato's vision of creation is the imposition of rational and orderly structure onto what is disorderly, to bring into being defined objects. Therefore, disorder precedes the cosmos and the Demiurge's work consists of fashioning a rational and orderly physical universe within and out of pre-existing entities that are non-rational and exist at random. In Part II, five figures together constitute this primeval disorder, namely: Necessity, the Wandering Cause, the Receptacle, Proto-Matter, and Space. 'Necessity' serves as a name for the random disorder facing the Demiurge, indicating the inevitability of its influence on creation. The 'Wandering Cause' is the specific cause of disorderly motion, standing in contrast to the cause of orderly motion, the Demiurge himself. The Wandering Cause is responsible for the disorderly motion of the Proto-Matter which is situated within the Receptacle of Becoming. Finally, the Receptacle itself is alternatively referred to as Space. From the point of view of essential narrative functions, these five together share the task of presenting the non-rational pre-cosmic existents that the Demiurge must work upon to create the physical universe. This distinct function is best represented, for me, by the figure of the Receptacle, on account of her central supporting role in Part II of the story. As the personification of the whole phenomenon of pre-cosmic disorder, then, the Receptacle is the third fundamental eternal figure. Therefore Form, Demiurge, and Receptacle can be identified as the three eternal entities fundamental to the creation story.[22] The Form is present in both Parts I and II.[23] The Demiurge is dominant in Parts I and III, but he is not named in Part II, where the main protagonist becomes the Receptacle.[24] Thus the male lead makes way for the female.

---

[22] Andrew Mason rightly pointed out (at a discussion during a seminar held at the Institute of Classical Studies in London in Autumn 2007) that the five primal figures of Part II can be further differentiated, since the Receptacle and Space are passive, while Necessity, the Wandering Cause, and disorderly Proto-Matter are active.

[23] The motif of form and copy is resumed in the final conclusion at 92c7.

[24] Where reference is needed to the creative divinity in Part II, the simple term 'the god' is used, e.g. 53b6, 55c5, and 56c5. The Demiurge reappears at 68e2, in the formal conclusion to Part II, where he is directly named (ὁ δημιουργός).

How, then, do Form, Demiurge, and Receptacle compare with Hesiod's primal figures? The first answer is that there is no direct or easy correspondence. I do not wish to claim that Hesiod's primal three of Chaos, Gaia, and Eros can be matched or specifically identified with this triad in *Timaeus*. Plato has his own, more complex, tale to tell and begins his account from very different starting points. Nevertheless, I venture to suggest that Hesiod is resonating in this and other triadic groupings in *Timaeus*.

Early in Part II, Timaeus looks back to the classification of the universe established in the Prelude (27d5–28a4) and says that two elements were distinguished—model and copy—which now require the addition of a third (48e2–49a4):

Our new starting point (ἀρχή) in describing the universe must, however, be a fuller classification than we made before. We then distinguished two things; but now a third must be pointed out. For our earlier discourse the two were sufficient: one postulated as model (παραδείγματος εἶδος), intelligible and always unchangingly real; second, a copy (μίμημα) of this model, which becomes and is visible. A third we did not then distinguish, thinking that the two would suffice; but now, it seems, the argument compels us to attempt to bring to light and describe a form difficult and obscure (χαλεπὸν καὶ ἀμυδρόν).

But in the Prelude model and copy *were* joined by a third—a cause (28a4–5) soon to be identified as maker, father, and Demiurge (28c3–29a3). What therefore happens here in Part II is that the Demiurge is excluded and replaced by a different third element, alongside model and copy—a third element of a new and quite different nature. Heralded as 'difficult and obscure', Timaeus now introduces, with something of a flourish, the Receptacle (49a4–6):

What nature must we, then, conceive it to possess and what part does it play? This, more than anything else: that it is the Receptacle—as it were, the nurse—of all Becoming (πάσης εἶναι γενέσεως ὑποδοχὴν αὐτὴν οἷον τιθήνην).

In addition to the rhetorical question, the delayed revelation, and the simile of the 'nurse', also notable at 48e2–49a4 is the reference back to the dialogue's striking opening—Εἷς, δύο, τρεῖς ('One, two, three': 17a1)—as the (new) triadic structure of the universe is identified.

As Timaeus continues to grapple with his demanding theme of the Receptacle (49a6–50c6; see e.g. 50c6: τρόπον τινὰ δύσφραστον καὶ θαυμαστόν),[25] he returns to his central point by using another triad (50c7–d2):

> Be that as it may, for the present we must conceive three things: that which becomes; that in which it becomes; and the model in whose likeness that which becomes is born.

After further difficult exposition on the Receptacle (50d4–51e6; see e.g. 51b1: ἀπορώτατά πῃ ... καὶ δυσαλωτότατον),[26] he then turns to a new formulation to summarize what he has been saying. Again there are three elements, this time Form, copy, and Space (51e6–52b1):

> This being so, we must agree that there is, first, the unchanging Form, ungenerated and indestructible ... Second is that which bears the same name and is like that Form; is sensible; is brought into existence; is perpetually in motion ... Third is Space, which is everlasting (ἀεί), not admitting destruction; providing a situation (ἕδραν) for all things that come into being.

Timaeus then settles on a summative classification of the universal order as consisting of Being, Space, and Becoming—again with an emphasis on the number three (52d2–4):

> Let this, then, be given as the tale summed (ἐν κεφαλαίῳ) according to my judgement: that there are Being, Space, Becoming (ὄν τε καὶ χώραν καὶ γένεσιν)—three distinct things—even before the Heaven (οὐρανόν) came into being.

So, in the Prelude to the cosmology there is a single triadic classification (model, copy, and cause: 27d5–28b2) which is used throughout Part I for the Demiurge's work of creation. This grouping is then modified in Part II so that the Receptacle/Space is used alongside model and copy in four further triadic classifications, thus replacing the cause. The substitution in the triadic arrangements of the Receptacle/Space for the cause/Demiurge is due to the exposition shifting its focus away from

[25] The processes of the Receptacle are described as happening 'in a strange manner that is hard to express'.

[26] The Receptacle is said to share in the intelligible 'in some very puzzling way ... and very hard to apprehend'.

the actions of the rational cause and onto the effects of non-rational 'Necessity'. Thus whereas the intelligible Form and the intelligent Demiurge are appropriate subjects in the Prelude and Part I, the non-rational Receptacle and her disorderly associates, all feminine in grammatical gender, must be left aside until the appropriate new beginning of Part II. Because of the divided structure of the myth, Demiurge and Receptacle do not appear together.

Within *Timaeus* as a whole, there are four constituents of the universal order: Form, copy, Demiurge/cause, and Receptacle/Space. So why then does Plato set up and keep revising a triadic structure? In these shifting schemata for the cosmic and pre-cosmic order, Plato seems to be making it difficult to fix on a final way of speaking about the primal entities. Indeed Timaeus seems to be tying himself in knots with his revisions. But throughout the cosmology there is an insistence on the number three. Perhaps the answer is that Plato, with the *Theogony* as his archetypal model, wants to utilize the triad as a successful narrative and explanatory motif, while recognizing that any single triadic group would simply prove insufficient to the needs of his own complex discourse. In short, Plato recognizes the power of the number three in telling a good creation story. Further, a triadic structure in which a male principle in Part I is replaced by, and so balanced against, a female principle in Part II allows him to revisit, in an original way, the male/female polarity so dominant in Hesiod's myth. Plato thus returns to the theme of the primal family but in place of Hesiod's dynastic strife creates a new and harmonious vision of how the cosmos is fathered and mothered.

## The cosmic family

Despite presenting a creation process quite unlike that of Hesiod's 'holy family', Plato follows the *Theogony* in making lineage the dominant motif in his cosmology. Indeed the image of the divine family, re-invented in surprising ways, plays an important part in Plato's story of the birth of the universe.

In Part I of the *Timaeus*, the sole agent of creation is the Demiurge, who is male. As well as being the craftsman of the universe, he is also simultaneously its father.[27] The personification of the Demiurge as a father is most pronounced when we hear of his emotional reaction to the birth of his child (37c6–d1):

When the father who had begotten it (ὁ γεννήσας πατήρ) saw it set in motion and alive, a shrine brought into being for the everlasting gods, he rejoiced and, being well pleased (ἠγάσθη τε καὶ εὐφρανθείς) he took thought to make it yet more like its pattern (τὸ παράδειγμα).

The Demiurge is also the father of the lesser gods.[28] It is notable that there is no mother of the universe in Part I of the myth, where the perfect, rational creatures are formed. But this situation changes with the introduction in Part II of the mysterious trio of Necessity (f), the Wandering Cause (f), and the Receptacle (f). These three non-rational but nevertheless eternal females are brought into view at the pivotal section of 47e–49a which introduces Part II and the creation of the physical universe.

　　When the Receptacle is first introduced, she is described in the arresting simile οἷον τιθήνην ('as it were a nurse': 49a6). A little later she is described explicitly as the 'mother' (μητέρα) of the sensible world (51a4–6):

For this reason, then, the mother and Receptacle (μητέρα καὶ ὑποδοχήν) of what has come to be visible and otherwise sensible must not be called earth or air or fire or water.

Moreover, in between these passages a more extended simile of a family is used to explain the triad of 'that which becomes', 'that in which it becomes', and the model (50d2–4):

Indeed we may fittingly compare the Recipient to a mother (μητρί), the model to a father (πατρί), and the nature that arises between them to their offspring (ἐκγόνῳ).

In Part I of the cosmology the Demiurge is the primal father, but here, following the idea of family likeness, the father of the cosmos is the Form. The Form as father cannot interact directly with the

---

[27] Demiurge as father of universe: 28c3, 32c1, 34a7, 34b9, 37a2, 37d4, 38b6, 38c4, 38e5, 39d7, and 68e4.

[28] *Timaeus* 41a7, 42e6 and 69c4.

mother, since it cannot act at all, and so in the story overall a dynamic cause is needed, which becomes in the figure of the Demiurge an alternative father. The Form as father cannot engage sexually with the mother and nurse of the universe, but can the Demiurge?

Zedda, in his illuminating treatment (2003), has argued that he can and does. The relevant passages are (a) 47e5–48a5 and (b) 56c3–7, the first of which occurs at the very opening of Part II:

(a) For the generation of this universe was a mixed result (μεμειγμένη) of the combination of Necessity and Reason (ἀνάγκης τε καὶ νοῦ). Reason overruled Necessity by persuading her to guide the greatest part of the things that become towards what is best (νοῦ δὲ ἀνάγκης ἄρχοντος τῷ πείθειν αὐτὴν τῶν γιγνομένων τὰ πλεῖστα ἐπὶ τὸ βέλτιστον ἄγειν); in that way and on that principle this universe was fashioned in the beginning by the victory of reasonable persuasion over Necessity (δι᾿ ἀνάγκης ἡττωμένης ὑπὸ πειθοῦς ἔμφρονος).

(b) And with regard to their numbers, their motions, and their powers in general, we must suppose that the god (τὸν θεόν) adjusted them in due proportion, when he had brought them in every detail to the most exact perfection permitted by Necessity willingly complying with persuasion (ὅπηπερ ἡ τῆς ἀνάγκης ἑκοῦσα πεισθεῖσά τε φύσις ὑπεῖκεν).[29]

Zedda's idea that the persuasion in both of these passages is to be understood as erotic is intriguing. This interpretation would present Reason/the god as sweet-talking and seducing non-rational Necessity into co-operating with him as he seeks to bring order. Since what is being ordered is the disorderly Proto-Matter moving *within* the Receptacle, the figures of Necessity and the Receptacle are being blurred. If we add in the Receptacle's role as 'mother' and 'nurse of Becoming', it is tempting to see this as an erotic persuasion that precedes the (metaphorical) birth of the physical cosmos, as Zedda claims (2003, 152–3):

My claim here is that Plato is deliberately using sexual reproduction as a paradigm for the interaction of the Demiurge and the Receptacle... The Demiurge and Necessity, through the act of persuasion, enter into a voluntary partnership. This partnership is a concept of fundamental importance,

---

[29] Cornford's translation masks the fact that the compliance of Necessity is with the 'god' who must be understood here as the Demiurge, although he is not named as such.

implying, on the one hand, that Necessity is willing to co-operate . . . On the other hand, it is clear that the Demiurge cannot, or will not, generate on his own any of the visible instantiations of the universal order he has devised . . . It is only as a combined effort by both rational and non-rational principles that recognizable objects can be built in the Receptacle.

Zedda rightly sees that Reason/the Demiurge cannot simply subordinate Necessity but has to work with it and that the result is a compromise. His conclusion is attractive (2003, 155–6):

> By having two such disparate entities work in partnership, the Demiurge can truly claim that the universe as generated is all-encompassing. Even more importantly, the maker can claim to have constructed a universe based on principles of true *harmonia*. The universe generated by the Demiurge and Necessity embodies all that exists, both rational and non-rational, into one single relationship: φιλία.

One drawback, however, with this interpretation is that *eros* is not formally introduced in the dialogue until 91a1–2, as the gods construct sexual intercourse at the point where women are differentiated from men (θεοὶ τὸν τῆς συνουσίας ἔρωτα ἐτεκτήναντο).[30] That said, it is still the case that sexual intemperance (ἀφροδίσια ἀκολασία) features in the account before the formal creation of *eros*, since it is presented at 86d3 as a disease of the soul (albeit with no explicit use of '*eros*' vocabulary). Given that *eros* is problematic,[31] one can see why Plato would not wish to introduce it overtly into his account of Demiurgic creation, but the procreative imagery nevertheless does seem to raise, albeit implicitly, the possibility of sexual attraction.

With the images of the Demiurge and Form as father and Receptacle as mother, the male/female relationship of *Timaeus* parallels the many liaisons of Hesiod's *Theogony*. While Hesiod's Gaia as planet earth has her own place in Plato's account of cosmogony, it is worth noting how she is also resonating in the female Receptacle out of which the material universe emerges.[32] Both

---

[30] I am grateful to Sarah Broadie for raising this point.

[31] As Diotima's speech in the *Symposium* makes clear, *eros* as lack is at odds with divine perfection.

[32] Sedley in this volume (Ch. 12) shows how Hesiod's Chaos anticipates Plato's Receptacle: both preceded the world but, once ordered, remain within it; and the Receptacle, like Chaos' family, 'represents the world's capacity for variation over

primal figures are mothers defined by their role as 'recipient' of matter—the Receptacle as 'all-receiving' ($\pi\alpha\nu\delta\epsilon\chi\epsilon\varsigma$: 51a7) echoes the ever-receptive Gaia (e.g. $\delta\epsilon\xi\alpha\tau o$: *Theogony* 184; and $\epsilon\delta\epsilon\xi\alpha\tau o$ at 479). The two are further connected when Timaeus refers to both planet earth and the Receptacle as 'nurses': $\tau\rho o\phi o\varsigma$ is used of earth at 40b8; $\tau\iota\theta\eta\nu\eta$ is used of the Receptacle at 49a6 and 52d5; and at 88d6 the Receptacle is both $\tau\rho o\phi o\varsigma$ and $\tau\iota\theta\eta\nu\eta$ of the universe. Like Gaia, the Receptacle seems to personify the 'female procreative drive' discussed by J. S. Clay, for she too is 'infinitely multiplying' as the nurse of ceaseless Becoming ($\dot{\alpha}\epsilon i$: 51a1, 52e5). Further, one may note that as Hesiod's Gaia is twice described as $\tilde{\epsilon}\delta o\varsigma$ $\dot{\alpha}\sigma\phi\alpha\lambda\epsilon\varsigma$ $\alpha i\epsilon i$ ('safe seat for ever': 117 and 128), so Plato's Receptacle/Space is said to provide an eternal $\tilde{\epsilon}\delta\rho\alpha$ ('seat': 52a8–b1) for becoming, since her space is 'everlasting' ($\dot{\alpha}\epsilon i$). Thus Plato follows Hesiod's personification of a primal mother who offers security and stability within her own sphere. Following this parallel, the *Timaeus* can be read as refashioning both Gaia and her partner. For, while Hesiod's Gaia and Ouranos set a template for power struggle and gender conflict amongst the gods, Plato's Demiurge (m) and Receptacle/Necessity (f) create a picture of greater harmony and co-operation at the birth of the universe. The process is not only more orderly and rational but also gentler—with persuasion instead of force and plotting. While the children of Ouranos are explicitly 'hated' by their father (155) who wants to stifle future generations, the Demiurge is joyful at the birth of his child (37c7). While Ouranos is 'jealous' of the strength, form, and stature of Briareus, Kottos, and Gyges (619), the Demiurge emphatically has no jealousy (29e1–2): 'He was good; and in the good no jealousy in any matter can ever arise.' The crucial difference, then, is that the Demiurge seeks to promote goodness and so creates harmony and order, even with his irrational female partner.

space and time' (p. 253). Reading the Receptacle as echoing both Gaia *and* Chaos does not seem to me problematic, since this sort of fluidity seems a familiar part of Plato's technique in creating allusions (see Pender 2007).

## THE TELEOLOGICAL ROLE OF THE MUSES

Plato's allusions to the *Theogony* in the *Timaeus* signal his respect for Greek literary and cultural tradition but also his distance from it. A final significant example of this double-edged technique is the philosopher's inspired re-working of Hesiod's Muses.

The Muses pervade the *Theogony*. Their name sounds the august opening (Μουσάων Ἑλικωνιάδων ἀρχώμεθ' ἀείδειν: 'From the Muses of Helicon, let us begin our singing'), they are a constant presence in the main text, and their sweet song closes the poem (965–6 and 1021–2). From line 25 onwards the Muses are repeatedly identified as Zeus' daughters ('Olympian Muses, daughters of Zeus, the aegis-bearer'),[33] and their closeness is apparent as they 'delight' him (37, 51) with their lovely sound. Born of Zeus and Mnemosyne, the story of their birth is told at 53–67, and then retold at 915–17, and the nine girls are named individually at 77–9.[34] Throughout, the poet attributes his song to the Muses themselves,[35] and thus obeys the goddesses' injunction that he sing of them 'first, last and always' (34).

Throughout the poem the gods in general are said to be 'givers of good things' (e.g. 46: δωτῆρες ἐάων),[36] but they also bestow evils, as with Pandora (570: κακόν; 585: καλὸν κακόν) and the Fates who send 'both good and ill' (906). The Muses, in contrast, stand as the epitome of heaven-sent goodness: their gifts are noted approvingly (e.g. 93: ἱερὴ δόσις 102: δῶρα θεάων), and their song offers 'oblivion of ills and respite from cares' (55), soothing the troubles of all (98–103). Their song is delightful because they 'sing in unison' (39: φωνῇ ὁμηρεῦσαι), and are 'united in purpose' (60: ὁμόφρονας). In contrast to the uproar of the mighty succession battles, the Muses symbolize the concord, peace, and friendship of Zeus' new order. Thus the Muses, and therefore the poem itself, celebrate Zeus' civilizing influence over primitive strife.[37]

---

[33] For the Muses as Zeus' daughters, see also 29, 36, 40, 52, 71, 104, 917, 966, 1022.

[34] Discussed by Regali, this volume, Ch. 13.

[35] Hesiod's song belongs to the Muses: *Theogony* 1, 22–4, 29, 33, 36–52, 75, 104–5, 114–15, 965–8, and 1021–2; cf. Haubold in this volume, Ch. 1.

[36] For the blessings given by the gods, see also 111 and 664.

[37] At *Theogony* 74 Zeus 'set in order' (διέταξεν) his constitution.

The narrative motif of the progressive achievement of order from disorder is replayed in Plato's story of the Demiurge and his harmonious cosmos.[38] Indeed, Plato seems to create an ironic allusion to the victory of Zeus by re-working the theme of bonds (δεσμοί). Zeus, following the example of his father Ouranos, is much given to imprisoning his enemies.[39] But the bonds of the Demiurge are part of his craftsmanship, since the binding of two separate entities to create a unity is a constant image of divine creation in *Timaeus*.[40] Further, the bonds of the Demiurge, achieved through geometrical proportion, unify the universe and bestow upon it an emotional concord (32b8–c4):

καὶ διὰ ταῦτα... τὸ τοῦ κόσμου σῶμα ἐγεννήθη δι᾽ ἀναλογίας ὁμολογῆσαν,
φιλίαν τε ἔσχεν ἐκ τούτων, ὥστε εἰς ταὐτὸν αὑτῷ συνελθὸν ἄλυτον ὑπό του
ἄλλου πλὴν ὑπὸ τοῦ συνδήσαντος γενέσθαι.

For these reasons... the body of the universe was brought into being, coming into concord by means of proportion, and from these it acquired Amity, so that coming into unity with itself it became indissoluble by any other save him who bound it together.

The triumph of the Demiurge's harmonious and unified creation is hymned in the final conclusion of the work (92c7–9)[41] and is also celebrated earlier at the close of Part I. In this structurally significant

[38] Vocabulary of ordering characterizes the Demiurgic arrangement of the universe. See e.g. διατάξας (42e5), διάταξιν (53b8), διατέτακται (75e1); ἀτάκτως, εἰς τάξιν... ἐκ τῆς ἀταξίας (30a5); ἀτάκτως (43b1 and 69b3); ἄτακτον (46e5); and προσέταξεν (69c5).
[39] Bonds and imprisonment in *Theogony*: 157; 501–2; 515; 521–2; 527–8; 616; 618; 651–3; 658–60; 669; 717–18; 729–33 and 868.
[40] *Timaeus* 31b8–c4: 'But two things alone cannot be satisfactorily united without a third; for there must be some bond (δεσμόν) between them drawing them together. And of all bonds the best is that which makes itself and the terms it connects a unity in the fullest sense; and it is of the nature of a continued geometrical proportion (ἀναλογία) to effect this most perfectly.' Bonds and binding in *Timaeus*: 32b1, b7, c4; 36a7; 37a4; 41a8–b6; 43a2–3, a5, d6–7; 44d5; 45a7; 45b4; 69e4; 70e3; 73c3; 74b5, d7; 81d6–7.
[41] In the closing lines the universe is hymned as 'a perceptible god, supreme in greatness and excellence, in beauty and perfection, this Heaven, single in its kind and one'.

passage, as the 'works of Reason' are completed, Plato reveals a new, teleological role for the Muses.

At 44d–46c, Timaeus sets out the structure of the human body, its limbs and organs. After explaining the eyes and vision, Timaeus identifies them as 'accessory causes', used by the creator to achieve 'the best result' (46c7–d1). In the *Timaeus*, the gods give *only* good things to man and, motivated purely by goodness, take care to design a universe where each element has its own and proper purpose. So we learn that the purpose of sight is to allow humans to observe the planets, to invent number, time, and natural science, and so discover philosophy, the greatest 'gift from heaven' (47b1–2: δωρηθὲν ἐκ θεῶν). Timaeus explains that the god gave us vision so that we might observe the revolutions of the planets and so set in order the 'wandering motions' within ourselves (47c2–4). The final lines of this section (47c4–e2) turn to sound, which is likewise identified as 'a gift from the gods' (παρὰ θεῶν δεδωρῆσθαι: 47c5–6). Although the topic of sound is appropriate alongside vision, this short account cannot match that of vision, which is far longer and more developed (45b2–47c4).[42] I suggest that Plato adds this brief discussion of sound in order to create a striking conclusion to Part I through the appearance of the divine Muses.

Sound and hearing, like vision, are designed for the same divine purpose. For philosophy is promoted not only by speech but also by the gift of harmonious music (47c7–d1: δοθέν). Thus the Muses enter the *Timaeus* (47d2–7):

ἡ δὲ ἁρμονία, συγγενεῖς ἔχουσα φορὰς ταῖς ἐν ἡμῖν τῆς ψυχῆς περιόδοις, τῷ μετὰ νοῦ προσχρωμένῳ Μούσαις οὐκ ἐφ' ἡδονὴν ἄλογον καθάπερ νῦν εἶναι δοκεῖ χρήσιμος, ἀλλ' ἐπὶ τὴν γεγονυῖαν ἐν ἡμῖν ἀνάρμοστον ψυχῆς περίοδον εἰς κατακόσμησιν καὶ συμφωνίαν ἑαυτῇ σύμμαχος ὑπὸ Μουσῶν δέδοται.

And harmony, whose motions are akin to the revolutions of the soul within us, has been given by the Muses to him whose commerce with them is guided by intelligence, not for the sake of irrational pleasure (which is now thought to be its utility), but as an ally against the inward discord that has

---

[42] The account of sound takes up *c*.12 lines, whereas that of vision takes up *c*.82 lines.

come into the revolution of the soul, to bring it into order and consonance with itself.

Therefore, the true gift of the Muses—as part of the divine strategy for guiding human beings—is to help the soul become orderly and harmonious. As Sedley has shown, *Timaeus* sets out how mortals can 'become like gods' by attaining inner harmony.[43] Thus the Muses for Plato play a teleological role in leading the human soul towards divine harmony and reason. Plato here pays respect to Hesiod but gives new significance to the poet's insights. At *Theogony* 26, through the gift of the Muses, shepherds may hope to be transformed from 'mere bellies' into poets. But for Plato, in a similar but more radical transformation, the gifts of the Muses are one of the many aspects of creation which offer human beings the chance to transcend entirely their physical limitations and thus become divine.

Setting aside the primitive family strife of the *Theogony*, Plato tells a new tale of first beginnings. Here the principle of goodness is eternally present, the triumph of order and reason is assured by design, and human beings have the means to become like gods. Plato's Muses thus symbolize a cosmos that is perfectly harmonious from the moment of its birth.

[43] Sedley (1997), 328: 'What emerges from the *Timaeus* is that the human soul's capacity to pattern itself after a divine mind is far from accidental, but directly reflects the soul's own nature and origins and the teleological structure of the world as a whole.'

# 12

## Hesiod's *Theogony* and Plato's *Timaeus*

### *David Sedley*

Plato's *Timaeus* could compete for the title of the single most seminal philosophical text to emerge from the whole of antiquity. That is surprising, because the *Timaeus* is Plato's dialogue on physics, a sub-discipline of philosophy which he appears to rank as intellectually inferior to others he practises. But the dialogue is unique in Plato's corpus in synthesizing a systematic world-view out of the disparate ideas that can be extracted from his other writings—in particular his psychology, his ethics, and his metaphysics. It thus came to serve as, in a way, the great manifesto of Platonism, which itself became in turn the most influential and prestigious philosophy that the ancient world produced.

And yet the *Timaeus*, for all its seminal influence, is also a uniquely difficult text to read and decode. It is written in a high-flown prose which shares many of the conventions of poetry, and it constantly shifts its generic register between creation myth, scientific treatise, hymn, dialectical argument, and aetiological fable. From its publication in the mid 4th century BC to the present day its meaning has been unflaggingly disputed, starting with radical disagreements among Plato's own pupils. To make headway with its decipherment is therefore a major desideratum for our understanding of ancient philosophy as a whole.

Hesiod's *Theogony* is among the earliest surviving Greek poems, datable perhaps to around 700 BC. Its narrative is in large measure the history of two divine families,[1] whose successive generations and their interactions can be taken to add up to a religious aetiology of how the world came to be as it now is. For all that it shares with the creation myths of neighbouring cultures, it acquired the status of the paradigmatic Greek creation myth. Hesiod's prestige was high by Plato's day, and there is abundant evidence (open to inspection throughout this volume) that he was close to the centre of Plato's cultural universe. However, Plato's most obvious and well-recognized interest is in Hesiod's other major poem, the *Works and Days*.[2] It is mainly when we turn to his *Timaeus* that the *Theogony* comes into focus. Although Hesiod is never directly referred to there,[3] he is an undoubted presence in the background.

My aim in this chapter is programmatic—to urge that we, classicists and historians of philosophy, spend more time discussing these two texts side by side. Our understanding of both cosmogonies will inevitably be enhanced when we take full account of their shared agenda, their shared problematic, and their shared theological modes

---

[1] For an understanding of the Chaos family, I have benefited a great deal from the introduction of Most (2006).

[2] See further the contributions to this volume by Ford and El Murr, Chs. 7 and 14 respectively.

[3] Hesiod's *Theogony* is, however, clearly in the frame at 40d6–41a3, where Timaeus, having described the creation of the main cosmic players, bows to the poets' authority regarding the genealogy of the lesser gods, the Olympians included:

'To speak of the other divinities and to know about their birth is too great a task for us, but we must believe those who have spoken of them before us. They were, on their own say-so, descendants of the gods, and presumably had clear knowledge of their own forebears. This fact makes it impossible to disbelieve the children of gods, even though they speak without likely and necessary proofs. On the ground that they claim to be reporting family matters, we should follow custom and believe them.'

What ensues is an outline synthesis of Hesiodic and Orphic theogony in five generations: Earth and Heaven; Okeanos and Tethys; Phorcys, Kronos, Rhea, etc.; Zeus, Hera, and the rest of their generation; and finally the offspring of these last. Although the attribution of divine descent to the poetic authorities strictly applies to Orpheus and Musaeus rather than to Hesiod, it can hardly be doubted that all are to some extent in view. The remark of nearly all commentators that the above words are 'ironic' should be resisted: Timaeus is, unlike Socrates, no ironist. His point is simply to make it clear that on the one hand he is not taking the radical step of excluding the traditional deities from his pantheon, but that on the other he has nothing to say about their genealogy beyond what can be read in the poets, since there is no Timaean-style argument from 'likelihood' available.

of representing cosmological truths. For example, there seems little chance of understanding Plato's representation of the world as an assemblage of created deities if we do not keep the Hesiodic model of the world as a divine family constantly in mind. And equally, we are unlikely to get an adequate conceptual grip on that Hesiodic model itself if we do not cast our minds forward to what was to become of it when fully reworked and articulated by Plato.

Did the world have a beginning, and will it one day come to an end? Most ancient thinkers maintained that it had both a beginning and an end, while Aristotle held that it had neither. According to one tradition,[4] this pleasing symmetry between beginning and end had been rejected by just two authorities, Hesiod and Plato, both of whom held that the world on the one hand had had a beginning but on the other hand would last for ever.

Hesiod's poem is all about the successive *births* of the *immortal* beings such as Heaven and Earth that constitute the world. So read at face value he is indeed committed to the asymmetric thesis of a created but immortal world. (In theory, Earth and Heaven could decouple and go their separate ways, but I do not for a moment think that the possibility of such a divorce is contemplated.) Plato's *Timaeus*, again taken at face value, is equally clear on the point. The world was created by an intelligent god, whose superiority as a creative artist guarantees that none but he would even be capable of destroying it, while his goodness guarantees that he will never in fact choose to do so. *Ergo* his creation will last for ever.

The asymmetry between beginning and end thus declared by Plato provoked outrage and controversy from the start. Aristotle thought he could show that it offended against the laws of modal logic, although his attempt to show how resulted in one of the most perplexing chapters he ever wrote (*On the Heavens* 1.12). Meanwhile many of Plato's more loyal pupils set out to show that their master's text, if properly scrutinized and deciphered, does not actually propound the asymmetric thesis after all, and that according to his subtext the world, which will indeed last for ever, was never created but has always existed. His apparent talk of divine creation of the

---

[4] See e.g. Philo, *On the Eternity of the World* 13–17. Sometimes, e.g. Philoponus, *On the Eternity of the World* 212.20–22 Rabe, Hesiod is joined with other 'theologians', such as Orpheus.

world, according to this lobby, is in reality no more than his way of indicating the world's dependence, since eternity, on a superior, intelligent cause. Their interpretation and variants on it continue to find innumerable champions to the present day.

The battle that rages around this question has come to focus largely on the incoherences that would allegedly follow from a literal reading of the creation described in the *Timaeus*. Plato, it is argued, intended us to notice those incoherences and to infer that his cosmogonic story could not be taken literally as a diachronic narrative.[5]

Here is one example. According to the literal reading of Plato's text, the world must have come to be, because it is perceptible, and all perceptible things are generated (28b7–c2). *How* did it come to be, then? Being a good product, it must have come to be as the deliberate act of a good creator, who imposed order on what had hitherto been material disorder. Later on in the dialogue we learn that that pre-cosmic disorder had consisted of chaotic motions in a universal substrate which Plato calls the 'receptacle'. This substrate, the receptacle, seems to combine the properties of what we would call matter and space.[6]

The threat of incoherence in Plato's narrative presents itself when we notice that the pre-cosmic disorder is itself described as having been perceptible (e.g. 30a3, 52e1). If so, by the same argument, that pre-cosmic disorder must itself at some time have come into being.[7] But out of what? Plato would no more than any other ancient thinker allow generation out of literally nothing;[8] but, equally, the disorder cannot have been generated out of previous *order*, since the good creator could never have allowed that to happen. It seems then that no coherent account can be given of the pre-cosmic disorder, if it is understood as a temporal phase in a sequential narrative.

---

[5] That the thesis there is in fact that the world had a beginning I argue in Sedley (2007), 98–107. For the ancient debate, see Baltes (1976–8); for modern arguments against literalism, see e.g. Baltes (1996), Dillon (1997).

[6] I agree with Algra (1995), Ch. 3, that neither aspect can be eliminated in favour of the other.

[7] It would not be sufficient to respond that each discrete *phase* of the pre-cosmic disorder came into being from a prior phase. The premise that 'perceptible' entails 'generated' has to apply to wholes as well as their parts, or the argument at 28b4–c2 for the world's having had a beginning would fail.

[8] The one reported exception is Xeniades, said to have held that everything comes into being out of nothing (Sextus Empiricus, *Against the Professors* 7.53).

This is a good moment to turn to Hesiod. Which of the gods was born first, he asks (*Theogony* 115). His answer is: Chaos. This noun does not mean 'chaos' in our sense. Its more literal meaning is a gaping space, not unlike the word 'chasm' with which it is cognate.[9] Nevertheless, from an early date Hesiod's interpreters also seem also to have associated it with *cheisthai*, 'to flow',[10] thus inaugurating a long semantic chain at the other end of which lies our modern use of the word 'chaos' for disordered flux.

Hesiod's Chaos is a god, despite being grammatically neuter, a grammatical privilege which in Hesiod's huge pantheon it shares with no one except its own offspring Erebos.[11] Being a god, Chaos certainly has not perished, and must therefore still be a presence in the world. Nor is it, like the Titans and other gods who lost the subsequent power struggles, one of the deities now imprisoned in Tartarus and therefore no longer in evidence or causally active in the world. What and where is it today, then? A natural guess is that, like Plato's receptacle, this mysteriously neuter power survives as the substrate on which subsequent deities such as heaven and earth have come to impose their own structure. If Plato's substrate combines the features of space and matter, the same might well be said of Hesiod's Chaos, especially if we suppose that its 'flowing' connotations were felt from the start and were therefore an antecedent of what, in Plato's narrative, reappears as the disorderly flux of pre-cosmic matter. Just as Hesiodic Chaos both preceded the world and remains present today but with order superimposed on it, so too Plato's receptacle has progressed from disorder in the pre-cosmic flux to a fully ordered structure today.

A couple of decades after Plato's death, a schoolboy in Samos named Epicurus, when presented with Hesiod's line 'The very first to come to be was Chaos' (116), asked his teacher in that case what Chaos had come to be *from*. The teacher replied evasively that this was a question for the so-called philosophers;[12] and so began

---

[9] Cf. *Theogony* 700, 814, and χάσμα at 740, with Pender p. 229 above.

[10] Cf. already Pherecydes 7 B1a DK.

[11] Cf. Pender, p. 229. Νείκεά τε Ψεύδεά τε at *Theogony* 229, kindly pointed out to me by Stavros Kouloumentas, are a partial parallel, but differ in that they get their neuter gender from their ordinary lexical usage, rather than as proper names.

[12] Sextus Empiricus, *Against the Professors* 10.18–19.

Epicurus' distinguished career in philosophy. Now young Epicurus' question was indeed a good one, and he himself, then or at any rate later, will have favoured the view that whatever fundamental state of things causally preceded our world had existed from the infinite past.[13] But Hesiod's poem is a 'theogony', literally an account of the 'birth' or 'coming to be' of the gods, and in accordance with his dominant genealogical model of the world's history he is quite explicit that even Chaos initially came to be.

If, as I have suggested, we take Plato's receptacle to fill the traditional role that Hesiod's Chaos had originally occupied, we can work out that, in the absence of any counter-indication by Plato, the default assumption was that the disorderly state of matter which preceded the world's creation had itself somehow at some prior time *come into being*. To recognize this as the default assumption inherited from the existing theogonic tradition is not, of course, to solve the problem of *why* or *how* in Plato's eyes the pre-cosmic flux came into being, let alone to answer the question what can possibly have preceded it. But it is a way of shifting the question with which we have to confront Plato's text. It may be—and the Hesiodic comparison supports the assumption—that Plato was not in the least bothered by his own argument's implication that the disorderly state of matter which preceded the world must have had its own temporal beginning. No doubt it did, because as he says experience confirms that everything perceptible has a temporal beginning, much as in Hesiod every component of the cosmos, the first included, had a birth. If Plato is prudent enough to halt the explanatory regress at this point, rather than embark on identifying a potentially unending chain of temporally prior explanatory principles, that is entirely in keeping with the methodological prospectus of the *Timaeus* (29c4–d3), where the limits of human understanding about the physical world, and the consequent impossibility of eliminating all incoherence from our conjectural reconstruction of its origin, are carefully spelled out. So the Hesiodic comparison offers us, not a resolution of the tensions within Plato's account, but rather

---

[13] Cf. the Epicurean criticism of the *Timaeus* on just these grounds at Cicero, *On the Nature of the Gods* 1.21.

their relocation to a more distant past, from where they can pose a much less immediate threat to the coherence of Plato's narrative.

Such a relocation is not a way of simply shutting one's eyes to the problem. The vast majority of successful historical explanations follow the same pattern, tracing a present explanandum back to some suitably primary state of affairs. The likelihood that the originating state of affairs itself is not one we have the resources to explain by a further journey backwards in time—if, for example, we can trace our own language back as far as, but no further than, a posited origin called Proto-Indo-European—does not undermine the success of our explanation. On the contrary, it encourages the assumption that, but for the remoteness of the events in question, we would be able to repeat that success by uncovering a yet earlier stage in the process. Very few successful historical explanations of anything aspire to go all the way back to the Big Bang, and even fewer to anything beyond it.

If, then, Plato assumes that the pre-cosmic disorder, like Hesiodic Chaos, must have had some origin, but does not aspire to discover what it is, he is to be commended for his prudence.

In this way, a perspective which takes due account of Hesiod offers both a potential gain for the internal intelligibility of Plato's cosmogony, and a cue for us to refocus our own discussions of it.

Let me return now to the intimate link between the twin functions of Hesiod's Chaos, as both space and fluid matter. The impression that it has this dual role is strengthened when we look at its progeny (123–5). Chaos reproduced asexually, giving birth to Erebos (roughly, darkness) and Night. These two siblings then copulated, giving birth to Aither—the bright upper atmosphere—and Day.[14] Thus by its third generation the entirely inbred Chaos family comprised personifications of (a) space, (b) darkness and night, and (c) brightness and day. It seems reasonable to suggest that the family in this way provides the world both with its spatio-temporal *dimensionality*, and with its capacity for change. Chaos itself corresponds to

[14] As I have mentioned, Erebos is, apart from Chaos, the only other grammatically neuter deity in Hesiod, but since it goes on to mate with Night in an explicitly sexual partnership it seems that this descendant of Chaos developed sexual differentiation which had been originally lacking.

the world's full spatial extent, onto which its individual structures have been subsequently superimposed. In addition, night and day jointly represent its temporal extension and variability. Darkness and brightness, for their part, accompany night and day as their respective siblings, being as it were the essential *constituents* of night and day, and thus the very stuff of the passage of time.

Much of the above anticipates in one way or another the role of the Platonic receptacle. In Plato's eyes it is precisely because the changeless Forms had to be imitated in this fluid substrate that our world is, unlike the Forms themselves, inherently subject to change. The creator has done everything possible to limit its liability to change, both by imposing the greatest possible regularity, and by protecting his creation from eventual dissolution. Nevertheless, it is the substrate that, much like Hesiod's Chaos family, represents the world's capacity for variation over space and time.

Is that a bad thing? Is the world a worse place for its unavoidable inherence in space and in changeable matter? In one sense yes, because according to Plato's metaphysics change is inferior to stability, and copy to original. But there is a very old tradition, probably traceable back to Aristotle,[15] of attributing to Plato the further view that matter is the direct cause of the world's imperfections, in the stronger sense that matter has to some extent successfully *resisted* the creator's imposition on it of rational order. In assessing the pros and cons of such an interpretation, it will pay once again to compare Hesiod.

We have so far taken the genealogy of the Chaos family down to its third generation, but there is more of that third generation, followed by a fourth generation, still to add to our list. Night, now reverting to the older family tradition of asexual reproduction, went on to become the mother of the following deities (211–32): hateful Doom, black Fate, Death, Blame, painful Woe, the Lots (*Moirai*), those pitiless punishers the Fates, Nemesis the bane of mortals, Deceit, terrible Old Age, and hard-hearted Strife. And through Strife she in turn became the grandmother of painful Toil, Forgetfulness, Hunger, tearful Griefs, Murders, Battles, Slaughters, Homicides,

---

[15] Cf. Aristotle, *Metaphysics* 988[a]14–17.

Discords, Lies, Disputes, Lawlessness, and Ruin (*Atē*). True, she also had a few less harmful-sounding offspring, namely Sleep, the tribe of Dreams, the Hesperides, and Friendship—and likewise her grandson Oath. But since even Oath is presented as the source of harm—for falsely sworn oaths are the greatest source of misery to mankind (231–2)—we need hardly doubt that taken as a whole the list represents the actual and potential forms of misery.[16]

At all events, there is no doubt that every one of the numerous negative qualities and forces whose personifications are included in Hesiod's divine genealogy is a descendant of Chaos, while none belongs to the other main lineage, the descendants of Earth and Heaven, an entirely separate line which never breeds with the Chaos descendants. If then, as I earlier suggested, Chaos has a role analogous to that of the receptacle in the *Timaeus*, are we to see this Hesiodic antecedent as favouring the traditional identification of matter as the source of evil in Plato's world as well?

We might set out to pursue the question by asking *why* Hesiodic Chaos should turn out to have such disagreeable descendants. Leaving aside for the moment Chaos' great-grandchildren, its grand-children—the offspring of Night—are roughly speaking those threa-tening things that structure and ultimately terminate the passage of a life, such as fate, old age, requital, and death. We might thus far take the picture of existence portrayed in this aetiological part of the genealogy to be one that associates evil with the inevitable passage of time. And that focus on transience fits comfortably enough both with the idea of Chaos as what underlies change, and with the intermediary role which the genealogy assigns to Chaos' daughter Night, the primeval representative of time.

As for Chaos' great-grandchildren, the offspring of its grand-daughter Strife, these can be summed up as the actual or potential sources of conflict, the things which blight lives by exposing and exploiting oppositions latent in them. As Heraclitus was to recognize, Night and her daughter Day in Hesiod already represent the polarization of opposites, which is why he criticized Hesiod for

---

[16] With the possible exception of the anomalously included Hesperides, whose genealogy as daughters of Night I assume to be a remnant of a different and probably non-aetiological tradition.

treating Night and Day as a discrete pair, rather than as the unity they in fact are.[17]

Chaos, then, appears to be the source of evil in Hesiod's universe because, as the substrate of change, it underlies both temporality and conflict. So when we turn back to Plato, it would be natural enough to see this Hesiodic background as lending support to the familiar interpretation according to which he too views the world's material substrate as its source of evil. But before endorsing such a parallelism we should pause for reflection. If Hesiod were indeed to make the most primeval of all deities, Chaos, a causally active presence in the world today, with disruptive effects, that need surprise no one (although I shall in fact argue below for a modification to that way of putting it). But Plato's material substrate, unlike Hesiod's Chaos, is not any kind of deity. The task of our intelligent creators was, according to Plato, to 'persuade' this inherently featureless material stuff to do their work, in other words to channel it into the smooth functioning of the beneficial structures that they devised. If matter had sometimes proved successfully resistant to divine persuasion, as the interpretation holds, the lowliest and most passive thing in the universe would be successfully resisting the best and most active one, god—a concession scarcely reconcilable with Plato's theology. I cannot believe that this is a coherent way to read Plato.[18] Plato may accept that matter is inherently a source of disorder, acknowledging as much by his nickname for it, the 'wandering cause' (48a7). But he also makes it very clear that this was its character *before* the divine creator imposed order on it, and he nowhere concedes that in the created world matter ever succeeds in defying the divine will.[19]

The emerging impression of disparity between the two writers should encourage us to return for a more careful look at Hesiod's

---

[17] Heraclitus 22 B57 DK.

[18] In Sedley (2007), esp. 113–27, I have argued that the text of the *Timaeus* does not support such a reading. Cf. also Lennox (1985).

[19] To pick just one example, the assumption that matter is to some extent recalcitrant has taken such a strong hold that 56c5–6 has regularly been mistranslated 'to the extent that the nature of necessity yielded under willing persuasion', implying that matter (= necessity) did not fully yield. The Greek, ὅπηπερ . . . ὑπεῖκεν, however, means merely 'in whatever way the nature of necessity yielded . . .' See further Sedley (2007), 119 n. 57.

aetiology of evil. This, on closer inspection, is a two-stage one. The actual entry of evil into the human realm belongs, not to the theogony proper, represented by the lineage of Chaos, but to a distinct and later episode (570–616), the creation of woman. This act of creative disruption was Zeus's revenge, expressing his anger at Prometheus' bestowal upon men of the stolen gift of fire. The nature of the troubles inflicted on men by the newly arrived women is set out only sketchily in the *Theogony* (590–612): you can't live with them, because they are parasites; nor can you live without them, however, since to do so condemns you to a childless old age. Hesiod's readers were familiar with the longer version famously set out in the *Works and Days* (53–105), recounting the heterogeneous jarful of troubles that Pandora opened and released into a previously blissful world. The contrast with that alternative version, which made woman above all the *conduit* of evils, brings into relief the distinctive emphasis that marks Hesiod's theogonic account: here women are not the mere conduit, but the very embodiment, of an unhappy human life.

Compare now Timaeus' counterpart to this, his own explanation of the arrival of evil in the world. The world's completeness required maximum likeness to its model, the genus Animal. This in turn required that it should contain all the animal kinds included in that genus (39e3–40a2). Since animals require souls, there had to be souls capable of becoming sufficiently degenerate to be appropriately reincarnated in species below the level of man. And the first stage of degeneration from man is woman, followed by lower and ever lower species (42b2–d2). Hence the creation of women very directly represents the planned (cf. 42d3–4) intrusion of moral badness into the world: in an important sense, women are its primary locus.

The close parallelism between Hesiod and Plato now begins to reassert itself. In both writers it is with the addition of women to the *scala naturae* that the degeneration sets in and unhappiness unmistakably enters the world. No doubt this parallelism should not be pushed too far, since the two authors' conceptions of unhappiness differ considerably. But Plato's story is, if nothing else, very naturally read as his reinterpretation of the Hesiodic aetiological myth, modified in the light of his own moral psychology. Many scholars will insist that in any case Plato's own narrative demands a non-literal reinterpretation on the part of the reader, and that he cannot seriously think that there was a time at which men already existed but women did not.[20] However, the two narratives, the Hesiodic and the Platonic, are precisely comparable in that regard. Each demands a choice between literal and non-literal readings of its chronology. And each, regardless of the reading chosen, retains a strong aetiological message regarding the sources of unhappiness.

What, then, are we to make of Hesiod's double aetiology of evil? On the one hand, the numerous kinds of evil are divinities, immortal offspring of the inbred Chaos family. On the other hand, evils originated from the inclusion of women in the human race. Forming as they do a single narrative, these are not two alternative aetiologies. Rather, we must take it, the proliferation of the Chaos family accounts for the multiplicity of kinds of evil, understood generically, whereas the advent of woman represents the first actual infliction of evils upon humanity. I suggested earlier that the successive generations of the Chaos family stand initially for temporal and spatial dimensionality, and thereafter for the specific kinds of instability (including mortality) and conflict between opposites that can take a hold in such an environment. We can now add that what was there being accounted for was no more than the world's *potentiality* to contain evils of these many kinds. The actual advent of the evils required in addition a specific genetic cause, the creation of woman.

Should we not say very much the same about Plato? The actual arrival of evil is the result of the planned degeneration of souls and the (necessary) creation of degenerate species for them to animate. Prior to that immediate cause, the potentiality for evil was already in place, thanks to the very fact of the world's creation with spatio– temporal dimensions. For it was by generating imitations of the Forms in the inherently changeable receptacle that the Demiurge made the world available as a locus of both good and evil; and the planned degeneration of species that ensued at a later cosmogonic stage depended on that inherent mutability.

If I am right, it is only in a very attenuated sense that matter is, for Plato, the source of evil. As in the *Theogony,* so too in the *Timaeus,*

---

[20] Cf. Baltes (1996), 85.

the world's substrate endows it merely with the formal capacity to contain evils. The substrate does not itself enforce the actualization of that capacity, an actualization which instead is divinely engineered only at an explanatorily posterior zoogonic stage. The substrate, matter, does not itself resist the divine creator, but complies with (is 'persuaded by') him in every phase of the cosmogonic process. And when evil is realized, it descends from a divine cause, rather than representing that divine cause's failure.

What has started to emerge here is a remarkably deep isomorphism between the Hesiodic and Platonic theogonies. There was no prior reason to insist that they must map so closely onto each other. But in the event, the policy of pushing the isomorphism as far as it will go has turned out to provide new perspectives on both Hesiod's and Plato's aetiology of evil.

My aim in this chapter has been to advertise how future discussions of the Hesiodic and Timaean cosmogonies are likely to be informed and enriched if we address the same questions to both in parallel. These two authors' shared agenda and assumptions, along no doubt with significant differences that in the last analysis separate their projects, promise to make the joint study of their cosmogonic myths much more than the sum of its parts.[21]

[21] The chapter by E. E. Pender (Ch. 11) in this volume is an outstanding example of what I have in mind. I also take the opportunity to thank the organizers of the Kyoto–Cambridge Symposium held at Cambridge in September 2006, for which this chapter was originally written, and members of the audience—especially Stavros Kouloumentas—for pressing me on various issues, both at the time and in subsequent discussion.

# 13

## Hesiod in the *Timaeus*: The Demiurge addresses the gods

*Mario Regali*

### INTRODUCTION

There are many ways in which Plato engages with the works of earlier poets, from fleeting allusions to the exegesis of extended portions of text, such as the passage from Simonides discussed in the *Protagoras*. Plato discusses at length the theory of poetry (e.g. Books 2 and 7 of the *Laws*),[1] and even when he does not make explicit connections between his own works and those of earlier poets he often incorporates scenes, motifs, and broader themes drawn from the literary tradition.[2] Thus, the first word of the *Republic*, κατέβην ('I went down'), famously evokes the underworld scenes of the *Odyssey*;[3] while the contest between Callicles and Socrates in the *Gorgias* takes as its model Euripides' *Antiope*.[4] The literary tradition clearly pervades Plato's works in various and often complex ways, despite the fact that he rejects it outright in *Republic* Books 3 and 10. Plato's reception of Hesiod too oscillates between appropriation and rejection: in Books 2–3 of the *Republic*, he criticizes the *Theogony*'s account of Ouranos, Kronos, and Zeus as violent and false (377e6–378b7); yet shortly after he borrows the Myth of Ages from Hesiod's *Works and*

---

[1] Cf. Giuliano (2005).
[2] Cf. Nightingale (1995).
[3] As Capra notes: above, p. 202, with Vegetti (1998*b*).
[4] Cf. Tulli (2007).

*Days* to fashion the so-called 'noble lie', which Socrates introduces as useful for the *polis* and acceptable to the guardians (414b7–415d5).

The *Timaeus* and the *Critias* in particular are good examples of how Plato engages with Hesiod. The *Timaeus*, like Hesiod's *Theogony*, charts the birth of the gods and the formation of the cosmos; and in *Critias* Plato recalls the heroes and their downfall rather as Hesiod does in the *Catalogue of Women*. We might speculate that the *Hermocrates* would have focused on Athens at the time of Plato rather as Hesiod's *Works and Days* focuses on Hesiod's own world.[5] Speculation aside, the overall narrative plan of *Timaeus* and *Critias* certainly looks Hesiodic. Within this larger context, my aim here is to look at one pivotal passage in which Plato establishes a particularly close connection with Hesiod: the moment when the Demiurge addresses the assembled gods in the *Timaeus*. The exceptional importance of this passage was already appreciated in antiquity. Iamblichus wrote an entire book about it,[6] and Proclus describes it as 'inspired, pure, dignified, impressive, and charming, full of beauty, and at the same time concise and elaborate' (ἐνθουσιαστικός ... καθαρός τε καὶ σεμνός, καταπληκτικός, καὶ χαρίτων ἀνάμεστος, κάλλους τε πλήρης καὶ σύντομος ἅμα καὶ ἀπηκριβωμένος).[7] Proclus' enthusiasm seems entirely appropriate, for Plato clearly fashioned the speech with exceptional care and attention.[8] Here, if anywhere, we are at the heart of what the *Timaeus* has to say about the role of the gods in the universe at large. The passage can thus offer a particularly rewarding route into thinking about Plato's relationship with Hesiod.

---

[5] Cf. Capra above, p. 203.

[6] See Proclus (*On the Timaeus* i. 308.19–20 Diehl) and Olympiodorus (*On the First Alcibiades* 2.4–5 Westerink), both of whom mention it. According to Proclus, the book was called 'The oration of Zeus in the *Timaeus*' (Περὶ τῆς ἐν Τιμαίῳ τοῦ Διὸς δημηγορίας). See also Clement of Alexandria *Stromata* 5.102.5 and Origen *Against Celsus* 6.10. Cf. Dörrie and Baltes (1993), 166, n. 4.

[7] Proclus *On the Timaeus* iii. 199.29–200.3 Diehl.

[8] Cornford (1937), 368 points out the careful rhythmic shape of the opening phrase. The rhythm of Θεοὶ θεῶν, ὧν ἐγὼ δημιουργὸς πατήρ τε ἔργων has parallels both in prose (cf. Demosthenes, *On the Crown* 1.1) and in lyric (Alcman fr. 58 *PMG* = 147 Calame). The following phrase has the same type of rhythmic structure. West (1982), 146 postulates a hymn tradition associated with Delphi based on the cretic and paeonian rhythms which Plato employs.

## THE NAME OF THE DEMIURGE

After recounting the making of the visible gods (*Timaeus* 38c3–40d5), and brushing up against traditional theogonic accounts very much in the mould of Hesiod (40d6–41a6), Timaeus introduces the Demiurge addressing the gathered gods (41a6–8):

Θεοὶ θεῶν, ὧν ἐγὼ δημιουργὸς πατήρ τε ἔργων, δι' ἐμοῦ γενόμενα ἄλυτα ἐμοῦ γε μὴ ἐθέλοντος.

Gods, children of gods, who are my works, and whose creator ['demiurge'] and father I am, my creations cannot be dissolved unless I wish to dissolve them.

Referring to himself as 'father', the Demiurge immediately recalls the Zeus of epic, father of gods and men; though the picture is complicated by the language of creation which is never applied to the Zeus of epic.[9] In the phrase that follows, the Demiurge claims that those beings that are born 'through' him cannot be dissolved unless he so wishes: δι' ἐμοῦ γενόμενα ἄλυτα. Careful readers of the passage are likely to notice an echo between the words ἔργων δι' ἐμοῦ and the designation δημιουργός. Indeed, the words can be read as an etymologizing gloss on the noun δημιουργός: the Demiurge is somebody *through whom* the works (ἔργα), which here coincide with the creation of the cosmos, are realized. To be sure, δι' ἐμοῦ does not sound exactly like δημιου-, and by the standards of modern etymology has nothing to do with it. But that is hardly the issue: in the *Cratylus*, Socrates explains that it is possible to add, subtract, or interchange individual letters in search of an etymology (394a1–c8).[10] The (pseudo-)etymology of δημιουργός that is implied here is of a piece with the many etymologies that Socrates suggests in the course of the *Cratylus*.[11]

---

[9] For the phrase ποιητὴν καὶ πατέρα which Timaeus uses to refer to the Demiurge at *Timaeus* 28c3, cf. F. Ferrari (2006).

[10] Sedley (2003), 80–82 rightly draws attention to Socrates' comparison between the smith who reproduces the same metal form from one occasion to the next and the lawgiver who imposes different names upon the same idea (*Cratylus* 389d4–390a2).

[11] Plato is interested in etymologies not just in the *Cratylus*: in the *Phaedrus*, for example, we see a marked interest in the word ὕβρις (238a1–5), and in the etymologies of μαντική and οἰωνιστική (244b6–d5). Cf. Sedley (2003), 33–4. The study of

Nor does it seem out of place in the context of the *Timaeus*, with its pronounced interest in language and the 'correctness' of names. In the introduction to the dialogue, Timaeus reflects on the appropriateness of the nouns οὐρανός and κόσμος (28b2–3),[12] recalling Aeschylus and his reflections on the names of Zeus at *Agamemnon* 160–62. A similar interest emerges when the genus of perceptible entities is said to be homonymous with the species of intelligible ones (52a5). Without establishing etymologies in a narrow sense, Timaeus also reflects on the meaning of the words αἴσθησις (43c5–7), ἡμέρα (45b4–6), θερμόν (62a2–5), and ἐγκέφαλον (73c6–d2).[13]

Etymological speculation was common in Greek literature at all periods, but in so far as it concerned the names and epithets of the gods it was above all associated with the work of Hesiod. The reasons are not difficult to see. The *Theogony* is not only the most famous Greek text about the gods but is also unusually explicit in its search for the true meaning of divine names. Thus, in the proem of the *Theogony*, Hesiod lists the Muses as follows (77–9):

> Κλειώ τ' Εὐτέρπη τε Θάλειά τε Μελπομένη τε
> Τερψιχόρη τ' Ἐρατώ τε Πολύμνιά τ' Οὐρανίη τε
> Καλλιόπη θ'· ἡ δὲ προφερεστάτη ἐστὶν ἁπασέων.

Clio and Euterpe and Thalia and Melpomene
and Terpsichore and Erato and Polymnia and Ourania
and Kalliope, who is foremost among them all.

Each of these names transparently describes its bearer and illustrates what individual Muses contribute to the art of song. By the time they are introduced, their names have already acquired resonance, for Hesiod has just described the power and areas of competence of the Muses in precisely the terms that make up their names. Thus, the name Clio recalls κλείουσιν at 67, that of Euterpe τέρπουσι at lines 37 and 51, while Thaleia takes up ἐν θαλίῃς at 65. Melpomene echoes

etymology helps to advance the cause of *logos*, though for Heitsch (1993, 92) recourse to etymology indicates a weakness in the argument.

[12] Taylor (1928), 65–6 sees οὐρανός as traditional, whereas he regards κόσμος as an innovation which he attributes to Pythagoras, following Aetius (2.1.1) and others. Compare, however, A. Finkelberg (1998), 108–9.

[13] See also Sedley (1998), 141 on *Timaeus* 90c5–6 (εὐδαιμονία/δαίμων).

μέλπονται (66), Terpsichore reminds us of several passages that describe the dancing of the Muses (4, 7, 63), as well as their ability to please, τέρπουσι (37 = 51). For Erato see ἐρατήν (65) and ἐρατός (70); for Polymnia, ὑμνεύσαις (70). Ourania recalls line 71, οὐρανῷ ἐμβασιλεύει; while Calliope, finally, echoes line 68: ὀπὶ καλῇ.[14] As has been pointed out, there is far more at issue here than mere wordplay: Hesiod carefully frames the list of divine names so that it comes to capture the essence of the Muses' nature and activities.[15]

The names of the Muses do not feature in Homer and may be Hesiod's own contribution to divine nomenclature. Yet he was also interested in the meaning of more traditional divine names. For example, he explains the name Aphrodite in his account of the goddess's birth (188–95):[16] Kronos castrates his father Ouranos and throws his genitalia into the sea, and Aphrodite is born from the foam that forms as a result. Perhaps because the etymological connection is less immediately obvious than in the case of the Muses, Hesiod this time spells it out for us (195–8):

> τὴν δ' Ἀφροδίτην
> ἀφρογενέα τε θεὰν καὶ ἐυστέφανον Κυθέρειαν
> κικλήσκουσι θεοί τε καὶ ἀνέρες, οὕνεκ' ἐν ἀφρῷ
> θρέφθη· ἀτὰρ Κυθέρειαν, ὅτι προσέκυρσε Κυθήροις·

> The gods and men call her Aphrodite,
> the goddess born of foam and Cythereia of the lovely wreath,
> because she was born in foam.
> And they call her Cythereia because she came ashore in Cythera.

Hesiod was of course famous for his knowledge of the gods, and his reputation seems to have been based at least in part on his ability to

---

[14] Cf. Friedländer (1931).

[15] Leclerc (1993), 293–6 discusses the order of the Muses and suggests that they are listed in four pairs, with Terpsichore on her own in the middle. The first pair would then represent song itself, the second its effects, the third its setting, and the fourth its form.

[16] The birth of Aphrodite has affinities with that of Pegasus (*Theogony* 280–86). Like Aphrodite, Pegasus springs from a wound (280–81); immediately after his birth, his name is explained by way of an etymology (282–3); he then joins the other gods (284–5) and acquires his place in the divine order (285–6). Cf. Walcot (1958), 9, and Arrighetti (1998), 331, who discusses the narrative function of Aphrodite's four names.

derive their true nature from their names and epithets by way of etymological speculation. We can observe a similar tendency to etymologize divine names in the *Homeric Hymns*,[17] but it was above all Hesiod who became associated with this practice. Plato himself certainly saw him as an expert in divine names and their 'true' meanings, as we can gather, for example, from the *Cratylus*.[18]

## THE SPEECH OF THE DEMIURGE AND THE *WORKS AND DAYS* PROEM

With his etymological play on δημιουργός, Plato takes up a tradition of divine etymologies that his readers would very probably have associated with Hesiod. Indeed, as well as adopting a Hesiodic technique, Plato alludes to a specific Hesiodic model. In the proem to the *Works and Days*, Hesiod describes the power of Zeus in the following manner (1–10):

> Μοῦσαι Πιερίηθεν ἀοιδῇσι κλείουσαι,
> δεῦτε, Δί᾽ ἐννέπετε σφέτερον πατέρ᾽ ὑμνείουσαι.
> ὅν τε διὰ βροτοὶ ἄνδρες ὁμῶς ἄφατοί τε φατοί τε,
> ῥητοί τ᾽ ἄρρητοί τε Διὸς μεγάλοιο ἕκητι.
> ῥέα μὲν γὰρ βριάει, ῥέα δὲ βριάοντα χαλέπτει,
> ῥεῖα δ᾽ ἀρίζηλον μινύθει καὶ ἄδηλον ἀέξει,
> ῥεῖα δέ τ᾽ ἰθύνει σκολιὸν καὶ ἀγήνορα κάρφει
> Ζεὺς ὑψιβρεμέτης, ὃς ὑπέρτατα δώματα ναίει.
> κλῦθι ἰδὼν ἀίων τε, δίκῃ δ᾽ ἴθυνε θέμιστας
> τύνη· ἐγὼ δέ κε Πέρσῃ ἐτήτυμα μυθησαίμην.

Muses of Pieria who give glory through song,
come, tell of Zeus your father and chant his praise—
through whom mortal men are famous or un-famed,

---

[17] E.g. *Hymns* 6.5: Aphrodite/ἀφρός; 19.47: Pan/πάντες; 26.1, 10: ἐρίβρομος, βρόμος (cf. Bromios); 27.5–6: the epithet ἰοχέαιρα implying both 'rejoicing in arrows' (χαίρω) and 'spreading arrows' (χέω); 28.9: Pallas/σείσασ᾽ ὀξὺν ἄκοντα (i.e. Pallas/πάλλω).

[18] For Hesiod's expertise in the correctness of names more generally see Koning in this volume, Ch. 5.

sung or unsung alike, as great Zeus wills.

For easily he makes strong, and easily he brings the strong
  man low;

easily he diminishes the conspicuous and raises the obscure,
and easily he straightens the crooked and deflates the proud,
Zeus who thunders aloft and has his dwelling most high.
Attend you with eye and ear, and make judgments straight
  with righteousness.
And I shall tell true things to Perses.

Having asked the Muses to sing about Zeus, Hesiod proceeds to describe the nature of that god in a protracted relative clause, as is usual in hexameter hymns. Less usual is the fact that the phrase ὅν τε διά offers a transparent etymological explanation for the name Zeus, which Hesiod has just mentioned in the preceding line, in the same metrical position and in the most relevant grammatical form, viz. the accusative Δί(α).[19] Etymological play on διά and Διός/Διί/Δία may already be present in the phrase Διὸς μεγάλου διὰ βουλάς, which is rare in epic but does occur in prominent position in the *Odyssey* and the *Theogony*.[20] Yet only in the *Works and Days* does it appear to take on a decisive function. In the proem to this work, Hesiod describes the power that Zeus wields over mortals, especially with regard to justice as a dominant theme in the poem. Zeus is the god who ultimately enforces respect for justice, and the etymology of his name thus illustrates his central role within the overall conception of the work, and indeed in the world it depicts: whether we take it as instrumental or causal, the word διά encapsulates the essence of Zeus

[19] Norden (1913), 259 n. 1 appears to have been among the first to appreciate this. His suggestion of wordplay is further developed by Deichgräber (1951–2), 19–28, Snell (1954), 111–12, and Verdenius (1962), 116–17, who discusses the epexegetic τε at line 3. West (1978), 138–9 remains noncommittal, but most scholars now accept that the passage amounts to etymological speculation: cf. Pfeiffer (1968), 4–5; Fehling (1969), 262; Arrighetti (1987), 23; J. S. Clay (2003), 76. See also Stanford (1981), 127–40, suggesting (at 132) that it creates an 'atmosphere of solemnity'.

[20] *Odyssey* 8.82, rounding off the first song of Demodocus; and *Theogony* 465, where the phrase describes the impending overthrow of Kronos at the hands of his son. The phrase is also attested in the vulgate text of *Works and Days* 122. For διά referring to the actions of a god from Homer onward see Kühner and Gerth (1898–1904), i. 483–4, and Fraenkel (1950), ii. 333–4. This use of διά seems ultimately to have inspired the etymology for the name Zeus proposed in the *Works and Days*.

(Δία) as arbiter of human destiny.[21] When Hesiod asks Zeus to straighten the judgments with justice (*Works and Days* 9–10) he adds a second striking pun (ἴθυνε . . . τύνη): Zeus is naturally, and appropriately, the god of justice.

When Plato's Demiurge glosses his own name in the *Timaeus*, he has a powerful model in the proem of the *Works and Days*. Plato was certainly familiar with Hesiod's etymology of the name Zeus as developed in the *Works and Days* (*Cratylus* 396a7–b3):

οὐ γὰρ ἔστιν ἡμῖν καὶ τοῖς ἄλλοις πᾶσιν ὅστις ἐστὶν αἴτιος μᾶλλον τοῦ ζῆν ἢ ὁ ἄρχων τε καὶ βασιλεὺς τῶν πάντων. συμβαίνει οὖν ὀρθῶς ὀνομάζεσθαι οὗτος ὁ θεὸς εἶναι, δι᾽ ὃν ζῆν ἀεὶ πᾶσι τοῖς ζῶσιν ὑπάρχει· διείληπται δὲ δίχα, ὥσπερ λέγω, ἐν ὂν τὸ ὄνομα, τῷ "Διὶ" καὶ τῷ "Ζηνί".

For there is nobody who is more the author of life to us and to all than the ruler and king of all. So we are right in calling him 'Zena' and 'Dia', which are one name despite being divided in two, meaning the god through whom all creatures always have life.

A little before the 'swarm' of wisdom,[22] Socrates has moved from Tantalus to the name of his father Zeus, introducing it as a paradigm of appropriate correspondence between the nature of a word and that which it signifies (395e5–396a2: φαίνεται δὲ καὶ τῷ πατρὶ αὑτοῦ λεγομένῳ τῷ Διὶ παγκάλως τὸ ὄνομα κεῖσθαι). That correspondence, however, is difficult to grasp (ἔστι δὲ οὐ ῥᾴδιον κατανοῆσαι), for the name Zeus is formed on the basis of two roots, each of which contributes towards explaining the nature of the god (*Cratylus* 396a2–7):

ἀτεχνῶς γάρ ἐστιν οἷον λόγος τὸ τοῦ Διὸς ὄνομα, διελόντες δὲ αὐτὸ διχῇ οἱ μὲν τῷ ἑτέρῳ μέρει, οἱ δὲ τῷ ἑτέρῳ χρώμεθα—οἱ μὲν γὰρ "Ζῆνα", οἱ δὲ "Δία" καλοῦσιν—συντιθέμενα δ᾽ εἰς ἓν δηλοῖ τὴν φύσιν τοῦ θεοῦ, ὃ δὴ προσήκειν φαμὲν ὀνόματι οἵῳ τε εἶναι ἀπεργάζεσθαι.

For the name of Zeus is really like a sentence, which is divided into two parts, for some call him 'Zena', and use the one half, and others who use the other half call him 'Dia'; the two together signify the nature of the god, and the business of a name, as we were saying, is to do that.

---

[21] Cf. Arrighetti (1998), 380–82. For a different approach see West (1978), 141–2.

[22] See *Cratylus* 397a3–421d6. For the order of the 'swarm', which tends towards encyclopaedic completeness, see Gaiser (1974), 54–9. Baxter (1992), 88–94 sees in it the chaos of mere opinion (δόξα).

Socrates considers the two roots of the noun Zeus in the accusative and dative, Δία/Διί and Ζῆνα/Ζηνί. These are the cases where they are both equally possible, and Socrates interprets the competing forms as indicating that it is on account of Zeus that living beings can live: δι' ὃν ζῆν ἀεὶ πᾶσι τοῖς ζῷσιν ὑπάρχει (396a2–b2). This etymology of the name Zeus (Δία ~ δι' ὄν) evidently recalls that of the *Works and Days*, and perhaps it also points ahead to the *Timaeus*, for the Demiurge too gives life and permanence to all things.[23]

Returning to the *Timaeus*, then, we may ask whether the discourse of the Demiurge has affinities with the *Works and Days* beyond the etymology discussed thus far. Let us take a closer look at the opening of his speech (41a8–b6):

Θεοὶ θεῶν, ὧν ἐγὼ δημιουργὸς πατήρ τε ἔργων, δι' ἐμοῦ γενόμενα ἄλυτα ἐμοῦ γε μὴ ἐθέλοντος. τὸ μὲν οὖν δὴ δεθὲν πᾶν λυτόν, τό γε μὴν καλῶς ἁρμοσθὲν καὶ ἔχον εὖ λύειν ἐθέλειν κακοῦ· δι' ἃ καὶ ἐπείπερ γεγένησθε, ἀθάνατοι μὲν οὐκ ἐστὲ οὐδ' ἄλυτοι τὸ πάμπαν, οὔτι μὲν δὴ λυθήσεσθέ γε οὐδὲ τεύξεσθε θανάτου μοίρας, τῆς ἐμῆς βουλήσεως μείζονος ἔτι δεσμοῦ καὶ κυριωτέρου λαχόντες ἐκείνων οἷς ὅτ' ἐγίγνεσθε συνεδεῖσθε.

Gods, children of gods, who are my works, and whose creator and father I am, my creations cannot be dissolved unless I wish to dissolve them. All that is bound can be undone, but only an evil being would wish to undo that which is harmonious and happy. Therefore, and because you are born creatures, you are not altogether immortal and indissoluble, but you shall certainly not be dissolved, nor be liable to the fate of death, having my will as a greater and mightier bond than those with which you were bound at the time of your birth.

What is immediately striking here is the emphasis on the opposing pair ἄλυτα–λυτόν (insoluble–soluble). The Demiurge is ultimately responsible for both categories of beings, those that can be dissolved and those that cannot; but he is above all associated with things that are permanent—or rather things that he cannot want to dissolve because of who he is. This carefully qualified and intellectually complex statement once again appears to hark back to the opening of the

---

[23] Already Proclus applied the etymology of the *Cratylus* to the *Timaeus* (*On the Cratylus* 48.1–12 Pasquali), because he saw in it a conception of Zeus as πατρικὸν αἴτιον. On the relationship which Proclus establishes between the *Cratylus* and the *Timaeus* on the issue of names see Romano (1987), 128–36.

*Works and Days.* The third and fourth lines of the *Works and Days* oppose ἄφατοι to φατοί, and ῥητοί to ἄρρητοι, as categories of being that Zeus can create at will. Hesiod constructs a chiastic sequence around the two positive members of the pairs, φατοί and ῥητοί,[24] and perhaps there is an echo of this structure when Plato's Demiurge points out that the gods are mortal because they are born, and that their death is only suspended by his continuing good will: compare 'you are not altogether immortal and indissoluble' (*Timaeus* 41b2–3) and 'you shall certainly not be dissolved, nor be liable to the fate of death' (41b4–5): in Plato too, the underlying pattern is A–B–B′–A′. To be sure, such affinities in structure and diction need not mean very much. After all, what we are dealing with here are fairly standard rhetorical tropes. Yet, in the present context the parallels do seem significant: whereas the *Works and Days* oscillates between the fame and obscurity which Zeus metes out among human beings, the *Timaeus* in a similar manner puts the Demiurge in charge of the cosmos and especially the gods.

Moving on in the speech, the Demiurge next explains the role of the gods, which he sees primarily in their attributing mortality to living beings. In such beings, mortality has to be interwoven with immortality, the latter a 'divine thing' (θεῖον λεγόμενον) that guides those who are willing to adhere to justice and respect the gods (τῶν ἀεὶ δίκῃ καὶ ὑμῖν ἐθελόντων ἔπεσθαι: 41c6–d3). The appearance of *dikē* (justice) in this context points once again to the *Works and Days* as a privileged point of reference. We need only think of the invitation to respect justice which Hesiod repeatedly extends to his 'foolish' brother Perses (27–39, 213–18, 274–5);[25] or of *dikē* personified, as she is violently dragged from the unjust city at *Works and Days* 220–24.[26] The violence of that scene suggests that justice could and should in fact be present among human beings, as illustrated at length in the vignette of the good city (225–37).[27] Hesiod returns to the theme of justice in his last address to the 'gift-devouring kings': Justice

---

[24] For the passage as an example of 'polare Ausdrucksweise' see Fehling (1969), 275.

[25] Cf. J. S. Clay (1993).

[26] Brisson (1992: 240, n. 236) recalls *Phaedrus* 248a1–5: the soul that follows the gods most closely ascends to the heavenly sphere.

[27] Cf. Erler (1987).

personified now acts as a bond between the human and divine spheres, sitting by the throne of Zeus and revealing to him the thoughts of humankind (256–62). In a similar manner, *dikē* in the speech of the Demiurge unites the worlds of gods and humans. Indeed, the divine aspects of all living beings manifest themselves precisely in their respect for justice, which, rather like the Hesiodic deity, takes pride of place among the anonymous mass of (other) gods.[28]

Those gods have the task of imitating the Demiurge: just as he manifests his power by creating them, so the gods manifest theirs by generating living beings. Their second task is to look after their creatures: having brought them into existence (ἀπεργάζεσθε ζῷα καὶ γεννᾶτε) they must nurture them (τροφήν τε διδόντες αὐξάνετε), see to it that they grow, and receive them after they have perished (φθίνοντα πάλιν δέχεσθε) (*Timaeus* 41d2–3). The way in which Plato describes the gods' task once again shows interesting parallels with the role of Zeus in the proem of the *Works and Days*. Zeus too is in charge of growth and decay (6), though unlike the gods of the *Timaeus* he acts with sovereign power. Again we encounter a mixture of similarity and difference which invites the reader to compare Plato's creation narrative with the opening lines of the *Works and Days*. At one level, the phrase 'nurture them and receive them again in death' (αὐξάνετε καὶ φθίνοντα πάλιν δέχεσθε) surely puts us in mind of the Hesiodic 'for easily he makes strong, and easily he brings the strong man low' (ῥεῖα δ' ἀρίζηλον μινύθει καὶ ἄδηλον ἀέξει) at *Works and Days* 6; but once acknowledged, the echo precisely emphasizes a crucial difference between the two texts, which is that the gods of the *Timaeus* merely administer an order that a superior power has imposed on them,[29] whereas the purpose of Zeus's actions remains opaque.

---

[28] In the *Critias*, the guardians of ancient Athens lead Attica and Greece on the basis of justice (112e2–6). By contrast, Atlantis is punished by the gods for its unjust acquisitiveness (πλεονεξία ἄδικος: 121b6–7). Cf. Nesselrath (2006), 240–41 and 430–42.

[29] This aspect of the gods' task recalls the *Politicus*: in the myth of the earthborn, the earth takes back the bodies of dead human beings and brings them back to life at the moment when the movement of the cosmos is reversed (271b5–c2). Cf. H. R. Scodel (1987), 79–80. In a sense, the earth in the *Politicus* carries out the task

We have seen that readers of *Timaeus* 41a7–d3 are invited to bear in mind the proem of the *Works and Days*; and that those readers who do take up the invitation are drawn into a complex intertextual relationship.[30] Much of that relationship turns on a comparison between Zeus and the Demiurge specifically as the patrons of an ordered world; and hence also as author figures that render possible any meaningful attempt to describe such a world. In the *Works and Days*, Zeus guarantees justice among human beings and thus ultimately the possibility of teaching Perses 'true things' (10). Although Hesiod distinguishes between Zeus' task of upholding justice and his own teachings in the last two lines of the proem, the two are in fact inextricably linked. As Hesiod himself points out later in the text, human beings, unlike animals, have justice and cannot simply eat one another (276–80). It follows that they must respect one another, work the land, and read their Hesiod. In so far as Zeus makes justice possible he also makes the *Works and Days* possible. In the *Timaeus*, the Demiurge assigns himself a similar role as author of the text. At a fairly basic level, he makes the gods and sees to it that they complete the creation of the cosmos. He is responsible for the cosmos as a whole, and because he acts and speaks in a rational way, Timaeus is in a position to give a plausible account of it.[31]

There is of course a wider context to all of this within the work of Plato. In Book 2 of the *Republic*, Plato modifies the portrayal of the gods found in the literary tradition, including the violent myth of succession as told in the *Theogony* (377e6–378b7). The resulting picture is compatible with that of the Demiurge in the *Timaeus*: god is 'truly good' ($\dot{a}\gamma a\theta\grave{o}s$ $\tau\hat{\omega}$ $\check{o}\nu\tau\iota$) and cannot be the source of

that the Demiurge assigns the gods in the *Timaeus*. For the chronological relationship between the *Politicus* and the *Timaeus* see Brandwood (1990), 249–52.

[30] The echoes that I have discussed suggest a model of reception as '*arte allusiva*': Pasquali (1968). See also Conte (1985), 5–14, in the context of Latin literature.

[31] The order which the Demiurge establishes in the cosmos at large is fundamental also to the story of Atlantis in the *Critias*: only in the world as the Demiurge conceived it can ancient Athens defeat Atlantis, which flourishes on the basis of injustice. The men of ancient Athens adhere to justice because the Demiurge sowed and inaugurated the divine element that guides those who follow justice (41c7–d1). Cf. Johansen (2004), 9. So it is ultimately by divine design that Atlantis is defeated in the *Critias* (121b7–c5). Cf. Brisson (1992), 10 and Nesselrath (2006), 442–50.

evil (379b1–c7). Socrates also rejects the possibility that the gods take different shapes, for god is perfect and cannot therefore undergo change. Already here in the *Republic* we find many of the ideas that are later formulated by the Demiurge in the *Timaeus*: god has no defects when judged by the criteria of beauty and excellence (κάλλος and ἀρετή), and he does not change shape because he is most beautiful (κάλλιστος) and altogether perfect (ἄριστος): 381b12–c8. In a sense we might say that the practice of the *Timaeus* is in accordance with the theory as formulated by Socrates in the *Republic*. That theory, we recall, was developed very much in contrast with the portrayal of the gods in the *Theogony*. When it is put into practice, Plato uses the *Works and Days* as an alternative point of departure.

Zeus as he appears in the proem to the *Works and Days* is seen in the context of the present world, where the violent conflicts of the *Theogony* have been settled and Zeus watches over human beings as they are 'now'.[32] Plato takes up the idea of a superior being in his description of the Demiurge, who unlike the gods comes to possess only positive qualities: he acts in accordance with his *nous*, is 'good' and lacks jealousy. He is 'best' and always adheres to what is most excellent (κάλλιστον: 29e1–30a7). Just as the actions of Zeus in the human sphere are determined by what is just, those of the Demiurge in the *Timaeus* are determined by what is κάλλιστον and according to ἀρετή. Yet the Demiurge, unlike the Hesiodic Zeus, does not need to acquire these qualities over the course of time: he has them already near the beginning of the world. In a sense, what we see here is Plato backdating and generalizing some of the characteristics of Zeus in the *Works and Days*: his central role in the world of human beings, as encapsulated by the etymology Δία/δι' ὄν, and his adherence to higher principles such as justice. In Hesiod, these qualities are the outcome of a long history of strife and cosmic upheaval, a history that Plato criticizes in the *Republic*. In criticizing the gods of the *Theogony*, Plato effectively blots out their history, as Xenophanes had already done when he complained that they did not behave properly (i.e. by human standards).[33] In the *Timaeus*, Plato gives this strategy

---

[32] Cf. Graziosi and Haubold (2005), 35–43.

[33] Xenophanes 21 B11 DK, esp. line 2: ὅσσα παρ' ἀνθρώποισιν ὀνείδεα καὶ ψόγος ἐστίν.

a more positive point: once we have done away with the *Theogony*, the much less offensive Zeus of the *Works and Days* can become a fruitful point of departure for thinking about divine activity near the beginning of the cosmos.

And another shift becomes possible, a shift in voice and perspective. As has often been pointed out, the *Works and Days* proem comes close in form and tone to being a hymn:[34] Hesiod asks the Muses to celebrate their father Zeus and follows his request with a long list of his attributes, a characteristic feature of Greek hymns (1–8).[35] In Book 10 of the *Republic* Socrates admits only praise poetry to the new *polis*: hymns for the gods and encomia for virtuous men (607a3–4). Not by coincidence, the discourses of Timaeus and Critias in Plato's *Timaeus* show clear characteristics of the hymn and the encomium. Socrates sets the tone by declaring himself unable to compose an appropriate encomium of the ideal city (19c8–d2) and by asking Timaeus and Critias to help him out. In reply, Critias takes up Socrates' language: he knows of the greatest deed that Athens has accomplished, and to tell of it would be a fitting way to show his gratitude to Socrates. Moreover, the occasion being the festival of Athena, it seems doubly appropriate to compose an encomium in the manner of a hymn (20e3–21a2). Once again we note the correspondences between the theory of the *Republic* and the practice of the *Timaeus*.

Within this larger context, the proem of the *Works and Days* becomes a natural point of departure for what is in many ways the hymnic core of a hymn-like text. The speech of the Demiurge is of course not technically a hymn, but rather like the proem of the *Works and Days* it shows close affinities with that form: like a hymn it defines the nature and sphere of the gods, though unlike most hymns it looks at the gods as a collective body. There are other differences too: Greek hymns are sung with hindsight by human beings or by the Muses on their behalf, whereas the Demiurge of *Timaeus* describes his own actions and prescribes those of the gods.

---

[34] Lenz (1980), 214–17 reviews the formal similarities as well as differences between the proem and hymns.

[35] Cf. Arrighetti (1998), 380. For the honours (τιμαί) of the gods in the *Homeric Hymns* see J. S. Clay (1989).

There are some famous precedents in the literary tradition, notably in the *Theogony* and the *Homeric Hymns.*[36] As we have seen, the Demiurge outlines the role of the gods and their relationship with living beings. That is broadly what Zeus does in the *Odyssey,* and what the Muses do in the *Theogony,* except that the Demiurge speaks from the vantage-point of an altogether superior being. This in a sense is the divine counterpart to the ideal Platonic hymn in the *Republic,* the ultimate source and model for all human hymns to come. As happens on a much more modest scale in the *Works and Days,* the traditional hymn form is recast and put to new and better use.[37]

That process is all the more revealing as Timaeus has just declined to account for the gods in the traditional way in a passage immediately preceding the speech of the Demiurge. His ostensible reason is that such an account would be too difficult to give (40d6–7). We must therefore, he says, believe those who have described the origin of the gods (γένεσις) in the past because as children of the gods they knew their ancestors (40d7–8).[38] The account of the gods' children cannot be rejected even though it lacks rigorous and plausible proof (40d9–e2). But it can be superseded, and that, surely, is the implication of the speech of the Demiurge which follows immediately after: for here we have an account of the gods that comes not from their sons but from their creator and father. Like any father, the Demiurge knows where his children came from, but more importantly, a father can instruct his children as to their role and nature. That is what the

---

[36] See *Theogony* 22–35, where the Muses explain their power and expertise to an audience of mortals; and *Homeric Hymn* 3 (*To Apollo*) 131–2 where Apollo does the same before an audience of gods. At *Odyssey* 1.32–43, Zeus explains the relationship between gods and humans to the assembled gods. We may also think more generally of the speeches that Zeus delivers in the assemblies of the *Iliad,* e.g. 8.5–27.

[37] Cf. Dalfen (1974), 287–304.

[38] In view of Plato's concept of inspiration (ἐνθουσιασμός) as developed in the *Ion,* the *Phaedrus,* and the *Laws,* the statement need not be taken as ironic: cf. Solmsen (1942), 117; Giuliano (1997), 156. Giuliano identifies a parallel in Aristotle, *Metaphysics* 1074ᵃ38–ᵇ14, which suggests that Timaeus is being quite serious. According to Aristotle, traditional accounts contain a kernel of truth: the divine nature of the first substances. Once that kernel is cleansed of mythical accretions, it has a place in philosophical enquiry. Timaeus' self-professed trust in the poets recalls that of Socrates in the *Philebus* (16c7–8) and the *Phaedrus* (274c1–3).

Demiurge does in his speech ($\mu\acute{a}\theta\epsilon\tau\epsilon$: 41b7). *Mutatis mutandis*, the same shift in emphasis from origins to ends ($\tau\acute{\epsilon}\lambda\eta$) characterizes the *Timaeus* as a whole: although Timaeus does not claim to offer more than a plausible myth ($\epsilon\grave{\iota}\kappa\grave{\omega}\varsigma\ \mu\hat{\upsilon}\theta\sigma\varsigma$),[39] he does give an account of the cosmos that explains not merely how the world came to be but also why it had to be the way it is.

## CONCLUSION

The discourse of the Demiurge enables Plato to comment on, and guide our reception of, the *Timaeus* at a crucial moment in the text. Readers of the *Timaeus* are encouraged to place the Demiurge at the centre of the world, transferring to him the role of father of the gods that had traditionally been reserved for Zeus. In the *Theogony*, Zeus asserts his power over the gods, while in the *Works and Days* he asserts his power over the world of humans with the help of justice ($\delta\acute{\iota}\kappa\eta$). In the *Timaeus*, the Demiurge forms the physical universe, just as he shapes the world of human beings in the *Critias*. At the crucial moment in the *Timaeus* where he clarifies his relationship with the gods—and the gods' relationship with living beings—Plato invites us to conjure up the figure of Zeus in the *Works and Days* proem.

The fact that Plato uses the *Works and Days* as a jumping-off point for his own reflections on the ruling god does not conflict with his ambition to supplant the literature of the past at every level, including that of language which is properly the domain of poetry. Yet Plato does not *simply* attempt to supersede Hesiod: rather, he offers us the figure of Zeus in the *Works and Days* as a model and foil for the Demiurge precisely because his readers recognized in Hesiod a knowledge of the gods that, however inchoate and partial, pointed towards the deeper understanding to which they aspired. Those readers who did make the connection were invited to embark on an intellectual journey from the *Works and Days* to the *Timaeus*, a

---

[39] Burnyeat (2005), 143–65.

journey that led them from outward appearances in the human world (famous vs obscure) to the very substance of the universe (permanent vs temporary); and from a ruling god who they hoped was going to uphold justice to one who painstakingly explains that he can only want what is good.

# 14

## Hesiod, Plato, and the Golden Age: Hesiodic motifs in the myth of the *Politicus*[1]

*Dimitri El Murr*

### INTRODUCTION

In his 1962 paper, 'Hesiodic Motifs in Plato', Friedrich Solmsen noted:

There are certain threads of continuity between Hesiod and Plato, and it may be more profitable by tracing them to study the changes in the pattern of ethical thought than to record the instances in which Plato quotes a line of Hesiod's poetry or endorses a minor item of his thought.[2]

Solmsen is surely right in claiming, first, that Hesiod's presence in the Platonic dialogues far exceeds the few passages where Plato quotes or alludes to some piece of Hesiodic poetry, some of which must have been *loci classici* in his time. Solmsen is surely no less right in claiming, secondly, that it is the ethical, or didactic, purpose of the

---

[1] For very interesting discussions during the conference on Plato and Hesiod, I wish to thank the organizers, also editors of this volume, George Boys-Stones and Johannes Haubold, as well as the participants. I am also grateful to the two anonymous referees for helpful bibliographical suggestions. My greatest debt goes to Paul Demont, who, commenting upon a previous draft of this paper, has made invaluable suggestions for improving it, and to Denis O'Brien, who has painstakingly read my tiresome prose and provided, as he always does, indispensable criticisms.
[2] Solmsen (1962), 179.

Hesiodic poems, especially of the *Works and Days*, that is of crucial interest to Plato. Both points are illustrated by the 'noble lie' of *Republic* Book 3, a classic example of the way Plato invests a Hesiodic motif with a brand-new meaning.[3] The Hesiodic Myth of Ages, which underlies the noble lie, also crops up not infrequently elsewhere. The Hesiodic background to the noble lie of the *Republic* has already been widely explored, but not the influence of Hesiod on the Platonic myth of the Age of Kronos in the *Politicus*, which has so far been surprisingly neglected. My aim, however, is not only to explore Hesiod's presence in the *Politicus* myth. My more specific aim will be to investigate how Plato inherited what was already by his time a traditional story, about life in the reign of Kronos (ἐπὶ Κρόνου βίος), which Roman writers were later to call the Golden Age (*aureum saeculum*).

The myth of the *Politicus* is admittedly one of Plato's more complex fictional stories; not surprisingly therefore it has given rise to numerous debates and controversies. Giving a full account of every textual and philosophical problem raised by the myth is obviously beyond the scope of this chapter. I do however hope to show that one of the crucial issues of the myth is directly connected to the interpretation of its Hesiodic background, and I shall therefore start by spelling out in more detail the issue in question and explain how Hesiod is involved in the controversy.

Determining the precise nature of the Age of Kronos and Plato's attitude to it in the myth of the *Politicus* is still a vexed question which has given rise to alternative accounts. On one traditional interpretation, which goes back at least to Proclus, the myth displays two opposite cosmic phases, each corresponding to a different era in human history.[4] During the age of Kronos, the world is under god's control and moves in one direction. The human herd is being looked after and every aspect of human life is taken care of. There is no need to work, since everything required for human sustenance springs spontaneously from the earth; men too arise directly from the soil, but they do so as old men. As the years pass by, their appearance is increasingly youthful, until the time comes for them

---

[3] On which see Van Noorden in this volume, Ch. 9.
[4] See Dillon (1995).

to disappear and to return to the earth from which they had arisen. The next age is controlled by Zeus. The world now rotates in the opposite direction, left more or less to its own devices. Human beings now have to take care of themselves: men and women give birth to children who grow old, as we do now. They have to work for their food and to protect themselves from other animals. When Kronos lets the rudder of his ship go, the age of Zeus follows, and the world suffers great catastrophes. Everything within the world—human beings, animals, plants—all follow this reversal of cosmic direction.

This account, however widely accepted it may still be, proves on reflection to be deeply problematic. Were it to be correct, then Plato's message would appear to be that the world is *either* controlled by god, *or* is as it is now,[5] with everything happening in a way contrary to that in which it would happen in a divinely ruled universe. Not only would this be blatantly at odds with the standard Platonic teleology, it would also contradict what we are told explicitly in both the *Timaeus* and the *Laws*.

To escape from this conundrum, some scholars, including Christopher Rowe in this volume, have sought to adopt a wholly different interpretation.[6] The age of Kronos, so they claim, cannot properly be read as both cosmologically and biologically opposed to our age, the age of Zeus. Plato's attitude to the primitive simplicity of the Age of Kronos is not sceptical, let alone hostile. The Golden Age of Kronos is an age of rational control which, so Plato implies, ought to be imitated by the human herd living under the reign of Zeus. On this interpretation, the account Plato gives of life under Kronos (ἐπὶ Κρόνου βίος) in the *Politicus* would be parallel to the one given in *Laws* Book 4. The problematic phenomena of biological reversal and catastrophes, traditionally placed in the age of Kronos, would then be confined to an intermediate cosmological phase where god has left the steering of the world. Taken in this way, the Age of Kronos turns out to be Plato's Hesiodic dream: a world totally governed by divinity and reason, where human beings grow up as we do now (albeit they

---

[5] For the difficult question of how to interpret the Stranger's frequent use of νῦν, see below, pp. 294–5.

[6] For Rowe see also his (1995a), 11–13 and (2002). Other scholars taking this position include Brisson (2000) and Carone (2004).

are born from the earth), do no work, suffer no pain, and even, so one may hope and expect, lead a life devoted to philosophy.

However, compelling as this reading may seem when presented so succinctly, the traditional two-phase interpretation is able, or so I shall argue, to do better justice to Plato's use of the Hesiodic Myth of Ages, and indeed to his appropriation of the traditional story of the Age of Kronos from sources other than Hesiod. For, as I hope to make clear, Plato does not inherit the motifs of the Golden Race and of the Life under Kronos only from Hesiod: the Golden Age had been a source of constant elaboration and parody in Plato's immediate past, at the end of the 5th century. Plato, far from taking for granted Hesiod's account of the Golden Race, is consciously depicting an ambiguous picture of life under Kronos, following in that respect a stock motif of Old Comedy. Perfectly good sense can be made of Plato's use, in the myth of the *Politicus*, of several specifically Hesiodic motifs (the Golden Race of Men, or Hesiod's worst night-mare: the grey-haired babies of the Iron Race) as well as more traditional motifs (life under Kronos), provided the role played by the two alternative cosmological phases of the world is accounted for within the dialogue as a whole. The art of statesmanship, which the *Politicus* aims at defining, is possible neither in a world governed by divinity nor in a godless world. The role played by the myth in the dialogue is to guard against both misconceptions.

## PLATONIC COMMENTS ON THE HESIODIC GOLDEN RACE

Although the *Theogony* forms the background to several passages in the dialogues,[7] Plato's interest in Hesiodic poetry is primarily direc-

---

[7] The *Theogony* is quoted only once in the dialogues (at *Symposium* 178b). In the *Cratylus* (396a–c), Socrates draws on Hesiodic genealogy (τὴν Ἡσιόδου γενεαλογίαν) to show up the difference between the instability of the names given to humans, where correctness depends on mere luck or poetic hindsight, and divine names which tell us something true of the unchanging and eternal nature of the gods in relation to the cosmos. On that topic, see Sedley (2003), 87. See also *Timaeus* 40d–41a.

ted towards Hesiod's didactic poem, the *Works and Days*, which he quotes more than a dozen times.[8] More often than not, Hesiod is quoted or referred to in support of a thesis that Plato dismisses.[9] Although Plato would surely not say that Hesiod is 'the best of all poets and the first of the tragedians',[10] he, no less than Homer, represents one of the bastions of traditional Greek education. As the *Republic* makes clear, Plato's view is that Hesiod portrays the gods as immoral and unstable beings,[11] imposing, as he does so, ethical paradigms which inevitably risk corrupting the youth. Moreover, Hesiod's praise of justice and the just life, as Adeimantus points out (*Republic* 363ab), is based on the advantages brought by a good reputation and not at all on the intrinsic value of justice. Hesiod has therefore the same ambivalent status as Homer:[12] his poems will always remain a great source of pleasure to old and learned ears, but they cannot properly be included in a virtuous education.[13]

Outside this criticism in the *Republic*, very few passages of the *Works and Days* give rise to full-scale treatment on Plato's part. One notable exception is his quotation of three verses of the *Works and Days*, crucial to my present topic, in so far as they give us some idea of the nature of a Hesiodic δαίμων.

As Socrates points out, the people of the Golden Race, when they have run their life on earth, become δαίμονες. The Hesiodic lines to which he refers, as recorded in our manuscripts, run as follows (*Works and Days* 121–3 with Most's translation):

---

[8] Cf. Most, Ch. 3 above. More significantly, there is evidence, in the dialogues and elsewhere, of a genuine Socratic interest in the *Works and Days*. See the debate over *Works and Days* 311 referred to in *Charmides* 163b and Xenophon, *Memorabilia* 1.2.56–7, and discussed by Graziosi in this volume, Ch. 6.

[9] Cf. *Lysis* 215cd, where *Works and Days* 25–6 will prove incapable of explaining what the *philon* really is; or *Republic* 363ab, where verses 232–4 are invoked by Adeimantus to account for the argument that justice is profitable for the good reputation it brings in the eyes of the gods.

[10] *Republic* 607a: ποιητικώτατος καὶ πρῶτος τῶν τραγῳδοποιῶν.

[11] See the Kronos/Zeus episode in *Theogony* 453–507, and its criticism in *Republic* 377e–378a.

[12] Hence the rather frequent occurrence of Hesiod's name in a classic sequence where it is usually associated with that of Homer and other poets. See *Apology* 41a; *Republic* 377d; *Symposium* 209d.

[13] On the poetic charm of Homer and Hesiod against whose spell elderly people are immunized by their old age, see *Laws* 658de.

αὐτὰρ ἐπεὶ δὴ τοῦτο γένος κατὰ γαῖα κάλυψε,
τοὶ μὲν δαίμονές εἰσι Διὸς μεγάλου διὰ βουλάς,
ἐσθλοί, ἐπιχθόνιοι, φύλακες θνητῶν ἀνθρώπων . . .

But since the earth covered up this race, by the plans of great Zeus they are fine spirits upon the earth, guardians of mortal human beings . . .

All three verses are quoted, with notable variants, at *Cratylus* 397e–398a (with Most's translations appropriately modified):

Αὐτὰρ ἐπειδὴ τοῦτο γένος κατὰ μοῖρ’ ἐκάλυψεν,
οἱ μὲν δαίμονες ἁγνοὶ ὑποχθόνιοι καλέονται,
ἐσθλοί, ἀλεξίκακοι, φύλακες θνητῶν ἀνθρώπων.

But since fate covered up this race, they are called fine, holy spirits, beneath the earth, defenders against evil, and guardians of mortal human beings.

The last two verses are quoted with two apparently minor differences in *Republic* 5 (469a):

οἱ μὲν δαίμονες ἁγνοὶ ἐπιχθόνιοι τελέθουσιν,
ἐσθλοί, ἀλεξίκακοι, φύλακες μερόπων ἀνθρώπων.

They are become fine spirits upon the earth, defenders against evil, and guardians of speech-endowed human beings.

The divergences between Plato's two quotations and Hesiod's text as recorded in the direct tradition are no doubt simply the result of Plato quoting from memory. The Platonic version, as Martin West has shown,[14] is unlikely to be authentic. Even so, a faulty memory does not, I suspect, explain convincingly the different choice of verb in the quotation in the *Cratylus* and in the *Republic*, neither of which repeats the text found in the manuscripts. In *Republic* 5, where Socrates is justifying the kind of honours due to soldiers who lose their lives in battle, there is no doubt that the verb τελέθουσιν ('are, become') suits his purpose better than the variant found in the *Cratylus* (καλέονται: 'are called'). Conversely, Socrates, in the *Cratylus*, is concerned with decoding the ancient wisdom supposedly encapsulated in the word δαίμων (supposedly derived from the verb δάω, to know) and with the relationship between the

---

[14] West (1978), 181–3, note *ad loc.* Plato's reading has been defended by some scholars: see, e.g., W. Ferrari (1939).

δαίμονες and the Hesiodic Golden Race. In this context, it is the very *name* δαίμων which is at stake. Hence the reading καλέονται. It seems to me that this discrepancy shows clearly enough how Plato may on occasion adapt his Hesiodic quotations to the specific context and purpose of his argument.

But there is more. In both quotations, again provided we adopt West's reading of the text, Plato avoided the stock Hesiodic phrase Διὸς μεγάλου διὰ βουλάς ('by the plans of great Zeus').[15] Is this a trivial lapse of memory? Here too I would venture to suggest that the change of text is deliberate. Significantly, Socrates comments in the *Cratylus* (398bc, trans. Reeve):

So Hesiod and many other poets speak well when they say that, when a good man dies (τις ἀγαθός), he has a great destiny and a great honor and becomes a 'daemon', which is a name given to him because it accords with wisdom (κατὰ τὴν τῆς φρονήσεως ἐπωνυμίαν). And I myself assert, indeed, that every good man, whether alive or dead, is daemonic, and is correctly called a 'daemon' (καὶ ὀρθῶς δαίμονα καλεῖσθαι).

Similarly, in the *Republic*, after having described the type of funerals and posthumous honours that are due to those who died in battle, Plato has Socrates say this (*Republic* 469b, trans. Grube/Reeve):

And we'll follow the same rites for anyone whom we judge to have lived an outstandingly good life, whether he died of old age or in some other way.

As both passages clearly demonstrate, the value attached to the δαίμονες is strictly dependent upon their intrinsic virtue. Obviously, Plato deliberately avoided any reference to the will of Zeus because it had nothing to do with his specific purpose in either passage. What matters to Plato, when the attribution of the name δαίμων is at stake, is not the mere decision of a god, but the rationale that lies behind that decision.

So it is too with the very description of the Golden Race. Bronze and Iron Races were so called by Hesiod because they made use of these metals (*Works and Days* 150–51). But was the same true of the

---

[15] Cf. *Theogony* 465, 572, 653, 730.

word 'golden'? Could this word too have been used literally? Hesiod
gives no explanation of the precise sense in which the first race was
'golden'. To the best of my knowledge, Plato is the first to pose the
question and to explain that 'golden' should not be taken literally to
mean 'made of gold', but rather as meaning 'noble' (ἀγαθόν τε καὶ
καλόν: *Cratylus* 398a). The *Cratylus* and the *Republic* passages may
therefore serve to alert us to the crucial issue at stake in the Age of
Kronos as depicted in the *Politicus*. It is true that Plato never, in the
*Politicus*, uses the language of a 'golden' race; nevertheless it seems
fair to ask whether the nurslings of Kronos lead a life devoted to
virtue and knowledge. More generally: is the Age of Kronos in the
*Politicus* meant to illustrate an age of moral perfection as opposed
to one of moral and political decline? Before pursuing that issue,
we need to engage in a more detailed examination of the life under
the reign of Kronos in pre-Platonic texts.

## THE GOLDEN AGE AND ITS CARICATURE
## IN OLD COMEDY

Let us start with Hesiod's account of the life of the Golden Race
(*Works and Days* 109–19, with Most's translation):

> Χρύσεον μὲν πρώτιστα γένος μερόπων ἀνθρώπων
> ἀθάνατοι ποίησαν Ὀλύμπια δώματ᾽ ἔχοντες.
> οἳ μὲν ἐπὶ Κρόνου ἦσαν, ὅτ᾽ οὐρανῷ ἐμβασίλευεν·
> ὥστε θεοὶ δ᾽ ἔζωον ἀκηδέα θυμὸν ἔχοντες
> νόσφιν ἄτερ τε πόνων καὶ ὀιζύος, οὐδέ τι δειλὸν
> γῆρας ἐπῆν, αἰεὶ δὲ πόδας καὶ χεῖρας ὁμοῖοι
> τέρποντ᾽ ἐν θαλίῃσι, κακῶν ἔκτοσθεν ἁπάντων·
> θνῆσκον δ᾽ ὥσθ᾽ ὕπνῳ δεδμημένοι· ἐσθλὰ δὲ πάντα
> τοῖσιν ἔην· καρπὸν δ᾽ ἔφερε ζείδωρος ἄρουρα
> αὐτομάτη πολλόν τε καὶ ἄφθονον· οἳ δ᾽ ἐθελημοὶ
> ἥσυχοι ἔργ᾽ ἐνέμοντο σὺν ἐσθλοῖσιν πολέεσσιν.

Golden was the race of speech-endowed human beings which the immortals,
who have their mansions on Olympus, made first of all. They lived at the
time of Cronus, when he was king in the sky; just like gods they spent their

lives, with a spirit free from care, entirely apart from toil and distress. Worthless old age did not oppress them, but they were always the same in their feet and hands, and delighted in festivities, lacking in all evils; and they died as if overpowered by sleep. They had all good things: the grain-giving field bore crops of its own accord, much and unstinting, and they themselves, willing and mild-mannered, shared out the fruits of their labors together with many good things.

As this passage makes clear, the men of the Golden Race live a blissful life: they do not have to work for a living since all good things spring automatically from the earth. Not only are they free from toil, but they know neither grief nor sorrow: they live at peace, in close companionship with the gods, and appear to spend their time feasting. Age does not wither them. When, for no obvious reason—unlike the other races, who perish as a consequence of their own inadequacy or folly—they disappear from the face of the earth, they continue to live eternally as guardian *daimones*.[16] From all this, we may infer that the men of the Golden Race led a simple and pastoral life, free from the burdens of life in the city and from the complexities of social organization that go with it.

Hesiod did not invent the idea of a lost age of happiness. That idea goes back a very long way indeed,[17] and was very probably already a well-established motif by the time Hesiod was writing.[18] But two features of this passage are specifically Hesiodic: the association of such a time with the epithet 'golden', and its inclusion in a series of increasingly degenerate 'ages'. Hesiod is also the first writer known to us to give a detailed explanation of how, in the Golden Age, fruits of the earth were produced spontaneously and with no human toil, in sufficient quantity to fulfil every man's need. Most, if not all, of the authors who later took over this myth are heavily indebted for such

---

[16] I will not consider the vexed question of the relationship between this account of the Golden Race and the reference to a quasi-Golden Age in a fragment of the *Catalogue of Women* (fr. 1 MW), when gods and men were dining and sitting in council together. See also *Theogony* 535–6: καὶ γὰρ ὅτ' ἐκρίνοντο θεοὶ θνητοί τ' ἄνθρωποι | Μηκώνῃ.

[17] Cf. Baldry (1952). On the possible oriental sources of Hesiod, see West (1978), 172–7 and West (1997), 312–24.

[18] See Baldry (1952), 84–6 and the useful analysis of Dillon (1992), 23–7.

ideas to the *Works and Days*. There is no need here to investigate in detail how all the salient features of the Hesiodic Golden Race were handled by post-Hesiodic authors.[19] But one detail is crucial for my thesis: the *bios automatos* (the idea that the necessities of life were spontaneously provided by nature)—a theme which attracted the attention first of the poets of Old Comedy, and then of Plato.

The relevant passages from Old Comedy are known to us only as fragments of plays and are recorded, for the most part, by Athenaeus in his *Deipnosophistae*. In Book 6 (267e–270a), the philosopher Democritus of Nicomedia tells us that there was a time when people had no slaves. To illustrate the point, he quotes in succession passages from Cratinus' *Pluti*, Crates' *Wild Animals*, Telecleides' *Amphyctions*, and Pherecrates' *Miners*. The passages he adduces do not specifically mention slaves, but they do depict various circumstances in which things happen 'of their own accord', without human toil.

This is particularly clear in the extracts from Cratinus.[20] Although we do not know much about the plot, it has been argued that the chorus of this play was made up of Titans who lived during the rule of Kronos and called themselves 'the wealthy ones' (*ploutoi*).[21] When they turn up in contemporary Athens it is to put on trial those who are now the wealthy ones in Athens. They have apparently come to see whether the distribution of wealth under the democratic consti-tution conforms to their standards. Especially significant for our purposes is the use of the adjective *automata* in fr. 172 KA, and the comic exaggeration of the idea in fr. 176 KA. Under the reign of Kronos, food was so plentiful that people could play at dice with loaves of bread and use barley-cakes to calculate the stakes. A similar comic fantasy may be found in two fragments of Crates' *Wild Ani-mals*.[22] Here too play is made of the idea of a time, but lying now in the future, when there will be a revival of the *bios automatos*: tables, saucepans, and food will lay on meals of their own accord; the

---

[19] For an exhaustive account of such details, see Gatz (1967).

[20] These are: fr. 172 KA: αὐτόματα τοῖσι θεὸς ἀνίει τἀγαθά; and fr. 176 KA: οἷς δὴ βασιλεὺς Κρόνος ἦν τὸ παλαιόν | ὅτε τοῖς ἄρτοις ἠστραγάλιζον, μᾶζαι δ᾽ ἐν ταῖσι παλαίστραις | Αἰγιναῖαι κατεβέβληντο δρυπεπεῖς βώλοις τε κομῶσαι.

[21] Cf. Baldry (1953), 52.

[22] Crates fr. 17.6–7 KA: ἔπειτ᾽ ἀλάβαστος εὐθέως ἥξει μύρου | αὐτόματος, ὁ σπόγγος τε καὶ τὰ σάνδαλα. See also fr. 16.4–10 KA.

oil-bottle, sponges, and sandals will automatically come forward and perform their specific tasks. In the same vein, an unnamed character in the *Amphyctions* of Telecleides, who could very well be Kronos himself, describes a past life of bliss where 'earth brought neither fear nor illness and the necessities of life were provided for spontaneously'.[23] Other specific features of the Golden Age, such as peace and the absence of illness and sorrow, are present in the rest of the fragment, and so too is their comic exaggeration, with the specific motifs of furniture obeying orders and food preparing and presenting itself to be eaten.

Much more could be said about the *bios automatos* in Old Comedy. A thorough examination would require reading many more fragments, including surviving verses from the *Miners* of Pherecrates, the *Sirens* of Nicophon, the *Thurio-Persians* of Metagenes, and the *Golden Race* of Eupolis. But the only point needed for my argument is that in all these fragments, and nowhere else in 5th-century literature, the Age of Kronos is depicted as a land of fantastic abundance, with the fantasy of spontaneous blessings showered on the Hesiodic Golden Race taken to absurd extremes.[24]

Comical and ludicrous as they are, these parodies of the Hesiodic Golden Age also serve a serious critical purpose. The plays to which the fragments belong all seem to have been performed within a fairly short period of time, some twenty years between 435 and 415 BC. The frequent use made of this theme is no doubt a sign that successive comic poets were aiming at upstaging their predecessors. But there is more to this phenomenon than just intertextuality. As has been argued convincingly, the Hesiodic motif of the *bios automatos* allowed comic poets to caricature and thus to criticize Pericles' thalassocratic regime in the war with Sparta.[25] Unlike the tragic poets, who favour the Olympian gods and the traditional heroes of the Homeric past,[26] the poets of Old Comedy not only focus on present-day Athens, but look with favour on the Kronian deities as opposed to their Olympian counterparts. The Kronian gods belong

---

[23] Telecleides fr. 1.3 KA: ἡ γῆ δ' ἔφερ' οὐ δέος οὐδὲ νόσους, ἀλλ' αὐτόματ' ἦν τὰ δέοντα.

[24] For a careful and suggestive study of these fragments, see Ruffell (2000).

[25] See Ceccarelli (1996).

[26] On this, see Carrière (1979), 90.

to a Golden Age identified as a land of Cockaigne, by comparison with which present-day Athens appears to be caught in the turmoil of Hesiod's Iron Race. For the comic poets, dreaming of a happier existence elsewhere is no longer a mere refuge from present ills: it functions as a satire on present times. The myth of the Kronian Age can hardly have been considered a serious historical thesis by them, and their frequent use of it may well show that the myth had moved from a simple 'utopia of escape' to a more complex 'utopia of reconstruction'.[27] No longer a mythic evocation of a lost paradise, the Age of Kronos has entered the realm of serious speculation about the conditions of an improved society.[28]

The satirical use of the myth in the concluding decades of the 5th century is essential for a clear appraisal of its use in a dialogue whose dramatic date falls just at that time. To explain Plato's use of the myth, it is too simplistic to appeal merely to Hesiodic elements of the Kronian age. Once we appreciate the satirical background attaching to the Hesiodic myth in the late 5th century, we recognize that there is no need at all to suppose that Plato shares Hesiod's unreservedly positive perspective when describing the nurslings of Kronos. Such a presupposition is adopted, with varying degrees of explicitness, by most of those who uphold the interpretation of the *Politicus* myth in which there are three distinct zoogonical stages.[29] By means of such an interpretation, they hope to insulate the Age of Kronos from its entanglement with features of the Hesiodic myth that would appear to be at odds with a life of unadulterated bliss. Once we take into

---

[27] I repeat Mumford's familiar terminology. See Mumford (1959) and Dillon (1992), 21–2.

[28] On the different types of 'automatist' utopias involved in the fragments of Old Comedy, see Ruffell (2000).

[29] See Rowe (2002), 169: 'Vielleicht ist das alles ja nur ein Teil der *paidiá*, mit der die Geschichte gewürzt ist. Doch in diesem Fall scheint sie denn doch etwas *zu viel* an Spielerei zu bieten: die halbe Weltgeschichte wirkt nun absurd—und da das Zeitalter des Kronos als besser hingestellt wird als das Zeitalter des Zeus, ist es eindeutig *unsere* Hälfte, von der ein solches Bild gezeichnet wird.' Carone (2004), 95 argues that the three-stage 'interpretation of the direction of ageing in the era of Cronus in the myth would in turn match its legendary background', i.e. would allow us to locate the grey-haired new-borns of Hesiod's Iron Race in the intermediate phase which, one might add, would in turn allow us to find in the myth a proper Golden Age, parallel to Hesiod's Age of the Golden Race.

account the satirical background, we no longer need to extract from the myth two distinct ages, one drawing on the Hesiodic Golden Age, the other including features taken from the Iron Age. Such seemingly disparate features are no longer incompatible.

No less erroneous is the claim that the god Kronos is portrayed by Plato as a god of beneficent intelligence. Kronos, as has been convincingly argued, is a deeply ambiguous figure throughout Plato's writings, and extant accounts of his reign are far from invariably favourable.[30] It is true enough that Kronos, in the *Cratylus* (396bc), is an emblem of rationality and divine intelligence. But in the *Gorgias* (523b–e), he is presented in quite a different light, as passing judgements that are arbitrary and superficial.[31] The disparity excludes any simple appeal to the presence of Kronos as decisive for Plato's conception of his rule in the *Politicus*.[32]

By contrast, the arguments in favour of the traditional two-stage view of the myth seem to me to be overwhelming. Plato took up and continued the attitude to the Age of Kronos with which his readers would have been familiar through Old Comedy.[33] Just as Old Comedy had recourse to the topsy-turvy world of the Kronian age as a means of social and political critique, so Plato's Age of Kronos in the myth of the *Politicus* is clearly intended as an era where everything is back-to-front. Instead of dismissing such a reading on the grounds of its supposed incompatibility with the teleology

---

[30]   On this, see Vidal-Naquet (1981) and Tulli (1990).

[31]   The versatility and double-sidedness of Kronos goes back at least to Homer and Hesiod. In the *Theogony*, as in Homer, Kronos is regularly described as 'crooked of counsel' (ἀγκυλομήτης: see *Theogony* 18, 137, 168, 473, 495; *Iliad* 2.205; *Odyssey* 21.415) and presented in an entirely negative light: his characteristics are parricide, infanticide, even cannibalism, and a complete absence of moral standards. Elsewhere, Kronos, the king *par excellence*, whom Hesiod calls 'the first king of the gods' (θεῶν πρότερος βασιλεύς: *Theogony* 486), is associated exclusively with a life of bliss and happiness. The ambiguity is to be seen in various cults and rites (the *Kronia*) surrounding the god. See Versnel (1987).

[32]   It is only because he takes no account of such diversity that Brisson (2000), 182–3 is led to make much of the figure of Kronos in *Laws* 4 in support of his three-stage interpretation of the myth of the *Politicus*.

[33]   The myth is not the only passage in the *Politicus* where Plato takes up motifs that are found in Old Comedy. The paradigm of weaving as a whole (*Politicus* 279a–283b) has to be read conjointly with its comic counterpart in Aristophanes' *Lysistrata*. See Lane (1998), 164–71 and El Murr (2002), 61–6.

displayed in the *Timaeus* or the Golden Age of the *Laws*, our study of the Hesiodic elements that Plato chose to combine in the *Politicus'* Age of Kronos should aim to make sense of them within the myth and the dialogue as a whole.

## MAKING SENSE OF HESIOD: THE AGE OF KRONOS IN THE MYTH OF THE *POLITICUS*

This is how the visitor from Elea depicts the life of the nursling of Kronos in the *Politicus* (271c–272b, trans. Rowe, slightly modified):

As for what you asked, about everything's springing up of its own accord for human beings (περὶ τοῦ πάντα αὐτόματα γίγνεσθαι τοῖς ἀνθρώποις), it belongs least to the period that now obtains; it too belonged to the one before. For then the god began to rule and take care of the rotation itself as a whole, and as for the regions, in their turn, it was just the same, each and every part of the world-order having been divided up by gods ruling over them. As for living things, divine spirits had divided them between themselves, like herdsmen, by kind and by herd, each by himself providing independently for all the needs of those he tended, so that none of them was savage, nor did they eat each other, and there was no war or internal dissent at all; and as for all the other things that belong as consequences to such an arrangement, there would be tens of thousands of them to report. But to return to what we have been told about a human life without toil, the origin of the report is something like this (τὸ δ' οὖν τῶν ἀνθρώπων λεχθὲν αὐτομάτου πέρι βίου διὰ τὸ τοιόνδε εἴρηται). A god tended them, taking charge of them himself, just as now human beings (καθάπερ νῦν ἄνθρωποι), themselves living creatures, but different and more divine, pasture other kinds of living creatures more lowly than themselves (ἄλλα γένη φαυλότερα αὐτῶν νομεύουσι); and given his attention, they had no political constitutions, nor acquired wives and children, for all of them came back to life from the earth, remembering nothing of the past. While they lacked things of this sort, they had an abundance of fruits from trees and many other plants, which grew not through cultivation but because the earth sent them up of its own accord (πολιτεῖαί τε οὐκ ἦσαν οὐδὲ κτήσεις γυναικῶν καὶ παίδων· ἐκ γῆς γὰρ ἀνεβιώσκοντο πάντες, οὐδὲν μεμνημένοι τῶν πρόσθεν· ἀλλὰ τὰ μὲν τοιαῦτα ἀπῆν πάντα, καρποὺς δὲ ἀφθόνους εἶχον ἀπό τε δένδρων καὶ πολλῆς ὕλης ἄλλης, οὐχ ὑπὸ γεωργίας φυομένους, ἀλλ᾽ αὐτομάτης ἀναδιδούσης τῆς γῆς). For the most part they would feed outdoors, naked and without bedding; for the blend of the seasons was without painful extremes, and they had soft beds from abundant grass that sprang from the earth.

As should now be clear, the similarities between the Hesiodic and the Platonic accounts of the Age of Kronos are obvious and numerous. Spontaneous growth from the earth, absence of agriculture, freedom from the need to work, no pain, no war, no political organization are all features common to both accounts. There is, furthermore, no doubt that for Plato, as for other authors before him, it is the *bios automatos* that constitutes the essential feature of the Hesiodic Golden Age. So much is clear from the repetition of the phrase in the *Politicus* passage just quoted (περὶ τοῦ πάντα αὐτόματα γίγνεσθαι τοῖς ἀνθρώποις at 271d1; τὸ . . . τῶν ἀνθρώπων λεχθὲν αὐτομάτου πέρι βίου at 271e4) as a way of describing the Golden Age as a whole.

At the same time, there is a striking difference in tone and scope between Hesiod's and Plato's accounts of the Kronian age. Where Hesiod is merely listing the essential aspects of such a life, Plato's account is explanatory. He is not merely following Hesiod, he is also out to explain how the life under Kronos should be understood. In this connection, Plato introduces distinctive features that have no counterpart in Hesiod's text.

First, and unlike the Golden Race of Hesiod, Plato's nurslings of Kronos do not live 'like the gods' (ὥστε θεοί: *Works and Days* 112), but like animals herded by the gods. There is therefore the same difference between the divine and the human as there is between a human herdsman and his animal flock. Secondly, the 'automatic' aspect of life does not concern plants and trees alone, nor the production of food in general; it concerns people too, who are born from the earth. In Hesiod, it is the gods who make the successive races of men (ποίησαν: *Works and Days* 110), whereas in Plato, men arise spontaneously from the earth. Just as the human flock seems closer to animals than to the gods, so too the generation of men, in the Platonic Golden Age, has more to do with the growing of plants than with any divine creation. Thirdly, and most importantly, people do not merely spring from the earth but are born fully grown and grey-haired, and grow *backwards* to infancy, until they disappear once again into the earth. As has long been recognized,[34] this is surely another reference to Hesiod and more precisely to the fate of our own iron race, which will be destroyed 'when the time comes for men to be born grey-haired' (εὖτ᾽ ἂν γεινόμενοι πολιοκρόταφοι τελέθωσιν: *Works and Days* 181).

The two idyllic pictures, although similar, are not identical. Hesiod's *bios automatos* is merely life in close association with the gods, where all good things spring from the earth, and where men can spend their time feasting, and are forever young (*Works and Days* 113–14). In Plato, men (who still do not suffer from thirst and hunger, nor from pain or war) do not live with the gods but are cared for by them. Everything, including the human race itself, springs automatically from the earth and, if men are spared the trials of old age, it is only because, though increasing in years, they are always becoming younger. By taking the 'automatic' aspect of life to its extreme so as to account for the birth of men, and by adding a significant feature taken from the Hesiodic Iron Race (the grey-haired new-born men) to his Age of Kronos, Plato's picture of mankind under Kronos is ambivalent. He has not drawn it exclusively from Hesiod's Golden Age, nor has he drawn it exclusively from its Iron counterpart.

So does Plato provide us with any indication as to how we should consider this surprising Age of Kronos? At the end of his portrait of the nurslings of Kronos, the visitor from Elea asks Young Socrates (*Politicus* 272b–d, trans. Rowe):

*Visitor*: Would you be able and willing to judge which of the two [lives] is the more fortunate?
*Young Socrates*: Not at all.
*Visitor*: Then do you want me to make some sort of decision for you?
*Young Socrates*: Absolutely.

---

[34] Cf. Adam (1891), 445.

*Visitor*:  Well then, if, with so much leisure (πολλῆς σχολῆς) available to
them, and so much opportunity to get together in conversation (διὰ λόγων
δύνασθαι συγγίγνεσθαι) not only with human beings but also with animals—
if the nurslings of Kronos used all these advantages to do philosophy, talking
both with animals and with each other, and enquiring from all sorts of
creatures whether any one of them had some capacity of its own that enabled
it to see better in some way than the rest with respect to the gathering of
wisdom, the judgement is easy, that those who lived then were far, far more
fortunate than those who live now. But if they spent their time gorging
themselves with food and drink and exchanging stories with each other and
with the animals of the sort that even now are told about them, this too, if I
may reveal how it seems to me, at least, is a matter that is easily judged. But
however that may be, let us leave it to one side, until such time as someone
appears who is qualified to inform us in which of these two ways the desires
of men of that time were directed in relation to the different varieties of
knowledge and the need for talk.

In this passage there is a clear opposition between alternative
visions of the Golden Age. The first is undoubtedly Platonic, an age
devoted to intelligence and philosophy, where men and animals talk
with each other and enquire about philosophical truth.[35] The second,
I venture to suggest, is Hesiodic, a time when people spend their
lives feasting, gorging themselves with food and drink. In the passage
quoted, the Stranger pointedly shies away from deciding whether
the age just depicted is a truly philosophical one or an absurd land of
Cockaigne. But are we to take him at his word? Does he really leave
the choice open? I suspect not. Had his implication been that the Age
of Kronos was an authentically philosophical Golden Age, in
the sense that Socrates gives to the epithet 'golden' in the *Cratylus*,
I hardly think he would have refrained from telling us so, clearly and
explicitly. Given that the happiness of the nurslings of Kronos is
strictly dependent upon their practice of philosophy, I suspect that

---

[35] Talking with animals is an aspect of the Golden Age that is absent from Hesiod's
account, but which may have its roots in Empedocles (see DK 31 B130) or in Orphic
vegetarian circles. This aspect of the Golden Age is also found in later accounts: see,
e.g. Babrius, *Aesopian Mythiambics prologue* 1–13 (esp. 5–8: ἐπὶ τῆς δὲ χρυσῆς καὶ τὰ
λοιπὰ τῶν ζῴων | φωνὴν ἔναρθρον εἶχε καὶ λόγους ᾔδει | οἵους περ ἡμεῖς μυθέομεν πρὸς
ἀλλήλους, | ἀγοραὶ δὲ τούτων ἦσαν ἐν μέσαις ὕλαις).

the question raised by the Stranger is merely rhetorical. The Age of Kronos does not allow of the 'leisure' (σχολή) intrinsic to philosophy which Socrates described earlier on, in the *Theaetetus* (172c–177b).[36] Even if, as happens all too often, Plato appears to leave the point in abeyance, the Stranger's implication that the Golden Age is not conducive to the philosophic life is all of a piece with the way he draws on heterogeneous features of the Hesiodic account, adding details taken from a very different moment in the story of the human race.

What sense can then be made of so extraordinary an interpretation of the Hesiodic text? In the *Politicus*, the two eras of the world are opposed as regards cosmology, zoogony, ethics, and politics. In the Age of Kronos, the world is led in its course by the god; in the Age of Zeus, the world is 'self-governing' (αὐτοκράτωρ: 274a5). Under Kronos, men are born 'put together in the earth from different elements' (ἐν γῇ δι' ἑτέρων συνισταντων: 274a3–4) and grow from apparent old age to apparent youth; under Zeus, they are born 'from one another' (ἐξ ἀλλήλων: 271a4), must 'bear, give birth, and rear ... themselves by themselves' (κυεῖν τε καὶ γεννᾶν καὶ τρέφειν ... αὑτοῖς δι' αὑτῶν: 274a6–7) and grow up as we do, passing from youth to old age. Under Kronos, god takes care of every aspect of human life;[37] under Zeus, men are deprived of divine guidance and have to fend for themselves (δι' ἑαυτῶν τε ἔδει τήν τε διαγωγὴν καὶ τὴν ἐπιμέλειαν αὐτοὺς αὑτῶν ἔχειν: 274d4–5). Finally and most importantly, under Kronos politics is not an issue at all, since cities and constitutions are not needed and do not exist; under Zeus, whether or not there were cities, the Stranger makes no mention of them. There is certainly a desperate need for statesmanship, but such an art, however indispensable, would seem to be a most ungrateful task, given that the world and its inhabitants cannot but fall gradually into chaos.

The whole myth is predicated on the opposition between the life under Kronos and that under Zeus, but what exactly are we to make of it? What is the underlying philosophical message that

---

[36] See Demont (1990), 303–10.
[37] Cf. the definition of herding at *Politicus* 268ab.

Plato would have his readers draw from the detailed opposition between the two ages? By contrasting two eras, Plato is contrasting two antithetical states of the universe and of the human condition. Neither allows for the art of statesmanship but not, I shall argue, for the same reason.

What would the world be like if an omnipotent and beneficent divine being was in charge of every aspect of human life? Certainly the world as a whole would be good, as the Stranger repeatedly claims it is (e.g. 273bc). Even so, human beings would be but pale shadows of themselves. They would certainly share common features with the men of the Hesiodic Golden Race, but would they be recognizably human at all? Their happiness would be comparable to that of an animal herd. This is why Plato manipulates Hesiod as he does. The Age of Kronos is an ambivalent age: it is good, in so far as god has made it to be so; but it is equally true that, under the reign of the divine shepherd, humans are 'virtuous', but with no mention made of the need for them to act rationally in order to be so. Therefore such people can hardly be said to be happy in any way that would be recognizably Platonic.[38]

What of the Age of Zeus? This age raises the converse question. What if the world were deprived of divine control and men left to their own devices? In a world where god is absent, humans would have to govern themselves with no help from the divine. Such a state, the Stranger claims, will inevitably bring them to the verge of chaos. So much the myth tells us and so much everyone, two-stagers and three-stagers alike, agrees on. Disagreement turns on the specific problem raised by the repeated use the Stranger makes of the adverb νῦν in his account of the Age of Zeus, so referring it to our present time.[39] What is the relation between the mythical 'now' of the cosmological phases and our supposed human historical time within the cycle? Is Plato, contrary to what he states explicitly in the *Timaeus*

---

[38] There is a useful analysis in Nightingale (1996), 76–91, even though her overall interpretation of the opposition between the two eras does not, I think, quite catch Plato's meaning.

[39] See 269a3, a5, 270b7, d4, 271d2, e6, 272b2-3, c5, c7, 273b6, 274d7, e10. I leave aside passages where νῦν is used to refer to the dramatic present of the discussion.

and the *Laws*, saying no more than that our age is not and cannot be political? I think not.

The *Politicus'* account of our age (the age of Zeus) coheres well enough with the *Timaeus* and the *Laws*, provided we understand that such an age is not political in Plato's own, heavily determined, sense of that word. Our present state is indeed the world the Stranger and Young Socrates live in. It is perhaps the world we live in too, a world which corresponds to the sort of humanism Protagoras would have defended.[40] In such a world, a true Platonic art of statesmanship is as impossible as it would be in the preceding age of Kronos, but not for the same reason. I have argued elsewhere that the entire division that unifies the *Politicus* as a whole is not at all a classification of existing constitutions and political organizations. These are all, in so far as they belong to our own age of Zeus, not πολιτικούς but στασιαστικούς (303c). What the rest of the division defines is the art of statesmanship as it should be, not as it is actually practised and considered in existing cities.[41] The art of statesmanship, so I would maintain, the true art of shepherding the human flock, as Plato likes to call it, has features in common both with the Age of Kronos and with the Age of Zeus, but would be equally impossible in either of them. The Age of Kronos, as I think everyone will agree, has no need of politics. The Age of Zeus, I venture to assert, has great need of politics, but politics, in the Age of Zeus, is impossible.

So radical an opposition may be thought far-fetched. Yet the alternative, three-phased, account of the myth fails to do justice to what I consider a very important point indeed. Is this interpretation of the myth compatible with the accounts given in the *Timaeus* and the *Laws*? Whatever the answer to that question, there remains a significant discrepancy. The myth of the *Politicus* relates a cyclical history, the indefinite repetition of identical phases in the history of the world.[42] The *Timaeus* and the *Laws* make no reference to such

---

[40] Hence the echoes between the Age of Zeus and the *Protagoras* Myth. See Miller (1980), 50–52.

[41] See El Murr (2005).

[42] Only once is this stated explicitly (274d) but the use of the adverb πάλιν (τὸν δὲ δὴ κόσμον πάλιν ἀνέστρεφεν εἱμαρμένη τε καὶ σύμφυτος ἐπιθυμία: 272e) has surely to be taken as an allusion to the eternal cyclical alternation, as does the use of ἀεί (273c5).

cyclical history at all. This need not mean that Plato was confused or
that he contradicted himself, but simply that there is no point in
trying desperately to make teleology coincide with what seems to be
an intrinsically anti-teleological device. Even though Plato depicted
an indefinite alternation of cosmic cycles, the two worlds within the
myth may well be intended as no more than two contradictory
aspects of one and the same world, our world. Such an idea fits in
happily with the end of the dialogue where the specific task of the
statesman is at last defined.[43] The king has to weave into one solid
fabric moderation and courage, two opposite tendencies of the
human soul. Moderation draws us to peacefulness but also to what
might now be called angelism, two features of the Age of Kronos.
Courage may lead us to impetuosity but also to war, as it risks doing
in the Age of Zeus. By reconciling these opposite tendencies, the
true art of statesmanship will no longer be caught in the web of a
cyclical myth.

There is another passage in Plato where the Age of Kronos again
appears free of its Hesiodic overtones. In the fourth book of the *Laws*,
life 'in the time of Kronos' is seemingly at odds with my interpretation of the Age of Kronos in the *Politicus*. The myth is the same, but
this age is now unambiguously depicted as a time of bliss (μακάρια
ζωή) where 'all things spring up of themselves and in profusion'
(ἄφθονά τε καὶ αὐτόματα πάντ᾽ εἶχεν: 713c). Why is this a time of
bliss for the human race in the *Laws*? The Athenian speaker argues
that, because men are incapable of governing themselves without
divine guidance, Kronos appointed *daimones* to rule over the cities of
men and to ensure justice and good legislation. The difference is
crucial. In the myth of the *Politicus*, so I argued, the *polis* was
significantly absent from the Age of Kronos, as also from the Age
of Zeus—so much so that the Age of Kronos as a whole was represented as non-political. In the *Laws*, by contrast, the Age of Kronos is
essentially political and serves to illustrate a key Platonic principle
(713e–714a, trans. Bury):

And even today this tale has a truth to tell, namely, that wherever a state has
a mortal, and no god, for ruler, there the people have no rest from ills and

---

[43] Cf. *Politicus* 305e–311c.

toils; and it seems that we ought by every means to imitate the life of the age of Kronos, as it is called, and order both our homes and our states in obedience to the immortal element within us, giving to reason's ordering the name of 'law'.

Again, these words enshrine a typical Platonic adaptation of 'what is usually called the life under Kronos' (ἐπὶ τοῦ Κρόνου λεγόμενος βίος). If the Age of Kronos is interpreted as the rule of the element of *nous* within us, there is certainly nothing to cavil at. But is it so in the *Politicus*? My claim is that it is not. At this point, one may indeed feel the temptation to read into the *Politicus* myth three phases rather than two, and in so doing to argue that the Age of Kronos in the *Politicus* is similar to the one depicted in the *Laws*. But even were one to yield to that temptation, there would still be no purpose for *poleis*, or for any other political organization in the Age of Kronos in the *Politicus*. From that point of view, the two passages remain irretrievably different. In the *Laws*, the Age of Kronos is introduced so as to explain what a truly political regime is, namely a constitution ruled by the power of intelligence. In the *Politicus*, nothing is said of the use of human *nous*, and we cannot be certain that the nurslings of Kronos lived a happy life by Platonic standards.

# 15

## On grey-haired babies: Plato, Hesiod, and visions of the past (and future)

*Christopher Rowe*

The immediate and particular subject of the present chapter is an aspect of the cosmic myth of Plato's *Politicus*; the larger subject is Plato's relationship to Hesiod. It is beyond doubt that Plato knows Hesiod's texts well, and that he frequently appropriates from them— as indeed he does from others, not least in the context that concerns me in this chapter—for his own writerly purposes. But how, exactly, does he use his Hesiod,[1] and for what purposes? The question arises with special urgency in the case of the *Politicus* myth; or at any rate,

---

[1] The following discussion may well turn out to have consequences for an understanding of Plato's relationship to other authors and texts, but in a chapter of a volume devoted specifically to Plato and Hesiod it seems reasonable enough to leave others to one side. One of the many sources of the present chapter was a dispute in 2000 between Denis O'Brien and myself, orchestrated by Suzanne Stern-Gillet, which turned out to centre on the influence of *Empedocles* on the myth. Empedocles' presence is plainly guaranteed, not just through the very idea of a cosmic cycle, but more directly by *Politicus* 269e–270a, where the speaker offers his own explanation of the two opposed movements of the heavenly bodies, rejecting *inter alia* the possibility that they might be caused by 'two gods, whichever they might be (τινέ), thinking opposite thoughts' (270a). But, equally plainly, it will be a separate question how closely Plato's own cosmic cycle imitates Empedocles'. In particular, is Plato's composed of balancing periods of 'forwards' and 'backwards' motion, or is backwards motion rather an anomalous state (as I myself suppose)? (If we do take the latter option, that will hardly suffice to rule out other Empedoclean connections, especially in relation to zoo- or anthropogony, but, again, such connections are beyond my brief in the present context.) For a nicely balanced approach to the issues here, see Viano (1994).

so it does on the commonest and simplest—or apparently sim-plest[2]—interpretation of the story as it is told. To put the problem succinctly: a feature that in Hesiod's account of the races of man[3] belongs not just to the present and distinctly unsatisfactory iron race, but even to the further *decay* of that race, appears in the *Politicus* myth—on the commonest type of interpretation of that myth—to belong rather to a time that is by and large marked as *preferable* to this age of ours. This is the 'age of Kronos', which precedes and will follow the present age, the 'age of Zeus'. Admittedly, the visitor from Elea who tells the story does not say outright that the Kronian era was/will be preferable; he rather says that it would have been/will be providing that a certain condition is fulfilled.[4] However, it is the time when the world is ruled directly by divine providence, and

---

[2] Only '*apparently* simplest', I propose, because the interpretation in question in fact leaves the story with a number of puzzling turns—on one of which the present paper will focus. The supporters of this interpretation—who represent the vast majority of those who have written about the myth apart from Lovejoy and Boas (1935), Brisson (2000), and Rowe (1995a, 2002)—will most probably claim that it is the most 'natural' reading, one that goes most with the grain of the story; more natural, at any rate, than the rival interpretation I shall offer, because it involves the reader's having to supply rather less by way of filling out the Eleatic Stranger's sketch. This rather depends, in my view, on how carefully one reads the story: no one has yet, to my knowledge, provided a step-by-step justification of the standard interpretation, of the kind offered in Rowe (1995a) for the rival interpretation. But in any case, as I have suggested in Rowe (1995a), (2002), and elsewhere, the problems that affect the standard interpretation should be more than enough to make us question why it has proved so popular. (For the standard, two-stage interpretation of the myth see e.g. McCabe 1997, 2000; Horn 2002; El Murr in this volume, Ch. 14. The Rowe version of a two-stage interpretation significantly differs from that in Brisson 2000; Lovejoy and Boas 1935 contains little by way of detailed commentary.)

[3] *Works and Days* 106–201. For commentary see especially Rosenmeyer (1957) and West (1978).

[4] Namely, that the people of that era used/will use the opportunities open to them to do philosophy, and to make better progress than 'the rest' (presumably their counterparts in the present era) in the gathering together of wisdom: 272bc. (These opportunities include especially having the time to 'get together in conversation not only with human beings but also with animals': 272b9–c1. The idea of conversations with the animals looks, and is, odd: why would the visitor want to suggest—if he represents a broadly Socratic/Platonic point of view, as he otherwise seems to do— that *animals* have any philosophical insight to share with humans? Or is there a covert allusion here to the kind of talking with animals that the Socrates of the *Phaedrus* proposes as a condition of the philosophical life: talking to the animal(s) in *us*?)

indeed it is this that constitutes the chief reason for its introduction, because the myth is intended precisely, or primarily, to illustrate the difference between divine and providential[5] rule and the kind of rule that human governors—statesmen—exercise.

Here is the point at issue. There was a period in world history,[6] according to the story, when (*Politicus* 270d–271a):

> ... the age[7] of each and every creature, whatever it was, stopped increasing, and everything that was mortal ceased moving in the direction of looking older, but changing back in the opposite direction grew as it were younger, more tender; the white/grey[8] hairs of older men became black, while in turn the cheeks of those who had their beards became smooth again, returning each to his past bloom, and the bodies of those in their puberty, becoming smoother and smaller each day and night, went back to the form of new-born children, becoming like them both in mind and in body; and from then on they proceeded to waste away until they simply disappeared altogether. As for those who died a violent death at that time, the body of the dead person underwent the same effects and quickly dissolved to nothing in a few days.

But now the visitor from Elea goes on to link this scenario with ancient accounts of people being born from the earth, which constituted one strand of what, according to his original suggestion at 269b, the myth—in its guise as a report of what actually happened—would turn out to explain (*Politicus* 271bc):[9]

---

[5] 'Providential', that is, to the extent that all human needs are taken care of by divine agency—except for those that ultimately determine the real quality of human life (as measured by its degree of rationality). See *Politicus* 268c, 274e–275c.

[6] And will be again (and again), since the story is of a recurring cycle; usually, however, like the teller of the story (the man from Elea), I shall refer to the cycle in the past tense—which will primarily pick out the parts of the cycle as instantiated in the times immediately preceding the present 'age of Zeus'.

[7] Or—for reasons that will emerge—as I supply in my published translations of the dialogue (which I shall for the most part follow, while sometimes diverging from them, and without warning), 'the *visible* age . . . '

[8] I.e. λευκοί: see n. 13 below.

[9] The other strands were (1) a story about the temporary reversal of the movements of the heavenly bodies, as a portent relating to the quarrel between Atreus and Thyestes (268e–269a); (2) the story about the time when Kronos was king (269a7–8: in the Hesiodic account, at *Works and Days* 111–20, associated with a golden race: following West (1978), I leave out of account the further reference to Kronos in the 'alternative version' in what he prints as *Works and Days* 173a–e); and (3) 'the report

I think we must reflect on what is implied by what we have said. It follows on the passage of old men to childhood that from the dead, lying in the earth, men should be put together again there and come back to life, following the direction of the reversal, with coming-into-being turning round with it to the opposite direction, and since they would according to this argument necessarily come into existence as earth-born, would thus acquire the name and have the report told about them[10]—all those of them, that is, whom god did not take off to another destiny.

Given that some of those who are reborn will have died in old age and with grey hair, there will have been some who were actually born—from the earth—already grey-haired; indeed, given that getting old is a normal part of human development, from our perspective,[11] one that occurs unless something goes wrong, it will be quite the normal and natural thing for 'new' humans, in the era in question, to be born with grey hair.

This, I propose (and my chapter depends on the proposal), is Plato's take on the Hesiodic idea of babies being born already grey-haired—that Zeus will destroy the iron race too, 'when they come to be born with grey hairs on their temples' (*Works and Days* 181). Given that the general connection with the Hesiodic story of the races is already established, from the beginning, with the reference to the 'age of Kronos',[12] Plato's earth-born grey-hairs will themselves be in direct line of descent from Hesiod's iron-age babies[13]—for they are babies themselves, despite being 'old men': this is the point of Plato's having the storyteller specify that 'everything that was mortal ceased

---

that earlier men were born from the earth and were not reproduced from one another' (269b2–3).

[10] That is, by people who lived at the beginning of our era, bordering on the time when things happened backwards (i.e. backwards from *our* point of view): 271a7–b3.

[11] Which is the relevant perspective, for the moment, in so far as what is being described is a reversal just from our point of view. The dead people who are coming back to life will be people who aged in the ordinary way before being buried (and so lived in the previous era, since dying in the new one is a matter of disappearing into thin air; no burial for them).

[12] See n. 9 above.

[13] Plato uses λευκός, whereas Hesiod has πολιός (πολιοκρόταφοι): πολιός, according to LSJ, is 'rare in Att. Prose', though in fact Plato does use it (as it happens, of Parmenides: *Parmenides* 127b). But here in the *Politicus* he needs λευκός in any case to contrast with μέλας ('white hairs became black': cf. e.g. *Lysis* 217d, where μέλας becomes substituted for ξανθός for the sake of the same opposition).

moving in the direction of *looking* older (ἐπὶ τὸ γεραίτερον ἰδεῖν), and instead changing back in the opposite direction grew as it were (οἷον) younger, more tender'. Time still moved forward then, so that what *we* now call younger-looking *they* called older. Certainly, time itself—history—is not reversed, as we can deduce from what happened to 'those who died a violent death at that time': they didn't get to live once more the lives they had before they were killed, but instead simply came back briefly to life in order to die in the way people at that time all died (by vanishing).[14] So although the earth-born would, for us, have been 'old', from the point of view of the Kronians themselves they are babies, and their old age will be our babyhood. *Ergo*: there was (and will be again)[15] a time, in the history of the universe as described by the Stranger, when babies were born 'with grey hairs on their temples'. There are important differences, to be sure, between the Stranger's version of the idea and Hesiod's: in Hesiod,[16] in particular, there is no reversal, only the implication of a quick end to an already unhappy era—in so far as *these* babies will have a very short life, whereas in Plato's version they will have a long one. But this connects with another, and more crucial difference: things that just happen, for no particular reason, in the Hesiodic version tend in the Platonic one to have rather particular, and openly stated, reasons for happening. As so often, Plato improves on (or at any rate changes) what he appropriates—here 'explaining' how it came about that people were once born 'old'.[17]

By now the problem should be plain enough. Given the standard interpretation, one of the very features that Hesiod uses to mark the catastrophic end to our era will be used, in Plato's version, as a central feature of the age of Kronos. Indeed, the situation will be even stranger than this, for the image of the grey-haired new-born is part of a description, in Hesiod, of an age that is in other respects

---

[14] I take it that they can't be reborn like the others, from the earth, for the simple reason that they were never *in* the earth (they died at or during the reversal, when there was no time to bury them—or else, in the cataclysm, people had other priorities). This is one of several places in the myth where seriousness is combined with what may be described, at the least, as a degree of playfulness.

[15] I.e. because Plato's story is one of a recurring cycle of ages/races.

[16] As McCabe, for one (2000, Ch.5), points out.

[17] For larger-scale 'improvements' on things appropriated, see below.

the mirror-image of the golden, Kronian age: thus the very first thing Hesiod tells us about the life of the iron men is that it was/is/will be a life of toil and trouble (*Works and Days* 176–8. True, 179 tells us there will be good things mixed with the bad, but these good things are to say the least somewhat underdetermined). Now of course, on the standard interpretation, the age of grey-haired babies in the *Politicus* myth is actually identical with the age of Kronos and physical ease, the description of which explicitly begins in 271c (at the Young Socrates' prompting); and the fact that people's basic needs were provided for without their having to lift a finger would not necessarily be a good thing, in strict Platonic terms; in itself, it would be no better than its opposite.[18] That indeed is one implication of the raising of the question: what exactly did the Kronians do with all that leisure the god afforded them?[19] In a way, then, a merging of Hesiodic golden and Hesiodic iron might itself be making a sound Platonic point. And at this stage one might even be tempted to argue that the very motif of grey-haired babies has by this point lost all its horror: why *not* imagine a past (and a future) when young was old already, and when things were better, not because it was paradise in material terms, but because material abundance—living in 'paradise'—gave more *opportunity* for a better life?[20]

However—once all this is granted[21]—there is one crucial respect in which the divine dispensation will evidently have contributed to a decrease rather than an increase in human capacity for fulfilment.

[18] Cf. El Murr, p. 294; and further n. 21 below.

[19] See p. 299 above.

[20] That is, in terms of greater leisure, and perhaps in the absence of the conditions for the growth of greed, lust, and so on (is that what permitted those 'conversations with the animals', in the sense suggested in n. 4 above?).

[21] Here I acknowledge a major debt to McCabe (1997) and (2000) which have belatedly brought me to see, in a way I had not seen before, that Plato's attitude towards the era of Kronos not only is, but must be, thoroughly ambivalent: that is, in so far as stories about Kronian times stress that it was a time of *abundance*, which is how the Stranger himself eventually introduces it (271c8–d1). 'Must be', because, according to the point of view continually associated with Plato's Socrates and in any case ubiquitous in the dialogues, abundance of material provision tells us nothing about the quality of the lives that enjoy it. In short, even if there was ever a time when everything 'sprang up of its own accord for human beings' (271c8–d1 again), and even if we may dream of such a world, the gods/god cannot himself determine how well or badly we will live.

Kronians (that is, again, on the standard interpretation: I stress that I am identifying a problem with *that*, not with the myth itself, as I propose it should properly be understood)[22] will grow or develop in the direction of a state that, whether it is described from their perspective as old age, or from ours as childhood, will nevertheless be one that is unavoidably associated with play rather than with seriousness—as the Stranger reminds us even as he ushers in his story: 'In that case pay complete attention to my story, as children do; you certainly haven't left childish games behind[23] for more than a few years' (268e). What is more, the description of the reversal of ageing, in 270d–271a (cited above), may reasonably be said to lay particular emphasis on the Kronians' movement from adulthood to childhood; at any rate, it cannot be said to downplay it ('. . . younger, more tender . . . the cheeks of those who had their beards became smooth again . . . and . . . those in their puberty . . . went back to the form of new-born children, becoming like them both in mind [i.e., presumably, childish, irrational] and in body'). In other words, in the era of Kronos, human life tends towards a condition in which philosophy is not only difficult but actually impossible. What does that say about divine providence?

My own response to this question is to suppose that either (a) Plato has nodded (by making Kronian life importantly, indeed crucially, worse), or else (b) the standard type of interpretation is wrong. But the difficulty with solution (a) is that it tends to make the feature in question—let us call it 'F'[24]—into no more than an unintended

---

[22] See further below, and especially Appendix B to this chapter, for an outline of the 'standard' interpretation, matched against my own.

[23] More literally, 'you haven't *escaped* . . .' (ἐκφεύγειν), underlining that childishness is something positively not to be wished for. McCabe (2000, 150, n. 46) acknowledges the point ('[the Stranger] wants to remind us that age and philosophy go together, but youth with the telling of stories'), but—I claim—without seeing its full implications for the story. Or does she claim that 'ageing in reverse' (ibid., n. 34) will also reverse the effects of youth and age? This hardly seems likely. Age is itself a prominent theme in the Hesiodic account: apart from those grey-haired iron babies, the golden race is forever spared old age, while the silver race has a hundred-year childhood and a short and stupid maturity (the stupidity deriving from all that time in the nursery?).

[24] That is (to recap), that Kronians—on the interpretation I am criticizing—become progressively *less* capable of doing the one thing on which their happiness depends.

consequence of the way Plato chose to construct the story; and in so far as F appears to work against one of the central aspects needed by the story in order to fulfil its central purpose (i.e., again, to illustrate the difference between divine and human government—or herdsmanship: at this point in the argument herding humans has not been separated off from herding other animals), it is hard to see how Plato could have failed to notice what he was doing, or to imagine how, when he did notice it, that in itself would not have been a sufficient reason for his *not* putting together the story in such a way that it involved F. To clarify: Kronians, it seems, will—in the most important respect of all—actually be worse off than we are. (At least many of us do get less childlike, whereas all the Kronians who survive long enough will become more so.) And yet ultimately 'the god'[25] is supposed to have to intervene to save us from ourselves, and stop things descending into complete chaos (273de). Of course, divine government will already be beneficial, just to that extent. But since the occasion of his intervention is our ultimate failure to save ourselves, that is, from within our own resources, it would be more than a little odd if a result of that intervention was to reduce the very resources the lack of which made it necessary. The Kronians too needed philosophy, if they were to be happy, no less than we need it. Divine rule by itself may not be enough to make us happy, but it should not have the effect of making us less capable of being so. Indeed, I venture that, from a Platonic point of view, the idea of humans being born grey-haired, in the version in which he has the Stranger develop it, is every bit as nightmarish as it was, in Hesiod's original version, for Hesiod. Part of the nightmare will be that the newly born, though grey-haired, will lack the experience of ordinary grey-hairs; for they have no past. So they lose out twice over: not only do they grow into—what we call—children, but their 'old age' (as we might be tempted to call it, from the perspective of our era) is robbed of *its* advantages.

[25] The Stranger never clearly commits himself to identifying the divine steersman with Kronos; the very name 'Kronos' probably belongs to the stories people tell (just as the present age is what people *call* the age 'of Zeus': 272b2). It is an important aspect of the Platonic story that there is only one (chief) god around: see n. 1 above.

But if that is so, (b) is evidently the only option available to us: what I have called the 'standard' type of interpretation must be mistaken.[26] The time when people are born already grey-haired, in the Stranger's story, cannot be the age of Kronos. And I suggest that the very motif is chosen as an early signal of that very point. When grey-hairs emerge from the earth, it is the time of reversal, but it is not the Kronian time: the age of Kronos, *pace* El Murr in this volume, but as I have argued elsewhere, is a *third* time or period, preceding that of my grey-haired babies (or 'babies'). I shall not repeat the case for this interpretation here.[27] Instead, I mean to exploit it.

That exploitation begins with the observation that a three-stage interpretation of the myth of the *Politicus*, which will give us three rather than two races of human beings, will allow a much closer comparison with the Hesiodic story. Indeed, it is part of my thesis in the present chapter that Plato's appropriation from Hesiod in this context extends considerably beyond the borrowing of an isolated motif. The *Politicus* myth is, in small part, Plato's own myth of the races—his own take on the human past (and future), which serves simultaneously to recall and improve upon Hesiod. To 'improve', specifically—to repeat a point introduced earlier—because Plato's version has a rationale behind it, in a way that Hesiod's does not, being for the most part an account of what happened after what ('next there came another race . . .'). Yet at the same time many of the basic elements out of which Plato constructs his rationale are them-selves—also—Hesiodic: the age of Kronos, the silliness of childhood, and so on.[28] The one central theme that is not Hesiodic (apart from

---

[26] It is not that Plato in principle could not have turned a Hesiodic motif upside down, or back to front; just that—I claim—he isn't in fact doing that. Grey-haired new-borns in Plato too are a bad thing.

[27] See especially Rowe (2002). For an outline (but no more) of how the inter-pretation will work, see Appendix B to this chapter.

[28] 271c2: 'all those of them [sc. the people who lived in the time of the reversed cosmos], that is, whom god did not take off to another destiny' itself plainly recalls *Works and Days* 167–73, where some of the heroic race escape death and are transported by Zeus to the ends of the earth/the isles of the blest. But once again, there is a rationale (presumably) to be supplied in the Platonic context which is signally missing in the Hesiodic: just why did some escape, when for all we are told they were just the same as the rest? Given Plato's known approval of philosophical lives, perhaps his escapees were those who succeeded in achieving such a life, against

that of the cosmic cycle itself,[29] and its ultimate causes), the idea of the earth-born, will be my next topic for discussion.

At least in a certain context, and at least by implication, the Athenians (whom I take to be Plato's first intended audience, as they are typically the immediate butt of his critiques) liked to think of themselves as autochthonous: born, that is, from the splendidly fertile soil of Attica, and so splendidly equipped by the very fact of being Athenian.[30] The context in question is, of course, that of the citizens' own self-image, most obviously and explicitly exemplified in the annual funeral oration.[31] However, the image of the earth-born that will be connected with *this* context (and so, for example, for the audience of the oration) will hardly be that of old people returning from the grave. Rather, the image will be of potent warriors, in the prime of their lives—or else of actual babies,[32] who grow into adulthood in the way we suppose to be normal. This seems to be how

all the odds. (Even when he has retired to his 'observation-post', god still looks after his own.) The short lives/extended deaths of 'those who died a violent death at that time' (270e10–272a2) might also—just possibly—be seen as a caricature of the career of the disastrous Hesiodic bronze race. However I should not want the wildness of this latter speculation to obscure the more fundamental proposal, that Plato is not just borrowing from, or even appropriating, Hesiod: he is setting out to better him, by providing a philosophically-founded version of a tale that would otherwise be suited to mere children. (Plato may appear to write off his own stories in just the same way, as in the *Politicus* itself: 268e again. But things are more complicated: as Books 2 and 3 of the *Republic* show, he—or his Socrates—hardly thinks even children deserve what mere poets give them.) For the central element in Plato's 'explanation' of the cosmic cycle, see 272e5–6 (the 'allotted and innate desire' of the physical cosmos), with 269d9–e1 (it 'has its share of body'). See below.

[29] *Pace* those who think such an idea implied by *Works and Days* 175: see West (1978), *ad loc.*

[30] The inference actually goes the other way (exceptionally good, because Athenian; therefore good because born in/from Attica). The 'accounts of the earth-born', the Stranger says (271b2–3), 'are nowadays wrongly disbelieved by many people': this is a typical Platonic double-take. 'People who call themselves sensible disbelieve such tales, when in fact they are true'; but the correction of course only holds good from within the framework of the myth. Cf. e.g. *Phaedrus* 229c–230a (on which see Rowe 1986, *ad loc.*).

[31] See Plato's parody of the genre in the *Menexenus*, especially at 237b–238b. Here parody and original will be scarcely distinguishable, to the extent that any tale of racial superiority (the superiority of a given city and its inhabitants) tends to identify that pretended superiority with excellence of *location*.

[32] Which it might be, in the *Menexenus*, is left nicely unspecified.

Critias, in the *Timaeus*, pictures the birth of those primitive Athenians who once defeated Atlantis: they are literally sown in the soil, by Hephaestus (*Timaeus* 23e).[33]

And this alternative vision of the earth-born is—so I claim—also present in the *Politicus* myth, alongside the nightmarish one. The Stranger's first topic, as he starts talking specifically about the Kronian era (the time when 'the god began to rule and take care of the rotation itself [sc. of the heavenly bodies]': 271d3–4), is what he expects his interlocutor, the young Socrates, to associate with that time: 'everything's springing up of its own accord for human beings' (271cd). Next, he spells out some of the consequences of divine 'herdsmanship': there were no political constitutions, nor was there any getting of wives and children, 'for all of [the people of that time] came back to life from the earth, remembering nothing of the past' (272a).[34] At first sight, it seems reasonable to presume[35] that the reference is to those grey-haired infants (or 'infants') again, who themselves 'came back to life' (271b7: the same term, ἀναβιώσκεσθαι, was used of them, and less than a Stephanus page earlier). But as we read on, I believe that this becomes a rather less reasonable presumption. First, we have the Stranger's judgement on the quality of life enjoyed by the Kronians—and here, by contrast with the earlier passage, there is no mention of growing childishness, only talk about the opportunities and choices then available. Then we reach the whole crux of the story (272de):

We must now state the point of our rousing our story into action ... When the time of all these things had been completed and the hour for change had

---

[33] Athena founded the city, having 'received from Earth and Hephaestus the seed from which your people were to come' (tr. Zeyl: given Athena's permanent virginity, Hephaestus must spill his seed upon the fertile earth).

[34] While they lacked all that, the Stranger goes on, they had 'an abundance of fruits from trees and many other plants, not growing through cultivation but because the earth sent them up of their own accord ...' (272a3–5). The description as a whole is strongly reminiscent of the original city, or 'city', of *Republic* 2, 369a–372d (what Glaucon, but not Socrates, calls the 'city of pigs'—because the inhabitants live on acorns: 'fruits from trees'?); the question whether people living like that could be *happy*, which the Stranger will immediately raise, is equally fundamental in the *Republic* context, and would, I think, by implication be answered in the same way as in the *Politicus*. ('Yes, they would be happy *if* they did philosophy.')

[35] As upholders of the 'standard' interpretation of the myth will (presumably) presume.

come, and in particular all the earth-born race had been used up, *each soul having rendered its sum of births, falling to the earth as seed* as many times as had been laid down for each, at that point the steersman of the universe, after letting go, as it were, of the bar of the steering-oars, retired to his observation-post, and as for the world-order, its allotted and innate desire turned it back again in the opposite direction.[36]

The crucial words here are the ones in italics: '*each soul having rendered its sum of births, falling to the earth as seed . . .*' If we go back to 271, and the description of the birth of those grey-haired babies, we find what is surely a quite different notion: 'It follows on the passage of old men to childhood that *from the dead, lying in the earth, men should be put together again there* and come back to life, following the direction of the reversal . . .' (271b4–7). Now it is evidently not impossible to read these two descriptions as being of the same event, since so many interpreters—all those who have adopted the 'standard' interpretation—will actually have done so, whether implicitly or explicitly.[37] The earlier passage (i.e. 271), we might suppose, to defend the standard account, gives a physical and mechanical description of the event (bodily parts being put back together), while the later one puts it into the larger Platonic context (living bodies include souls, and souls have histories . . . ). But this seems to me highly implausible. In 271, for all we are told, people come back to *life just because of the reversal of the cosmos*; that is, the cause is itself purely mechanical—or at least, that is the impression the Stranger gives, and does nothing to correct. Objection: why isn't that exactly what he does in 272 (i.e. point out that there was more to it than that)? Response: the idea of a sowing of souls is fundamentally different from that of a reassembly of body parts. Souls will of course

---

[36] This, then, is the great reversal: caused by the 'innate desire' of the cosmos (272e6), which takes it immediately in the reverse direction to that imparted to it by the god. But after a relatively short period (short, that is, in cosmic terms, though still from our point of view an *age*), the cosmos began to 'remember so far as it could the teaching of its craftsman and father' (273b2–3)—so, according to the interpretation I have proposed, reversing direction once more. Thus reason—this time, the cosmos' own—reasserts itself, in the same way that the arts and sciences (including, by implication, statesmanship), constructed by us as 'gifts of the gods', make up for the absence of Kronian, divinely caused, abundance. See Appendix B to this chapter.

[37] Thus the 'putting together' in the earth might require a Hephaestus—the 'father' in the *Timaeus–Critias*; but his fatherhood seems there to have more to do with his semen than his craftsmanship, and souls 'falling to earth as seed' seem equally capable of doing without a craftsman (unless as father).

have to fall back into the reassembled bodies if those bodies are to be revived. But this is hard to reconcile with the idea of their 'falling to [into] earth as seeds', which looks rather more like what Critias said happened in primitive Athens with Hephaestus' seed (which then grew up in the 'right' direction, i.e. to adulthood).

This juxtaposition—if it can be called that[38]—of two different ideas of the earth-born is, I propose, quite deliberate; indeed, it represents one of the main functions of the myth.[39] The actual story of autochthony, as told by the Athenians themselves (as well as others) to themselves, is linked, in the Stranger's story, to a time of horror and chaos (271ab):

> The earth-born race said to have existed once was this one, the one that existed [during the period of reversal], turning back again from the earth; it was remembered by our first ancestors, who bordered on the previous period as it ended, living in the succeeding time, and grew up at the beginning of the present one . . .

So the reversal explains the origins of *that* story, as the Stranger said it would (269b2–5). But if so, Athenian autochthony is nothing to be proud of; rather the reverse, since it means that the Athenians are descended from ancestors who were no better than silly children, indeed who *were* silly children, from the perspective of the present.[40] So much for the idea, parodied in the *Menexenus*, that Attica herself guarantees the quality of her inhabitants, by being the womb from which their ancestors were born. For *that* scenario, or for the closest to it that real conditions (!) will allow, one needs to go much further back: to the time *preceding* the time when things went into reverse— or, in the parallel story of the *Timaeus–Critias*, to the period when Athens defeated Atlantis, before itself being destroyed by another kind of cataclysm (earthquake and floods).[41] But even this other,

---

[38] One of the two ideas, after all, is clearly advertised—as *the* explanation of talk about 'earth-born' people; the other comes in merely as one among many aspects of a work-free age (new people born without even the need for copulation).

[39] See Appendix A to this chapter.

[40] That is, they were children from that perspective (not from their own); they were silly in any case.

[41] True, in the latter case present-day Athenians will turn out to be the ultimate descendants of the better kind of earth-born. But Critias' story has its own mechan-

different kind of autochthony brings no solutions with it. Quality, and quality of life, have still to be worked for.

Question: why does Plato not mark the difference between the two sorts of autochthony more clearly?[42] My reply to this question is twofold. First, I believe that Plato does in fact clearly distinguish between the age of reversal and the age of Kronos. The Stranger and (Young) Socrates do the job together. Immediately after the passage last cited, Socrates asks when the time of Kronos' power was 'in those turnings ($\tau\rho\sigma\pi\alpha\hat{\iota}s$) or these? Because clearly the reversal in the movements of the heavenly bodies must take place in either.' By this, I take him to mean: 'Did Kronos rule in the period you've just described [= 'these turnings': the period of grey-haired babies] or the one before [= 'those turnings']?'—on the basis, as he more or less says, that there must have been two reversals, one taking things[43] backwards, the other taking them back again in their usual direction.[44] To this, the Stranger replies: if you mean the time when things sprang up of their own accord, 'it belongs least to the movement that now obtains' (272d1–2): that is, I suppose, 'least' to the 'movement' ($\phi\sigma\rho\acute{\alpha}$) obtaining since the god retired from the 'steering-oar' of the universe, where the 'movement' in question is constituted by 'these turnings'—'in' which the second reversal took place—plus the time following them. This may well not be the most straightforward reading of the Greek of the passage taken just by itself, but I believe that it is workable enough once we fully understand the overall argument of the myth.[45]

ism for separating present-day Athenians from the wisdom and valour of their ancestors.

[42] The question was actually put at the Durham conference behind this volume; I now offer a more considered response.

[43] Specifically: the heavenly bodies.

[44] The whole myth, we should remember, is introduced by a story (that of Atreus and Thyestes) involving a *temporary* reversal—a portent: 268e.

[45] See Appendix A to this chapter. In 2000, Denis O'Brien (see n. 1 above) claimed that the passage just discussed was enough by itself to undermine completely the three-stage interpretation I then proposed and continue to propose. I persist in maintaining that O'Brien's position underestimates the difficulties posed by the Greek of the passage (and particularly of young Socrates' intervention) *for the two-stage interpretation itself*, as it certainly underestimates the difficulties that interpretation faces from the detail of other parts of the myth. (The present chapter, of course, starts from some of those difficulties, and argues that they fall away if the three-stage interpretation is adopted.) What is still missing, from the proponents of the two-

Yet to make such a concession is in effect already to invite the same question again: if that is what Plato had in mind, why does he not put it *more clearly?* Here is the second, and rather more speculative, part of my answer: that he is positively inviting his readers to misinterpret the story— just as those who believe in the myth of autochthony in fact misinterpret the story they tell themselves. 'We were born Athenians, and that's enough, because the Attic soil is so good . . . Once upon a time (so Plato allows their story to develop), it was even an earthly paradise, an era truly governed by Kronos; and we are descended from that time.' But there in the text, beside that version, is another one, which tells these Athenians that they are and always were separated from paradise,[46] and that their future depends on the extent to which they can recreate some kind of resemblance to divine governance from within their own resources. That is what separates us, and mythically saved us, from a state of chaos and nightmare induced by innate (and unreasoning) desire in which everything was and will again go into reverse, or as we might prefer to put it, be turned upside down.[47]

# APPENDIX A

The shape[48] of the Stranger's exposition of the myth in 268e–274e:

1. The story of the reversal of the movement of the heavenly bodies.
2. Reports of a 'rule of Kronos'.
3. Reports of earth-births.

stage reading, is a complete, step-by-step account of the way their reading deals with each of the many details of a very complex myth: that is, a rival to the kind of account I offer in Rowe (1995a) and its successors (including my 1999).

[46] As, again, they are separated from that better Athens that defeated Atlantis. On why—for Plato—the real Athens' defeat of Persia is no real parallel to that feat, see Rowe (2007b).

[47] For other instances of this kind of phenomenon, in which Plato appears to buy in to ordinary assumptions even while in the process of undermining them, see Rowe (2007a).

[48] Slanted, inevitably, in the direction of a three-stage interpretation of the myth as a whole.

4. In fact, it is the reality underlying 1 that underlies 2 and 3.

5. Description, and explanation, of the reversal; the upheavals it caused (and will cause again).

6. One such consequence of the reversal: people grow 'younger', etc.; people are reborn from the earth—giving the explanation of 3.

7. What about 2? When did the 'Kronian' age occur? Before this one. Description of that time.

8. Were people happier then? It depends...

9. In any case, at the end of this—Kronian—age, god retired, leaving the world to its own devices, with disastrous consequences, though after a while it—the world—started remembering what it had previously been taught, and moved back to its proper and accustomed course.[49] Eventually, however, things begin to break down again, and god has to intervene once more...

10. The world after the second reversal, i.e. after the period of backward rotation: the present age; the present; the development of different kinds of expertise (including, by implication, the art of statesmanship).

---

[49] This, crucially, is my reading of 273a4–b3: 'After this, when sufficient time had elapsed, [the cosmos] began to cease from noise and confusion and attained calm from its tremors, and set itself in order, into the accustomed course that belongs to it, taking charge of and mastering both the things within it and itself, because it remembered, so far as it could, the teaching of its craftsman and father.' 'Its proper and accustomed course' is East to West, i.e. in the same direction as the god impelled it in the 'age of Kronos'; this is its 'proper' course because it is the one on which reason takes it, whether divine reason or its own, and it is its 'accustomed' course because the period of reversal is an aberration, even if it lasts for 'many tens of thousands of revolutions' (270a7): long enough for people to move from 'old age' to 'babyhood' (and ultimate disappearance), but short enough, in relation to the total length of the cosmic cycle, for it to be treated, on occasion, just as a small—and purely temporary—aspect of god's 'letting go' of things (thus at 273c4–d1; contrast especially 270a, where the focus is on the reversal itself, and the cause of the reversal).

## APPENDIX B

Two interpretations of the myth in outline. Here the 'standard' type of interpretation[50] is contrasted with my own (separated in each case, where appropriate, by '//'):

268e4–269c3: the three 'sources' of the myth.

269c4–d2: alternation of opposite movements // existence of opposite movements as cause of the three types of phenomena referred to in the stories.

269d2–270b2: the necessity of circular movement (269d2–e4); the cause of the alternation of opposite movements (269e5–270b2) // why *reversal* is necessary (whole passage).

270b3– 271c2: turbulence during the changeover from one movement to the other (270b3–d1); beginning of movement from West to East: a zoogony opposite to ours (270d1–271a1); the birth of men from the earth (271a2–c2) // description of the events following the catastrophe (that occurrence of the catastrophe) which caused the stories with which the Stranger began; including reversal of cosmos, i.e. a period of West-to-East movement, plus rebirth of the dead from the ground (whole passage).

271c3–7: the question asked by Young Socrates ('So [he says] we have the reversal of the heavenly bodies and the earth-born; where does the third story, about the age of Kronos, come in?').

271c8–d2: reply—the reign of Kronos occupies the period of movement from West to East // Kronos' reign was the era prior to the period of movement, West to East, just described, and prior to the reversals with which that period began and ended (so it was a period, like ours, of East-to-West movement).

271d3–272d4: further description of the age of Kronos (271d3–272b3); presence (or absence) of philosophy in the reign of Kronos (272b3–d4) // description of the age of Kronos (271d3–272b3); presence (or absence) of philosophy in the reign of Kronos (272b3–d4).

---

[50] As based (now at several removes) on an original handout of Denis O'Brien's: see n. 1 above. I hope and expect the discussion that this handout helped to launch will continue.

272d5–273b2: the end of movement from West to East (272d5–273a1); turbulence separating movement from West to East from movement East to West (our own period); the world starts to adapt itself to movement from East to West (273a4–b2) // the age of Kronos ends (275d5–273a1), followed by the/a period of reversal (273e5–6, 273a1–6), followed by the restoration of East-to-West movement (273a4–b2).

273b2–d4: movement from East to West is a degradation // the age of Zeus, which begins well but gradually goes to the bad.

273d4–e4: the end of movement from East to West and the beginning of contrary movement (from West to East) // the god resumes control, and the age of Kronos begins again—without any contrary movement, because the heavenly bodies were still moving from East to West (which is also the direction of divinely-caused movement).

273a4: the tale of a single 'cycle' is thus completed.

273e5–274e4: relevance of the tale to the discussion of political theory (273e5–6); origins of human society at the beginning of the period of movement from East to West (our own period) (273e6–274a1); births in our world: and therefore a zoogony the opposite of that related at 270d1–271a1 (274a2–b1); the human condition in our world (274b1–d6); conclusion (274d6–e4) // the story picked up from the second reversal, i.e. at the end of the period of West-to-East movement, which is the part relevant to showing the nature of the king (273e5–6); we have to learn —like the cosmos itself (274d6–7)—how to do everything for ourselves, in the absence of gods to do it for us (we even have to procreate for ourselves, though this is less relevant to the argument: see 274a2–b1, b1–2): and that (the story leaves us where we are now, in the 5th century BC) is what we need to use to put our account of the king and statesman right . . . (274e1–4).

## Summary

—On the standard interpretation, there are two movements, two zoogonies // [whereas]
—On my interpretation the myth describes *three* periods of movement, *three* modes of procreation/coming to life of human beings:

one, sexual, belonging to our era, that of Zeus. But in the age of
Kronos, there was no sexual coupling, because 'everyone was reborn
from the earth' (272a1)—I take it, like plants, their souls being 'sown'
as seeds for an appointed number of times (272d6–e3; for the whole
set of ideas, see esp. *Phaedrus* 248cd). These new/old humans (who
however remember nothing of their previous lives: 272a2) emerge as
babies and grow in the normal direction, i.e. so as to appear as well as
to become older, from our perspective (just as the cosmos itself is
presently travelling in the normal direction, i.e. East to West—and as
the plants evidently also grow in the usual directions, and get bigger,
not smaller). However, there is also a third mode by which human
beings come into being, or rather into life: in the transitional period,
that of the reversal of the cosmos, the dead lying in their graves/in
the ground come back to life, and appear, from our perspective, to
grow younger.[51]

[51] I do not suggest that my own account of the structure of the myth is even now
complete and satisfactory: in particular, as was shown in the course on an excellent
discussion at the 2009 May Week Seminar, on the *Politicus*, in Cambridge, I need a
more persuasive explanation of 274e10–275a1 and 273e6–7—which happen to be two
of the strongest *prima facie* pieces of evidence for the 'standard' three-stage reading of
the myth. But my account overall is at least in better shape than my opponents', which
is sketchy, and unsupported by the kind of detailed analysis that Plato's text seems to
me always to demand—and nowhere more than in the present case.

# References

## 1. Ancient authors

Where not listed here, editions of Greek texts used in this volume are as detailed in L. Berkowitz and K. A. Squitier, *Thesaurus Linguae Graecae: Canon of Greek Authors and Works*. 3rd edn. New York/Oxford, 1990.

Acusilaus: R. L. Fowler, *Early Greek Mythography*. Oxford, 2000.

Alcman: C. Calame (ed.), *Alcman: Introduction, texte critique, témoignages, traduction et commentaire*. Rome, 1983.

—— M. Davies (ed.), *Poetarum Melicorum Graecorum Fragmenta*. Oxford, 1991–. [*PMGF*]

*Contest of Homer and Hesiod*: M. L. West (ed.), *Homeric Hymns, Homeric Apocrypha, Lives of Homer*. (Loeb Classical Library 496.) Cambridge, Mass., 2003.

Cratinus: R. Kassel and C. Austin (eds.), *Poetae Comici Graeci*. Berlin, 1983. [KA]

Hermogenes: L. Spengel (ed.), *Rhetores Graeci*. 3 vols. Leipzig, 1854.

Hesiod, *Catalogue*: A. Rzach (ed.), *Hesiodi carmina*. Leipzig, 1902.

Hesiod, *fragments* and *testimonia*: G. W. Most (ed. and trans.), *Hesiod*. Vol. 1: *Theogony, Works and Days, Testimonia* (Loeb Classical Library 57). Vol. 2: *The Shield, Catalogue of Women, Other Fragments* (Loeb Classical Library 503). Cambridge, Mass. 2006–7.

Hesychius, *Vita Aristotelis*: V. Rose, *Aristotelis qui ferebantur librorum fragmenta*. 3rd edn. Leipzig, 1886.

Orphica: A. Bernabé (ed.), *Orphicorum et Orphicis similium testimonia et fragmenta* (*Poetae Epici Graeci* II.1), Munich/Leipzig, 2004.

## 2. Modern authors

Adam, J. (1891), 'The Myth in Plato's *Politicus*', *Classical Review* 5: 445–6.

—— (1902), *The Republic of Plato*. 2 vols. Cambridge.

Algra, K. (1995), *Concepts of Space in Greek Thought*. Leiden.

Allen, R. E. (2006), *Plato: The Republic*. New Haven, CT.

Anceschi, B. (2007), *Die Götternamen in Platons Kratylos. Ein Vergleich mit dem Papyrus von Derveni*. Frankfurt.

Annas, J. (1981), *An Introduction to Plato's Republic*. Oxford.

Annas, J. (1982): 'Plato on the Triviality of Literature' in J. Moravcsik and P. Temko (eds.), *Plato on Beauty, Wisdom, and the Arts* (Totowa, NJ), 1–28.

Arrighetti, G. (1978), 'Uomini e dei in Esiodo', *Grazer Beiträge* 7: 15–35.

—— (1987), *Poeti, eruditi, e biografi. Momenti della riflessione dei Greci sulla letteratura.* Pisa.

—— (1991), 'Platone fra mito, poesia e storia', *Studi classici e orientali* 41: 13–34.

—— (1998), *Esiodo. Opere.* Turin.

Assmann, J. (2000), *Religion und kulturelles Gedächtnis; zehn Studien.* Munich.

Ayache, L. (1997), 'Est-il vraiment question d'art médical dans le Timée?', in Calvo and Brisson 1997: 55–63.

Bachofen, J. J. (1861), *Das Mutterrecht. Eine Untersuchung über die Gynaikokratie der alten Welt nach ihrer religiösen und rechtlichen Natur.* Stuttgart.

Bakker, E. J. (1990), 'Homeric Discourse and Enjambment: A Cognitive Approach', *Transactions of the American Philological Association* 120: 1–21.

Balaudé, J.-F. (2006), 'Hippias le passeur' in M. M. Sassi (ed.), *La Costruzione del discorso filosofico nell' età dei Presocratici/The Construction of Philosophical Discourse in the Age of the Presocratics* (Pisa, 2006), 287–304.

Baldry, H. C. (1952), 'Who Invented the Golden Age?', *Classical Quarterly* 2: 83–92.

—— (1953), 'The Idler's Paradise in Attic Comedy', *Greece and Rome* 22: 49–60.

Baltes, M. (1976–8), *Die Weltentstehung des platonischen Timaios nach den antiken Interpreten.* 2 vols. Leiden.

—— (1996), 'Γέγονεν (Platon, Tim. 28 B 7). Ist die Welt real entstanden oder nicht?' in K. Algra, P. van der Horst, and D. Runia (eds.), *Polyhistor: Studies in the History and Historiography of Ancient Philosophy* (Leiden), 76–96. Reprinted in M. Baltes, *ΔΙΑΝΟΗΜΑΤΑ. Kleine Schriften zu Platon und zum Platonismus.* edited by A. Hüffmeier, M.-L. Lakmann, and M. Vorwerk (Stuttgart, 1999), 303–25.

Bárány, I. (2006), 'From Protagoras to Parmenides: A Platonic history of Philosophy' in M. M. Sassi (ed.), *La Costruzione del discorso filosofico nell' età dei Presocratici/The Construction of Philosophical Discourse in the Age of the Presocratics.* (Pisa, 2006), 305–27.

Bate, J. (1993), *Shakespeare and Ovid.* Oxford.

Baxter, T. M. S. (1992), *The Cratylus: Plato's Critique of Naming.* Leiden.

Beazley, J. D. (1948), 'Hymn to Hermes', *American Journal of Archaeology* 52: 336–40.

Belfiore, E. (1985), '"Lies Unlike the Truth": Plato on Hesiod, *Theogony* 27', *Transactions of the American Philological Association* 115: 47–57.

Benardete, S. (1963), 'Some Misquotations of Homer in Plato', *Phronesis* 8: 173–8.

Bergren, A. T. (1989), 'The Homeric Hymn to Aphrodite: Tradition and Rhetoric, Praise and Blame', *Classical Antiquity* 8: 1–41.

Berti, E. (1997), 'L'oggetto dell' εἰκὼς μῦθος nel *Timeo* di Platone' in Calvo and Brisson 1997: 119–31.

Betegh, G. (2004), *The Derveni Papyrus: Cosmology, Theology, and Interpretation*. Cambridge.

Blondell, R. (2002), *The Play of Character in Plato's Dialogues*. Cambridge.

Bonitz, H. (1870), *Index Aristotelicus*. Berlin.

Borgeaud, P. (1999), *La mythologie du matriarcat: l'atelier de Johann Jacob Bachofen*. Avec la collaboration de Nicole Durisch, Antje Kolde et Grégoire Sommer. Geneva.

Boys-Stones, G. R. (2001), *Post-Hellenistic Philosophy: A Study of its Development from the Stoics to Origen*. Oxford.

Brandwood, L. (1976), *A Word Index to Plato*. Leeds.

—— (1990), *The Chronology of Plato's Dialogues*. Cambridge.

Brisson, L. (1970), 'De la philosophie politique à l'épopée. Le *Critias* de Platon', *Revue de Métaphysique et de Morale* 75: 402–38.

—— (1992) (ed.), *Platon. Timée/Critias*. Paris.

—— (2000), 'Interprétation du mythe du *Politique*' in L. Brisson (ed.), *Lectures de Platon* (Paris, 2000), 169–205. Originally pubished in Rowe 1995*b*: 349–63.

Broadie, S. (2001), 'Theodicy and Pseudo-History in the *Timaeus*', *Oxford Studies in Ancient Phlosophy* 21: 1–28.

Brown, A. S. (1977), 'Aphrodite and the Pandora Complex', *Classical Quarterly* 47: 26–47.

—— (1998), 'From the Golden Age to the Isles of the Blest', *Mnemosyne* 51: 385–410.

Brown. L. (1998), 'Innovation and Continuity: The Battle of Gods and Giants in Plato's *Sophist* 245–249' in J. Gentzler (ed.), *Method in Ancient Philosophy* (Oxford, 1998), 181–207.

Burkert, W. (1987), 'The Making of Homer in the 6th Century BC: Rhapsodes versus Stesichorus' in *Papers on the Amasis Painter and his World* (Malibu, 1987), 43–62.

—— (1990), 'Herodot als Historiker fremder Religionen' in *Hérodote et les peuples non grecs* (*Entretiens sur l'antiquité classique* 35) (Geneva, 1990), 1–32.

Burkert, W. (1999), 'The Logic of Cosmogony' in R. Buxton (ed.), *From Myth to Reason? Studies in the Development of Greek Thought* (Oxford, 1999), 87–106.

Burnet, J. (1899–1907) (ed.), *Platonis Opera.* (*Scriptorum classicorum bibliotheca Oxoniensis.*) 5 vols. Oxford.

Burnyeat, M. F. (1999), 'Culture and Society in Plato's Republic' in G. B. Peterson (ed.), *The Tanner Lectures on Human Values 20* (Salt Lake City, UT, 1999), 215–324.

—— (2005), '*ΕΙΚΩΣ ΜΥΘΟΣ*' *Rhizai* 2: 143–65.

Burston, D. (1986), 'Myth, Religion and Mother Right: Bachofen's Influence on Psychoanalytic Theory', *Contemporary Psychoanalysis* 22: 666–87.

Bury, R. G. (1929) (ed. and trans.), *Plato.* Vol. ix: *Timaeus, Critias, Cleitophon, Menexenus, Epistles.* (Loeb Classical Library 234). Cambridge, Mass.

Butler, S. (1898) (trans.), *The Iliad of Homer, Rendered into English Prose for the Use of those who Cannot Read the Original.* London.

Butti de Lima, P. (2002), *Platone. Esercizi di filosofia per il giovane Teeteto.* Venice.

Buzio, C. (1938), *Esiodo nel mondo greco sino alla fine dell'età classica.* Milan.

Calabi, F. (2005), 'Timocratia' in Vegetti 2005*a*: 263–93.

Calame, C. (2004), 'Succession des âges et pragmatique poétique de la justice. Le récit hésiodique des cinq espèces humaines', *Kernos* 17: 67–102.

Callataÿ, G. de (2005), 'Il numero geometrico di Platone' in Vegetti 2005*a*: 169–87.

Calvo, T. and Brisson, L. (1997) (eds.), *Interpreting the Timaeus-Critias.* (*Symposium Platonicum* 4.) Sankt Augustin.

Cameron, A. (1995), *Callimachus and his Critics.* Princeton, NJ.

Campbell, L. (1883), *The Theaetetus of Plato.* With a Revised Text and English Notes. 2nd edn. Oxford.

Capra, A. (2001), *Ἀγὼν λόγων: Il Protagora di Platone tra eristica e commedia.* Milan.

—— (2005), 'Protagoras' Achilles: Homeric Allusion as a Satirical Weapon (Pl. Prt. 340a)', *Classical Philology* 100: 274–7.

Carone, G. R. (2004), 'Reversing the Myth of the *Politicus*', *Classical Quarterly* 54: 88–108.

Carrière, J.-C. (1979), *Le carnaval et la politique: Une introduction à la comédie grecque, suivi d'un choix de fragments.* Paris.

Casertano, G. (2000) (ed.), *La struttura del dialogo platonico.* Naples.

Ceccarelli, P. (1996), 'L'Athènes de Périclès: un "pays de cocagne"? L'idéologie démocratique et l' *automatos bios* dans la comédie ancienne', *Quaderni Urbinati di Cultura Classica* 54: 109–59.

Cerri, G. (2000), 'Dalla dialettica all'epos: Platone, "Repubblica" X, "Timeo", "Crizia"' in Casertano 2000: 7–34.

Cerutti, M. V. (1998), 'Mito di distruzione, mito di fondazione. Hes. fr. 204, 95–103 M.-W.', *Aevum antiquum* 11: 127–78.

Clark, M. (1994), 'Enjambment and Binding in Homeric Hexameter', *Phoenix* 48: 95–114.

—— (1997), *Out of Line: Homeric Composition Beyond the Hexameter.* Lanham, MD.

Classen, C. J. (1962), 'The Creator in Greek Thought from Homer to Plato', *Classica et Mediaevalia* 23: 1–22.

Clay, D. (1994), 'The Origins of the Socratic Dialogue' in P. A. Vander Waerdt (ed.), *The Socratic Movement* (Ithaca, NY, 1994), 23–47.

—— (1997), 'The Plan of Plato's *Critias*' in Calvo and Brisson 1997: 49–54.

—— (2000), 'Plato's Atlantis: The Anatomy of a Fiction', *Proceedings of the Boston Area Colloquium in Ancient Philosophy* 15: 1–21.

Clay, J. S. (1989), *The Politics of Olympus: Form and Meaning in the Major Homeric Hymns.* Princeton, NJ.

—— (1993), 'The Education of Perses: From "Mega Nepios" to "Dion Genos" and Back' in A. Schiesaro, P. Mitsis, and J. Strauss Clay (eds.), *Mega Nepios. Il destinatario nell'epos didascalico* (*Materiali e discussioni per l'analisi dei testi classici* 31) (Pisa, 1993), 23–33.

—— (2003), *Hesiod's Cosmos.* Cambridge.

—— (2005), 'The Beginning and End of the *Catalogue of Women* and its Relation to Hesiod' in Hunter 2005: 25–34.

Coby, J. P. (1993), 'Socrates on the Decline and Fall of Regimes: Books 8 and 9 of the *Republic*', *Interpretation* 21: 15–39.

—— (2001), 'Why are there Warriors in Plato's *Republic?*', *History of Political Thought* 22: 377–99.

Collins, D. (2001*a*), 'Improvisation in Rhapsodic Performance', *Helios* 28: 11–27.

—— (2001*b*), 'Homer and Rhapsodic Competition in Performance', *Oral Tradition* 16: 129–67.

—— (2005), *Master of the Game: Competition and Performance in Greek Poetry.* Cambridge, Mass.

Conte, G. B. (1985), *Memoria dei poeti e sistema letterario. Catullo, Virgilio, Ovidio, Lucano.* 2nd edn. Turin.

Cooper, J. M. (1997) (ed.), *Plato: Complete Works.* Indianapolis, IN.

Cornford, F. M. (1937), *Plato's Cosmology. The Timaeus of Plato.* London.

Craig, L. H. (1994), *The War Lover. A Study of Plato's Republic.* Toronto.

Cribiore, R. (2001), *Gymnastics of the Mind: Greek Education in Hellenistic and Roman Egypt.* Princeton, NJ.

D'Alessio, G. B. (2005), 'The *Megalai Ehoiai*: A Survey of the Fragments' in Hunter 2005: 176–216.

Dalfen, J. (1974), *Polis und Poiesis. Die Auseinandersetzung mit der Dichtung bei Platon und seinen Zeitgenossen.* Munich.

—— (2002), 'Platons Jenseitsmythen: eine "neue Mythologie"?' in Janka and Schäfer 2002: 214–30.

David, E. (1984), 'The Problem of Representing Plato's Ideal State in Action', *Rivista di filologia e di istruzione classica* 112: 33–53.

Deichgräber, K. (1951–2), 'Etymologisches zu Ζεύς, Διός, Δία, Δίκη', *Zeitschrift für vergleichende Sprachforschung* 70: 19–28.

Demont, P. (1990), *La cité grecque archaïque et classique et l'idéal de tranquillité.* Paris.

Demos, M. (1999), *Lyric Quotation in Plato.* Lanham, MD.

Derrida, J. (1981), 'Plato's Pharmacy' in his *Dissemination.* Trans. B. Johnson (Chicago, 1981), 63–171.

Detienne, M. (2002), 'Even Talk is in Some Ways Divine' in his *The Writing of Orpheus: Greek Myth in Cultural Context.* Trans. J. Lloyd (Baltimore, MD, 2002), 70–77. First published in French as 'La rumeur, elle aussi, est une déesse', *Le genre humain* 5 (1982), 71–80.

Dillon, J. (1992), 'Plato and the Golden Age', *Hermathena* 153: 21–36.

—— (1995), 'The Neoplatonic Exegesis of the *Statesman* Myth' in Rowe 1995*b*: 364–74.

—— (1997), 'The Riddle of the *Timaeus*: Is Plato Sowing Clues?' in M. Joyal (ed.), *Studies in Plato and the Platonic Tradition* (Aldershot, 1997), 25–42.

Donini, P. (1988), 'Il *Timeo.* Unità del dialogo, verisimiglianza del discorso', *Elenchos* 9: 5–52.

Dörrie, H. and Baltes, M. (1993), *Der Platonismus im 2. und 3. Jahrhundert nach Christus* = *Der Platonismus in der Antike* vol. 3. Stuttgart/Bad Cannstatt.

Dover, K. J. (1980) (ed.), *Plato: Symposium.* Cambridge.

Dräger, P. (1997), *Untersuchungen zu den Frauenkatalogen Hesiods.* Stuttgart.

duBois, P. (1992), 'Eros and the Woman', *Ramus* 21: 97–116.

Dusanic, S. (1982), 'Plato's Atlantis', *L'Antiquité Classique* 51: 25–52.

Edelstein, L. (1945), 'The Rôle of Eryximachus in Plato's Symposium', *Transactions of the American Philological Association* 76: 83–103.

—— (1949), 'The Function of the Myth in Plato's Philosophy', *Journal of the History of Ideas* 10: 463–81.

Edwards, M. J. (1992), 'Protagorean and Socratic Myth', *Symbolae Osloenses* 67: 89–102.

El Murr, D. (2002), 'La *symplokè politikè*: le paradigme du tissage dans le *Politique* de Platon, ou les raisons d'un paradigme arbitraire', *Kairos* 19: 49–95.

—— (2005), 'La division et l'unité du *Politique* de Platon', *Les Études philosophiques* 3: 295–324.

Erler, M. (1987), 'Das Recht (*ΔIKH*) als Segensbringerin für die Polis. Die Wandlung eines Motivs von Hesiod zu Kallimachos', *Studi italiani di filologia classica* 80: 5–36.

—— (2007), *Platon (Grundriss der Geschichte der Philosophie: Die Philosophie der Antike.* vol. 2/2) Basel.

Fago, A. (1991), 'Mito esiodeo delle razze e logos platonico della psychè: una comparazione storico-religiosa', *Studi e materiali di storia delle religioni* 15: 221–51.

Fakas, C. (2001), *Der hellenistische Hesiod. Arats Phainomena und die Tradition der antiken Lehrepik.* Wiesbaden.

Feeney, D. (forthcoming), 'Horace on his Own Reception' in L. Houghton and M. Wyke (eds.), *Perceptions of Horace: A Roman Poet and his Readers* (Cambridge, forthcoming).

Fehling, D. (1965), 'Zwei Untersuchungen zur griechischen Sprachphilosophie', *Rheinisches Museum* 108: 212–29.

—— (1969), *Die Wiederholungsfiguren und ihr Gebrauch bei den Griechen vor Gorgias.* Berlin.

Ferrari, F. (2006), '*Poietes kai pater*: esegesi medioplatoniche di Timeo, 28c3' in G. De Gregorio and S. M. Medaglia (eds.), *Tradizione, ecdotica, esegesi. Miscellanea di studi* (Napoli, 2006), 43–58.

Ferrari, G. R. F. (2003), *City and Soul in Plato's Republic.* Sankt Augustin.

Ferrari, W. (1939), 'Esiodo, *Erga* 122 sg.', *Studi italiani di filologia classica* 16: 229–48.

Finkelberg, A. (1998), 'On the History of the Greek κόσμος', *Harvard Studies in Classical Philology* 98: 103–36.

Finkelberg, M. (1998), *The Birth of Literary Fiction in Ancient Greece.* Oxford.

Fisher, N. R. E. (1992), *Hybris. A Study in the Values of Honour and Shame in Ancient Greece.* Warminster.

—— (2001), *Against Timarchos: Translated with Introduction and Commentary.* Oxford.

Ford, A. L. (1992), *Homer: The Poetry of the Past.* Ithaca, NY.

—— (1997), 'Epic as Genre' in I. Morris and B. Powell (eds.), *A New Companion to Homer* (Leiden, 1997), 396–414.

—— (1999), 'Reading Homer from the Rostrum: Poems and Laws in Aeschines' *Against Timarchus*' in S. Goldhill and R. Osborne (eds.),

*Performance Culture and Athenian Democracy* (Cambridge, 1999), 231–56.

—— (2002), *The Origins of Criticism: Literary Culture and Poetic Theory in Classical Greece.* Princeton, NJ.

Fowler, H. N. (1921) (ed. and trans.), *Plato.* Vol. vii: *Theaetetus, Sophist.* (Loeb Classical Library 123.) Cambridge, Mass.

Fowler, R. L. (2000), *Early Greek Mythography.* Vol. 1: *Text and Introduction.* Oxford.

Fraenkel, E. (1950), *Aeschylus. Agamemnon.* 3 vols. Oxford.

Friedländer, P. (1931), review of Jacoby (1930) in *Göttingische Gelehrte Anzeigen* 92: 241–6. Reprinted in E. Heitsch (ed.), *Hesiod* (Darmstadt, 1966), 100–30.

Gaiser, K. (1974), *Name und Sache in Platons Kratylos.* Heidelberg.

Gatz, B. (1967), *Weltalter, goldene Zeit und sinnverwandte Vorstellungen.* Hildesheim.

Giannantoni, G. (1990), *Socratis et Socraticorum reliquiae.* 4 vols. 2nd edn. Naples.

Gifford, M. (2001), 'Dramatic Dialectic in *Republic* Book 1', *Oxford Studies in Ancient Philosophy* 20: 35–106.

Gill, C. (1977), 'The Genre of the Atlantis Story', *Classical Philology* 72: 287–304.

—— (1980), *Plato: The Atlantis Story.* Bristol.

Giuliano, F. M. (1997), 'L'*enthousiasmos* del poeta filosofo tra Parmenide e Platone', *Studi classici e orientali* 46: 515–57. Reprinted in Giuliano 2004: 137–79.

—— (2004), *Studi di letteratura greca.* Pisa.

—— (2005), *Platone e la poesia. Teoria della composizione e prassi della ricezione.* Sankt Augustin.

Grafton, A. (1992), *New Worlds, Ancient Texts: The Power of Tradition and the Shock of Discovery.* Cambridge, Mass.

Graziosi, B. (2001), 'Competition in Wisdom' in F. Budelmann and P. Michelakis (eds.), *Homer, Tragedy and Beyond. Essays in Honour of P. E. Easterling* (London, 2001), 57–74.

—— (2002), *Inventing Homer: The Early Reception of Epic.* Cambridge.

—— (2006), 'Il rapporto tra autore ed opera nella tradizione biografica greca' in D. Lanza and S. Roscalla (eds.), *L'autore e l'opera nella Grecia antica* (Pavia, 2006), 155–74.

—— and Haubold, J. H. (2005), *Homer: The Resonance of Epic.* London.

Griffith, M. (1983), 'Personality in Hesiod', *Classical Antiquity* 2: 37–65.

—— (1990), 'Contest and Contradiction in Early Greek Poetry' in M. Griffith and D. J. Mastronarde (eds.), *Cabinet of the Muses: Essays on*

*Classical and Comparative Literature in honor of Thomas G. Rosenmeyer* (Atlanta, GA, 1990), 185–207.

Grube, G. M. A. and Reeve, C. D. C. (1992) (trans.), *Plato: Republic*. 2nd edn. Indianapolis, IN.

Guthrie, W. K. C. (1962–81), *A History of Greek Philosophy*. 6 vols. Cambridge.

Hackforth, R. (1944), 'The Story of Atlantis: Its Purpose and its Moral', *Classical Review* 58: 7–9.

Hadot, P. (1983), 'Physique et poésie dans le Timée de Platon', *Revue de Théologie et de Philosophie* 115: 113–33.

Halliwell, S. (1984), 'Plato and Aristotle on the Denial of Tragedy', *Proceedings of the Cambridge Philological Society* 30: 49–71.

—— (1993), *Plato: Republic 5*. Warminster.

—— (2000), 'The Subjection of Muthos to Logos: Plato's Citations of the Poets', *Classical Quarterly* 50: 94–112.

Hamilton, E. and Cairns, H. (1961) (eds.), *The Collected Dialogues of Plato*. Princeton, NJ.

Hamilton, R. (1989), *The Architecture of Hesiodic Poetry*. Baltimore, MD.

Hanasz, W. (1997–8), 'Poetic Justice for Plato's Democracy?', *Interpretation* 25: 37–57.

Hardwick, L. (2003), *Reception Studies*. (*Greece and Rome New Surveys in the Classics* 33.) Oxford.

—— and Stray, C. A. (2008) (eds.), *A Companion to Classical Receptions*. Oxford.

Hartman, M. (1988), 'The Hesiodic Roots of Plato's Myth of the Metals', *Helios* 15: 103–14.

Hartog, F. (2001), *Memories of Odysseus: Frontier Tales from Ancient Greece*. Trans. J. Lloyd. Edinburgh.

Haslam, M. W. (1976), 'A Note on Plato's Unfinished Dialogues', *American Journal of Philology* 97: 336–9.

Haubold, J. H. (2000), *Homer's People: Epic Poetry and Social Formation*. Cambridge.

—— (2002), 'Greek Epic: a Near Eastern Genre?', *Proceedings of the Cambridge Philological Society* 48: 1–19.

Heitsch, E. (1993), *Platon: Phaidros*. Göttingen.

Herbermann, C.-P. (1996), 'Antike Etymologie' in P. Schmitter (ed.), *Geschichte der Sprachtheorie*. Vol. 2: *Sprachtheorien der abendländischen Antike* (Tübingen, 1996), 353–76.

Higbie C. (1990), *Measure and Music: Enjambment and Sentence Structure in the Iliad*. Oxford.

Hirschberger, M. (2004), *Gunaikon Katalogos und Megalai Eoiai: Ein Kommentar zu den Fragmenten zweier hesiodeischer Epen*. Munich.

Hobbs, A. (2000), *Plato and the Hero: Courage, Manliness and the Impersonal Good*. Cambridge.

Horn, C. (2002), 'Warum zwei Epochen der Menschheitsgeschichte? Zum Mythos des Politikos' in Janka and Schäfer 2002: 137–59.

Hornblower, S. (2001), 'Epic and Epiphanies: Herodotus and the "New Simonides"' in D. Boedeker and D. Sider (eds.), *The New Simonides. Contexts of Praise and Desire* (Oxford, 2001), 135–47.

Howes, G. E. (1895), 'Homeric Quotations in Plato and Aristotle', *Harvard Studies in Classical Philology* 6: 153–237.

Howland, J. (1993), *The Republic: The Odyssey of Philosophy*. New York.

Hunter, R. L. (2004), 'Homer and Greek Literature' in R. Fowler (ed.), *The Cambridge Companion to Homer* (Cambridge, 2004), 235–53.

—— (2005) (ed.), *The Hesiodic Catalogue of Women: Constructions and Reconstructions*. Cambridge.

—— (2008), 'Hesiod, Callimachus and the Invention of Morality' in G. Bastianini and A. Casanova (eds.), *Esiodo: cent' anni di papiri* (Florence, 2008), 153–64.

Hunter, V. J. (1990), 'Gossip and the Politics of Reputation in Classical Athens', *Phoenix* 44: 299–325.

—— (1994), *Policing Athens: Social Control in the Attic Lawsuits, 420–320 BC*. Princeton, NJ.

Iannucci, A. (2002), *La parola e l'azione. I frammenti simposiali di Crizia*. Bologna.

Irwin, E. (2005a), *Solon and Early Greek Poetry: The Politics of Exhortation*. Cambridge.

—— (2005b), 'Gods among Men? The Social and Political Dynamics of the Hesiodic *Catalogue of Women*' in Hunter 2005: 35–84.

Iser, W. (1978), *The Act of Reading: A Theory of Aesthetic Response*. Baltimore, MD.

Jacoby, F. (1930) (ed.), *Hesiodi Carmina. Pars I: Theogonia*. Berlin.

Janka, M. and Schäfer, C. (2002) (eds.), *Platon als Mythologe. Neue Interpretationen zu den Mythen in Platons Dialogen*. Darmstadt.

Jauss, H. R. (1982), *Toward an Aesthetic of Reception*. Trans. T. Bahti. Minneapolis, MN.

Johansen, T. K. (2004), *Plato's Natural Philosophy. A Study of the Timaeus–Critias*. Cambridge.

Jonkers, G. (1989), *The Manuscript Tradition of Plato's Timaeus and Critias*. Diss. Amsterdam.

Kahn, C. H. (1981), 'Did Plato write Socratic Dialogues?', *Classical Quarterly* 31: 305–20. Reprinted in H. H. Benson (ed.), *Essays on the Philosophy of Socrates* (Oxford, 1992), 35–52.

—— (1996), *Plato and the Socratic Dialogue: The Philosophical Use of a Literary Form.* Cambridge.

Kambylis, A. (1965), *Die Dichterweihe und ihre Symbolik. Untersuchungen zu Hesiodos, Kallimachos, Properz und Ennius.* Heidelberg.

Kerferd, G. B. (1981), *The Sophistic Movement.* Cambridge.

Keyser, P. M. (1992), 'Stylometric Method and the Chronology of Plato's Works' (review of Brandwood 1990), *Bryn Mawr Classical Review* 03.01.12.

Kiberd, D. (2008), 'Joyce's Homer, Homer's Joyce' in R. Brown (ed.), *A Companion to James Joyce* (Oxford, 2008), 241–53.

Kindstrand, J. F. (1973), *Homer in der zweiten Sophistik: Studien zu der Homerlektüre und dem Homerbild bei Dion von Prusa, Maximos von Tyros und Ailios Aristeides.* Uppsala.

Kirk, G. S. (1966), 'Studies in some Technical Aspects of Homeric Style II: Verse Structure and Sentence Structure in Homer', *Yale Classical Studies* 20: 105–52. Reprinted with modifications in his *Homer and the Oral Tradition* (Cambridge, 1976), 146–82.

—— (1970), *Myth, its Meaning and Functions in Ancient and Other Cultures.* Berkeley, CA and Cambridge.

—— (1972), 'Greek Mythology. Some New Perspectives', *Journal of Hellenic Studies* 92: 74–85.

Knight, R. C. (1950), *Racine et la Grèce.* Paris.

Koning, H. and Most, G. W. (forthcoming), *The Scholia to Hesiod's Theogony.* Atlanta, GA.

Kotsidu, H. (1991), *Die musischen Agone der Panathenäen in archaischer und klassischer Zeit. Eine historisch-archäologische Untersuchung.* Munich.

Krause, W. (1958), *Die Stellung der frühchristlichen Autoren zur heidnischen Literatur.* Vienna.

Kühner, R. and Gerth, B. (1898–1904), *Ausführliche Grammatik der griechischen Sprache.* 3rd edn. 2 vols. Hannover.

Kurke, L. (1990), 'Pindar's Sixth Pythian and the Tradition of Advice Poetry', *Transactions of the American Philological Association* 120: 85–107.

Labarbe, J. (1949), *L'Homère de Platon.* Liège.

Lane, M. S. (1998), *Method and Politics in Plato's Statesman.* Cambridge.

Laplace, M. (1984), 'Le "Critias" de Platon, ou l'ellipse d'une épopée', *Hermes* 112: 377–82.

Lear, J. (1992), 'Inside and Outside the *Republic*', *Phronesis* 37: 184–215.

Leclerc, M.-C. (1993), *La parole chez Hésiode: à la recherche de l'harmonie perdue*. Paris.

Ledbetter, G. M. (2003), *Poetics before Plato: Interpretation and Authority in Early Greek Theories of Poetry*. Princeton, NJ.

Ledger, G. R. (1989), *Re-Counting Plato: A Computer Analysis of Plato's Style*. Oxford.

—— and Keyser, P. (1992), 'Responses', *Bryn Mawr Classical Review* 03.06.19.

Lefkowitz, M. (1981), *The Lives of the Greek Poets*. London.

Lennox, J. (1985), 'Plato's Unnatural Teleology' in D. O'Meara (ed.), *Platonic Investigations* (Washington, 1985), 195–218. Reprinted in J. Lennox, *Aristotle's Philosophy of Biology: Studies in the Origins of Life Science* (Cambridge, 2001), 280–302.

Lenz, A. (1980), *Das Proöm des frühen griechischen Epos. Ein Beitrag zum poetischen Selbstverständnis*. Bonn.

Lev Kenaan, V. (2008), *Pandora's Senses: The Feminine Character of the Ancient Text*. Madison, WI.

Levin, S. B. (2001), *The Ancient Quarrel between Philosophy and Poetry Revisited: Plato and the Greek Literary Tradition*. Oxford.

Liatsi, M. (2008), *Die semiotische Erkenntnistheorie Platons im Siebten Brief. Eine Einführung in den sogenannten philosophischen Exkurs*. (*Zetemata* 131.) Munich.

Livingstone, N. (2001), *A Commentary on Isocrates' Busiris*. Leiden.

Lloyd, G. E. R. (1966), *Polarity and Analogy. Two Types of Argumentation in Early Greek Thought*. Cambridge.

Lord, A. B. (1960), *The Singer of Tales*. Cambridge, Mass.

Lovejoy, A. O. and Boas, G. (1935), *Primitivism and Related Ideas in Antiquity*. Baltimore, MD.

Lovelock, J. (1979), *Gaia: A New Look at Life on Earth*. Oxford.

—— (1988), *The Ages of Gaia: A Biography of Our Living Earth*. New York.

Marsilio, M. S. (2000), *Farming and Poetry in Hesiod's Works and Days*. Lanham, MD.

Martin, R. P. (1992), 'Hesiod's Metanastic Poetics', *Ramus* 21: 11–33.

Martindale, C. (1993), *Redeeming the Text: Latin Poetry and the Hermeneutics of Reception*. Cambridge.

—— and Martindale, M. (1990), *Shakespeare and the Uses of Antiquity: An Introductory Essay*. London.

—— and Taylor, A. B. (2004) (eds.), *Shakespeare and the Classics*. Cambridge.

—— and Thomas, R. F. (2006) (eds.), *Classics and the Uses of Reception*. Oxford.

Mayer, K. (1996), 'Helen and the *ΔΙΟΣ ΒΟΥΛΗ Dios Boulé*', *American Journal of Philology* 117: 1–15.

McCabe, M. M. (1997), 'Chaos and Control: Reading Plato's *Politicus*', *Phronesis* 42: 94–115.

—— (2000), *Plato and his Predecessors. The Dramatisation of Reason*. Cambridge.

Merkelbach, R. and West, M. L. (1967) (eds.), *Fragmenta Hesiodea*. Oxford.

Mesch, W. (2002), 'Die Bildlichkeit der platonischen Kosmologie. Zum Verhältnis von Logos und Mythos im Timaios' in Janka and Schäfer 2002: 194–213.

Midgley, M. (2001), *Gaia: The Next Big Idea*. London.

—— (2007) (ed.), *Earthy Realism: The Meaning of Gaia*. Exeter and Charlottesville, VA.

Miller, M. H. (1980), *The Philosopher in Plato's* Statesman. The Hague.

—— (2001), '"First of All": On the Semantics and Ethics of Hesiod's Cosmogony', *Ancient Philosophy* 21: 251–76.

Momigliano, A. (1929–30), 'Prodico da Ceo e le dottrine sul linguaggio da Democrito ai Cinici', *Atti della Reale Accademia delle Scienze di Torino* 65: 95–107.

Mordine, M. J. (2006), 'Speaking to Kings: Hesiod's αἶνος and the Rhetoric of Allusion in the *Works and Days*', *Classical Quarterly* 56: 363–73.

Morgan, K. A. (1998), 'Designer History: Plato's Atlantis Story and Fourth-Century Ideology', *Journal of Hellenic Studies* 118: 101–18.

—— (2000), *Myth and Philosophy from the Pre-Socratics to Plato*. Cambridge.

—— (2004) 'Plato' in I. J. F. De Jong, R. Nünlist, and A. M. Bowie (eds.), *Narrators, Narratees and Narratives in Ancient Greek Literature* (Leiden, 2004), 357–76.

Most, G. W. (1989), 'The Structure and Function of Odysseus' *Apologoi*', *Transactions of the American Philological Association* 119: 15–30.

—— (1992), 'Il poeta nell'Ade: catabasi epica e teoria dell'epos tra Omero e Virgilio', *Studi italiani di filologia classica* 10: 1014–26.

—— (1993), 'Hesiod. Textualisation of Personal Temporality' in G. Arrighetti and F. Montanari (eds.), *La componente autobiografica nella poesia greca e latina fra realtà e artificio letterario* (Pisa, 1993), 73–92.

—— (1994), 'Simonides' Ode to Scopas in Contexts' in I. J. F. De Jong and J. P. Sullivan (eds.), *Modern Critical Theory and Classical Literature* (*Mnemosyne Supplementum* 130) (Leiden, 1994), 127–52.

—— (1997), 'Hesiod's Myth of the Five (or Three or Four) Races', *Proceedings of the Cambridge Philological Society* 43: 104–27.

—— (2001), *Leggere Raffaello. La Scuola di Atene e il suo pre-testo*. Turin.

Most, G. W. (2005), 'How many Homers?' in A. Santoni (ed.), *L'Autore multiplo* (Pisa, 2005), 1–14.

—— (2006) (ed. and trans.), *Hesiod, Theogony, Works and Days, Testimonia.* (Loeb Classical Library 57.) Cambridge, Mass.

—— (2007) (ed. and trans.), *Hesiod, The Shield, Catalogue of Women, Other Fragments.* (Loeb Classical Library 503.) Cambridge, Mass.

Mumford, L. (1959), *The Story of Utopias.* 2nd edn. Gloucester, Mass.

Murdoch, I. (1977), *The Fire and the Sun: Why Plato Banished the Artists.* Oxford.

Murray, P. (1996) (ed.), *Plato on Poetry: Ion, Republic 376e–398b, Republic 595–608b.* Cambridge.

—— (2004) 'The Muses and their Arts' in P. Murray and P. Wilson (eds.), *Music and the Muses. The Culture of Mousike in the Classical Athenian City* (Oxford, 2004), 365–89.

Musäus, I. (2004), *Der Pandoramythos bei Hesiod und seine Rezeption bis Erasmus von Rotterdam.* Göttingen.

Naddaf, G. (1994), 'The Atlantis Myth: An Introduction to Plato's Later Philosophy of History', *Phoenix* 48: 189–209.

—— (1997), 'Plato and the *peri physeos* tradition' in Calvo and Brisson 1997: 27–36.

Nagy, G. (1979), *The Best of the Achaeans: Concepts of the Hero in Archaic Greek Poetry.* Baltimore, MD.

—— (1990), *Pindar's Homer: The Lyric Possession of an Epic Past.* Baltimore, MD.

—— (1996), 'Autorité et auteur dans la Théogonie Hésiodique' in F. Blaise, P. Judet de La Combe, and P. Rousseau (eds.), *Le métier du mythe. Lectures d'Hésiode* (Lille, 1996), 41–52.

—— (2002), *Plato's Rhapsody and Homer's Music. The Poetics of the Panathenaic Festival in Classical Athens.* Cambridge, Mass.

Nails, D. (1992), 'Platonic Chronology Reconsidered' (review of Ledger 1989 and Thesleff 1982), *Bryn Mawr Classical Review* 03.04.17.

Nauck, A. (1889) (ed.), *Tragicorum Graecorum Fragmenta.* 2nd edn. Leipzig.

Nehamas, A. and Woodruff, P. (1989), *Plato: Symposium.* Indianapolis, IN.

Nelson, S. (1998), *God and the Land: The Metaphysics of Farming in Hesiod and Vergil.* Oxford.

—— (2003), review of Marsilio (2000), *International Journal of the Classical Tradition* 10: 279–81.

Nesselrath, H.-G. (2006), *Platon, Kritias: Übersetzung und Kommentar.* Göttingen.

Niderst, A. (1978), *Racine et la tragédie classique,* Paris.

Nietzsche, F. (1870–73), 'Der florentinische Tractat über Homer und Hesiod, ihr Geschlecht und ihren Wettkampf', *Rheinisches Museum* 25: 528–40 + 28: 211–49.

Nightingale, A. W. (1995), *Genres in Dialogue: Plato and the Construct of Philosophy.* Cambridge.

—— (1996), 'Plato on the Origins of Evil: The *Statesman* Myth Reconsidered', *Ancient Philosophy* 16: 65–91.

Norden, E. (1913), *Agnostos Theos. Untersuchungen zur Formengeschichte religiöser Rede.* 2nd edn. Leipzig.

Nussbaum, M. C. (1986), *The Fragility of Goodness: Luck and Ethics in Greek Tragedy and Philosophy.* Cambridge.

O'Connor, D. K. (2007), 'Rewriting the Poets in Plato's Characters' in G. R. F. Ferrari (ed.), *The Cambridge Companion to Plato's Republic* (Cambridge, 2007), 55–89.

O'Sullivan, N. (1992), *Alcidamas, Aristophanes and the Beginnings of Greek Stylistic Theory.* (*Hermes Einzelschriften* 60.) Stuttgart.

Olick, J. K. and Robbins, J. (1998), 'Social Memory Studies: From "Collective Memory" to the Historical Sociology of Mnemonic Practices', *Annual Review of Sociology* 24: 105–40.

Ophir, A. (1991), *Plato's Invisible Cities: Discourse and Power in the Republic.* London.

Pappas, N. (1995), *Routledge Philosophical Guidebook to Plato and the Republic.* London.

Parry, A. (1965), 'A Note on the Origins of Teleology', *Journal of the History of Ideas* 26: 259–62.

Parry, M. (1929), 'The Distinctive Character of Enjambment in Homeric Verse', *Transactions of the American Philological Association* 60: 200–20. Reprinted in A. Parry (ed.), *The Making of Homeric Verse* (Oxford, 1971), 251–65.

Partenie, C. (1998), 'The "Productionist" Framework of the *Timaeus*', *Dionysius* 16: 29–34.

Pasquali, G. (1968), 'Arte allusiva' in his *Pagine stravaganti.* 2nd edn. (Florence, 1968), 275–82. First published in *L'Italia che scrive* 25 (1942): 185–7.

Patzer, A. (1986), *Der Sophist Hippias als Philosophiehistoriker.* Freiburg.

Pender, E. E. (2000), *Images of Persons Unseen. Plato's Metaphors for the Gods and the Soul.* Sankt Augustin.

—— (2007), 'Poetic Allusion in Plato's *Timaeus* and *Phaedrus*', *Göttinger Forum für Altertumswissenschaft* 10: 51–87.

Penner, T. and Rowe, C. J. (2005), *Plato's Lysis.* Cambridge.

Perlman, S. (1965), 'Quotations from Poetry in Attic Orators of the Fourth Century BC', *American Journal of Philology* 85: 155–72.

Pfeiffer, R. (1968), *History of Classical Scholarship: From the Beginnings to the End of the Hellenistic Age*. Oxford.

Pontani, F. (2000), 'Catullus 64 and the Hesiodic *Catalogue*. A Suggestion', *Philologus* 144: 267–76.

Pradeau, J.-F. (1997), *Le monde de la politique. Sur le récit atlante de Platon, Timée (17–27) et Critias*. Sankt Augustin.

—— (2001), 'L'Atlantide de Platon, l'utopie vraie', *Elenchos* 22: 75–98.

Press, G. A. (2000) (ed.), *Who Speaks for Plato? Studies in Platonic Anonymity*. Lanham, MD.

—— (2007), *Plato: A Guide for the Perplexed*. London.

Prier, R. A. (1989), *Thauma Idesthai: The Phenomenology of Sight and Appearance in Archaic Greek*. Tallahassee, FL.

Pucci, P. (1977), *Hesiod and the Language of Poetry*. Baltimore, MD.

Querbach, C. W. (1985), 'Hesiod's Myth of the *Four* Races', *Classical Journal* 81: 1–12.

Reinsch-Werner, H. (1976), *Callimachus Hesiodicus. Die Rezeption der hesiodischen Dichtung durch Kallimachos von Kyrene*. Berlin.

Richardson, N. J. (1981), 'The Contest of Homer and Hesiod and Alcidamas' *Museion*', *Classical Quarterly* 31: 1–10.

Robb, K. (1994), *Literacy and Paideia in Ancient Greece*. Oxford.

Romano, F. (1987), 'Proclo lettore e interprete del Cratilo' in J. Pépin and H. D. Saffrey (eds.), *Proclus: Lecteur et interprète des anciens. Actes du colloque international du CNRS, Paris, 2–4 octobre 1985* (Paris, 1987), 113–36.

Roochnik, D. (2003), *Beautiful City: The Dialectical Character of Plato's Republic*. Ithaca, NY.

Roscalla, F. (2005), 'La città delle api' in Vegetti 2005*a*: 397–422.

Rosen, R. (1990), 'Poetry and Sailing in Hesiod's *Works and Days*', *Classical Antiquity* 9: 99–113.

Rosen, S. (1988), *The Quarrel Between Philosophy and Poetry: Studies in Ancient Thought*. London.

Rosenmeyer, T. G. (1957), 'Hesiod and Historiography (*Erga* 106–201)', *Hermes* 85: 257–85.

Rowe, C. J. (1983), 'Archaic Thought in Hesiod', *Journal of Hellenic Studies* 103: 124–35.

—— (1986), *Plato, Phaedrus*. Edited with translation and commentary. Warminster.

—— (1995*a*), *Plato, Statesman*. Edited with translation and commentary. Warminster.

—— (1995*b*) (ed.), *Reading the Statesman* (*Symposium Platonicum* 3). Sankt Augustin.

—— (1998*a*) (ed.), *Plato, Symposium*. Edited with translation and commentary. Warminster.

—— (1998*b*), 'On Plato, Homer and Archaeology', *Arion* 6: 134–44.

—— (1999), *Plato: Statesman*. translated with introduction, Indianapolis, IN.

—— (2002), 'Zwei oder drei Phasen? Der Mythos im *Politikos*' in Janka and Schäfer 2002: 160–75.

—— (2006) 'The Literary and Philosophical Style of the *Republic*' in G. X. Santas (ed.), *The Blackwell Guide to Plato's Republic* (Oxford, 2006), 7–24.

—— (2007*a*), *Plato and the Art of Philosophical Writing*. Cambridge.

—— (2007*b*), 'Plato and the Persian Wars' in E. Bridges, E. M. Hall, and P. J. Rhodes (eds.), *Cultural Responses to the Persian Wars* (Oxford, 2007), 85–104.

Rubinstein, L. (1998), 'The Athenian Political Perception of the Idiotes' in P. Cartledge, P. Millett, and S. von Reden (eds.), *Kosmos: Essays in Order, Conflict and Community in Classical Athens* (Cambridge, 1998), 125–43.

Ruffell, I. (2000), 'The World Turned Upside Down: Utopia and Utopianism in the Fragments of Old Comedy' in F. D. Harvey and J. Wilkins (eds.), *The Rivals of Aristophanes: Studies in Athenian Old Comedy* (London, 2000), 473–506.

Rutherford, R. B. (1995), *The Art of Plato: Ten Essays in Platonic Interpretation*. London.

Rzach, A. (1902) (ed.), *Hesiodi Carmina, editio maior*. Leipzig.

Saïd, S. (2000), 'Dio's Use of Mythology' in S. Swain (ed.), *Dio Chrysostom: Politics, Letters, and Philosophy* (Oxford, 2000), 161–86.

Sanford, E. M. (1941), 'The Battle of Gods and Giants', *Classical Philology* 36: 52–7.

Sassi, M. M. (1986), 'Natura e storia in Platone', *Storia della Storiografia* 9: 104–28.

—— (1997), 'Sulla conoscibilità di Dio secondo Timeo' in A. Fabris, G. Fioravanti, and E. Moriconi (eds.), *Logica e teologia. Studi in onore di Vittorio Sainati* (Pisa, 1997), 229–34.

Schmidt, J.-U. (1986), *Adressat und Paraineseform. Zur Intention von Hesiods 'Werken und Tagen'*. Göttingen.

Schneider S. H., Miller, J. R., Crist, E., and Boston, P. J. (2004) (eds.), *Scientists Debate Gaia: The Next Century*. Cambridge, Mass.

Schofield, M. (2006), *Plato: Political Philosophy*. Oxford.

References

Schofield, M. (2007), 'The Noble Lie' in G. R. F. Ferrari (ed.), *The Cambridge Companion to Plato's Republic* (Cambridge, 2007), 138–64.

—— (2009), 'Fraternité, inegalité: la parole de Dieu': Plato's Authoritarian Myth of Political Legitimation', in C. Partenie (ed.), *Plato's Myths* (Cambridge, 2009), 101–15.

Schwartz, J. (1960), *Pseudo-Hesiodeia. Recherches sur la composition, la diffusion et la disparition ancienne d'œuvres attribuées à Hésiode.* Leiden.

Scodel, H. R. (1987), *Diaeresis and Myth in Plato's Statesman.* Göttingen.

Scodel, R. (1982), 'The Achaean Wall and the Myth of Destruction', *Harvard Studies in Classical Philology* 86: 33–50.

—— (2002), *Listening to Homer: Tradition, Narrative, and Audience.* Ann Arbor, MI.

Sedley, D. N. (1997), '"Becoming like God" in the *Timaeus* and Aristotle' in T. Calvo and L. Brisson (eds.), *Interpreting the Timaeus–Critias* (Sankt Augustin, 1997), 327–39.

—— (1998), 'The Etymologies in Plato's *Cratylus*', *Journal of Hellenic Studies* 118: 140–54.

—— (2003), *Plato's Cratylus.* Cambridge.

—— (2004), *The Midwife of Platonism. Text and Subtext in Plato's Theaetetus.* Oxford.

—— (2006), 'The Speech of Agathon in Plato's *Symposium*' in B. Reis (ed.), *The Virtuous Life in Greek Ethics* (Cambridge, 2006), 47–69.

—— (2007), *Creationism and its Critics in Antiquity.* Berkeley/Los Angeles, CA.

Segal, C. (1978), 'The Myth was Saved: Reflections on Homer and the Mythology of Plato's *Republic*', *Hermes* 106: 315–36.

—— (1994), *Singers, Heroes and Gods in the Odyssey.* Ithaca, NY.

Shorey, P. (1938), *Platonism, Ancient and Modern.* Berkeley, CA.

Slaveva-Griffin, S. (2005), '"A Feast of Speeches": Form and Content in Plato's *Timaeus*', *Hermes* 123: 312–27.

Sluiter, I. (1997), 'The Greek Tradition' in W. van Bekkum, J. Houben, I. Sluiter, and K. Versteegh (eds.), *The Emergence of Semantics in Four Linguistic Traditions. Hebrew, Sanskrit, Greek, Arabic* (Amsterdam, 1997), 147–224.

Snell, B. (1944), 'Die Nachrichten über die Lehren des Thales und die Anfänge der griechischen Philosophie und Literaturgeschichte', *Philologus* 96: 170–82. Reprinted in C. J. Classen (ed.), *Sophistik* (Wege der Forschung 187) (Darmstadt, 1976), 478–90.

—— (1953), *The Discovery of the Mind: The Greek Origins of European Thought.* Trans. T. G. Rosenmeyer. Oxford.

—— (1954), 'Die Welt der Götter bei Hesiod' in *La notion du divin depuis Homer jusqu'à Platon* (*Entretiens sur l'antiquité classique* 1) (Geneva, 1954), 97–117.

Solmsen, F. (1942), *Plato's Theology.* Ithaca, NY.

—— (1962), 'Hesiodic Motifs in Plato' in *Hésiode et son influence* (*Entretiens sur l'antiquité classique* 7) (Geneva), 171–211.

—— (1970) (ed.), *Hesiodi Theogonia, Opera et Dies, Scutum*. Oxford.

Stanford, W. B. (1981), 'Sound, Sense, and Music in Greek Poetry', *Greece and Rome* 28: 127–40.

Steiner, D. (1996), 'For Love of a Statue: A Reading of Plato's *Symposium* 215a–b', *Ramus* 25: 89–111.

Stoddard, K. J. (2004), *The Narrative Voice in the Theogony of Hesiod*. Leiden.

Stokes, M. C. (1962), 'Hesiodic and Milesian Cosmogonies – I', *Phronesis* 7: 1–37.

—— (1963), 'Hesiodic and Milesian Cosmogonies – II', *Phronesis* 8: 1–34.

—— (1997) (ed.), *Plato, Apology of Socrates*. Warminster.

Strauss, L. (1964), *The City and Man*. Chicago.

Szlezák, T. A. (1993), 'Atlantis und Troia, Platon und Homer: Bemerkungen zum Wahrheitsanspruch des Atlantis-Mythos', *Studia Troica* 3: 233–7.

Taylor, A. E. (1926), *Plato, the Man and his Work*. London.

—— (1928), *A Commentary on Plato's Timaeus*. Oxford.

Thesleff, H. (1982), *Studies in Platonic Chronology*. Helsinki.

Tulli, M. (1990), 'Età di Crono e ricerca sulla natura nel *Politico* di Platone', *Studi classici e orientali* 40: 97–115.

—— (1994), 'Il Crizia e la famiglia di Platone', *Studi classici e orientali* 44: 95–107.

—— (2007), 'Il Gorgia e la lira di Anfione' in M. Erler and L. Brisson (eds.), *Gorgias-Menon*. (*Symposium Platonicum* 7) (Sankt Augustin, 2007), 72–7.

Untersteiner, M. (1954), *The Sophists*. Trans. K. Freeman. Oxford.

Van Noorden, H. (forthcoming), *Playing Hesiod: The 'Myth of the Races' in Classical Antiquity*. Cambridge.

Vasunia, P. (2001), *The Gift of the Nile: Hellenizing Egypt from Aeschylus to Alexander*. Berkeley, CA.

Vegetti, M. (1998*a*) (ed.), *Platone, La Repubblica: traduzione e commento*. Vol. 1: *Libro I*. Naples.

—— (1998*b*), 'Katabasis' in Vegetti (1998*a*), 93–104.

—— (2000), 'Società dialogica e strategie argomentative nella Repubblica' in Casertano 2000: 74–85.

—— (2005*a*) (ed.), *Platone. La Repubblica: traduzione e commento*. Vol. 6: *Libri VIII e IX*. Naples.

—— (2005*b*) 'Il tempo, la storia, l'utopia' in Vegetti 2005*a* 137–68.

—— (2006), 'La letteratura socratica e la competizione tra generi letterari' in F. Roscalla (ed.), *L'autore e l'opera: attribuzioni, appropriazioni, apocrifi nella Grecia antica* (Pisa, 2006), 119–31.

Verdenius, W. J. (1962), 'Aufbau und Absicht der Erga' in *Hésiode et son influence* (*Entretiens sur l'antiquité classique* 7) (Geneva, 1962), 111–59.

—— (1985), *A Commentary on Hesiod Works and Days, vv. 1–382*. Leiden.

Vernant, J.-P. (1960), 'Le mythe hesiodique des races. Essai d'analyse structurale', *Revue de l'histoire des religions* 157: 21–54.

—— (1980) *Myth and Society in Ancient Greece*. Trans. J. Lloyd, Brighton.

—— (1990), 'One . . . Two . . . Three: Erōs' in D. M. Halperin, J. J. Winkler, and F. I. Zeitlin (eds.), *Before Sexuality: The Construction of Erotic Experience in the Ancient Greek World* (Princeton, NJ, 1990), 465–78.

Versnel, H. S. (1987), 'Greek Myth and Ritual: The Case of Kronos' in J. Bremmer (ed.), *Interpretations of Greek Mythology* (London/Sydney, 1987), 121–52.

Veyne, P. (1988), *Did the Greeks Believe their Myths? An Essay on the Constitutive Imagination*. Trans. P. Wissing. Chicago.

Viano, C. (1994), 'Aristote, *De coel.* I 10: Empédocle, l'alternance et le mythe du *Politique*', *Revue des études grecques* 107: 400–13.

Vidal-Naquet, P. (1981), 'Le mythe platonicien du *Politique*. Les ambiguïtés de l'âge d'or et de l'histoire' in his *Le Chasseur noir* (Paris, 1981), 361–80.

—— (1986), *The Black Hunter: Forms of Thought and Forms of Society in the Greek World*. Trans. A. Szegedy-Maszak. Baltimore, MD.

—— (2005), *L'Atlantide. Petite histoire d'un mythe platonicien*. Paris.

—— (2007), *The Atlantis Story: A Short History of Plato's Myth*. Trans. of Vidal-Naquet (2005) by J. Lloyd, Exeter.

Wakker, G. (1990), 'Die Ankündigung des Weltaltermythos (Hes. Op. 106–108)', *Glotta* 68: 86–90.

Walcot, P. (1958), 'Hesiod's Hymns to the Muses, Aphrodite, Styx and Hecate', *Symbolae Osloenses* 34: 5–14.

Wayte, W. (1854) (ed.), *Platonis Protagoras: The Protagoras of Plato*. Cambridge

Welliver, W. (1977), *Character, Plot and Thought in Plato's Timaeus–Critias*. Leiden.

West, M. L. (1966) (ed.), *Hesiod, Theogony*. Oxford.

—— (1967), 'The Contest of Homer and Hesiod', *Classical Quarterly* 17: 433–50.

—— (1978) (ed.), *Hesiod, Works and Days*. Oxford.

—— (1982), *Greek Metre*. Oxford.

—— (1985), *The Hesiodic Catalogue of Women: Its Nature, Structure, and Origins*. Oxford.

—— (1988) (trans.), *Hesiod, Theogony and Works and Days*. Oxford.

—— (1992), *Ancient Greek Music*. Oxford.

—— (1997), *The East Face of the Helicon. West Asiatic Elements in Greek Poetry and Myth.* Oxford.

—— (2003) (ed.), *Homeric Hymns, Homeric Apocrypha, Lives of Homer.* (Loeb Classical Library 496.) Cambridge, Mass.

Wilamowitz-Moellendorff, U. von (1920), *Platon.* 2 vols. 2nd edn. Berlin.

—— (1928), *Hesiodos, Erga,* Berlin.

Young, C. M. (1994), 'Plato and Computer Dating', *Oxford Studies in Ancient Philosophy* 12: 227–50.

Zanker, P. (1995), *The Mask of Socrates: The Image of the Intellectual in Antiquity.* Trans. A. Shapiro. Berkeley, CA.

Zedda, S. (2003), *Theory of Proportion in Plato's Timaeus: The World-Soul and the Universe as Structure.* PhD diss., University of Exeter.

Zeitlin, F. I. (1996), *Playing the Other: Gender and Society in Classical Greek Literature.* Chicago, IL.

—— (2001), 'Visions and Revisions of Homer' in S. Goldhill (ed.), *Being Greek under Rome. Cultural Identity, the Second Sophistic and the Development of Empire* (Cambridge, 2001), 195–266.

# General Index

# Index locorum